Intercom:

*Readings in
Organizational Communication*

Intercom:

Readings in Organizational Communication

STEWART FERGUSON

Associate Professor
Communication Studies Department
University of Windsor

SHERRY DEVEREAUX FERGUSON

Communication Consultant

HAYDEN BOOK COMPANY, INC.
Rochelle Park, New Jersey

√

Library of Congress Cataloging in Publication Data

Main entry under title:

Intercom: Readings in Organizational Communication

   Includes bibliographies.
   1. Communication in organizations—Addresses, essays,
lectures. 2. Communication in management—Addresses,
essays, lectures. I. Ferguson, Stewart. II. Ferguson, Sherry.
HD30.3.I55   658.4'5   80-13146
ISBN 0-8104-5127-1

1	2	3	4	5	6	7	8	9	PRINTING
80	81	82	83	84	85	86	87	88	YEAR

Acknowledgments

Lesley A. Albertson, "Telecommunications as a Travel Substitute: Some Psychological, Organizational, and Social Aspects." Reprinted from "Telecommunications as a Travel Substitute: Some Psychological, Organizational, and Social Aspects," by Lesley A. Albertson in *The Journal of Communication* (27:2).

Steven H. Appelbaum, "A Model of Managerial Motivation." Reproduced by special permission from the March 1975 *Training and Development Journal.* Copyright 1975 by the American Society for Training and Development Inc.

David L. Austin, "Transactional Interviewing or, Who Does What to Whom?" Reprinted with permission *Personnel Journal* copyright June 1974.

Warren Bennis, "Leadership—A Beleaguered Species." Reprinted by permission of the publisher, from *Organizational Dynamics* (Summer 1976) © 1976 by AMACOM, a division of American Management Associations. All rights reserved.

Robert R. Blake and Jane Srygley Mouton, "An Overview of the Grid.®" Reproduced by special permission from the May 1975 *Training and Development Journal.* Copyright 1975 by the American Society for Training and Development Inc.

Richard N. Bolles, "The Job-Hunt As an Information Search." Copyright © 1977 by Richard Nelson Bolles. Excerpted from *What Color Is Your Parachute?* 1978 edition, published by Ten Speed Press, Box 7123, Berkeley, Ca. 94707. Reprinted with permission of the author.

Patricia Hayes Bradley, "Socialization in Groups and Organizations: Toward a Concept of Creative Conformity." Original essay prepared for *INTERCOM.*

David S. Brown, "Macrobarriers to Successful Communication." Reprinted by permission of the publisher, from *Management Review* (December 1975) © 1975 by AMACOM, a division of American Management Associations. All rights reserved.

Michael Burgoon, Judee K. Heston, and James McCroskey. "Communication Roles in Small Group Interaction." From *Small Group Communication: A Functional Approach* by Michael Burgoon, Judee K. Heston, and James McCroskey. Copyright © 1974 by Holt, Rinehart and Winston, Inc. Reprinted by permission of Holt, Rinehart and Winston.

John Cowan, "A Human-Factored Approach to Appraisal." Reprinted, by permission of the publisher, from *Personnel* (November–December 1975) © 1975 by AMACOM, a division of American Management Associations. All rights reserved.

Olga L. Crocker, "Conflict: An Overview." Original essay prepared for *INTERCOM.* All rights reserved by author.

ACKNOWLEDGMENTS

Keith Davis, "Management Communication and the Grapevine," *Harvard Business Review,* September–October 1953, Copyright © 1953 by the President and Fellows of Harvard College; all rights reserved.

Richard V. Farace, Peter R. Monge, and Hamish M. Russell, "Communication in Micro-Networks." Farace/Monge/Russell, *Communicating and Organizing,* © 1977, Addison-Wesley, Reading, Massachusetts. Pp. 158–162. Reprinted with permission.

Stewart Ferguson and Sherry Devereaux Ferguson, "Assessing Information Load." Original essay prepared for *INTERCOM.*

Stewart Ferguson and Sherry Devereaux Ferguson, "The Physical Environment and Communication." Original essay prepared for *INTERCOM.*

Fred E. Fiedler, "Style or Circumstance: The Leadership Enigma." Reprinted from *Psychology Today,* Copyright © 1969, Ziff-Davis Publishing Company.

Thomas J. Freeman, "Leadership Models," reprinted with permission of the author.

Thad B. Green and Paul H. Pietri, "Using Nominal Grouping to Improve Upward Communication," pp. 37–43, *MSU Business Topics,* Autumn 1974. Reprinted by permission of the publisher, Division of Research, Graduate School of Business Administration, Michigan State University.

Walter A. Jablonski, "How Useful Are Exit Interviews?" Reprinted by permission of the publisher, from *Supervisory Management* (May 1975) © 1975 by AMACOM, a division of American Management Associations. All rights reserved.

Bonnie McDaniel Johnson, "Characteristics of Effective Decision Building." From Bonnie McDaniel Johnson, *Communication, the Process of Organizing,* Copyright © 1977 by Allyn and Bacon, Inc., Boston. Reprinted with permission of the publisher.

Bonnie McDaniel Johnson, "Phases of Decision Building." From Bonnie McDaniel Johnson, *Communication: The Process of Organizing,* Copyright © 1977 by Allyn and Bacon, Inc., Boston. Reprinted with permission of the publisher.

M. Blaine Lee and William L. Zwerman, "Developing a Facilitation System for Horizontal and Diagonal Communications in Organizations." Reprinted with permission *Personnel Journal,* copyright July 1975.

William B. Lee and John T. Small, "In Search of an MIS," pp. 47–55, *MSU Business Topics,* Autumn 1975. Reprinted by permission of the publisher, Division of Research, Graduate School of Business Administration, Michigan State University.

Joseph Leese, "The Bureaucratic Colander." Reprinted with permission *Personnel Journal,* copyright October 1974.

Will Lorey, "Mutual Trust Is the Key to Open Communication." Republished with permission from *Administrative Management,* copyright © 1978 by Geyer-McAllister Publications, Inc. New York.

V.P. and L.L. Luchsinger, "Transactional Analysis for Managers or How to be More OK with OK Organizations," pp. 5–12, *MSU Business Topics,* Spring 1974. Reprinted by permission of the publisher, Division of Research, Graduate School of Business Administration, Michigan State University.

Norman R.F. Maier, "Assets and Liabilities in Group Problem-Solving: The Need for an Integrative Function," *Psychological Review,* Vol. 74, 1967, pp. 239–49. Copyright 1967 by the American Psychological Association. Reprinted by permission.

Robert Minter, "The Hiring Interview." Reprinted, by permission of the publisher, from *Supervisory Management,* (December 1974) © 1974 by AMACOM, a division of American Management Associations. All rights reserved.

David Oates, "The Boom in Creative Thinking." Reprinted by special permission from the December 1972 issue of *International Management.* Copyright ©. McGraw-Hill International Publications Company Limited. All rights reserved.

ACKNOWLEDGMENTS

Carl Rogers and Richard E. Farson, "Active Listening." Reprinted by special permission of the author and The Industrial Relations Center, University of Chicago.

Everett M. Rogers and Rekha Agarwala-Rogers, "Three Schools of Organizational Behavior." Reprinted with permission of Macmillan Publishing Co., Inc., from *Communication in Organizations* by Everett M. Rogers and Rekha Agarwala-Rogers. Copyright © 1976 by The Free Press, a Division of Macmillan Publishing Co., Inc.

John Senger, "Seeing Eye to Eye: Practical Problems of Perception." Reprinted with permission *Personnel Journal,* copyright October 1974.

Michael Z. Sincoff, Dudley A. Williams, and C.E. Tapie Rohm, Jr., "Steps in Performing a Communication Audit." Reprinted by permission of the authors. Dr. Sincoff is with Mead Corporation, Dayton, Ohio; Mr. Williams and Dr. Rohm are with Ohio University, Athens, Ohio.

Charles B. Smith, "Communication—An Essential of Reality." Reprinted with permission *Personnel Journal,* copyright August 1974.

Irvin Summers and David E. White, "Creativity Techniques: Toward Improvement of the Decision Process," *Academy of Management Review* (April 1976). Copyright © 1976. Reprinted by permission of the publisher and the author.

James Allen Taylor and Linda Joy Eagle, "Communication Networks and Organizational Structure." Original essay prepared for *INTERCOM.*

Richard J. Tersine and Walter E. Riggs, "The Delphi Technique: A Long-Range Planning Tool," *Business Horizons,* Vol. 19, April 1976, pp. 51–56. Copyright, 1976, by the Foundation for the School of Business at Indiana University. Reprinted by permission.

Jacques Vallee, Robert Johansen, and Kathleen Spangler, "The Computer Conference—An Altered State of Communication," from *The Futurist* (June 1975), published by the World Future Society, P.O. Box 30369 (Bethesda), Washington, D.C. 20014. Reprinted with permission of the publisher.

Abraham Zaleznik, "Managers and Leaders: Are They Different?" *Harvard Business Review,* May–June 1977, Copyright © 1977 by President and Fellows of Harvard College; all rights reserved.

Preface

In 1978 the Nobel prize in economics was awarded to Professor Herbert A. Simon for his work on decision making in organizations. This recognition marks the coming of age of a relatively new discipline, the study of communication in organizations.

The purpose of this collection of readings is to offer a focus for the study of organizational communications. Although *INTERCOM* may easily be used as a supplementary text in undergraduate or graduate courses, it was organized with the aim of presenting a comprehensive and coherent introduction to the field at whatever level the subject is being studied. The quality of the articles included justifies its use at the graduate level, and the readability justifies its use at the undergraduate level. Students of communication in industrial and business settings will find the material equally appropriate.

The parameters have not yet been set on communication issues and concerns of interest and relevance to the organizational specialist. For that reason, this collection offers an alternative to other texts and collections presently on the market. The readings included are drawn from psychology, communication, and management literature.

The book is divided into thirteen sections, intended to correspond with a semester's program in a college or university. Part One, an introductory article by Everett and Rekha Agarwala-Rogers, considers the role of communication in the organization from three points of view: the Scientific Method School, the Human Relations School, and the Systems School.

Part Two looks at the functions of formal and informal networks in the organization and the relationship between structure and communication. An article by Keith Davis discusses the operation of the grapevine.

In general, the articles in Part Three deal with the analysis and monitoring of information flow through the system. Specifically, they are concerned with information load control, steps in performing a communication audit, and the function of management information systems.

The relationship between the physical environment and communication is discussed in the introductory article to Part Four. It focuses on the open organization, an environment in which a high level of disclosure is possible with minimum penalties. Will Lorey's article stresses mutual trust as the key to open communication. The concluding article makes suggestions for facilitating horizontal and diagonal communications in organizations.

Part Five discusses barriers to effective interpersonal communication, barriers that may derive from the organizational environment or from the perceptual frame of the individual.

The nature of leadership draws the interest of most management specialists. Changing views of what makes an effective leader or a successful manager make the topic a controversial one. In Part Six, the opinions and research of Warren Bennis, Abraham Zaleznik, Fred Fiedler, Robert Blake, and Jane Mouton are presented. A closing article by Thomas Freeman summarizes some of the most popular leadership theories.

A brief section on the psychology of managerial motivation and the utilization of transactional analysis comprises Part Seven.

Still maintaining a focus on the responsibility of the manager or supervisor, Part Eight considers techniques for effective interviewing. The first article on transactional interviewing and Carl Rogers' and Richard Farson's discussion of active listening provide a general context for the more specific discussions of the hiring interview, the appraisal interview, and the exit interview that follow.

Part Nine contrasts the assets and liabilities in the face-to-face group problem-solving situation with those of the computer conference and the teleconference or videoconference. Norman Maier's article on face-to-face interaction has long been recognized as a valuable contribution to the literature. The futurist approaches of the other authors in this section offer good departure points for discussion.

The articles in Part Ten examine in more detail the dynamics of small group interaction with an emphasis on the decision-making process. Richard Farace, Peter Monge, and Hamish Russell contribute a summary of the classical literature on communication in micro-networks. Bonnie Johnson discusses phases of decision building and characteristics of effective decision building. Michael Burgoon, Judee Heston, and James McCroskey define communication roles assumed in small group interaction.

Creativity techniques is the subject of Part Eleven with discussion of brainstorming, nominal grouping and the Delphi method.

In any organization there is the potential and the likelihood for conflict. Part Twelve gives an overview of the literature on conflict and discusses socialization processes that operate in groups and organizations. Patricia Bradley's article advocates the concept of creative conformity.

Seeking affiliation with the organization is the final topic of discussion, and Richard Bolles gives specific suggestions for conducting a job-hunt through information search techniques. Although this section is presented last for organizational purposes, instructors may prefer to teach the unit first. There are many interesting films that can be used in conjunction with this section.

We would like to express our appreciation to Robert Boynton of Hayden Book Company for his cheerful and competent handling of all editorial matters and to Dianne Littwin of Hayden for her support of our project in its early stages. One of the editors would like to acknowledge her debt to Professor J. Jeffery Auer, who for more than 20 years as chairman of the Speech Communication Department at Indiana University did much to encourage the study of communication in society.

STEWART FERGUSON
SHERRY DEVEREAUX FERGUSON

Contents

Intercom:

Readings in
Organizational Communication

Part One

The Role of Communication in the Organization

1

Three Schools of Organizational Behavior

EVERETT ROGERS *and* REKHA AGARWALA-ROGERS

"The Scientific . . . Management [School] is in bad repute these days. The principles and rules which earlier in the century marked the beginning of the management movement today appear to many, in the light of our present knowledge of human relations, as a hopelessly inadequate guide to organization and management."

—John T. Diebold

"Too often it is assumed that the organization of a company corresponds to . . . an organization chart. Actually, it never does."

—Fritz J. Roethlisberger and William J. Dickson

"The open system does not run down, because it can import energy from the world around it."

—Daniel Katz and Robert Kahn

There is a tremendous volume of books and other literature published on the topic of organizations, and even the specialty of communication in organizations is represented by over 1,200 books and articles in a recent bibliography (Carter 1972). In dealing with this enormous volume of literature, it is useful to describe the three theoretical viewpoints that have predominated in the study of organizational behavior. These three "schools"—groups of scholars who shared a common viewpoint about organizational behavior—go by the names of Scientific Management, Human Relations, and Systems. The Scientific Management School originated in 1911 and was popular until the 1930s; the Human Relations School then predominated until the 1960s, when the Systems School became preeminent. While each of the first two approaches to organizational theory had its "day," neither has faded completely from sight nor been completely replaced by the school that followed it. In fact, there are still followers of the Scientific Management School today, and the Human Relations School has by no means been made completely obsolete by the Systems viewpoint. Indeed, each of the earlier schools had a strong influence on the now-dominant Systems School. So it will be useful to understand each of these theoretical positions in order to have a complete grasp of how organizations function, and the role of communication in organizations.[1]

Revolutionary Paradigms and Invisible Colleges

Any given field of scientific research begins with a major breakthrough of reconceptualization which provides a new way of looking at some phenomenon (Kuhn 1970). This so-called "revolutionary paradigm" is often a universally recognized scientific achievement that for a time provides model problems and solutions to a community of scholars. Famous examples are associated with names like Copernicus, Newton, Darwin, Pasteur, and Freud. The paradigm typically sets off a furious amount of intellectual effort as promising young scientists are attracted to the field, either to advance the new conceptualization with their research or to disprove certain of its aspects. Gradually, a scientific consensus about the field is developed.

An "invisible college" forms around the revolutionary paradigm, consisting of "an unofficial establishment based on fiercely competitive excellence. [The members] send each other duplicated preprints of papers yet to be published, and for big things they telephone and telegraph in advance. . . . They keep warm the seats of jet planes and commune with each other at small select conferences and seminars" (Price 1970).

Why do scientists band together in invisible colleges? Because science is a puzzle-solving process, and each scientist is faced with a tremendous amount of uncertainty in seeking to cope with the unknown in his or her discipline. A revolutionary paradigm provides a temporary sense of order, and a starting place for empirical investigation.

Furthermore, scientists are faced with an information explosion of books, journal articles, and research reports in their field (Price 1963). It is impossible for them to keep abreast of all of this scientific literature unless they somehow narrow it down. The invisible college, centering around a revolutionary paradigm, provides a means for doing so. It defines for the scientist what is relevant, and irrelevant, to his or her special research interests.

Research studies of invisible colleges in several fields show that they provide a structure and continuity to scientists with like interests (Crane 1972). There are respected leaders within an invisible college; usually they are the high producers of scholarly publications in the field.

The history of scientific research on organizational behavior presents a good illustration of the formation of an invisible college—or, more accurately, of three subcolleges. Each centered around a revolutionary paradigm that was initially proposed by one or more founders. The Scientific Management School was launched by Frederick W. Taylor in 1911; many books and other publications soon appeared dealing with his paradigm of human behavior in organizations. But in the 1930s, Chester Barnard and Elton Mayo found Taylor's paradigm unsatisfactory in explaining the nature of organizational behavior as they understood it—from Barnard's personal experience as a business executive and Mayo's empirical research at the Western Electric Company's Hawthorne plant near Cicero, Illinois. So Barnard and Mayo set forth a new paradigm, around which the invisible college that we call the Human Relations School grew.

An intellectual watershed occurred in the 1960s, when growing dissatisfaction with the Human Relations paradigm, along with the attractive alternative of general systems theory, led to the formation of the Systems School of organization theorists.

The main elements of each of these viewpoints are set forth in Table 1-1.

Scientific Management School

This school is sometimes called the "machine-theory" school, and is also known as "Taylorism" (after its founder), but it is usually called "Scientific Management" because it marked the introduction of scientific methods into the managing of organizations.

The Scientific Management School was preceded by the development of a body of management principles by the managers of businesses and industries and by professors at the business schools in U.S. universities, influenced somewhat by European authors like Henri Fayol.[2] Most of these principles were very simple by today's standards, such as the admonition to "plan ahead." There was almost no social science component in this early period, as social scientists were not much interested in studying organizations in general, or business firms in particular. Social science thinking had not yet begun to invade the fledgling business schools. In fact, there was very little science of any kind in the study of organizational behavior in this era; it was a time of learning mainly from experience. Management principles were pragmatic, and they seemed to work.

But all that changed in 1911, when Frederick W. Taylor published his influential book, *Scientific Management.* Taylor's basic approach to organizational research was extremely atomistic and mechanical: he analyzed each job in terms of its smallest aspect. For instance, Taylor would observe a work task in great detail by measuring and timing (with a stopwatch) each of the worker's movements that were involved. Repeated time-and-motion studies would be made of each action required to complete the task. Then Taylor would analyze the capacities of the worker as a "human machine" just as carefully, and seek to fit the worker and the task together.[3] The assumption of the Scientific Management School was that work operations could best be understood by breaking the whole down into its basic parts, and then aggregating these tiny bits and pieces back together into the whole system. This assumption was strongly challenged by the Systems School over fifty years later.

Taylor was able to achieve some spectacular results with his method. For example, he studied coal shoveling at the Bethlehem Steel Works, where he was employed for many years. His time-and-motion studies indicated that the average weight of coal scooped by a shovel ranged from 16 to 38 pounds. His experiments showed that a good worker could load twice as much coal in one work shift if he used a relatively small shovel holding 21 to 22 pounds. Fifteen different types of shovels were provided for loading different kinds of materials; workers were issued written instructions as to which shovel to use for each purpose. Within a few years, 140 workers were doing the same work that previously had required 400 to 600 workers (Gvishiani 1972, p. 179).

These time-and-motion experiments soon created considerable interest in the scientific management approach on the part of industrial managers and owners. But Taylor advocated far more than just efficiency studies such as these. He claimed that every worker should be paid according to his individual output, rather than that of the gang or shop of which he was a part. That is, the reward system should be tied to individual, not group, performance. So Taylor's approach was actually a combination of (1) studying the physical capabilities of workers, and (2) designing industrial reward systems around a conception of "economic man."[4]

The main tenets of Taylorism were summed up as: "Science, not rule of. thumb. Harmony, not discord. Cooperation, not individualism. Maximum output, in place of restricted output. The development of each man to his greatest efficiency and prosperity" (Taylor 1911, p. 140). This approach assumed that the worker was deeply irrational if left on his own, but would respond properly to money rewards. Man was made for the organization, and through cooperation with its objectives his maximum productivity could be achieved. Thus the worker was essentially perceived as a human appendage to the industrial machine (Etzioni 1964, p. 21).

Critical Reactions to Taylorism

"Scientific management will mean, for the employers and the workmen who adopt it, the elimination of almost all causes of dispute and disagreement between them" (Taylor 1911). Unfortunately, this sanguine vision of mutual worker-employer benefits from scientific management was not appreciated by the workers, who reacted bitterly to what they perceived as the inhumanity of Taylor's system. They did not like being reduced to the level of efficiently functioning machines. Scientific management was thus bitterly opposed by labor unions in the 1920s and 1930s.[5] The unions saw it as a means of employer exploitation of workers, leading to higher unemployment as a result of the greater efficiency that was attained. "All the time study in the world could not say how much ought to be paid for a job; it can only show the length of time a job ought to take" (Cole 1917, p. 13).

Table 1-1. The Three Main Schools of Organizational Behavior

	1. SCIENTIFIC MANAGEMENT SCHOOL	2. HUMAN RELATIONS SCHOOL	3. SYSTEMS SCHOOL
1. *Basic principles and assumptions about human behavior*	A mechanistic view of behavior: man is economically motivated, and will respond with maximum performance if material rewards are closely related to work efforts. Favors human engineering of worker effort and time in order to achieve maximum production, efficiency, and profit for the managers/owners.	A social view of man: informal groups affect production rates; attention to workers' needs and job satisfaction can motivate higher performance; worker participation in decision making; realization that the individual's goals may differ from the organization's goals; workers motivated by social needs and by their peer relationships.	The organization is an open system in continuous interaction with its environment; the system and its environment co-determine each other. The system must be analyzed as a whole in order to be understood properly. The organization is composed of subsystems, which are interdependent; individuals are the carriers of the organization.
2. *Main research methods used*	Observation (including time-and-motion studies); participation; some surveys.	Survey interviews and questionnaires; observation; participation; diary keeping; sociometric analysis of leadership and communication patterns.	Network analysis of sociometric data from survey interviews and questionnaires; systems analysis; computer simulation.
3. *Main types of organizations studied*	Industrial firms and public utilities.	Manufacturing plants (especially assembly-line operations), including some outside of the U.S.	Industrial, military, and government organizations; hospitals; educational and mental institutions; prisons.
4. *Bias of the school*	Pro-management; "management knows best."	Pro-workers; sympathetic to them. Attempts to help employees and employers solve their problems through understanding.	Pro-"organization"; the organization exists as an entity that consists of more than just its present individual members.

5. *View of organizational communication*	Emphasis on written, formal channels of communication: impersonal, work-related messages initiated by higher-ups and sent down the chain of command. The role of communication is not considered especially important.	Informal communication as well as formal; stress on interpersonal channels, especially with peers. Rumor and the grapevine exist.	Communication is crucial, as it holds the organization together and interrelates the subsystems. Communication across organization's boundary with its environment is also important.
6. *Founder or dominant figures*	Frederick W. Taylor.	Chester I. Barnard; Elton Mayo.	Herbert A. Simon; Daniel Katz and Robert L. Kahn; James G. Miller
7. *Landmark books*	Frederick W. Taylor (1911), *Scientific Management.* Henri Fayol (1949), *General and Industrial Management.* Luther Gulick and Lyndall F. Urwick (1937), *Papers on the Science of Administration.*	Chester I. Barnard (1938), *The Functions of the Executive.* Fritz Roethlisberger and William Dickson (1939), *Management and the Worker.* Elton Mayo (1960), *The Social Problems of an Industrial Civilization.* Rensis Likert (1961), *New Patterns of Management,* and (1967), *The Human Organization.* George C. Homans (1950), *The Human Group.*	Daniel Katz, and Robert L. Kahn (1964), *The Social Psychology of Organizations.* James G. Miller (1972), *Living Systems: The Organization.* Joan Woodward (1958), *Management and Technology,* and (1965), *Industrial Organization: Theory and Practice.* Paul R. Lawrence and Jay W. Lorsch (1967), *Organization and Environment: Managing Differentiation and Integration.* Herbert A. Simon (1947), *Administrative Behavior,* and (1956), *Models of Man.*

Today, we know the Scientific Management School best as a set of principles of management that grew out of the work of Taylor, Fayol, and other representatives of the school: span of control (each supervisor should manage the work of only a handful of subordinates, usually five or six at most), unity of command (each individual should have only one direct boss), and delegation of authority to subordinates. The Taylor School denied the importance of noneconomic motivations and discounted the influence of informal work groups.[6] The organization's formal structure was the main tool for achieving maximum performance and efficiency. People were adapted to this structure; organizations hired only the parts of people that related to their task.

Today, the shortcomings of Taylorism are thought to outweigh its strong points. "This school of thought is fighting a rear-guard action in the groves of academe, if not in the stony field of actual organization" (Perrow 1970a, p. 16). Few advocates of the Scientific Management School can be found to trumpet its principles today, although certain vestiges of its thinking may be seen in assembly-line production and in military organizations.

Taylorism and Communication

Frederick Taylor actually had little to say about communication in his book *Scientific Management.* His emphasis was on organizational structure and on individual behavior. Communication was to be formal, hierarchical, and planned; its purpose was to get the work done, to increase productivity and efficiency. In sum, Taylorism viewed communication as one-sided and vertical (top-down) and task-related.

Henri Fayol (1949) most clearly elaborated the role of communication flows in organizations, and the restrictions placed on communication by the organizational structure. Fayol illustrated this problem of restricted communication flows, and suggested a solution. If communication is required between individuals L and M (see Fig. 1-1), who are at the same hierarchical level but in two different departments, they can formally contact each other only by sending a message up and down the long, twelve-step ladder of command. It is obviously much more sensible, and much quicker, for L and M to communicate directly, even though this action bypasses their eleven superiors. Fayol argued that such direct, horizontal communication ought to be allowed in an organization, at least in crisis situations when rapid action is essential. His special-purpose bypassing device today bears the name of "Fayol's Bridge"; it represents recognition by the Scientific Management School that the formal structure may unduly impede useful communication flows, and that special exceptions ought to be allowed (we return to this point in Chapter 4).

The Scientific Management School recognized that communication problems occurred in organizations, at least when certain management "principles" were not followed correctly. For instance, if the span of control of a manager became too wide because he or she had more than five or six subordinates, ability to communicate effectively with underlings was likely to suffer (Gulick and Urwick 1937; Mooney and Reiley 1939). The solution to this problem, the Taylorists claimed, was the delegation of authority by the manager to lower levels in the hierarchy, with an accompanying decrease in the span of control.[7]

Scientific Management also distinguished between the communication functions of "line" and "staff." Staff officials were usually specialists in certain matters (like personnel, accounting, and supply), and their communication function was thought to consist in persuading their executive head to accept their advice. Line officials were cogs in the chain of command, and so their function was to communicate orders from their boss to their subordinates, and to see that such instructions were properly carried out.

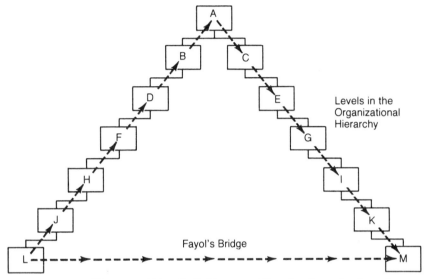

Fig. 1-1 Diagram of Fayol's Bridge, providing for direct horizontal communication between individuals L and M

Overall, *the Scientific Management School did not accord a very significant role to communication, and it conceived of communication as limited to command and control through vertical, formal channels.* This viewpoint assumed that those at the top possessed all the relevant information, and the function of communication was to disseminate their knowledge.

We know today that communication operates in many ways in an organization. But it was not until the 1940s that these came to be more fully realized with the advent of the Human Relations School.

Human Relations School

The Human Relations School grew out of the thinking of two founders: Chester I. Barnard, who had been president of the New Jersey Bell Telephone Company, and Elton Mayo, a professor of industrial research in the Harvard University Graduate School of Business. Barnard authored a tremendously influential book, *The Functions of the Executive,* published in 1938; Mayo headed a series of researches by Harvard professors in the Hawthorne plant of the Western Electric Company that revolutionized conceptions of human behavior and motivation in organizations. Mayo is generally recognized as the founder of the Human Relations School (and of industrial sociology), although he and Barnard were in close touch at the time, and probably both deserve about equal credit for leading the scientific revolution against the Scientific Management School.

The frontal attack on the Scientific Management School reached a peak in the late 1940s and 1950s. Barnard's book and the findings from the Hawthorne studies (see below) were crucial, but changes in the industrial landscape were also involved. The proportion of white-collar workers in the work force increased tremendously during the economic boom following World War II; these professionals at lower- and middle-management levels were not hired because they were a relative of the owner, nor did most of them rise through the ranks. Rather, they were flowing out of engineering and business schools into the corporations. Government and other nonindustrial organizations had also begun to hire large numbers of professionals. The cost of hiring these well-educated employees helped make organizations more aware of employees' needs; they were treated with consideration in order to keep them in the organization. No longer were workers viewed by management as quiescent extensions of the company's machines.

The studies that were most important in rediscovering human motivation at work, and which became a cornerstone of organizational behavior theory, are known as the Hawthorne studies.

Illumination at the Hawthorne Plant

In the mid-1920s, the National Research Council's Illuminating Engineering Society conducted a series of industrial lighting studies. The results were rather surprising, as they indicated that "it was clear that a direct relationship between illumination and production was non-existent" (Snow 1927). Additional studies were planned on the relationship between illumination on the job and workers' productivity. One of the participating firms was the Western Electric Company.

In the late 1920s, that firm, in collaboration with the Committee on Work in Industry of the National Research Council, initiated a series of such studies at the Western Electric Hawthorne plant in Cicero, Illinois, outside of Chicago. These researches were begun by William J. Dickson, a Western Electric manager. The Hawthorne plant employed about 4,000 workers in manufacturing equipment for the telephone industry. Its name was to become famous as the site of a classic social science investigation that was to revolutionize conceptions of organizational behavior.

The research at the Hawthorne plant began with a number of field experiments on improved illumination,[8] all of which ended in surprising and intellectually frustrating results. In one experiment, for example, workers were divided into two groups: a control group in which the regular level of lighting was maintained, and an experimental group in which the lighting was increased, first from 24 to 46, and then to 70 footcandles. As expected, production increased under these brighter conditions. But, amazingly, production also increased by about the same amount in the control group!

Then the lighting was diminished in the experimental room, first to 10 and then to 3 footcandles. Production went up, not down (as expected). In the control room, where lighting remained constant, production went up.

In yet another experiment, the illumination was reduced to .06 of a footcandle, approximately equivalent to moonlight; not until this very dim condition was reached did production begin to decrease.

Something very strange was going on, and the researchers tried to figure out exactly what it was. Clearly they could not conclude from their investigations that illumination was directly related to the level of production of the workers. Rather, production seemed to be related to the workers' perception of the special attention they were getting from the investigators. Whether they were in the experimental or in the control group, the workers knew they were respondents in a research study, and this realization apparently inspired them to greater production. In honor of the study in which this effect was first noticed and so dramatically demonstrated, social scientists have called it the "Hawthorne effect" (defined as the tendency for individuals to behave in an artificial way when they know they are subjects in an experiment).

One of the Hawthorne researchers, Fritz J. Roethlisberger (1941, p. 15), an industrial psychologist from Harvard University, concluded that "in most work situations the meaning of a change is likely to be as important, if not more so, than the change itself. This was . . . the new illumination that came from the research. It was an illumination quite different from what . . . had [been] expected from the illumination studies."

Enter the Professors

When the results of the illumination experiments appeared mysterious to the investigators, they called in Professor Elton Mayo from the Harvard University Business School, an industrial sociologist who had had previous research experience in studying workers' productivity. Professor Mayo and his colleagues, Fritz Roethlisberger and William Dickson, along with several others carried out a series of researches between 1927 and 1932 that are today referred to as the "Hawthorne studies."

In one experiment, the researchers set up a small work room called the Relay Assembly Test Room. Six female workers were assigned to assemble telephone relays. A variety of experimental treatments were introduced: a group payment incentive, rest pauses, shorter working hours, and refreshments. Production increased with each of these treatments. Then the Relay Assembly Test Room reverted to a 48-hour, six-day week, with no incentives, no rest pauses, and no refreshments. Production went up to the highest level yet recorded!

Next, Mayo and his research group set up the Bank Wiring Observation Room, in which the researchers could closely observe and record the behavior of the workers. The latter constituted a highly integrated group, with their own norms and code of behavior. The production rate of this work group seldom varied, and the social scientists soon learned why: the work group had its own standards of production, and group pressure was exerted to achieve and maintain this standard, despite the efforts of management to increase production.

Rediscovering Informal Communication

This serendipitous rediscovery of the roots of worker motivation in informal social relationships was to become the most famous product of the Hawthorne studies.[9] In their review of social science research literature, Katz and Lazarsfeld (1955, pp. 33–42) consider the Hawthorne studies one of the main empirical investigations leading to the "rediscovery" of the primary group (a relatively small-sized group of individuals in intimate relationships, such as a family or a friendship network): a belated recognition of the importance of informal interpersonal relationships in situations formerly conceptualized as strictly formal and atomistic.[10]

The Hawthorne studies marked an important intellectual watershed in conceptions of organizational behavior, leading to an entire recasting of assumptions about human behavior in organizations. The resulting new paradigm was called the "Human Relations" School, because of its emphasis on employee relationships as the determining factor in production. Concepts like worker satisfaction and morale rose to the fore in this school, which was individual-centered rather than organization-oriented.

In contrast to the Scientific Management School's conception of the worker as an economic man who responded directly to monetary incentives, the Human Relations School perceived the worker as a *social* man, responding to the interpersonal influences of the informal work group. "The emotional, unplanned, nonrational elements in organizational behavior" were stressed (Etzioni 1964, p. 20). One noted example of such group influence on worker productivity was observed in the Bank Wiring Observation Room of the Hawthorne plant. The workers produced at a rate established not by their supervisors, not by time-and-motion experts, but *by themselves as a group*. If a worker did not produce up to this standard, the group would exert pressure on him to work harder, and they might even pitch in to help the slow producer (thus confounding the official work production records kept on the individual). At the same time, an overproducer (called a "speed king" or "rate-buster") was also pressured by his peers, and might even be physically assaulted until his work output returned to the group-sanctioned norm.

Changing Organizational Behavior Through the Human Relations Approach

Clearly, the Human Relations scholars argued, conducting time-and-motion studies of individual workers and offering them cash incentives as individuals would, in such a group-centered work situation, be futile. A more appropriate strategy would be to assess the workers' needs and then seek to satisfy them; the increased job satisfaction would presumably lead to higher production. The message of the Human Relations School was that "tender loving care" of the workers by their supervisors, and by higher management, would pay off in higher production. The Human Relations viewpoint ultimately led organizational scholars to focus on leadership as a means of attaining greater job satisfaction and thus greater productivity.

Organizational researchers at the Institute for Social Research at the University of Michigan, one of the academic centers for Human Relationists in the 1950's and 1960's, were generally not able to prove that satisfied workers produce more than dissatisfied workers (Tannenbaum and Seashore, no date).[11] In fact, sometimes the least satisfied workers are the highest producers. This unreasonable finding led researchers to investigate supervisory leadership, and a common research finding was that style of supervision (such as showing a concern for subordinates as human beings) was related to production. Training programs for work leaders were subsequently designed, emphasizing the human relations approach, as a means of raising production.

The Human Relations School advocated the use of such training programs to change human behavior and thus solve organizational problems. This approach amounts to altering individual behavior in order to bring about change in the system. An alternative approach would, of course, be to change the organizational structure or goals (Perrow 1970b). In many cases, both individual training programs and changing the organizational structure are needed. In fact, a common experience is that a new trainee, when returned to his or her old job in an existing structure, quickly slides back into his or her old behavior.

The Scanlon Plan: An Operationalization of the Human Relations Approach

The most famous participation and incentive system growing out of the Human Relations movement is called the Scanlon Plan, after its founder, Joseph N. Scanlon. Scanlon was a laborer in the 1930s on an open-hearth blast furnace in a steel company that was rapidly slipping into bankruptcy. Its equipment was obsolete, its profits were nil, and the labor union was demanding higher wages. Scanlon was a union leader in this steel mill, and he convinced the company executives and his fellow workers to try a cooperative work-management productivity plan to meet the immediate financial crisis. Thus was born the Scanlon Plan (Lesieur 1958).

The employees agreed to make an all-out effort to improve production, and offered numerous suggestions for reducing costs, decreasing waste, and improving efficiency and quality. Management agreed to grant the union's demands for higher wages as soon as improved production made such increases possible.

The story ended happily, as the steel company pulled out of its financial nose dive and the workers soon received their salary boost. Joe Scanlon became famed as a consultant who could rescue failing companies with his radical plan for labor-management cooperation. He took a staff position with the United Steelworkers Union, where he promoted the Scanlon Plan, and then he joined the faculty of MIT, although he still continued his consulting activities in the field of labor-management relations.

At the heart of the Scanlon Plan are two essential elements: (1) that all members of the organization participate in improving productivity by offering suggestions, and (2) that all members are rewarded equitably for improving productivity (Frost and others, 1974, p. 5). The first tenet of the plan is achieved by utilizing an open suggestion system, with a set of "production committees" throughout the organization (composed of one manager and a small number of representatives elected by the workers) to screen the suggestions. For example, in the Atwood Vacuum Machine Company of Rockford, Illinois, over 28,000 suggestions were received from its 2,000 employees during the first fourteen years of the Scanlon Plan (Lesieur and Puckett 1969). At the Stromberg-Carlson Company, 1,300 suggestions were received during the first eighteen months of the plan; half of these suggestions were accepted and implemented in order to improve production. The suggestion system provides a means for upward feedback from the workers to management; the fact that these messages get through and are acted upon encourages the feeling that making suggestions is worthwhile. From time to time, special campaigns are organized in order to obtain even more suggestions, sometimes by offering prizes and other benefits.

Each production committee has the authority to immediately implement in its shop or division any suggestions it considers reasonable, except for relatively high-cost suggestions, which are passed on to the company's "screening committee" (composed equally of top executives and elected workers) for action. This committee also computes and allocates a monthly bonus to all employees on the basis of the current increase in total company productivity as compared with a previous time period, which implements the second element of the plan. The bonus is not an *individual worker* incentive, as the Scientific Management School advocated, but a *group* incentive, paid on the basis of the performance of the total organization; the purpose of this bonus system is to encourage all parts of the organization to work together cooperatively for higher performance. Thus the employee suggestions and the extensive committee work that is required by the Scanlon Plan pay off in improved welfare for all.

For example, the Parker Pen Company of Janesville, Wisconsin, initiated the Scanlon Plan among its 1,000 workers in 1955. Monthly bonuses, ranging from 6 to 20 per cent, have been earned in about 85 percent of the months since (Lesieur and Puckett 1969). Today, a number of North American and European companies use some version of the Scanlon Plan. It is not always successful, and it has failed in some organizations.

The Scanlon Plan operationalizes in a specific and useful form many of the key tenets of the Human Relations School: a participatory management style in which the workers are involved,[12] bottom-up communication flows in the form of employee suggestions about how to improve organizational performance, and a bonus system that encourages cooperative activities by groups of workers and managers. Its relative success to date is one evidence that the Human Relations viewpoint has some validity, at least in certain organizations.

Criticisms of the Hawthorne Studies

The data base from the Hawthorne studies was actually rather inadequate for the broad assumptions and claims of the Human Relations School, and a number of scholarly criticisms along this line have appeared in recent years.[13] These criticisms claim that the methodology of the Hawthorne studies was inadequate or defective (for example, they cite faulty sampling as a basis for generalization of the research results), and question the resulting philosophy of the Human Relations School, such as that satisfying workers' needs leads to higher production.

Some critics of the Human Relations School have charged that it is manipulative, in that involving the workers in participatory decision making may be used by management only to gain the facade of democracy, while in fact the decisions have already been made. "It has been charged that providing workers with 'gripe sessions' and suggestion boxes . . . may reduce their alienation without improving their lot" (Etzioni 1964, p. 45).

Other critics object to the purpose of management's ostensible concern for, and communication with, workers. "Those who favor the syrupy form of human relations—being friendly, knowing each worker's name and how many children he has, distributing selectively a little bag of rewards—have done a great disservice to management by obscuring its real responsibilities and the real needs of workers" (Mott 1972, p. 183).

Managers and work supervisors became the focus of interest of the Human Relations School and the vehicles for changing worker behavior, as we showed previously. To maximize production, they needed to pay attention to employees' social needs. "In effect, they took a bagful of cookies along when they took the child to the dentist. Instead of scolding, they would now be modern and sensible. They would distract the kid, and, if necessary, bribe him" (Leavitt and others 1973, p. 130).

Much research on organizational behavior seems to have been conducted by gathering data from workers in order to obtain understanding mainly for the benefit of management. This elitist bias in social science research is especially apparent in the Human Relations School. There is never really much doubt, when one reads the various books and other publications growing out of the Hawthorne studies, as to whom they are expected to benefit. The researchers seem to be rather firmly enlisted on the side of management, in a cozy partnership of Harvard University professors and Western Electric captains of industry. Of course the workers benefit also, if the executives really listen to the professors' research results about the importance of their needs and satisfaction, but management seems to definitely come first.[14]

The Contribution of Chester Barnard

In addition to the Hawthorne studies, the other main intellectual input to the Human Relations School was Chester Barnard's (1938) book *The Functions of the Executive.* Actually, Barnard was in close contact with Elton Mayo and his research group at Harvard University, and so it is not surprising that they agreed in putting forward a "social" worker in place of the "economic man" of the Scientific Management School. Instead of calling on empirical research studies, however, as did Professor Mayo and his group, Barnard depended upon his extensive and insightful experience as the top executive of the New Jersey Bell Telephone Company.

Barnard was not satisfied with the traditional definition of an organization. To him, the most essential characteristic of an organization was communication. He gave considerable attention to both the formal and the informal aspects of organizations. "Informal organizations," he wrote, "are necessary to the operations of formal organizations" (Barnard, 1938, p. 123): informal groups establish attitudes, norms, and individual codes of conduct within the formal system. Communication, cohesion, and protection of individual integrity are the main functions of informal organization. Barnard was one of the first organization theorists to give importance to human motivation as a crucial factor in production, and to recognize that economic motives were sometimes of minor significance.

"Though I early found out how to behave effectively in organizations, not until I had much later relegated economic theory and economic interests to a secondary—though indispensable—place did I begin to understand organizations or human behavior in them" (Barnard 1938, p. xxxi). Thus Barnard raised noneconomic motives to much greater attention than they had received at the hands of the Scientific Management School. Previously, most business managers thought that if they waved a fistful of green stuff in front of their workers' eyes, the latter would produce more. But Barnard's position flew in the face of this conception of economic man.

Barnard envisioned an essentially cooperative relationship between the individual and the organization. There are certain needs that any given individual cannot attain alone, hence he or she must cooperate with others in an organized way to achieve them. So the organization simply helps the individual do what he or she could not otherwise accomplish.

Publication of Barnard's book marked the beginning of the realization of the importance of communication in organizations. "The first executive function," he wrote, "is to develop and maintain a system of communication" (Barnard 1938, p. 226). Although communication was emphasized throughout his book, Barnard's conception of communication was a limited one, with the focus on its use by authority. To Barnard, communication was mainly what a source (usually a manager or executive) did *to* a receiver (a subordinate).

Barnard set forth a series of principles of communication in organizations, which today we would recognize as dealing mainly with formal, one-way communication. For example, he proposed (1938, pp. 175–181) that:

1. Communication channels should be clearly established through organization charts.
2. No "bypassing" of formal channels should be allowed.
3. Formal channels of communication must exist for everyone; each individual must report to someone and be subordinate to someone.

Other Human Relationists: The Human Resources Subschool

While Barnard and Mayo-Roethlisberger-Dickson were the kingpins in the Human Relations School, several scholars, such as Professor Douglas McGregor of MIT, Rensis Likert of the University of Michigan, and Chris Argyris (formerly of Yale, and now at Harvard University), made important contributions in carrying on, expanding, and refining the main tenets of the Human Relations movement. These latter-day scholars are often labeled the "Human Resources" group, because they assumed that all segments of the organization (workers and managers) could benefit from more appropriate human relationships in the organization.

McGregor (1960) contrasted Theory X (based on the classical notion of a rational economic man) with Theory Y, a view of man as independent, responsible, and growth-oriented. Likert (1961, 1967) argued for a participatory style of organizational management, in which the workers are involved in decision-making processes. Argyris (1957, 1960) claimed that the employees' struggle for need satisfaction within an organizational structure often led to a conflict between the goals of the organization and those of the individual member.

The participatory management approach, promoted by Likert and other Human Relationists in the United States, may be culture-bound. Is a participatory leadership style appropriate, for example, in certain Asian nations where an authoritarian relationship between a boss and a subordinate has been institutionalized for centuries? If a superior in such a situation treated his employees as coequal participants in decisionmaking, he would probably be ridiculed by them.

However, the scarce evidence available to date suggests that a somewhat higher degree of participatory management may perhaps be related to organizational effectiveness, even in Asia. For example, one study shows that those family planning clinics in the Republic of Korea and in Singapore which were more participatory were somewhat higher in effectiveness.[15] Perhaps Likert-style participatory leadership is not so culture-bound after all.

In recent years, the "contingency" viewpoint that no one type of organizational structure or leadership style is most appropriate for all situations—has gained much credence. Such variables as the organization's objectives, its size, and the culture in which it operates must be considered in specifying its most effective organizational structure and communication behavior. In other words, what "works" in Keokuk may not work in Allahabad, and vice versa. Participatory management style may be appropriate in the General Motors plant in Flint, Michigan, but less so in the Singhania Textile Mills in Kanpur.

From S–M–C–R to R–M–C–S

With the Hawthorne studies came the realization that informal group functioning was very much a part of the total organizational landscape. Attaining participation, strengthening commitment to the organization, and maintaining group cohesion were seen as important functions of communication within informal work groups. Barnard perceived of communication as an essential characteristic of an organization: "In any exhaustive theory of organization, communication would occupy a central place" (1938, p. 8). Generally, *the Human Relationists saw communication as relatively more important than had the Taylorists. And they perceived of organizational communication, not just as a means of sources (that is, management) talking to workers, but of management listening to what the workers were saying.* The workers came first in the receiver-oriented approach to communication advocated by the Human Relations School.

In 1958, the American Management Association published "Ten Commandments for Successful Communication," an article addressed to business executives. An emphasis on communication, in the broadest sense of the term, was justified by the argument that efficient management depended on it. The ten principles of "good" communication dealt with planning, analysis, purpose, meaning and intent, receiver orientation, a long-range viewpoint, the consonance of actions with communication, and the virtues of being a good listener. The trend was toward a humanistic view of communication, in order to achieve "satisfied" workers. The informal communication system was understood and accepted. Focus was upon superior-subordinate interaction, and hence communication became almost synonymous with motivation and leadership in organizations. Participatory management became popular, and the Human Relationists believed that a high degree of interaction among individuals and groups, as exemplified by the Scanlon Plan, was needed for a truly "democratic" organization (Likert 1967).

"Many of the actually existing patterns of human interaction have no representation in the formal organization at all, and others are inadequately represented by the formal organization. . . . *Too often it is assumed that the organization of a company corresponds to . . . an organization chart.* Actually, it never does" (Roethlisberger and Dickson 1939, p. 559). This statement by the Hawthorne researchers illustrates their realization that communication in organizations was informal and interpersonal (actually, the Human Relationists may have overemphasized informal communication to the neglect of formal structure).

Because of their ubiquity in empirical investigations like the Hawthorne studies and the many researches that followed it, rumors[16] came in for heavy attention. Formal, vertical communication channels are often short-circuited or negated by the "grapevine"—as was shown in a noted study of rumoring conducted in the "Jason Company," a leather manufacturing firm (Davis 1953a). The lesson for business managers, presumably, was to understand and use informal channels, rather than to ignore rumors and have their plans wrecked by them. Because rumors spread interpersonally and across hierarchical levels, the overwhelming importance ascribed to formal, vertical channels by the Scientific Management School came to be doubted by the Human Relationists. Their focus on the worker and on satisfying his or her needs as a means of achieving higher production led to their taking the worker's view of the organization, and of organizational communication as well. *The Human Relation School focused attention on informal communication among peers in an organization.*

"The Plant Is Closing, the Plant Is Closing"

In a spoof of the Human Relations approach, Etzioni (1964, p. 43) asks us to imagine a training movie in which we see "a happy factory in which the wheels hum steadily and the workers rhythmically serve the machine with smiles on their faces." But then a truck driver arrives and mysteriously unloads large crates containing new machines. "A dark type with long sideburns who sweeps the floor in the factory spreads a rumor that firing is imminent since the new machines will take over the work of many of the workers. The wheels turn slower, the workers are sad." That evening they carry their gloom home to their wives and families.

The next morning, however, the workers are reassured by the voice of their boss over the intercom system in the plant. "He tells them that the rumor is absolutely false; the machines are to be set up in the new wing and more workers will be hired since the factory is expanding its production. Everybody sighs in relief, smiles return, the machines hum speedily and steadily again." Only the floor sweeper is saddened, as nobody will listen to his rumors anymore.

The moral of this film is clear: had management adequately communicated its expansion plans to the workers, the near-crisis could have been averted. Or perhaps the workers should have been involved in making the decision to expand in the first place. In any event, a participatory-management would have considered the feelings and reactions of the workers.

The Human Relations ethic did transfer some degree of authority and power from the formal organizational structures to the peer group at the operational level. But management still wanted the game played according to the organization's rules, not just the workers'. The individual was considered and invited to participate in decision making, but with the main objective of attaining greater work performance. Unfortunately, there was an inauthentic quality to organizational communication as viewed in this light: "A major effect [of the Human Relations movement] was to reduce the honesty of communication; it led people to play games, to delude one another, to talk at one level while communicating at another" (Leavitt and others, 1973, p. 42).

The Systems School

In the 1960s and 1970s a synthesis of the Scientific Management and Human Relations Schools began to emerge, as part of a gradual realization that the assumptions of the first school best fit some types of organizations, while the conceptions of the second school were more appropriate to other structures. The Systems School that emerged represented a more eclectic and encompassing viewpoint; in fact, the general systems theorists claimed that their theoretical approach could be applied to any living system (any biological or social system). That is, general systems theory is a general theory of systems (Laszlo 1975). It conceptualizes an organization as a system of interrelated components, and stresses the orchestration of these parts as the key to maximizing performance.

The empirical scope of the Systems School was wider than that of the Scientific Management and Human Relations Schools. The latter had focused mainly on factories in their empirical studies; only later was this limited data base somewhat broadened. In contrast, a variety of types of organizations were studied by the Systems researchers: prisons, schools, armies, hospitals, and many kinds of business firms.

General Systems Theory

Unlike its predecessors, which arose mainly from practical experience and empirical research, the Systems School was grounded in a theoretical perspective called "general systems theory." This intellectual viewpoint has been the single most influential theory in contemporary scientific thought, especially in the social sciences. Key figures in launching this scientific revolution were the biologist and philosopher Ludwig van Bertalanffy, the logician Anatol Rapoport, the philosopher-economist Kenneth Boulding, and the sociologist Talcott Parsons.[17]

Theorists of this school conceived of a system as a set of interdependent parts (Bertalanffy 1956, 1962, 1968). One essential element of a system is communication, which links the parts or subsystems so as to facilitate their interdependence. This focus on interaction as the lifeblood of a system was, of course, completely compatible with the view of organizations held by communication scientists. Hence general systems theory was welcomed by the field of communication in general, and has had a strong impact on the study of human communication. It also revolutionized organizational theory and has remained the dominant viewpoint in the field.

General systems theory had been defined as the "science of 'wholeness'" (Bertalanffy 1968, p. 37). It contends with wholes and how to deal with them, relationships between parts, interaction of wholes with the environment, the creation and elaboration of structures, adaptive evolution, goal seeking, and the control or self-regulation of direction (Buckley 1967, p. 2). The central credo of the systems viewpoint is the statement that the whole is more than the sum of its parts. The systems approach arose, and achieved a following in each of the social sciences, because it represented an alternative to the mechanistic atomism then common in most research on human behavior. The atomistic approach assumed that explanation is achieved by breaking down a phenomenon into its parts, and then understanding the parts. The whole was assumed to be just the sum of its parts. In contrast, systems theory is holistic.

It assumes that the complex interactions among the parts of a given system are destroyed by the dissection of the system through atomistic research procedures. Instead, wholes have to be studied and understood as total units, as systems.

The Unfulfilled Potential of Systems–Oriented Research in Organizations

It was an easy and natural move for organization theorists and communication scientists in the Systems School to apply the concepts and viewpoints of general systems theory to the study of organizations, and to the analysis of organizational communication. The systems approach to the study of organizations proceeds from the premise that an organization is a system, composed of a series of definite elements having limited goals. The organization's goal is to achieve optimal efficiency as a whole. Maximum efficiencies on the part of all of its elements are not so important, as the whole is more significant.

The new perspective in analyzing organizations provided by general systems theory, however, had little impact on the actual operations of research. Although social science systems theory provided a new and useful sensitizing orientation to the study of human behavior in organizations (in that it encouraged thinking in holistic terms), the needed research methods for studying behavior in a total-system context were not readily available.

The problem with the systems approach is precisely that it is difficult to effectuate in actual research operations. The vocabulary of systems theory ("structure," "feedback," "input-output," "open systems," "boundary maintenance") infected social scientific thinking in the mid-1960s, and provided a sensitizing function in the intellectual analysis of human behavioral problems (Buckley 1967, p. 7). But social scientists generally proceeded to use their previously existing research techniques within the new theoretical perspective of systems theory. For example, researchers would typically single out for research attention one or two variables that were easily measured, and ignore all other variables that might also be involved in the situation studied. The resulting research results fell far short of the promising potential of the systems approach.

Social science research has usually been concerned with trees rather than forests. Largely owing to influences from the physical sciences, the social sciences have generally studied specific parts of a system, in order to then proceed to understand the whole system. Or so they thought.

Most past communication research has been of this limited nature, and hence has been rather uninteresting from a systems perspective. Laboratory/experiment research methods in communication (and in other fields) have been relatively atomistic, while field studies have generally tended to be somewhat more holistic, but even they have been much less so than a true systems approach would demand.

We utilize a systems framework in this book to order and present our synthesis of what is currently known about organizational communication. Specifically, we follow an open system approach.

An Open System Approach

A *system* is a set of units that has some degree of structure, and that is differentiated from the environment by a boundary. The system's boundary is defined by communication flows; the units in the system have a greater degree of communication with each other than—across the boundary—with units in the external environment. But this does not mean that communication across the boundary is any less important for the system's maintenance than information exchanges within the system. In fact, any system that does not input matter, energy, and information *from* its environment and output messages *to* its environment will soon run down and eventually cease to exist.

The Systems School of organization theorists focused especially on *open* systems, because most organizations are relatively "open." What do we mean by open and closed systems?

A *closed* system is completely isolated from its environment. Its boundaries are closed to the exchange of information and energy with the environment.

By contrast, an *open system* continuously exchanges information with its environment. It imports information from its environment, transforms or processes this "raw material," and exports the finished product back into its environment.

A closed system does not admit matter-energy[18] from external sources, and therefore it is subject to "entropy" and the Second Law of Thermodynamics, which states that all (closed) systems move toward disorganization or death (Buckley 1968, p. xviii). *Entropy* is a measure of the degree of disorder in a system.

Open systems do not behave according to the Second Law of Thermodynamics, because they import matter-energy from their environments. If open systems became closed, they would eventually run down and die. "The open system does not run down, because it can import energy from the world around it. Thus the operation of entropy is counteracted by the importation of energy and the living system is characterized by negative rather than positive entropy" (Katz and Kahn 1966, p. 19).

An open system employs feedback mechanisms in order to provide a certain degree of self-regulation, so that deviations from equilibrium are constantly being corrected. Such mechanisms help the system achieve and maintain a *steady state,*[19] in which some aspect of the system remains constant in spite of its importing and exporting of information. Open systems tend toward increased specialization and differentiation. Open systems are capable of reaching the same end state despite different initial conditions (this quality is called "*equifinality*").

Most *living systems* (that is, human or other types of biological systems, as opposed to physical systems) are thought to be open rather than closed. Certainly most communication systems, including organizations, are relatively open (Thayer 1972, p. 116; Katz and Kahn 1966). "Social organizations are flagrantly open systems in that the input of energies and the conversion of output into further energic input consist of transactions between the organization and its environment" (Katz and Kahn 1966, pp. 16–17).

The openness of open systems implies that a fast-changing environment causes appropriately rapid change in the organization. The open system approach pictures organizations as constantly changing—unlike the Human Relations School, which hardly allowed for change.

"Open system theory is not a theory at all" (Katz and Kahn 1966, p. 452), at least in the sense of providing a set of specific hypotheses that can be tested in empirical research. But the open system approach was certainly theoretical, in the sense that it provided an integrated body of concepts constituting a framework for the study of organizational communication. And the Systems School was thus distinctive in its foundations from the Scientific Management and Human Relations Schools, both of which arose inductively out of experience and empiricism.

Looking Outward

So *the Systems School of organization theorists view an organization as an open system that inputs and outputs to the environment across its boundary* (Fig. 1-2). Until the mid-1960s most organization scholars looked within the system for factors explaining the behavior of the organization and of its members. Their analyses usually stopped at the boundary. The organization was treated as an isolated entity; little attention was given to the environment, and to what went on in the environment as an explanation of changes in the organization. The open system view implied the importance of the organization's environment, and led to intellectual attempts to classify environments.[20] *Openness,* the degree to which a system exchanges information with its environment, became an important variable in organization research.

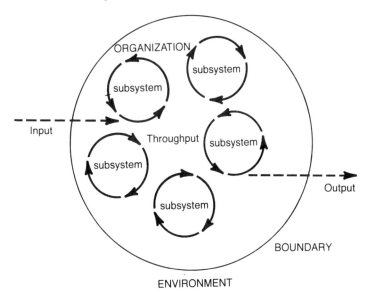

Fig. 1-2 Main elements in an open system conceptualization of an organization

An organization is a system composed of a set of subsystem components that each serve certain functions, and that are each in interaction with the other subsystems. An organization inputs information and matter-energy from its environment, and, after processing these elements, outputs them. Thus changes in the environment have a continuous impact on the organization, so that it is constantly adjusting to environmental change; contrariwise, the organization's internal changes have a continuous impact on its environment (Katz and Kahn 1966). The systems viewpoint, as we have seen, emphasized the interrelationships and exchanges between an organization and its environment; the Scientific Management and Human Relations Schools often studied an organization as an isolated entity, looking within the organization for explanations of organizational behavior. The Systems School also looked outside, to the organizational environment.

The Internal Function of Communication

The Systems School focuses upon the interdependency of the subsystem components of the system. Most organizations have, at the least, a production subsystem, a maintenance subsystem, and an adaptation or innovation subsystem. Each subsystem has certain goals, and each seeks to contribute to the system's overall objective, thus encouraging the interdependency of the subsystems. This interdependency depends on communication.

The units in a system do not all have an equal amount of communication with each other, and so it is useful to speak of subsystems within a system. A *subsystem* is a set composed of those units within a system that have more frequent communication with other units in their subsystem than with those units not in their subsystem. Thus subboundaries exist within the system's boundary that mark off the system's subsystems.

One problem is to specify exactly where a system's boundary is. This difficulty occurs because every system is part of a larger system, which is in turn a subsystem of a still larger system. The problem is to know where to stop. A similar problem occurs in specifying the subsystems within a system. Each of these subsystems, in turn, has subsystems.

The point here is that every organization is a nesting of systems, composed of systems within systems. There are levels of systems, and the choice of what level to consider *the* system is somewhat arbitrary, depending in part on the purpose of the analyst. Often in research in organizations the system is specified by the identity of the organization.

Daniel Katz and Robert Kahn

After general systems theory was begun by a small group of scientists at the University of Chicago, the University of Michigan became one of the academic centers of the general systems theorists. Professors Anatol Rapoport and Kenneth Boulding, for example, were faculty members, and it was natural that open systems thinking would be applied by their colleagues in Ann Arbor to the study of organizations. Professor James G. Miller at Michigan authored a series of influential articles in the mid-1960s and early 1970s on the theory of living systems; one of these dealt with organizations as living systems (Miller 1972). But probably the greatest boost to applying open system theory to organizations came from two University of Michigan professors, Daniel Katz and Robert Kahn, through publication of their book *The Social Psychology of Organizations* (Katz and Kahn 1966). This volume, based indirectly on the authors' extensive experience in investigating organizational behavior, set forth and illustrated the main credo of open system theory. Publication of the Katz and Kahn book marked the real beginning of the application of systems thinking to the study of organizations, and launched what we have called in this chapter the Systems School.

The "Technology" Subschool

During approximately the same period in which the open system theorists of organization were at work in the United States, especially at the University of Michigan, a related theoretical development in organizations theory was underway in England, centering around Joan Woodward and other researchers.[21] This approach focused on "technology" as the defining characteristic of organizations. "Technology" was used here not in the usual sense of machinery, but rather, more broadly, as referring to the tasks that organizations perform. Woodward (1958) classified technology as to whether an industrial production process was (1) unit or small-batch (like making custom suits), (2) mass or large-batch (like automobile assembly lines), or (3) continuous flow process (as in chemical companies). In her sample of 100 English manufacturing firms, Woodward found that organizations in a similar category of technology had similar organizational structures. For example, supervision was more direct in the small-batch technology companies and less direct in the continuous-process firms, where the structure had more hierarchical layers. The higher degree of specialization in the continuous-process technology meant that a greater number of specialized work units, and hence more communication among them, was needed.

The technology approach to studying organizations is consistent with the general viewpoint of the Systems School, in that interdependence among subsystems is emphasized, but it differs in the heavy emphasis put upon the organization's task (its "technology") as an independent variable explaining other aspects of the system's structure and its members' communication behavior. It is not yet known whether Woodward's approach is applicable to people-processing organizations, such as a government welfare agency, as well as to industrial firms.[22]

Out of these studies has come the realization that there is no one best structure for an organization, as an organization's structure should be suited to its "technology," environment, and goals (we previously termed this viewpoint the contingency approach to organizational theory). There are a great variety of organizations, and no one approach to organization theory will be useful in all of them. Scientific Management may still apply today to military organizations and assembly-line industries, and perhaps to hierarchical churches like the Roman Catholic. The Human Relations approach is more applicable to other types of organizations, especially those in which large numbers of professionals are employed at the lower operational levels, such as schools and universities and research and development firms. The Systems School provides a theoretical perspective that can be fruitful in understanding any organization.

The Systems View of Communication

As the Systems School recognizes the need to study interactions of the subsystems in an organization, it focuses on communication as the key to analyzing and understanding organizations as social systems. Consequently, communication and information theory were central in the development of systems theory (Wiener 1950—see Table 1-2).

Communication is the basic process facilitating the interdependence of the parts of the total system; it is the mechanism of coordination. The role of communication is to be a "harmonizer" of the organization, an orchestrator of its parts.

"Organizations draw their nourishment from information. They depend for their life on networks and systems of communication that make it possible for many people to work in concert. It is this flow of information that binds an organization together into a single, coherent unit" (Leavitt and others, 1973, p. 57). Information was seen by Systems theorists as "the glue that holds organizations together." In fact, *information processing came to be seen by the Systems School as the main function performed by all organizations; organizational systems were essentially communication systems.*

"The portals and orifices of the organization cannot be sealed off to ensure stability and predictability; instead, the environment must be allowed inside, to ensure adaptability" (Perrow 1970a, p. 179). As we pointed out previously, Systems theorists were paramount in recognizing the importance of external communication with the organization's environment; and they looked to the environment to find explanations for organizational behavior change.

Summary

There are three main "schools" identified in the study of organizational behavior: Scientific Management, Human Relations, and the Systems School. An understanding of these three theoretical positions is important in gaining an understanding of how organizations function, and of the role of communication in organizations. The three schools are examples of "invisible colleges" composed of scholars of similar outlook who are in close communication with each other.

The Scientific Management School, initiated by Frederick W. Taylor, contributed a set of principles to guide the actions of those who manage organizations. Taylorism viewed workers as human extensions of their machines, responsive to individual economic incentives. The Human Relations School

Table 1-2. Comparison of the Nature of Organizational Communication as Seen by the Three Schools

	SCIENTIFIC MANAGEMENT SCHOOL	HUMAN RELATIONS SCHOOL	SYSTEMS SCHOOL
1. *Importance of communication*	Relatively unimportant, and largely restricted to downward communication from management workers.	Relatively important, but mainly limited to peer communication; some attention to communication of needs from workers to management.	Very important; communication is considered the cement that holds the units in an organization together.
2. *Purpose of communication*	To relay orders and information about work tasks, and to achieve obedience and coordination in carrying out such work.	To satisfy workers' needs, to provide for lateral interaction among peers in work groups, and to facilitate the participation of members in organizational decision making.	To control and coordinate, and to provide information to decision makers; and to adjust the organization to changes in its environment.
3. *Direction of communication flows*	Downward (vertical), from management to workers, in order to persuade or convince them to follow instructions.	Horizontal among peers who belong to informal work groups; vertical between workers and management (1) to assess worker needs, and (2) to make possible participatory decision making.	All directions within the system, including downward and upward across hierarchical levels, and across the organization's boundary with the environment.
4. *Main communication problems thought to exist*	Breakdowns in communication due to (1) bypassing a hierarchical level, and (2) a too-large span of control.	Rumors, which are communicated through the "grapevine"; a partially ineffective formal communication structure that is thus supplemented by informal communication.	Overload, distortion, and omission; unresponsiveness to negative feedback.

was founded by Chester I. Barnard and Elton Mayo. The latter rediscovered the importance of informal work groups within the formal structure of the organization in the so-called Hawthorne studies; these researches paved the way for other empirical studies of organizational behavior. Unlike the Scientific Management School, the Human Relationists emphasized communication (especially that among peers) as a key to understanding organizational behavior. Along with the Hawthorne studies, a main intellectual input to the Human Relations School was provided by Barnard's book *The Functions of the Executive,* based upon his personal experience as president of the New Jersey Bell Telephone Company.

The Systems School arose in the late 1930s though the writings of the general systems theorists such as Ludwig van Bertalanffy, who argued for a science of "wholeness"; they conceived of a system as a set of interdependent parts connected by communication flows. The scientific revolution caused by the systems paradigm led to a reorientation of organizational research. Unfortunately, the intellectual potential of systems theory had not yet been fully realized in the operations of organizational research, which are still mainly atomistic and mechanistic.

A *system* is a set of units that has some degree of structure, and that is differentiated from the environment by a boundary. An *open system* continuously exchanges information with its environment. The Scientific Management and Human Relations Schools focused their main attention on the internal functioning of organizations, while the Systems School stressed the crucial role of external communication flows with the environment (in addition to analyzing internal communication).

The three schools of organizational behavior differ in their conceptions of communication. The Scientific Management School placed greater emphasis on vertical, downward flows; the Human Relations School stressed the crucial role of horizontal flows among peers; and the Systems School argues that all flows are important, some being more so for certain purposes or at certain times. Systems theorists give particular attention to communication with the environment and communication flows to link the subsystems within the organization.

So the Scientific Management School arose from an influential book about intuitively derived principles of management; the Human Relations School grew out of a classic empirical investigation; and the Systems School stemmed from a theory.

Notes

[1] The story of the passing intellectual prominence enjoyed by the three schools of organizational behavior is related in numerous books, among them Etzioni (1964), Mouzelis (1967), Perrow (1972), and Pugh and others (1971). For a review by a Russian author, see Gvishiani (1972).

[2] Fayol was a French engineer who had managed Commentary–Fourchamboult–Decazeville, a giant mining and metallurgical compa-

ny, taking it almost from bankruptcy to where it had become one of the most powerful concerns in France by the time of his retirement in 1918. His theory of management was based upon fourteen administrative principles, presumably derived mainly from his personal experience. His book *General and Industrial Management* was published in French in 1916, although it was not available in English until thirty-three years later (Fayol 1949).

[3] Among the followers of Frederick W. Taylor were Frank and Lillian Gilbreth (of *Cheaper by the Dozen* fame). Frank Gilbreth had been a brickwork contractor, who became interested in scientific management about 1906 when he read some of Taylor's early writings. Gilbreth specialized in time-and-motion studies, often using motion pictures of a worker performing a task in order to break it down into its basic parts.

[4] The Taylorist spirit of rationalization was extended from the individual worker to the organization as a whole through the influence of Henri Fayol (Mouzelis 1967, p. 2).

[5] As depicted in the play and film *The Pajama Game,* about the introduction of Taylorism in a pajama factory in Dubuque, Iowa.

[6] In fact, it tended to deal with worker behavior as if it did not occur within an organizational context. Taylorism was "more concerned with the worker as an isolated unit . . . than as an organizational member" (Mouzelis 1967, p. 79).

[7] More recently, it has been recognized that the span of control may include more or less than five to seven individuals, depending on such factors as the nature of the organizational task and the capacity of the leader.

[8] A research approach that was initially quite in line with the Taylor approach of the Scientific Management School.

[9] The main book reporting the results of the Hawthorne studies is Roethlisberger and Dickson (1939); other publications about this investigation are Mayo (1933), Roethlisberger (1941), Whitehead (1938), Landsberger (1958), and Homans (1950).

[10] Other "rediscoveries" of the importance of informal communication included (1) the Erie County study in which Lazarsfeld and others (1948) found that the effects of the mass media in a political election campaign were mediated by opinion leaders in a two-step flow of communication, thus destroying the "hypodermic needle" model of mass media effects, and (2) *The American Soldier* studies in World War II by Stouffer and others (1949), which found

that soldiers were motivated in combat not by the coercion of discipline and of formal orders from above, but by loyalty to a peer group of buddies. In each of the three investigations, informal communication had to be rediscovered because more formal and atomistic conceptualizations left too much unexplained.

[11] Vroom (1964) found a consistent but weak correlation between worker satisfaction and performance. Lawler and Porter (1967) concluded that satisfaction might be a consequence, rather than a cause, of high performance. There are hundreds of other investigations of job satisfaction and its correlates in organizational settings. Most such studies do not find strong evidence for the satisfaction-production hypothesis of the Human Relationists.

[12] Research studies in several companies that have adopted the Scanlon Plan show that their management style is indeed highly participatory (Likert 1967, p. 40).

[13] Some of the most penetrating criticisms of the Hawthorne studies—and, more broadly, of the Human Relations School—are: Argyle (1953), Carey (1967), Mouzelis (1967), Perrow (1972), Cook (1967), Baritz (1961), and Sykes (1965).

[14] This pro-management tilt on the part of organization researchers is paralleled by the source bias on the part of most past communication research. As a result, much research on communication in organizations is directed mainly toward the management of communication for the benefit of the organization's leaders. Too bad.

[15] This investigation, whose results are not yet published, was coordinated by Dr. Hirofumi Ando of the Population Division of the United Nations ECAFE (Economic Commission for Asia and the Far East).

[16] A *rumor* is an unconfirmed message passed from person to person.

[17] They helped move the study of social systems from a *closed system* to an *open system approach* (see below).

[18] We use the concept of "matter-energy" because matter can be converted into energy, and vice versa. *Matter* is anything that has mass and occupies physical space; *energy* is the ability to do work (J.G. Miller 1971).

[19] A *steady state* occurs in a system when a slight disturbance in an equilibrium is counteracted so as to restore the previous state. So energy and activity are required to maintain a steady state.

[20] As, for example, to their degree of turbulence (Terreberry 1968).

[21] Other scholars whose work is somewhat related to Woodward's include: Perrow (1970a), Gouldner (1954), Burns and Stalker (1962), Lawrence and Lorsch (1967), Agarwala-Rogers (1973), and Hage and Aiken (1969).

[22] Yet another "subschool" of organization theory has many aspects of a systems approach, but tends to focus particularly on decision making as a means of understanding organizational behavior. Leading representatives of the decision-making subschool are Simon (1947, 1956) and Cyert and March (1963).

References

Agarwala-Rogers, Rekha. "Technology and Communication Behavior in an Organization: A Case Study in India." Ph.D. thesis, Allahabad, India: University of Allahabad, 1973.

Argyle, Michael. "The Relay Assembly Test Room in Retrospect." *Occupational Psychology* 27 (1953): 98–103.

Argyris, Chris. *Personality and Organization.* New York: Harper, 1957.

———.*Understanding Organizational Behavior.* Homewood, Ill.: Dorsey, 1960.

Baritz, Loren. *The Servants of Power.* Middletown, Conn.: Wesleyan University Press, 1961.

Barnard, Chester J. *The Functions of the Executive.* Cambridge, Mass.: Harvard University Press, 1938.

Bertalanffy, Ludwig von. "General Systems Theory." *General Systems* 1 (1956): 1–10.

———. "General Systems Theory: A Critical Review." *General Systems* 7 (1962): 1–20.

———. *General Systems Theory.* New York: Braziller, 1968.

Buckley, Walter. *Sociology and Modern Systems Theory.* Englewood Cliffs, N.J.: Prentice-Hall, 1967.

Buckley, Walter, ed. *Modern Systems Research for the Behavioral Scientist: A Sourcebook.* Chicago: Aldine, 1968.

Burns, Tom, and Stalker, G. M. *The Management of Innovation.* London: Tavistock, 1961.

Carey, Alex. "The Hawthorne Studies: A Radical Criticism." *American Sociological Review* 32 (1967): 403–16.

Carter, Robert M. *Communication in Organizations: A Guide to Information Sources.* Detroit: Gale Research, 1972.

Cole, G. D. H. *Reorganization of Industry,* Series II. Oxford, England: Ruslan College, 1917.

Cook, Desmond. *The Impact of the Hawthorne Effect on Experimental Design in Educational Research.* Columbus, Ohio: Ohio State University, 1967.

Crane, Diana. *Invisible Colleges: Diffusion of Knowledge in Scientific Communities.* Chicago: University of Chicago Press, 1972.

Cyert, Richard M., and March, James G. *A Behavioral Theory of the Firm.* Englewood Cliffs, N.J.: Prentice-Hall, 1963.

Davis, Keith. "Management Communication and the Grapevine." *Harvard Business Review* 31 (1953): 43–49.

Etzioni, Amitai. *Modern Organizations.* Englewood Cliffs, N.J.: Prentice-Hall, 1964.

Fayol, Henri. *General and Industrial Management.* London: Pitman, 1949.

Frost, Carl F., et al. *The Scanlon Plan for Organization Development: Identity, Participation, and Equity.* East Lansing, Mich.: Michigan University Press, 1974.

Gouldner, Alvin. *Patterns of Industrial Bureaucracy.* New York: Free Press, 1954.

Gulick, Luther, and Urwick, Lyndall F. *Papers on the Science of Administration.* New York: Columbia University, Institute of Public Administration, 1937.

Gvishiani, D. *Organization and Management: A Sociological Analysis of Western Theories.* Moscow: Progress, 1972.

Hage, Gerald, and Aiken, Michael. "Routine Technology, Social Structure, and Organization Goals." *Administrative Science Quarterly* 14 (1969): 366–76. In *The Formal Organization,* edited by Richard H. Hall. New York: Basic Books.

Homans, George C. *The Human Group.* New York: Harcourt, Brace, 1950.

Katz, Daniel, and Kahn, Robert L. *The Social Psychology of Organizations.* New York: Wiley, 1966.

Katz, Elihu, and Lazarsfeld, Paul. *Personal Influence: The Part Played by People in the Flow of Mass Communications.* New York: Free Press, 1955.

Kuhn, Thomas S. *The Structure of Scientific*

Revolutions. Chicago: University of Chicago Press, 1970.

Landsberger, Henry. *Hawthorne Revisited.* Ithaca, N.Y.: Cornell University Press, 1958.

Laszlo, Erwin. "The Meaning and Significance of General System Theory." *Behavioral Science* 20 (1975): 9–24.

Lawler, Edward E., and Porter, Lyman W. "The Effect of Performance on Job Satisfaction." *Industrial Relations* 7 (1967).

Lawrence, Paul R., and Lorsch, Jay W. *Organization and Environment: Managing Differentiation and Integration.* Boston: Harvard University Press, 1967.

Lazarsfeld, Paul F., et al. *The People's Choice.* New York: Columbia University Press, 1948.

Leavitt, Harold J., et al. *The Organizational World.* New York: Harcourt Brace Jovanovich, 1973.

Lesieur, Fred G. *The Scanlon Plan: A Frontier in Labor-Management Relations.* Cambridge, Mass.: Massachusetts Institute of Technology Press, 1958.

Lesieur, Fred G., and Puckett, Elbridge S. "The Scanlon Plan has Proved Itself." *Harvard Business Review* 47 (1969).

Likert, Rensis. *New Patterns of Management.* New York: McGraw-Hill, 1961.

———. *The Human Organization.* New York: McGraw-Hill, 1967.

McGregor, Douglas. *The Human Problems of Enterprise.* New York: McGraw-Hill, 1960.

Mayo, Elton. *The Human Side of an Industrial Civilization.* New York: Macmillan, 1933.

Miller, James G. "The Nature of Living Systems." *Behavioral Science* 16 (1971): 277–301.

———. "Living Systems: The Organization." *Behavioral Science* 17 (1972): 1–182.

Mooney, J. D., and Reiley, A. C. *The Principles of Organization.* New York: Harper, 1939.

Mott, Paul E. *The Characteristics of Effective Organizations.* New York: Harper and Row, 1972.

Mouzelis, Nicos P. *Organization and Bureaucracy: An Analysis of Modern Theories.* Chicago: Aldine, 1968.

Perrow, Charles. *Organizational Analysis: A Sociological Perspective.* Belmont, Calif.: Wadsworth, 1970.

———. *Complex Organizations: A Critical Essay.* Glenview, Ill.: Scott, Foresman, 1972.

Price, Derek J. de Solla. *Little Science, Big Science.* New York: Columbia University Press, 1963.

———. "The Scientific Foundations of Science Policy." *Nature* 206 (1970): 233–38.

Pugh, Diane S., et al. *Writers on Organizations.* London: Penguin, 1971.

Roethlisberger, Fritz J. *Management and Morale.* Cambridge, Mass.: Harvard University Press, 1941.

Roethlisberger, Fritz J., and Dickson, William J. *Management and the Worker.* Cambridge, Mass.: Harvard University Press, 1939.

Simon, Herbert A. *Administrative Behavior.* New York: Macmillan, 1947.

———. *Models of Man.* New York: Wiley, 1956.

Snow, C. E. "Research on Industrial Illumination." *Technical Engineering News* (1927) 257–82.

Stouffer, Samuel A., et al. *The American Soldier: Studies in the Social Psychology of World War II.* Princeton, N.J.: Princeton University Press, 1949.

Sykes, A. J. "Economic Interest and the Hawthorne Researches: A Comment." *Human Relations* 18 (1965): 253–63.

Tannenbaum, Arnold, and Seashore, Stanley. *Some Changing Conceptions and Approaches to the Study of Persons in Organization.* Ann Arbor, Mich.: University of Michigan, Survey Research Center.

Taylor, Frederick. *Scientific Management.* New York: Harper and Row, 1911.

Terreberry, Shirley. "The Evolution of Organizational Environments." *Administrative Science Quarterly* 12 (1968): 590–613.

Thayer, Lee. "Communication Systems." 1972. In E. Laszlo, ed. *The Relevance of General Systems Theory.* New York: Braziller, 1972.

Vroom, Victor. *Work and Motivation.* New York: Wiley, 1964.

Whitehead, T. N. *The Industrial Worker.* Cambridge, Mass.: Harvard University Press, 1938.

Wiener, Norbert. *The Human Use of Human Beings: Cybernetics and Society.* Boston: Houghton Mifflin, 1950.

Woodward, Joan. *Management and Technology.* London: Her Majesty's Stationery Office, 1958.

Part Two

Communication and Organizational Structure

2

Communication Networks and Organizational Structure

JAMES ALLEN TAYLOR and LINDA JOY EAGLE

...The inclination to aggression is an original self-subsisting instinctual disposition in man, and I return to my view that it constitutes the greatest impediment to civilization. At one point in the course of this inquiry I was led to the idea that civilization was a special process which mankind undergoes, and I am still under the influence of that idea. I may now add that civilization is a process in the service of Eros, whose purpose is to combine single human individuals, and after that families, then races, peoples and nations, into one great unity, the unity of mankind. Why this has to happen, we do not know; the work of Eros is precisely this. These collections of men are to be libidinally bound to one another. Necessity alone, the advantages of work in common, will not hold them together.

—Sigmund Freud[1]

Freud observes that civilization can be viewed as collectivities or groupings of people bound to one another in such a way that progressive groupings embrace larger and larger numbers of people, until the whole of the species may be seen as having unity. Another way of making this point, however less elegantly, is to say that we are all ultimately connected one to the other by virtue of our communication. Believe it or not, you are probably no more than a few links from the President of the United States if you have a message of sufficient importance. An example will help explain what we mean. Recently, an executive of a large corporation asked us to find a citizen of Ghana with a doctorate in mass media, someone who could direct a public information program in Africa. After pondering our best moves, it took just two telephone calls to find such a person working in Hawaii. Because we are members of the field of communication, we participate in its communication network; and thus we have access to the resources of the field—even those of which we are unaware. What lies at the root of the collectivities that form our civilized order is communication networks—patterns of prevailing social, political, and organizational relationships.

Freud says that civilization is impeded by our disposition to aggress. We think that he can be appreciated both literally and figuratively on this point. We join groups. We form political parties; and we create rules and laws to restrain our aggressions so that we all may function with as much individual freedom as possible. We also join these groups because we have discovered that in working together we can accomplish things that we cannot accomplish when working alone. The twin motives of organizing are the same. First, we restrict the variance in behavioral characteristics among people (the notion of control and coordination). Second, we organize to achieve an interdependence which enables us to accomplish mutually beneficial, common goals.

In this chapter we are going to describe networks as they relate to organizations. It is our contention that organizations constitute the zenith of man's social planning efforts in his attempt to develop relatively enduring social relationships, which are the grand metaphors for civilization itself. We will try to explain what networks are, why you eagerly participate in them, and perhaps why you don't. We will try to explain how they work; and we will try to make clear how you might be able to see them, for sometimes they are obscured by our deep-seated preferences. Finally, we will suggest principles for making the networks in which you participate work for you.

Networks Defined

Peter Monge and his colleagues define networks as a "set of stable person-to-person relationships through which information flows in an organization."[2] The concept of networks may be generalized beyond the organization. If you are reading this early in the semester as part of your course work, you will find that by the end of the semester a set of interpersonal relationships will have developed allowing you to reach every other person in your class. This does not mean you will know everyone; it means instead that you can reach anyone by using intermediaries. By the end of the term you will be hearing gossip about classroom personalities, rumors about grading policies, and other kinds of information concerning your class. This can only happen after enduring, situation-bound relationships develop.

By *enduring* we mean that certain interactions (incidents of particular people talking) are more likely to take place than others, usually because they've taken place in the past. This is an important characteristic of all networks, since in a large system it would be impossible for all possible pairs of individuals to have an equal likelihood of communicating. Such factors as proximity, opportunity, perceived similarity, common interests, and most especially attractiveness make it likely that you will be *linked* only with a particular set of people. Moreover, it is not enough just to meet someone; you must participate in a series of communication events over some extended period of time. When you speak to someone for a while, trust develops, and information of consequence begins to flow.

If, in a class of thirty, each person communicated with three others, it is very likely that everybody would be linked by no more than two or three intermediaries. Also, because of the patterns of interaction, it is likely that stories would be carried across intermediaries. You would be provided with information about classmates with whom you have no direct contact, and they would be provided with information about you.

Situation/Context

We noted that networks are situation bound. This means that a particular network develops in a particular place—literally in a geographic space. We call this an environment and admit from the start that it is sometimes hard to pin down. In a sense, if the place where the network functions is relatively stable, the network is relatively enduring. By place or space, we mean not only the geography but also the elements which occupy the space—such as people, appliances, and objects. Your class, for example, will become a network. When your class breaks up, does the network dissolve? Well, there is a simple answer and a complicated answer. The simple answer is yes because the reason that you occupied a classroom as a unique group has been withdrawn. But you are all part of the same college; and if we expand the environment to embrace everybody in the college, we would say no. In fact, since some of you have established friendships that will continue outside of the class, we would say that the classroom provided an opportunity to augment the network of students on your campus. A crucial decision, then, is how we define the environment.

Both these above mentioned points become more important when we consider large, complex organizations. Since large organizations are complex by virtue of the differentiation that is present (Fig. 2-1), it becomes a question

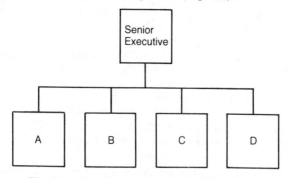

Fig. 2-1 Organizational sub-unit differentiation

of whether we're interested in the whole organization, individual subunits, or even small office groupings. Changing the size of the group we characterize as a *network* allows us to ask different questions and to place behavior in different perspectives. For example, in our hypothetical organization, a person in subunit A, the research department, may be absolutely critical to the flow of information within that unit. However, this person may not have any contacts outside that unit; so when we consider information flow throughout the organization, his importance diminishes greatly. Thus, as observers we have changed our perspective and the question we are asking. In the former case we are interested in the structure of the subunit. In the latter case we are interested in the structure of the organization.

Structure

We have used the term structure several times and have deliberately left it undefined up to this point. This is because we think that an organization's structure is synonymous with its prevailing communication network. Structure implies ordered, predictable patterns of interpersonal and mediated communication behavior. The term connotes the way individuals are organized to accomplish the tasks that justify their common efforts. Traditionally organizational theorists—and in particular Max Weber—conceived of an organizational structure as a pyramid of supervisor-subordinate relationships. Your position on the pyramid would dictate both to whom you report and who reports to you (Fig. 2-2). The pyramid is said to be the *formal structure*. The pyramid, or hierarchy, has three properties of interest to us. First, a pyramid

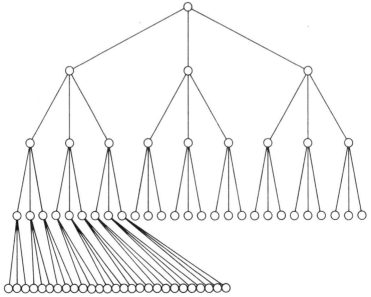

Fig. 2-2 Bureaucratic hierarchy: Pyramid structure

suggests that all information flows vertically to and from the top and that ultimately all information is collected at the top, since everybody is connected along the chain of command to the senior executive. Second, the formal structure indicates who has what power over which people. If you are a vice-president in our figure, you control the behavior of three assistant vice-presidents, nine middle level managers, and twenty-seven production personnel. Third, the formal structure is fundamentally a depiction of communication relationships, which allow productive processes to take place and which are required by the formal rules of the organization.

It is obviously very necessary for a manager to have an understanding of networks. The rules that prescribe how you behave toward your supervisor and your subordinates are in large part communication rules. The norms that augment or replace rules elaborate the deviations by which you might violate the formal pattern of supervisor-subordinate communication. It is communication and the rules governing it that lie at the heart of all administrative processes. This may seem like a bold claim because so much of our behavior seems to be task-oriented; however, if you consider the tasks a manager is asked to perform, you will see that these tasks have to do with communication and the management of communication. Further, if you consider the tasks the subordinates must accomplish, it becomes obvious that the rules and patterns by which the subordinates communicate dictate the processes by which they coordinate and implement their strategies for productivity. Chester Barnard in his standard work entitled *The Functions of the Executive* stated the point better than we can. He wrote, "In an exhaustive theory of organization, communication would occupy a central place, because the structure, extensiveness and scope of the organization are almost entirely determined by communication techniques."[3]

Informal Structure

Most traditional scholars of organizational behavior focus their attention on the properties of formal structure. Researchers have found, however, that on close examination almost everybody violates the formal pattern of prescribed relationships. Looking at our pyramid, we can detect a flaw in the assumptions that govern the construction of formal structures, and we can understand why so much *informal* communication takes place.

When all relationships are pyramid-like, ultimately all the information generated by all the people in the organization arrives in one massive pile on the desk of the senior executive. It is immediately obvious, then, that mechanisms are needed to allow people to screen information at various points along the pyramid or to reduce the volume of information.

Since it is difficult for the organization to generate rules other than accounting rules to screen all possible information, individuals at the same level need to communicate with one another to develop norms so that they can coordinate their *gatekeeping* activities. In particular, if the left side of our pyramid is sales and the right side is production, the best way for sales to discover the minimal amount of information required for production to operate efficiently is for the two vice-presidents to get together. Since the assistant vice-presidents might be coordinating sales for a specific product (for example, in a ball-point pen factory, sales of felt-tipped pens and the production of felt-tipped pens), they may have an even greater need to communicate directly. The hierarchy would require that they always communicate through their superiors and their superiors always communicate through the president or senior executive. Clearly, this is inefficient.

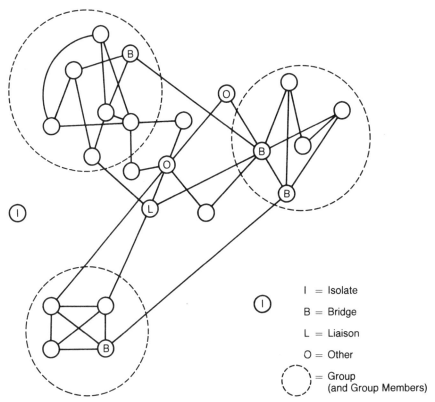

I = Isolate
B = Bridge
L = Liaison
O = Other
= Group (and Group Members)

Fig. 2-3   A typical communication network

Thus individuals may violate the hierarchy to achieve their own goals. If the violations result in improved performance for the organization, they will be tolerated and eventually encouraged. Today the vast majority of communication in modern organizations is informal.[4] In fact, we have arrived at the point where it makes very little sense to maintain the distinction between formal and informal communication. In most cases managers are rewarded through promotions and raises for their informal contacts (what we might call connections). By virtue of recognition, informal contacts are rendered formal.

If we can accept this argument, we can accept the statement that the communication network within an organization *is* the organization's structure. *Structure, then, is the prevailing pattern of information flow within an organization.* It is controlled by rules and informal norms, which govern *how* people behave, and by role assignments, which indicate *with whom* they so behave.

What then dictates the form of networks? Figure 2-3 is an example of a typical communication network as we have observed them in our research. It no longer looks like a pyramid, but instead it resembles a kind of sociometric map. The circles represent individuals (nodes) and the lines represent the existence of a communication link or a relationship between the nodes joined by the line. An interesting observation is that the clusters of people within the dotted circles generally represent people with relatively equal hierarchical position. If we were to cluster the pyramid, the groupings would likely be broken by task and by supervisor-subordinate relationships. Instead we find that senior officials interact most often with senior officials, middle managers interact with middle managers, and low-level managers interact with other low-level managers.[5]

We call this form of structure *organic-adoptives,* in contrast to the pyramid or bureaucratic structure. By organic-adoptive we mean that the organization changes its structure to meet emergent needs. All organizations are somewhat bureaucratic and somewhat organic; however, most are more one than the other. The difference between the inflexibility of the bureaucracy and an organic organization seems to be the kind of task an organization characteristically performs, its technological sophistication, its size, and the uncertainty of its environment. In general we can say that as organizations become technologically complex with rapidly changing markets, large in size, and as production processes become complicated, the organization will be more organic. This is because, under these conditions, an organization experiences uncertainty in unpredictable ways at unpredictable points. Therefore, we try to make it possible for people to contact one another and exchange information as rapidly as possible so we can solve problems quickly and efficiently.

Rules and Roles

At the beginning of this chapter we noted Freud's observation that civilization acts to restrain our aggressiveness—our urge to undo collective order. How does organized society order people's behavior so that the aggressiveness of everyone is held at least partly in check? What we do is nominate, in one way or another, individuals to create rules that specify acceptable behavior. In effect, rules smooth the variance among us according to two criteria that we try to optimize simultaneously: (1) the freedom of each individual to act and (2) the restriction of behaviors that are defined as destructive to the goals of the collective. The irony of civilization is that by ruling some behavior as antisocial, we make it possible for people to be free. This also applies to organizations. If organizations provide us the opportunity to maintain a standard of living that enables us to enjoy freedom outside the organization, it does so by limiting freedom within the organization.

Note that when we nominate individuals—and again, never mind how they are chosen for the moment—we differentiate (or create differences) between those who make the rules and those for whom the rules are made. Crudely, we create roles and even more important, status. Interestingly, even those members with little status and with relatively unimportant roles ordinarily feel that this is fair. Because of the status system that has developed, even lower status members of an organization regard as fair the fact that some members of the firm receive more benefits than others.

Roles

Every individual in society plays many different roles. The use of the term *role* to describe the way people behave is genuinely analagous to the use of the term in drama. In the dramatic arts a role is a very predictable behavior set. It is predictable by virtue of the specifications contained in the script. While most of the roles we play are not so clearly specified, they are still predictable patterns of behavior, and it is predictability that lends the concept of role its power. A role can be defined as the specification of behavior appropriate to particular circumstances. When we observe the same response to similar stimuli by the same person acting at different points in time, we begin to be able to anticipate the response; in the operant sense, we condition the response by reinforcing it. We do this because patterned responses to common stimuli make the world much more understandable, particularly in terms of the consequences of our behavior. Repeated over and over again, a behavioral *set* becomes institutionalized or formalized.

In the organizational sense, a role is simply an expectation of how we are to behave. In the most formal case, a role is a behavior set prescribed in a job description. A supervisor is given the role of assigning work to subordinates, of interviewing job applicants, of reporting to superiors, and the like.

The assignment of responsibilities, which individually and collectively comprise the role we play, is not new to organizational theory. Weber argued that by carefully describing the role each individual is to play in the production processes, it is possible to reduce the amount of attention managers must pay to subordinates. By specifying how each actor is to behave and the conditions under which a person merits a particular role, uncertainty is resolved in favor of what we might term behavioral protocols. A protocol is a patterned behavior shared among a number of individuals that, when applied to a production process, yields what we term a heteromerous competency. A heteromerous competency is an outcome of the interaction of a group of role players that would not be possible if each of the individuals acted independently. The term heteromerous refers to the fact that the contribution of individual actors may vary in quality or value, but all contributions add to the collective competency. Because all the people involved are playing roles, variance among the individuals is restricted; each person can rely on everyone else to fulfill his responsibility. Thus because the group plays roles, the behavior of the group is predictable for the group and for those who supervise the group's behavior.

In the network sense, formal roles account for a portion of the communication behavior taking place within the firm. The president fulfills his/her obligation to maintain at least symbolic contact with the employees by making site visits to the plant. We can all imagine that contacts during such a visit are brief and communication is probably trivial. Still, the role leads one to expect the visit; and if the president fails to visit, he/she becomes suspect.

Note that roles are expectations. An expectation is a probability that event A will be associated with event B for a given stimulus. Expectations cause two related problems. First of all, an expectation often gets translated into a demand that cannot always be satisfied. For example, your teacher has the role of assisting you in understanding these materials. It is not at all unlikely that your teacher has research interests different from ours and has only a little more knowledge of these ideas than you. Your expectation cannot be satisfied even though it is natural and reasonable that your teacher should not know everything. You will be disappointed. You will question your teacher's competency because your teacher has failed to satisfy a role expectation.

The second major problem is what is referred to as role ambiguity. This comes either from confusion about what role you are playing or from confusion about what role is appropriate in a particular circumstance because of a lack of *role definition*. In the former case, an example might be a supervisor who has worked with a subordinate for a long period of time and developed a friendship as well as a working relationship. If the supervisor is called upon to criticize the subordinate's behavior, it might be difficult to determine whether he ought to behave as a friend by withholding the criticism and not jeopardize the friendship or behave as a supervisor and criticize. Notice that neither individual is likely to understand clearly the appropriate behavior.

In the second case, role ambiguity occurs when a responsibility has not been clearly defined. For instance, in some organizations a manager is encouraged to have an open relationship with subordinates. The manager tries to *keep an open door*. Since this implies a trusting relationship, the manager experiences ambiguity when faced with a problem that ought to be reported to superiors. If the manager reports the situation, a trust is violated. If the manager does not, the organization suffers. The ambiguity stems from the failure to identify clearly the parameters governing the openness with which the manager relates to the subordinate. In both cases, role ambiguity produces stress.

Roles govern the probabilities of communication taking place. We have noted that the basic distinction between informal and formal communication is whether or not a communication act is mandated by the organizational chart. In studying networks, we have discovered that roles have similar properties—i.e., there are both formal and informal roles—and as with communication acts, the two overlap.

Informal communication roles, however, result not from prescriptions but rather from the prevailing pattern of communication contacts. Some individuals have uniquely important contacts and, by virtue of that fact, acquire information and hence power far beyond that which would be expected from their formal roles alone. In one case, a governmental agency was undergoing a power struggle over budgetary priorities. Several assistant directors were in active conflict over the distribution of discretionary program development funds. One of the assistant directors found that every time he attempted a ploy, his opposites seemed to know exactly what was going on and often counteracted the strategy in advance. As in most organizations, memos from the assistant director were routed through a secretary. The secretary was an employee of long standing, while the assistant director was an aggressive younger man who had replaced a well-liked senior person. The secretary strongly disliked her new supervisor; and despite her low status, her position in the flow of information gave her the power to manipulate the outcome of a major bureaucratic struggle. She accomplished this by sending copies of her boss's memoranda to his rivals.

Network Analysis

Various network analysis techniques—or methods of graphing the prevailing communication relations—exist. The one most often used in the communication field was developed by William Richards.[6] This technique looks at people's reports of those with whom they talk about particular subjects and then assigns them communication roles. Without going into much detail, we would like to describe briefly these roles (Figure 2–3).

Nodes—individual members of the system—are assigned one of five possible communication roles. These roles are as follows:

1. Group members—nodes with more than some minimal percentage of interaction within the group
2. Bridges—nodes who are members of groups but who are also connected to other groups and, hence, serve to link two or more groups
3. Liaisons—nodes who link two or more groups but who are not themselves members of any group
4. Isolates—nodes that have no links (Type I Isolates) or nodes that are connected to only one other node (Type 2 Isolates)
5. Others—nodes that fail to meet the criteria for a particular role assignment

Of particular interest are the classification of bridges and liaisons. Bridges and liaisons allow information to flow among large groups of people. A bridge who is a member of a particular group, for example, can serve as a source of information from that group and a receiver of information from the rest of the network. At his/her discretion, the individual who is the bridge can facilitate or block information flow and thus influence the course of events in the network. Similarly, liaisons, by virtue of their positions between two or more groups, can significantly influence the flow of information.

Likert[7] noted the position of the individual who links large chains or groups of other nodes. He described such an individual as a *linking pin* and attributed to that individual authority independent of hierarchical position. Like the bridge, the linking pin can facilitate or impede the flow of information and, since information is the mechanism of control and coordination within organizations, can effectively manipulate information flow to personal ends. The liaison controls the flow in two ways. First, a liaison can delay messages so that the value of the information declines substantially. Second, the liaison can interdict the flow, stopping a message altogether. If the liaison is the only link or pathway between the groups, and the liaison recognizes that fact, the liaison can actually control the two groups' perceptions of one another. This capacity, of course, varies from organization to organization and depends upon the degree of autonomy, flexibility, and coercion within a system.

A second consideration concerns the nature of the groups that these liaisons link. Network theorists would argue that if the liaisons are exercising significant control over the flow of information, the groups are likely to reflect the attitudes of the liaisons eventually. In a study of special education networks, Taylor[8] also found that one could predict almost exactly the attitudes of group members by looking at the attitudes of liaisons and bridges who link the groups.

Isolates are those individuals who report no contact with anybody and are not reported by others. It is hard to explain how this is possible, but two factors may account for the existence of isolates. First, when we measure networks, we ordinarily ask individuals to whom they talk about a particular topic. It is possible that the topics we select for measurement purposes are so specific that they exclude certain individuals who do interact on other topics. Second, it is possible that some individuals, for their own reasons, have disassociated themselves from the organization and left the mainstream of the organization's information flow. We suspect that personality factors play a role in such behavior patterns, and we also suspect that these individuals might be ostracized by virtue of their unique task or by virtue of their deviant behavior.[9]

Rules

Rules are statements of prescribed or proscribed behavior. A communication rule is, analogously, a rule which governs communication among individuals. In organizations, communication rules underlie network development since they specify who may talk to whom, under what conditions, and on which topics.

Rules abound in everyday life. Obviously the applicability of a particular rule depends upon one's status, the role one is performing, and the exigencies of the situation. Since people are so governed by rules, it is safe to say the organizational structure is largely a consequence of *the rules which exist* and the *degree to which they are enforced.* The differences between bureaucracies and organic organizations are reflected in both the number of communication rules that exist and the degree to which violations are tolerated.

Bureaucracies are likely to have many rules because the response of managers to contingencies that arise is likely to be a new rule. To return to our example of the pen company, if the company is bureaucratic, the senior manager may recognize the need for the assistant vice-president of sales to communicate with his/her equal on the production side. We would expect that a rule would be created sanctioning communication between the two individuals, but no others. The advantage of the rule is that it facilitates productivity and still allows for the appearance of control. The disadvantage is that as more and more contingencies arise, more and more rules are generated until no one can follow them all. As the number of rules gets large relative to the size of an organization, the utility of additional rules becomes very low.

This compounding of rules accounts for the seemingly overwhelming complexity of governmental agencies. Private organizations, however, have been able to avoid this problem by eliminating many of the rules (often through the use of what is called organizational development). In so doing, managers increase organizational flexibility, often improve employee morale and motivation, and change the structure of the firm.

We note that when rules are dispensed with, another kind of rule emerges. These *rules* are referred to as norms. A rule is ordinarily codified with an attached explanation of associated punishments. A norm is a prescribed behavior arising from the mutual interests of members of a social system. A norm is less formal than a rule, and its interpretation is more open to question. This is not to say that norms are not enforced, but rather that the lack of specificity allows for discretion in application and enforcement. *All organizations are characterized by both rules and norms.*

Procedure and Content

Cushman and Whiting[10] make an important distinction between two kinds of rules: procedural rules and content rules. A procedural rule specifies the *way* in which a communication act will take place—the methods to be followed. For example, most organizations have a rule that communication about a grievance or a dispute between a supervisor and a subordinate will be referred to a grievance arbitrator who is charged with (whose role is) adjudicating such differences. Procedural rules govern flow up and down the pyramid, the medium to be used, and the circumstances in which communication will take place. Note that the rules affect the network by dictating relationships.

Content rules specify the content that may be discussed by a particular dyad, or two persons. Content rules are important to us for two reasons. First, content rules provide the basis for energizing communication procedures. For example, discovering fraud in your department (content) will allow you to use existing protocol (procedures) to bypass your superiors and to contact the senior executive of your organization directly.

More important, however, is that content rules allow us to have multiple networks within a single organization. A content rule specifies the topics you can discuss with another individual. Different rules cover different relationships. David Berlo argues that organizations are characterized by three separate networks, depending upon the content of typical communications: a production network, a maintenance network, and an innovation network.

The production network enhances communication about task achievement. It is the network that is most similar to the formal hierarchy, and all members of an organization are likely to have a role in it. (It is the case, however, that when we study specific organizations, we often find isolates even in the production network.)

The maintenance network is the network of social relationships or communication events that reinforce the value of continued participation in the firm. This network would also tend to include everyone, although some individuals might choose not to participate.

The innovation network is the prevailing pattern of communication about new ideas or new technologies. All organizations have some form of innovation network. Larger, more conservative organizations recognize, however, that new ideas imply creativity, and creativity suggests deviance. Thus they separate their innovators from the bulk of the organization and place them in research and development areas.[11]

Concluding Remarks

We have tried to explain what a network is, and we have tried to show how the form of the network is governed by organizational processes having to do with rules and roles. Now we will provide some insights and some general principles that can help you make the networks in which you participate work for you.

Social Exchange

We suggest that the underlying explanation for how people become effectively embedded in networks can be found in ideas developed in theories of social exchange.[12] Social exchange theories are based on an analogy between economic transactions and other kinds of social interaction. They see human beings as "reward-seeking and punishment-avoiding creatures."[13] The idea is that people undergo psychological costs to get psychological rewards, always attempting to maximize rewards and minimize costs to obtain most profitable outcomes. When two people interact, each gets his rewards and punishments directly from the other. Each chooses one action or message over another if it is more profitable or less costly than the other.

The spectrum of social exchange episodes may be seen as an array of business deals. Even the vocabularies of the theories smack of business. Homans,[14] for example, not only defines rewards, costs, and profits but speculates about diminishing marginal utility, increasing marginal costs, and scarcity.

In the case of the network, the economic analogy helps us predict and understand our co-workers' expectations of our communication acts and our expectations of theirs. When a person is hired into an organization (we call this person a novice), this person's communication is greatly determined by the social exchanges in which he/she engages with superiors. The trade offs might work in such a way that the novice gives the boss status and assistance in return for explanations of unstated and non-obvious rules and norms and, hopefully, for acceptance into the network. As time goes on, the quality of the service rises (the novice develops competency). In addition, the novice develops the ability to gather quality information through the novice's own contacts. The novice then has currency of greater value to exchange. At this point, if the supervisor is sensitive and the novice is smart, a relationship can develop based on trust and resulting in the emergence of heteromerous competency. This means that the success of both supervisor and subordinate depends upon maintaining the relationship. The supervisor confirms the status of the novice by offering the defined role of *colleague*. The novice ceases to be a novice, and all social exchanges are subtly altered. Note that the transition from novice to organizational member can only be ordained by an established member. We think, in fact, that the power to ordain others requires not only status conferral, but the attainment of public rewards such as raises and promotions.

The trade off one will be expected to make in order to receive status conferral will usually be energy and forfeiting of idiosyncratic attitudes and beliefs. In order to receive attention from supervisors, one is expected to become more like them.

We suggest that you prepare yourself for the cost of network participation. Part of this cost is a willingness to trade parts of yourself for parts of others.

Some Working Principles

The following principles help us understand how and why people behave in particular networks.

1. The first of these principles is what has been called the *iron law of oligarchy.*[15] The iron law of oligarchy holds that whenever a new group takes control of a social system, that group acts in such a way that its power is retained and sustained. This means that as new managers gain control of large organizations, they will alter the mode of operation to gainsafe not only their power but their right to nominate successors. Weber noted that bureaucracy, and hence all organizations, are power instruments of the first order, at least for those who control the bureaucracy. The role for you, then, is to hitch your wagon to a rising star. If you open your eyes, you can identify the key actors and serve them.

2. The second principle was developed by Anthony Downs in his highly regarded work, *Inside Bureaucracy.*[16] Downs created the law of *increasing conservation.* This law holds that as time goes by, organizations will become increasingly skeptical of change in procedure, process, or technology. This means that it is much more difficult to penetrate the communication network of old firms than of newer firms. The trade off is that the probability of survival in an older firm is much greater since there is less instability. Also, older firms are much more likely to have a rule to cover every situation and to have managers who manage by the book.

3. Downs also created what we call the rule of *subformality*. In his research he found that the vast majority of communication acts in organizations are subformal or, in the way we use the term, informal. That is, communication does not follow the formal information pathways. This is true; but the novice should bear in mind that one is known for what one says, bad news travels faster than good news, and in a time of crisis the organization will revert to formality. If your influence derives solely from your informal role, you will be seen as unreliable when the chips are down.

4. The fourth principle is what Downs referred to as the law of *counter-vailing goal pressures*. This law holds that every organization is continuously experiencing pressures to maintain traditional forms (e.g., rules, policies, procedures, operating protocols), while at the same time pressures are being exerted to change. The clearest example of this might be the organizational goal of growth. Almost all enterprises maintain a constant goal of growth. This means conservative forces act to sustain a goal that, if achieved, results in change. Networks are often characterized by *political camps* which differ in their support of the two countervailing pressures. Be sensitive to your position and to those of others.

5. Finally, the law of counter-vailing goal pressures suggests what we call the rule of *dynamic instability*. Networks are constantly changing. A liaison gets promoted or transferred. A group conflicts and dissolves. New power elites emerge. Things change all the time. The wise student will learn to be flexible.

We believe that the successful person will understand networks, organizational rules, formal and informal roles, behavioral exchanges and trade offs, and other concepts explained and discussed in this chapter. But understanding a chapter in a book will not guarantee personal success. Knowing a set of principles is not the same as having the ability to act upon them. Knowledge and understanding are necessary, but not sufficient, elements of success.

We suggest, if you are seriously intent on succeeding as a member of a particular organizational network, that you pay careful attention to the behavior of others while monitoring your own behavior. Though you will enter the organization with a unique history and set of values, you will need to be conscious of how you and your ideas, biases, abilities, resources, and predispositions mesh with those sought and valued by the organization. The bottom line is this: the organization will reward you commensurate with your contributions. To the extent that the organization's success depends upon your presence and input, and to the extent that this is recognized by those around you, you will be seen and eventually treated as an integral part of its structure.

Notes

[1] S. Freud, *Civilization and Its Discontents* (New York: W.W. Norton & Company, Inc., 1961), p. 69.

[2] P. Monge, J. A. Edwards, and K. K. Kirste, "The Determinants of Communication and Communication Structure in Large Organizations: A Review of Research." In B. D. Rubin (ed.), *Communication Yearbook II* (New Brunswick, N.J.: Transaction Books).

[3] C. Barnard, *The Functions of the Executive* (Cambridge, Mass.: Harvard University Press, 1933).

[4] A. Downs, *Inside Bureaucracy* (Boston: Little-Brown, 1967).

[5] M. A. Pacanowsky and R. V. Farace, "An Instructional Simulation for Organizational Communication." Paper presented at the Annual Meeting of the International Communication Association, Chicago, 1975.

[6] W. D. Richards Jr., "A Coherent Systems Methodology for the Analysis of Human Communication Systems, Report No. 25," Center for Interdisciplinary Research, Stanford University, Palo Alto, California, 1976.

[7] R. Likert, *New Patterns of Management* (New York: McGraw-Hill, 1961).

[8] J. A. Taylor, "Communication and Organizational Change: A Case Study and Empirical Analysis." Unpublished doctoral dissertation, Michigan State University, 1978.

[9] This is a brief overview of the notion of communication rules. For a more extensive discussion, the reader is directed to *Communicating and Organizing* (R.V. Farace, P. Monge, and H. Russell, Boston: Addison-Wesley, 1977). A fundamental understanding of the issues discussed here can be obtained by reading *Inside Bureaucracy* (A. Downs, Boston: Little-Brown, 1967) and *Social Theory and Social Structure* (R. Merton, rev. ed., Glencoe, Ill.: Free Press, 1957).

[10] D. Cushman and G. C. Whiting, "An Approach to Communication Theory: Toward Consensus on Rules," *Journal of Communication* 22 (1972): 217–238.

[11] V. Thompson, *Bureaucracy and Innovation* (Alabama University Press, 1969).

[12] P. M. Blau, *Exchange and Power in Social Life* (New York: Wiley, 1964).

[13] R. L. Simpson, "Theories of Social Exchange." In J. W. Thibaut, J. T. Spence, R. C. Carson, eds., *Contemporary Topics in Social Psychology* (New Jersey: General Learning Press, 1976).

[14] G. C. Homans, *Social Behavior: Its Elementary Forms* (New York: Harcourt, Brace & World, 1961).

[15] R. Michels, *Political Parties,* translated by Eden and Cedar Paul (New York: Dover Press, 1959).

[16] A. Downs, *Inside Bureaucracy* (Boston: Little-Brown, 1967).

3

The Bureaucratic Colander

JOSEPH LEESE

In the classic bureaucracy, messages are supposed to travel up and down the chain of command. In the industrial establishment the superintendent tells the foreman who tells the employee. The machine operator communicates his needs, his ideas, and his complaints to his boss, who passes the information on to the more general supervisor. In the public schools the assistant superintendent conveys to the principal and then to the department chairman the answer and explanation to the problems which have emerged for the teacher in the classroom or in the staff room; that is, if the assistant superintendent ever hears about them.

Most are familiar now with the informal system of communication which has developed in nearly every hierarchical operation to make up for the fact that the information transmission-system dependent on going through channels doesn't work. Employees long since have found out how to learn about "what's cookin' " and how to stir the soup behind the cook's back. The waiters often know "what's for dinner" before the daily menu has been delivered to the kitchen, and they tell the proprietor what the clients like before they tell the headwaiter.

Happily these informal arrangements for passing along correct information and rumor alike work quite well in many situations. They give a knowingness to employees that they like, and they keep the middle managers less arrogant than they might otherwise be. The car pool, chatty wives, not-so-confidential secretaries, extremely intuitive sign readers, et al, keep the grapevine supplied, and juicy morsels plucked from the most secret places exhilarate the organization, even if they annoy the manager of the vineyard.

But even if it is more of a help than a hindrance, most would agree that as a creative antidote for organization sickness, the informal system may be a kind of medicine worse than the illness. The informal system has its own peck order of transmission; the nosey get their information first, and they distribute it as nectar to their favorites; the trouble-makers and obstructionists get a head start in crystallizing opposition; the naive and last to know increase their isolation and frustration; and the middle managers feel like the farmer at the barn door with the key and lock after the horse has been stolen. On the other side, the by-pass process upward leaves bosses carrying coals to Newcastle, lamely reporting or recommending what has already been slipped under the door or whispered in an attentive ear. The middle manager who has already been beaten to the superintendent by a shop steward, or an association representative, or top bowler in the twilight league knows he has been had.

We know some of the reasons why there are rumor-bearers and self-appointed town criers. John as well as Mary likes tid-bits, and spies and informers get well paid by newspapers, as well as by those neighborhood wives who assemble in the half-past-nine coffee klatch. Secrets itch to be shared, and ego grows from the telling, with elaboration added.

But what do the gossips and the bold who take the bits in their teeth to circumvent the organizational structure thrive on? What creates the need for them and what brings them honor?

All too clearly it is the selecting and sieving process employed by the intermediaries along the communication routes. Bosses send upward only what they want to or cannot avoid, and supervisors distribute faithfully only that which they cannot edit and interpret. Interfering and draining in both directions, they allow to go freely and rapidly through the colander only that which is unimportant anyway. The rest they taste carefully before they pass it on.

This straining prerogative vastly increases the power of the bureaucrat. He can pass along someone else's ideas, particularly upward, without identifying the source; he can retain information about plans for reassignment of personnel; he can wait until an announcement comes too close to action to permit the affected any leeway, any response, or any alternative suggestion; he can decide whether his boss needs to know about employee illness or aggravation or ambition; he can separate explanation from decision and thereby increase misunderstanding and dissatisfaction. And through these moves or lack of action he can control and affect responsible decisions and steps by supraordinates and manipulate and disempower subordinates. He also can and does drive the uninformed out in search of data and influence, and he interferes with and impairs organizational effectiveness.

The points at which information is blocked and distorted varies in organizations. Pyramided structure provides many levels for communication clog. It is not uncommon in establishments operated through many layers for there to be at one step after another a great wailing that "they never tell me anything. I'm always the last to hear *what,* and I never hear why." Nothing could be calculated to better block upward transmission, for if you don't tell me all I need to know, why should I tell you?

All too many level executives who lecture about not hearing from the ranks and who shake their agreeing heads about communication would be well advised to ask about the widespread malaise they spread themselves. More often than not they have sent along less information than has been needed, and they have started the information reduction process themselves. If everyone in the kitchen picks out a little from the colander as it passes by, one could well predict little on the plate for the hungry worker at the table.

The very top man seldom has less information than anyone else. Because he has so much, he worries little about passing along a very large share of it. But like well-mauled peaches in a supermarket, picked over and bruised, what is left solid and sweet down at the end of the line is much less satisfying, but much more valuable. It can be jealously guarded.

The motives for sorting and selecting are the same, however, at any echelon. Subordinates can't be trusted to use the information; they don't need the information; the information will disturb and distress them; the information will increase their appetite to know and to respond with suggestions. Superordinates will want to have a further look; they might recognize merits they would never otherwise hear about; they could espouse suggestions that mean more work for their lieutenants; they themselves could get a promotion for it.

This suggests that supervisors look out for number one. They want to be safe and secure. They need to be one step ahead and be ready to have an answer. They need to be sought out for decisions their special knowledge permits to be made. They enjoy being "in the know." They like to play cat and mouse with the critical and creative but uninformed. What a pleasure to tease the upstart with a proposal when one knows a plan is already in the works or has already been rejected. What a temptation to dismiss the plan when its conception should have come from the ambitious superior to whom it is presented.

To be sure, some of the communication loss comes because the willing are word bound. Neither able to write or to talk simply and cogently, they distort the direct and contort the complex. More confusion than clarity comes out of meetings. Memos and newsletters obfuscate in pursuit of orientation. And announcements are anticlimactic because they are poorly timed and ineptly placed.

Fortunately these faults can be corrected, but much more difficult is the task of discovering and treating the individuals who bury information and ideas like squirrels do nuts. Their behavior seldom arises from intuition. It generates more often out of pervasive attitudes about others and gnawing needs in themselves to protect against the consequences of openness and objectivity. Schutz[1] some time ago proposed a thesis about human behavior which he called *F*undamental *I*nterpersonal *R*elationship *O*rientation.

In his FIRO theory Schutz proposed that affectation, belonging, and control are two-way streets. All of us want to be liked by others, to be accepted by them, and to be controlled by others. But equally, wholesome and balanced people want to like others, to accept others, and to control them. Some variations along continua in each of these categories are to be expected, but excessive expectation in any of the three, and particularly pronounced demand at one end of the scale in one, and at the opposite end in the others, may be so injurious to personal and institutional service as to be disastrous.

The manager who has very substantial need to control and little need to be liked or to be accepted has high potential for frustrating the common organization communication system. His personality orientation yields easily to neither exhortation nor explanation.

In the last five years a continuing study was made of the communication flow in an organization involving three levels: workers, supervisors, and general superintendent. The general superintendent provided the organizational link with the next echelon. That echelon met regularly with the next level chief officer to hear about, to examine, to discuss and to evaluate institutional conditions, problems, responses, intentions and decisions. Items of the same kind were the content of transmissions from the chief officer to the general superintendent via conference, telephone, memo, and directive.

There was no access to these latter communications nor to individual communications of similar type to department supervisors, but there were general memoranda from the regular meetings of the general superintendent with the department supervisors. The content of these memoranda and of announcements, decisions, plans, was thus available.

The study undertaken sought to determine the extent to which there was transmission and filtration of the "information" possessed by each of those supervisors to the workers who reported to them. The information was categorized into areas identified above, that is, conditions, problems, responses, intentions and decisions.

It is obvious that the lieutenants were at liberty to select for distribution what information they wished except that held to be confidential or for their purposes alone.

Preparation for the possible transmission was easily observable in the supervisor group. Some supervisors took voluminous and careful notes; some took none; most took a few. One supervisor distributed organized notes at a meeting of his subordinates the next day. One supervisor seldom met with his group, but casually passed along information to confidants.

The upshot proved to be an extremely uneven information transmission; widespread misinformation, a sick rumor mill, contentment in pussy cats treated to the cream and indignation and apathy among the old toms that finally got the skim.

Obviously, there can be too much information as well as too little. In certain kinds of organizations the volume made available in behalf of enlightenment can be overwhelming. The appetite for knowledge also can vary appreciably. Some employees simply do not care about either the number currently employed in another plant or unit elsewhere or about retirements and awards for secretaries and sales managers they never have known. It may be necessary from an over-all vantage to carry acknowledgments and pictures of employee recognitions in a company newspaper. It then cannot be said that management is oblivious of faithful service and unaware of historical past events. Twilight league success in the third inning or at third base builds up personal ego and expectation. But that kind of information does not suffice.

What most employees do care about is information on matters which affect them personally or upon which their personal influence can be exercised.

From time to time one does not care, and in situations where there is great confidence in the objectivity and honesty of the supervisor, employees would occasionally prefer not to be bothered with information necessary to administrivia. For instance, some university professors may not particularly care to know that supervisors are authorized to send secretaries home on extremely hot days at four when the ordinary work day runs to five. But an interesting aspect of confidence is that it needs periodic reinforcement and subordinates need periodic reassurance. If "not to bother'" on some items comes to result in not providing information on more and more items over time, it can be anticipated that there will be an increment of distress in the ranks.

The art, then, once there is honest commitment to the responsibility of information flow, is to judge wisely and well what information is useful, important and meaningful, and to whom and to how many. The transmission needs to be general or limited or individual, but swift and clear. Those in the family of supervisors and workers should know before or at the same time as those who are outside. Of course, certain gross policy statements of very large organizations, which affect many within the organization, cannot be controlled by this criterion. Decisions may have to precede machinery and may require action within time requirements which do not permit notification, explanation and action effect. Great apprehension and anxiety, protestation and hostility may and do arise from such constraints in the management of large complexes. There seems no way to avoid having some decisions dropped like a bomb.

But the effect from such necessity, even in massive organizations, can be softened through a general practice at all levels of judicious and considerate, objective and generous decisions about the information others want and need. Even though group decisions may bind supervisor members to use prescribed media and procedures for transmitting agreed-upon summaries, announcements and explanations, every organization will very often have to depend upon officers and representatives at all levels to make individual and independent decisions about what to pass down. No specification will control what will be passed upward.

In either case the intermediary has to be one determined to use information as a positive productive resource, not as a weapon. In almost any setting supervisors can be helped to understand better what can and should be passed on and how. They also can be given insight into why they strain more thoroughly or block entirely the communication the lieutenancy system was designed to facilitate. Unfortunately, few organizations provide a thorough training program and a systematic monitoring and evaluation of the communication flow. Their chief officers just pronounce periodically how important it is to know, and think a house newspaper and a bulletin board will do the job. They won't.

Notes

[1] W. C. Schutz, *FIRO: A Three Dimensional Theory of Interpersonal Behavior* (New York: Holt, Rinehart and Winston, 1958).

4

Management Communication and the Grapevine

KEITH DAVIS

Communication is involved in all human relations. It is the "nervous system" of any organized group, providing the information and understanding necessary for high productivity and morale. For the individual company it is a continuous process, a way of life, rather than a one-shot campaign. Top management, therefore, recognizes the importance of communication and wants to do something about it. But what? Often, in its frustration, management has used standard communication "packages" instead of dealing situationally with its individual problems. Or it has emphasized the means (communication techniques) rather than the ends (objectives of communication).

One big factor which management has tended to overlook is communication *within its own group.* Communication to the worker and from the worker is dependent on effective management communication; and clearly this in turn requires informal as well as formal channels.

The Grapevine

A particularly neglected aspect of management communication concerns that informal channel, the grapevine. There is no dodging the fact that, as a carrier of news and gossip among executives and supervisors, the grapevine often affects the affairs of management. The proof of this is the strong feelings that different executives have about it. Some regard the grapevine as an evil—a thorn in the side which regularly spreads rumor, destroys morale and reputations, leads to irresponsible actions, and challenges authority. Some regard it as a good thing because it acts as a safety valve and carries news fast. Others regard it as a very mixed blessing.

Whether the grapevine is considered an asset or a liability, it is important for executives to try to understand it. For one thing is sure: although no executive can absolutely control the grapevine, he can *influence* it. And since it is here to stay, he should learn to live with it.

Perspective

Of course, the grapevine is only part of the picture of communication in management. There is also formal communication—via conferences, reports, memoranda, and so on; this provides the basic core of information, and many administrators rely on it almost exclusively because they think it makes their job simpler to have everything reduced to explicit terms—as if that were possible! Another important part of the picture is the expression of attitudes, as contrasted with the transmission of information (which is what we will be dealing with in this article). Needless to say, all these factors influence the way the grapevine works in a given company, just as the grapevine in turn influences them.

In this article I want to examine (a) the significance, character, and operation of management communication patterns, with particular emphasis on the grapevine; and (b) the influence that various factors, such as organization and the chain of procedure, have upon such patterns. From this analysis, then, it will be possible to point up (c) the practical implications for management.

As for the research basis of the analysis, the major points are these:

1. *Company studied*—The company upon which the research is based is a real one. I shall refer to it as the "Jason Company." A manufacturer of leather goods, it has 67 people in the management group (that is, all people who supervise the work of others, from top executives to foremen) and about 600 employees. It is located in a rural town of 10,000 persons, and its products are distributed nationally.

   In my opinion, the pattern of management communication at the Jason Company is typical of that in many businesses; there were no special conditions likely to make the executives and supervisors act differently from their counterparts in other companies. But let me emphasize that this is a matter of judgment, and hence broader generalizations cannot be made until further research is undertaken.

   As a matter of fact, one of the purposes of this article is to encourage businessmen to take a close look at management communication in their own companies and to decide for themselves whether it is the same or different. In many companies, men in the management group now follow the popular practice of examining and discussing their problems of communicating with workers, but rarely do they risk the embarrassment of appraising their communications with each other.

2. *Methodology*—The methods used to study management communication in the Jason Company are new ones. Briefly, the basic approach was to learn from each communication recipient how he first received a given piece of information and then to trace it back to its source. Suppose D and E said they received it from G; G said he received it from B; and B from A. All the chains or sequences were plotted in this way—A to B to G to D and E—and when the data from all recipients were assembled, the pattern of the flow of communication emerged. The findings could be verified and developed further with the help of other data secured from the communication recipients.

This research approach, which I have called "ecco analysis," is discussed in detail elsewhere.[1]

Significant Characteristics

In the Jason Company many of the usual grapevine characteristics were found along with others less well known. For purposes of this discussion, the four most significant characteristics are these:

1. *Speed of transmission*—Traditionally the grapevine is fast, and this showed up in the Jason Company.

   For example, a certain manager had an addition to his family at the local hospital at 11 o'clock at night, and by 2:00 p.m. the next day 46% of the whole management group knew about the event. The news was transmitted only by grapevine and mostly by face-to-face conversation, with an occasional interoffice telephone call. Most communications occurred immediately before work began, during "coffee hour," and during lunch hour. The five staff executives who knew of the event learned of it during "coffee hour," indicating that the morning rest period performed an important social function for the staff as well as providing relaxation.

2. *Degree of selectivity*—It is often said that the grapevine acts without conscious direction or thought—that it will carry anything, any time, anywhere. This viewpoint has been epitomized in the statement that "the grapevine is without conscience or consciousness." But flagrant grapevine irresponsibility was not evident in the Jason Company. In fact, the grapevine here showed that it could be highly selective and discriminating.

   For example, the local representative of the company which carried the employee group insurance contract planned a picnic for company executives. The Jason Company president decided to invite 36 executives, mostly from higher executive levels. The grapevine immediately went to work spreading this information, but it was carried to *only two of the 31 executives not invited*. The grapevine communicators thought the news was confidential, so they had told only those who they thought would be invited (they had to guess, since they did not have access to the invitation list). The two uninvited executives who knew the information were foremen who were told by their invited superintendent; he had a very close working relationship with them and generally kept them well informed.

Many illustrations like the above could be gathered to show that the grapevine can be discriminating. Whether it may be *counted on* in that respect, however, is another question. The answer would of course differ with each case and would depend on many variables, including other factors in the communication picture having to do with attitudes, executive relationships, and so forth.

3. *Locale of operation*—The grapevine of company news operates mostly at the place of work.

Jason managers were frequently in contact with each other after work because the town is small; yet grapevine communications about company activities predominantly took place at the plant, rather than away from it. It was at the plant that executives and supervisors learned, for instance, that the president was taking a two weeks' business trip, that the style designer had gone to Florida to study fashion trends, and that an executive had resigned to begin a local insurance business.

The significance of at-the-company grapevines is this: since management has some control over the work environment, it has an opportunity to influence the grapevine. By exerting such influence the manager can more closely integrate grapevine interests with those of the formal communication system, and he can use it for effectively spreading more significant items of information than those commonly carried.

4. *Relation to formal communication*—Formal and informal communication systems tend to be jointly active, or jointly inactive. Where formal communication was inactive at the Jason Company, the grapevine did not rush in to fill the void (as has often been suggested[2]); instead, there simply was lack of communication. Similarly, where there was effective formal communication, there was an active grapevine.

Informal and formal communication may supplement each other. Often formal communication is simply used to confirm or to expand what has already been communicated by grapevine. Thus in the case of the picnic, as just described, management issued formal invitations even to those who already knew they were invited. This necessary process of confirmation results partly because of the speed of the grapevine, which formal systems fail to match, partly because of its unofficial function, and partly because of its transient nature. Formal communication needs to come along to stamp "Official" on the news and to put it "on the record," which the grapevine cannot suitably do.

Spreading Information

Now let us turn to the actual operation of the grapevine. How is information passed along? What is the relationship among the various people who are involved?

Human communication requires at least two persons, but each person acts independently. Person A may talk or write, but he has not *communicated* until person B receives. The individual is, therefore, a basic communication unit. That is, he is one "link" in the communication "chain" for any bit of information.

The formal communication chain is largely determined by the chain of command or by formal procedures, but the grapevine chain is more flexible. There are four different ways of visualizing it, as Fig. 4-1 indicates:

1. *The single-strand chain*—A tells B, who tells C, who tells D, and so on; this makes for a tenuous chain to a distant receiver. Such a chain is usually in mind when one speaks of how the grapevine distorts and filters information until the original item is not recognizable.
2. *The gossip chain*—A seeks and tells everyone else.
3. *The probability chain*—A communicates randomly, say, to F and D, in accordance with the laws of probability; then F and D tell others in the same manner.
4. *The cluster chain*—A tells three selected others; perhaps one of them tells two others; and then one of these two tells one other. This was virtually the only kind of chain found in the Jason Company, and may well be the normal one in industry generally.

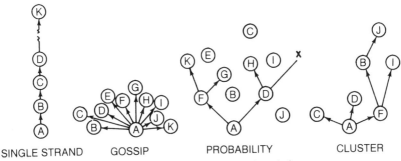

SINGLE STRAND   GOSSIP   PROBABILITY   CLUSTER

Fig. 4-1   Types of communication chains

Active Minority

The predominance of the cluster chain at the Jason Company means that only a few of the persons who knew a unit of information ever transmitted it—what Jacobson and Seashore call the "liaison" individuals.[3] All others who received the information did not transmit it; they acted merely as passive receivers.

For example, when a quality-control problem occurred, 68 percent of the executives received the information, but only 20 percent transmitted it. Again, when an executive planned to resign to enter the insurance business, 81 percent of the executives knew about it, but only 11 percent passed the news on to others. Those liaison individuals who told the news to more than one other person amounted to less than 10 percent of the 67 executives in each case.

These active groups varied in membership. There was no evidence that any one group consistently acted as liaison persons; instead, different types of information passed through different liaison persons. However, as will be shown later, some individuals were invariably communication "isolates"; they received and transmitted information poorly or not at all.

The above findings indicate that if management wants more communication, it should increase the number and/or effectiveness of its liaison individuals. This appears to be a large order, but it is entirely possible. Liaison individuals tend to act in a predictable way. If an individual's unit of information concerns a job function in which he is interested, he is likely to tell others. If his information is about a person with whom he is associated socially, he also is likely to tell others. Furthermore, the sooner he knows of an event after it happened, the more likely he is to tell others. If he gets the information late, he does not want to advertise his late receipt of it by telling it to others.

In other words, three well-known communication principles which are so often mentioned in relation to attitudes also have a major influence on the spread of information by liaison individuals:

1. Tell people about what will affect them (job interest).
2. Tell people what they want to know, rather than simply what you want them to know (job and social interest).
3. Tell people soon (timing).

Organizational Effects

The way an organization is divided horizontally into organizational levels and vertically into functions, such as production and sales, obviously has effects on management communication, for it cuts each company's over-all administrative function into small work assignments, or jobs, and sets each management person in certain relationships to others in his company.

Horizontal Levels

Organizational levels are perhaps the more dramatic in effect because they usually carry authority, pay increases, and status. From the communication point of view, they are especially important because of their number. In a typical firm there are usually several management levels, but only one or two worker levels; furthermore, as the firm grows, the management levels increase in number, while the worker levels remain stationary.

Communication problems are aggravated by these additional levels because the chain of communication is lengthened and complicated. Indeed, just because of this, some companies have been led to try to reduce the number of intermediate management levels. Our concern here is with the patterns of communication among individuals at the different levels.

At the Jason Company, executives at *higher* levels communicated more often and with more people than did executives at *lower* levels. In other words, the predominant communication flow was downward or horizontal.

When an event happened at the bottom level, usually the news did reach a high level; but a single line of communication sufficed to carry it there, and from that point it went downward and outward in the same volume and manner (cluster chain) as if it had originated at the top.

Accordingly, the higher an executive was in the organizational hierarchy (with the exception of nonresident executives), the greater was his knowledge of company events. This was true of events which happened both above his level and below his level. Thus, if the president was out of town, a greater proportion at the fourth level knew of it than at the sixth level. Or—and this is less to be expected—if a foreman at the sixth level had an accident, a larger proportion of executives at the third level knew of it than at the fourth level, or even than at the sixth level where the accident happened. The more noteworthy the event, of course, the more likely it was to be known at upper levels—but, in a company of this size, it had to be quite trivial indeed before it failed to reach the ears of top executives.

The converse follows that in terms of communications transmitted and received the sixth and lowest level of supervision, the foreman level, was largely isolated from all other management. The average foreman was very hesitant to communicate with other members of management; and on the rare occasions when he did, he usually chose someone at his own level and preferably in his own department. Members of this group tended to be the last links in management communication, regardless of whether the chains were formal or informal.

A further significant fact concerns the eight departmental superintendents at the fourth level. Six of them supervised foremen directly; two others, with larger departments, each had a single line assistant between him and his foremen. The two who had line assistants were much more active in the communication chains than were the six others; indeed, all but one of the six appeared to have little to do with their foremen except in a formal way.

Perhaps the clue is that, with increased organizational levels, those at the higher (and hence further removed) levels both recognize a greater need for communication and have more time to practice it!

Functional Groups

Functionalization, the second important way in which an organization is "cut up," also has a significant impact on communication in management. The functions which are delegated to a manager help to determine the people he contacts, his relationships with them, his status, and, as a result, the degree to which he receives and transmits information. More specifically, his role in communication is affected (a) by his position in the chain of command and (b) by his position in the chain of procedure, which involves the sequence of work performance and cuts across chains of command, as when a report goes from the superintendent in one chain of command to the chief engineer in another chain of command and to the controller in still another.

In the Jason Company, the effects of functionalization showed up in three major ways:

1. *Staff men "in the know"*—More staff executives than line men usually knew about any company event. This was true at each level of management as well as for the management group as a whole. For example, when the president of the company made a trip to seek increased governmental allotments of hides to keep the line tannery operating at capacity, only 4 percent of the line executives knew the purpose of the trip, but 25 percent of the staff men did. In another case, when a popular line superintendent was awarded a hat as a prize in a training program for line superintendents, within six days a larger proportion of the staff executives than of the line executives knew about this event.

The explanation is not just that, with one staff executive to every three line executives, there were more line executives to be informed. More important is the fact that the *chain of procedure* usually involved more staff executives than line executives. Thus, when the superintendent was awarded his hat, a line executive had approved the award, but a staff personnel executive had processed it and a staff accounting executive had arranged for the special check.

Also the staff was more *mobile* than the line. Staff executives in such areas as personnel and control found that their duties both required and allowed them to get out of their offices, made it easy for them to walk through other departments without someone wondering whether they were "not working," to get away for coffee, and so on—all of which meant they heard more news from the other executives they talked with. (In a larger company staff members might be more fixed to their chairs, but the situation in the Jason Company doubtless applies to a great many other businesses.)

Because of its mobility and its role in the chain of procedure, the staff not only received but also transmitted communications more actively than did the line. Most of these communications were oral; at least in this respect, the staff was not the "paper mill" it is often said to be. It seems obvious that management would do well to make conscious use of staff men as communicators.

2. *Cross-communication*—A second significant effect of functionalization in the Jason Company was that the predominant flow of information for events of general interest was between the four large areas of production, sales, finance and office, and industrial relations, rather than within them. That is, if a production executive had a bit of news of general interest, he was more likely to tell a sales, finance, or personnel executive than another production executive.

Social relationships played a part in this, with executives in the various groups being lodge brothers, members of the same church, neighbors, parents of children in the same schools, and so on. In these relationships the desire to make an impression was a strong motivation for cross-communication, since imparting information to executives outside his own area served to make a man feel that the others would consider him "in the know." Procedural relationships, discussed earlier, also encouraged the executives to communicate across functional lines.

Since communications tended not to stay within an area, such as production, they tended even less to follow chains of command from boss to sub-boss to sub-sub-boss. Indeed, the chain of command was seldom used in this company except for very formal communications. Thus Fig. 4-2 reproduces a communication chain concerning a quality control problem in production, first brought to the attention of a group sales manager in a letter from a customer. Although it was the type of problem that could have been communicated along the chain of command, the exhibit shows that, of 14 communications, only 3 were within the chain of command and only 6 remained within one functional area—sales—where the information was first received.

The fact that the chain of command may affect management communication patterns less than procedural and social influences—which has shown up in other companies too[4]—means that management needs to devote considerably more attention to the problems and opportunities of cross-communication.

3. *Group isolation*—The research in the Jason Company revealed that some functional groups were consistently isolated from communication chains. Also, there were other groups which received information but did not transmit it, and thus contributed to the same problem—the uneven spread of information through the company. Here are three examples at the foreman level illustrating different degrees of failure to participate in the communication process and different reasons for this failure:

(a) The foremen in one group were generally left out of communication chains. These men were of a different nationality from that of the rest of the employees, performed dirty work, and worked in a separate building. Also, their work fitted into the manufacturing process in such a way that it was seldom necessary for other executives to visit their work location.

(b) Another group often was in a communication chain but on the tail end of it. They were in a separate building some distance from the main manufacturing area, their function was not in the main manufacturing procedure, and they usually received information late. They had little chance or incentive to communicate to other executives.

(c) A third group both received and transmitted information, but transmitted only within a narrow radius. Although they were in the midst of the main work area, they failed to communicate with other functional groups because their jobs required constant attention and they felt socially isolated.

In sum, the reasons for group isolation at the Jason Company were: geographical separation; work association (being outside the main procedures or at the end of them); social isolation; and organizational level (the lower the level of a group, the greater its tendency to be isolated).

Obviously, it is not often feasible for management to undertake to remove such causes of group isolation as geographical or social separation. On the

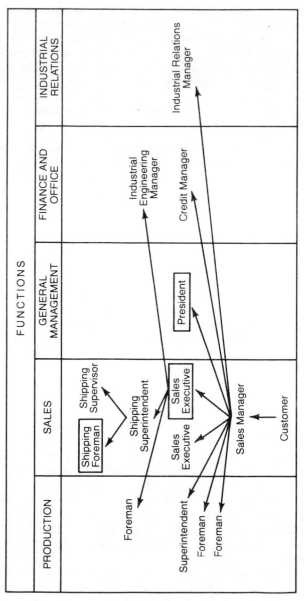

NOTE: Executives in boxes received chain-of-command communications.

Fig. 4-2 Communication chain for a quality-control problem

other hand, it may well be possible to compensate for them. For example, perhaps the volume of formal communication to men who happen to be in a separate building can be increased, or arrangements can be made for a coffee break that will bring men who are isolated because of the nature of their work or their nationality into greater contact with other supervisors. In each situation management should be able to work out measures that would be appropriate to the individual circumstances.

Conclusion

The findings at the Jason Company have yet to be generalized by research in other industries, but they provide these starting points for action:

1. If management wants more communication among executives and supervisors, one way is to increase the number and effectiveness of the liaison individuals.
2. It should count on staff executives to be more active than line executives in spreading information.
3. It should devote more attention to cross-communication—that is, communication between men in different departments. It is erroneous to consider the chain of command as *the* communication system because it is only one of many influences. Indeed, procedural and social factors are even more important.
4. It should take steps to compensate for the fact that some groups are "isolated" from communication chains.
5. It should encourage further research about management grapevines in order to provide managers with a deeper understanding of them and to find new ways of integrating grapevine activities with the objectives of the firm.
6. "Ecco analysis," the recently developed research approach used at the Jason Company, should be useful for future studies.

If management wants to do a first-class communication job, at this stage it needs fewer medicines and more diagnoses. Communication analysis has now passed beyond "pure research" to a point where it is immediately useful to top management in the individual firm. The patterns of communication that show up should serve to indicate both the areas where communication is most deficient and the channels through which information can be made to flow most effectively.

In particular, no administrator in his right mind would try to abolish the management grapevine. It is as permanent as humanity is. Nevertheless, many administrators have abolished the grapevine from *their own minds.* They think and act without giving adequate weight to it or, worse, try to ignore it. This is a mistake. The grapevine is a factor to be reckoned with in the affairs of management. The administrator should analyze it and should consciously try to influence it.

Notes

[1] Keith Davis, "A Method of Studying Communication Patterns in Organizations," to be published in *Personnel Psychology* (Fall 1953).

[2] For example, see National Industrial Conference Board, *Communicating with Employees,* Studies in Personnel Policy, No. 129 (New York: 1952), p. 34.

[3] Eugene Jacobson and Stanley E. Seashore, "Communication Practices in Complex Organizations," *The Journal of Social Issues* 7 (No. 3, 1951): 37.

[4] See Carroll L. Shartle, "Leadership and Executive Performance," *Personnel* (March 1949): 377–378.

Part Three

Analyzing Communication Flow

5

Assessing Information Load

STEWART FERGUSON *and* SHERRY DEVEREAUX
FERGUSON

Designing communication systems that efficiently meet the needs of organizations and institutions has been the concern of policy makers since the
evolution of organizations. Whether the communication system involves the
moving of information or the moving of things or people, the problem is in
many ways the same.

Consider the difficulty of designing a mass transit system in a city like
London. Literally millions of people have to be transported in the morning
and evening rush hours. The problem is to have sufficient service to fill the
peak demand, but not too much for the rest of the day. The same kind of
problem is reflected in the sliding scale of telephone charges for off-peak
times and in the reduced utility rates in some areas for late night use.

These examples demonstrate the concepts of overload and underload.
When the system cannot reasonably meet the demands made on it, we have
overload; and when the system is grossly underutilized, we have underload.
Both of these states are clearly inefficient.

Information systems are also subject to underload and overload. For the
purposes of clarity and organization, information load can be discussed at
two levels—in terms of how the system copes, as above, and in terms of how
the individual within the system copes.

How the Individual Copes

An example often used to illustrate information overload is the Japanese
attack on Pearl Harbor. It is said that the attack was successful not because
the Americans did not have enough information on the likelihood of such an

attack, but because they had too much information and were unable to differentiate between the significant information and the trivia!

The Pearl Harbor example introduces two important concepts in communication and information theory. The first of these concepts is *noise,* and the second is *pattern recognition.* In communication theory, *noise* refers to any part of a transmitted message that does not contribute to the transfer of the *intended* meaning in the communication. This noise could be static or mechanical or electrical distortion. Noise could also be symbolic content, such as superfluous or distracting information.

Contained in this second aspect of noise is our second concept of pattern recognition. The information theorist (or learning theorist) looks at information as being made up of packages of building blocks. The smallest unit or block is called a bit. Collections of related bits are known as chunks.[1] When information is assembled in a library, or in a computer memory bank, or in an individual's cognitive data bank, it is brought together in packages of related bits. For instance, the library will group its data by subject and author, and experience in using the card index can bring a searcher to the right shelf very quickly. Another network is accessible through reference to bibliographical notes or through subject indices; and by a series of associated steps, it is possible to locate data of a very precise nature.

Computer information is stored in a similar way and is retrieved on the presentation of *descriptors.* These descriptors are words that describe the contents of certain packages, or chunks. When a package of information is stored, it is given a number of descriptors; and when a search is called and one of these descriptors is fed into the computer, the package will be drawn. The usefulness of the data bank will depend on the skill with which descriptors are initially *assigned* and on the skill with which the descriptors are *used* by the searcher.[2]

Anyone who has done any research work in the Library of Congress will understand the meaning of information overload. It is of little comfort to the uninitiated to know that he is in one of the most comprehensive libraries in the world if he does not know how to locate the material he needs. Whether the individual regards the situation as presenting chaotic information overload or an abundance of useful information will depend on his ability to locate and to extract from the vast array of information available the precise information he requires. Overload then is a characteristic of the individual reacting with information, rather than of the information itself.

The individual assembles his personal information program in a way very similar to the librarian or the computer programmer. Experiences and impressions are categorized and stored in chunks and bundles of related chunks. They are recallable under the stimulation of trigger signals similar to the descriptors the computer uses. An individual stores his information and makes connecting cross-reference networks. The skill with which he assembles and activates the appropriate networks is what we generally regard as his level of intelligence.[3]

The more networks are utilized, the more accessible they become. They may indeed become so accessible that they can be drawn on and used without conscious effort. This is what is known as learned or reflexive response. The instantaneous response to an emergency situation, which we generally call reflexive, is far from a mindless response. Indeed, it is a demonstration of the mind working at the highest level. The reflexive response demonstrates a lesson so well learned that it can be applied instantly without the need for conscious step-by-step analysis. Conscious analysis would generally involve so much time that it would be difficult, if not impossible, to drive an automobile or to type a letter at any reasonable speed if only conscious awareness were involved.

To relate these points to the subject of this chapter, the learner-driver who finds that he does not have enough feet, hands, or eyes to fulfill the demands that the machine and the environment are making on him is suffering from information overload. The experienced driver, on the other hand, may choose to drive, rather than take a plane or train, so that he can relax or have some time to think out a solution to a problem. The situation in both of these instances is the same; but the load is heavy or light depending on the individual's capabilities, which in turn are dependent on his past experience and training.

An individual who is a specialist in some field will have organized his information according to context, and he will have arranged various contexts according to some priority scale. Fitting a concept to the appropriate context is what we mean by pattern recognition. The non-specialist being confronted with a total cargo of information on a subject may be confused by the seeming lack of form or the seemingly contradictory nature of some of the information.

The problem-solving techniques used by an electronics engineer illustrate this distinction. Faced with a non-functioning piece of equipment, the engineer enters the problem through a series of steps that move from the very general to the very specific. First he will check for power at the wall outlet and then test the supply cord to note whether or not the power is reaching the equipment—two steps that any intelligent person would take. The next step, however, will distinguish the specialist from the non-specialist. The non-specialist will remove the back of the piece of equipment and look inside at the mass of intimidating wires, resistors, capacitors, and transistors (after the fashion of those perplexed bodies we see on the shoulders of highways, peering under gaping car hoods), hoping for some divine inspiration. The specialist, on the other hand, will seek out a diagram of the system and study it. Given the schematic, he sees sets of subsystems assembled according to principles he is familiar with. These subsystems are linked together in dependent ways. Following the chain of dependency and checking on successive subsystems leads the specialist to the faulty subsystem. Once he has located the faulty subsystem, he tracks down the faulty component in the same way.

The schematic on which the specialist depends would probably serve only to intimidate the non-specialist. The procedure followed by the engineer is dependent on his information *chunking* background. These successive processes operate on the same principle as the parlor game of twenty questions. The series of answers to yes-no questions can either answer twenty questions or, by elimination, reduce over half a million possible questions to one yes-no question. The specialist, by the use of a series of dependent chunking decisions, moves very rapidly to a decision. The non-specialist does not have the chunking ability and so, in effect, asks twenty questions randomly out of a possible universe of half a million questions.

In short, a person's capacity to organize the information that is impinging on him will depend on his ability to recognize the appropriate context to which the information belongs. Only by having an understanding of various patterns of context will a person recognize whether a piece of information is vital or trivial. Without the capacity to recognize vital clues, all information must be regarded as vital, and thus we have a Pearl Harbor situation of overload.

Whether an individual in an organization has a high or low load potential is important or not important depending on his function in the system. If he is a linking agent between two subsystems, then it could be imperative that he have a high level of chunking ability to be able to isolate the essential elements of communication. Failing to do so, he may transfer noise instead of information from one subsystem to another.

It would seem to be futile to try to prescribe ways an individual may cope with overload. Acquisition of chunking skills is a long-term process dependent on background, education, experience, and in many regards, on personality. A more fruitful approach may be to examine how the system deals with the problem through its control of load and its placement of individuals in the system. The second part of this article will address itself to these issues.

How the System Copes

It has been said that the primary function of organizational structure is to restrict communication.[4] By so doing, the organization can control information load on members of the system. Restricting flow to formal channels and placing gatekeepers in strategic positions are fundamental to maintaining control. Gatekeepers serve an important screening function. They act as checks against the inundation of management by irrelevant information, information that would constitute overload. As liaison figures, it is essential that persons acting in gatekeeper capacities be able to adapt to high load work demands. If they fail to do so, the work load on other members of the organization may result in unnecessarily chaotic conditions.

Other strategies the organization may use in its efforts to cope with overload are working to rule, queuing or assigning priority to certain categories of messages during high load periods and delaying handling others, hiring additional assistants to help those on whom the heaviest load falls (especially those in linking capacities), adopting self-service techniques, subcontracting extra load, creating branch offices, and reducing service standards and/or performance standards.[5]

Many of these strategies have the potential to generate bad morale among employees and ill will among customers. In implementing strategies designed to avoid problems of information overload, the organization brings other problems upon itself.[6] It is generally agreed that any person who handles and transmits information modifies it in some way. Thus, information that must pass through different layers in an organizational hierarchy will change in character as it is passed from one individual to the next. In some cases, the changes will be intentional; in other cases, unintentional. Either out of self-interest or because the gatekeeper does not recognize the significance of an information item, he may omit or distort some part of a message. In so doing, he may be inhibiting the flow of information essential to the well-being of the organization. It is sometimes proposed, and only part in jest, that by virtue of his office, the President of the United States is among the least well-informed people on earth. Because of the vast amount of information relevant to his position and because of the enormous bureaucracy that he heads, the President's information may well be more characteristic of the gatekeepers through which it has passed than of the information events in question.

Everett and Rekha Agarwala-Rogers discuss the 1968 My Lai massacre of Vietnamese civilians by American troops as an example of the distortion that can occur with messages flowing through the formal hierarchy:

> Newspaper reporters in Vietnam at the time observed that Army orders tended to be interpreted quite broadly, and frequently with distortion, as they passed from echelon to echelon down the chain of command. For instance, a war correspondent was present when a hamlet was burned down by the United States Army's First Air Cavalry Division. Inquiry showed that the order from division headquarters to the brigade was: "On no occasion must hamlets be burned down."
>
> The brigade radioed the battalion: "Do not burn down any hamlets unless you are absolutely convinced that the Vietcong are in them."
>
> The battalion radioed the infantry company at the scene: "If you think there are any Vietcong in the hamlet, burn it down."
>
> The company commander ordered his troops: "Burn down that hamlet."[7]

Most organizations recognize the possibilities for distortion, omission, and bad morale inherent in attempts to monitor and control information flow in the system. Attempts to compensate may take the form of (1) redundancy, or repetition of a message in more than one form or through more than one channel or at different times, (2) verification, or checking out the accuracy of a message by reference to additional persons or documents, and (3) bypassing individuals who act as gatekeepers in the organizational chain of authority. Such bypassing may be encouraged by an organization's expressed commitment to an open door policy, use of suggestion boxes, and/or employment of ombudsmen who function as independents in a liaison capacity, hearing complaints from employees and resolving differences between employees and administration.[8]

The difficulty with these approaches is that the solution again becomes the problem. While redundancy, verification, and bypassing procedures help the organization to cope with distortion, omission, and the potential for low morale, these practices generate more messages and new information overload problems. Bypassing individuals in the organizational chain of authority can also undermine the self-image of supervisory staff.

Figure 5-1 illustrates the cyclical nature of overload coping strategies.[9]

Viewed from this perspective, it is clear that any strategy employed by the organization has its price, and the organization's successes in coping with information load will always be costly ones. The choices the organization makes in its efforts to set policies for dealing with information load will, in many regards, reflect the basic values of the organization.

Fig. 5-1 The cyclical nature of overload coping strategies

Notes

[1] Information theory is described in Claude E. Shannon and Warren Weaver, *The Mathematical Theory of Communication* (Urbana, Ill.: University of Illinois Press, 1964).

[2] For development of the computer analogy, see Allen Newell, Herbert A. Simon, and John C. Shaw, "Elements of a Theory of Human Problem Solving," in *Readings in the Psychology of Cognition,* edited by Richard C. Anderson and David P. Ausubel (New York: Holt, Rinehart and Winston, Inc., 1965), pp. 136–37.

[3] For further discussion of ideas see Carl I. Hovland, "Computer Simulation of Thinking," *Psychology of Cognition,* 158–64.

[4] Everett M. Rogers and Rekha Agarwala-Rogers, *Communication in Organizations* (New York: The Free Press, 1976), p. 91.

[5] Richard V. Farace, Peter R. Monge, and Hamish M. Russell, *Communicating and Organizing* (Reading, Mass.: Addison-Wesley Publishing Company, 1977), pp. 115–24, discuss various strategies that they classify as minimal effort, moderate effort, and major effort strategies for coping with information overload. They credit these strategies to Campbell (1958), Meier (1972), Weick (1970), J. G. Miller, (1960), Galbraith (1973), Prince (1970), Dearden, McFarlan, and Zani (1971).

[6] Rogers and Rogers, pp. 93–94.

[7] Ibid., p. 93.

[8] Ibid., pp. 93–94.

[9] The ideas presented in the diagram derive from a discussion by Everett Rogers and Rekha Agarwala-Rogers, *Communication in Organizations* (New York: The Free Press, 1976), pp. 90–95.

6

Steps in Performing a Communication Audit[1]

MICHAEL Z. SINCOFF, DUDLEY A. WILLIAMS, *and* C. E. TAPIE ROHM, JR.

As managerial thought has evolved, the result has been the continual redefinition, expansion, and description of a growing number of functions identified as responsibilities of the modern manager (Wren, 1972). According to many management professionals (Miner, 1973; Weisman, 1974), the manager today is responsible not only for facilitating effective and efficient operation of each functional area, but also for insuring their timely and continual mutually supportive interrelation within an organization.

Nearly 70 years ago Frederick W. Taylor, the founder of the school of scientific management, identified the primary functions of a manager as planning, organizing, controlling, scientifically selecting the right man for the right job, and facilitating cooperation between employee and employer (Miner, 1973). Since that time, the conception of management has enlarged Taylor's list of functions to include planning, organizing, staffing, coordinating, controlling, investigating, communicating, formulating goals and objectives, directing, motivating, evaluating, innovating, decision-making, listening, and administering (Koontz & O'Donnell, 1964; Redding, 1972; Drucker, 1974).

Associated with the widening scope of managerial functions has been an increasing awareness that communication is a key function among the others, and is, in fact, the "linkage" binding the other functions (Haimann & Scott, 1970; Weisman, 1974). As that linkage, communication is depicted as having the objective of interrelating and providing the mutual support among the other functions within an organization.

As the significance of the communicative function emerges, common sense and logic indicate that management must accept the inherent responsibility to become personally involved with communication activities (Townsend, 1965; Weisman, 1969). The effectiveness of an organization's communication is directly related to implicit and explicit organizational objectives and accomplishment of the organizational mission (Redding & Sanborn, 1964). The very important relationship among managerial functions is allowed and provided for through communicative activity and the resultant organizational cohesiveness.

In the past, top management through its supervision and direct involvement in selective functional areas, has initiated studies, inquiries, reviews, financial audits, or analyses to determine organizational problem areas. Unfortunately, such investigations usually focused upon the dominantly recognized managerial functions and excluded communication. When communication appeared to be involved in the area of scrutiny, then the communication activity was included within the scope of the study, but generally only as a component or sub-element of the more traditional system. Since the proper instrumentation to conduct research in, on, or about communication systems had not been developed and refined, communication was the lesser part of any particular analysis.

Only recently has a technique begun to be developed and tested to permit thorough and accurate evaluation of the effectiveness of communications systems and activities within the organization. The technique is the *communication audit*. Previously, managers used questionnaires, interviews, administrative logs, flow-charts, ECCO analysis, card sorts, participant-observation, content analyses, or any number of research techniques adapted to investigate separate functions and their particular problems. While any of these research techniques can be used to determine communication variables within an organization, until the recent advent of the communication audit, no single integrated and standardized procedure had been developed. Partial approaches generally focused on previously discovered problems and their impact. Seldom did these approaches address either the effectiveness of the organization's communication climate as a whole, separately, or by component. The currently developing communication audit technique provides a sophisticated approach for the capability of determining communication effectiveness.

This paper reviews current knowledge of the procedures for preparing for and conducting a communication audit so that managers, management, and outside consultants can become aware of the audit as a key supportive activity, how it is accomplished, and what benefits develop from its proper use.

The concept of the communication audit is explained best through a schematic (see Fig. 6-1) which depicts the stages of the audit from initiation to completion. The flow chart and accompanying text address the communication specialist since he, either as a member of the particular organization, or as a member of an outside organization specializing in audit services, must obtain the permission and support of top management in an organization, conduct the audit, and evaluate data obtained.

The schematic traces the major steps from inception to conclusion of the audit: introductory contacts between the auditor and management, the conduct of the audit, and final evaluations of communication effectiveness as revealed by the audit. Comments are general, since no two organizations are identical, and as such will require some special planning and tailoring of the audit. Both auditor and client must be able to conceptualize the audit within the special areas and environmental characteristics of the respective organizations.

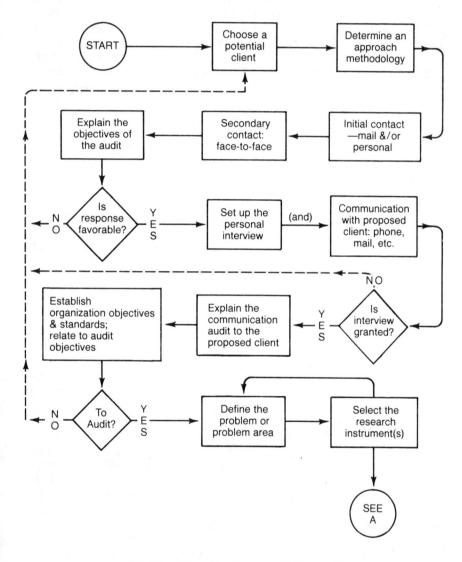

Fig. 6-1 Schematic of communication audit

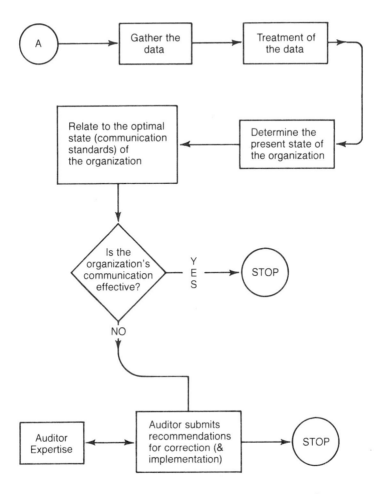

Fig. 6-1   Schematic of communication audit (cont'd)

Approach to Organizational Problems

Choosing the Potential Client

To establish potential target markets for implementation of the communication audit, consideration of several factors is necessary. They include: (1) Determination of any restrictions to be placed on the market; for instance, if the target market encompasses an industrial, governmental, or religious organization, an essential requirement is to identify the specific levels and communication activities that the audit will address. Legal and political considerations must also be included in selection criteria if these pose operational constraints within which the audit must be conducted. (2) Establishment of restrictions as to size, geographical location, industrial limitations, or number of employees. (3) Clearly establishing the relationship between the term "communication"/"communication audit" and the organization(s) under consideration. (4) Establishment of an operational definition for the terms "communication" and "communication audit." Attending to the criteria above will facilitate the selection of target markets, or of those segments of the available population with which the communication audit will be concerned.

Determining Approach Methodology

Upon the selection of a prospective client and a particular segment of the client population, a final decision must be made concerning what initial approach(es) will be taken to reach him. Alternatives include: Contact through advertisement mail and/or brochures containing an attractive outline of the proposed audit; telephone; interview; personal appearance; referral; or, any combination of the above. The financial cost of contact incurred by the auditor should be considered, however, before any meaningful decision along these lines is implemented.

Secondary Contact

Due to the lack of any established contact at the outset, the initial contact is a critical step in the entire contact/sell approach in the audit business. Therefore, in the secondary contact, care should be taken to expand on the theme which was utilized in the approach campaign; e.g., if a brochure were received by the prospective client, the auditor, in his follow-up contact, would take care to provide supplementary information about the materials received. Additionally, he would expand the concept, definition, and operational procedure of the communication audit. Obviously, this is the marketing phase of the operation, since failure to impress the organizational management is likely to elicit an unfavorable response.

Explaining the Objectives of the Communication Audit

A communication audit must have objectives. An important part of the sales promotion of the pre-audit phase is the establishment of objectives in a clear, concise manner to which management can relate. Several objectives for conducting a communication audit are: (1) assessing the effectiveness of the organizational communication system; (2) mapping the communication flows within an organization; (3) pin-pointing weak and/or undesirable areas in the system; (4) ascertaining whether or not the appropriate elements are present within the existing organizational structure; (5) assembling information through data gathering instruments, in order to measure and compare that information within standards previously set by the organization, and, (6) developing recommendations for the correction of apparent deficiencies and preparing plans for implementation of these recommendations.

Is Response Favorable?

If the response from the prospective client is unfavorable, then the auditor must begin the whole process again, i.e., repeat the initial and secondary contact procedures.

Setting Up the Personal Interview and the Communication Form Used

If the response from the prospective client is favorable, then the auditor needs to set up an interview in order to explain what a communication audit is, and how it will benefit the particular organization. Several alternatives are suggested to set up the personal interview: a personal telephone call, a letter, a face-to-face interaction, referral, or any combination thereof.

Is the Interview Granted?

If the interview is not granted, this would necessitate starting at the beginning of the diagrammed procedure.

Once the appointment for the interview is arranged, the auditor should intensify his research of the organization (i.e., obtain general knowledge of it, perhaps through its public financial statement, annual report, and/or any published listing of a given organization's characteristics) and establish his approach for the interview, before the next contact can be made. Preparation for this sales interview requires a complete analysis of the client organization. Since this interview determines whether or not permission is granted to conduct the audit, the client must be convinced of the need for, and benefits derived from the audit, along with the compatability of organizational objectives and those of the audit. How well the auditor analyzes the particular organization and the problem will largely determine his chance for success in the coming interview. This is the critical point where all excellent principles of interviewing should be appropriately chosen and executed (Goyer, Redding, & Rickey, 1968).

Explaining the Communication Audit

Answers to the following questions should be provided by the auditor: What is the communication audit? What can a communication audit do for the organization in question to help identify and solve some of its problems? How can a communication audit check for potential problems in the organization?

Goldhaber (1974) explained: "A communication audit is a research procedure which assesses the effectiveness of the organizational communication system according to a set of standards." When explaining the audit, the auditor should include mention of areas where communication problems are frequently encountered: horizontal (Townsend, 1965), vertical (Chase, 1970), and diagonal communication (Hulbert & Capon, 1972); the grapevine (Davis,

1961); bypassing, allness, and frozen evaluation (Haney, 1967); and, specific formal and informal communication patterns (Bavelas & Barrett, 1951).

Showing Alignment of Organizational Objectives With Audit Objectives and Establishing Standards

As the interview takes place, the auditor should elicit management's organizational objectives and determine what the organization's communication standards are. At this time a joint decision is made by client and auditor to proceed with the audit.

Definition of the Problem

At this stage in the pre-communication audit strategy, attention is directed toward identification of specific area(s) within the organization to be audited through specially selected instruments and methods chosen by the audit team (auditor and associates).

Within this framework, further definition of the problem occurs. Having some idea of the number and classification of employees who will be informants in the audit will allow for further specification of instruments and techniques useful in obtaining the information desired. Should the focus of the audit be in a production department, for example, only foremen might be made aware of the presence of an audit team, and a participant observer will be used to collect data. If the informants are vice-presidents or directors perhaps an information-giving interview should be chosen as one means of gathering data. Because many types of information-gathering devices are used in communication auditing, the audit team should have some knowledge of the number and types of employees who will be serving as informants in the study in order to select the most appropriate methods and instruments.

In addition to numerical and geographic information, the audit team must also be aware of the current communication climate within the area involved (Redding, 1966; Hunt, 1972; Dennis, 1974). Whether or not the atmosphere is one that would facilitate or hinder honest open communication is an extremely important factor in determining the methods to be used for information gathering (Sincoff, 1969). Tensions and jealousies must be taken into consideration in an analysis of communication climate. Previous exposure to communication surveys and reactions to them by the client sample are appropriate data to obtain.

Selection of the Instruments

Following definitions of the audit objectives, the auditor should select the data gathering instrument(s), a process involving three phases: (1) Determination of the instrument's relevance to a particular purpose; (2) estimation of cost factors (temporal and monetary) which are involved in using the particular instrument; and, (3) evaluation of the strengths and weaknesses of each instrument.

Since a variety of data gathering instruments are available, the auditor has to decide which ones will provide the desired information about the problem under study. The auditor should determine the scientific usefulness of the instrument considered, i.e., its reliability and validity. Since many instruments (commercially prepared questionnaires) neither consistently nor accurately measure the constructs they purport to measure, determining reliability and validity of the instrument becomes a critical step. Relative cost factors must be considered when determining the extent to which reliability and validity need to be demonstrated.

Having narrowed the selection of data gathering instruments, the auditor compares the strengths and weaknesses of the remaining instruments by looking for answers to the following questions: (1) Can the instrument be easily used? (2) Is it objectively scored? (3) Is it available for use? (4) Is is easily explained? Some common weaknesses of which the auditor should be aware are biased or leading questions, subjectivity in scoring, and data which are subject to only unfamiliar forms of statistical procedures. These and other comparisons will lead the auditor to choose the optimum data gathering instruments.

Although many instruments can be employed in the communication audit, most of them are representative of one of the three major types of data gathering techniques: the questionnaire, the interview, and observation. Since the auditor needs to be familiar with all three if he desires proficiency in his task, they are explained here briefly.

The Questionnaire

The questionnaire is a written instrument which attempts to secure information concerning an individual's attitudes, knowledge, and perceptions on a particular topic or activity. In most cases, the questionnaire is self-administered—the individual providing information completes the questionnaire without assistance from the auditor.

The ease with which the questionnaire is administered is one of its main advantages. Other inherent advantages are its flexibility, low cost, the wide variety of information obtainable, and the relatively short period of time necessary for its administration.

The major disadvantages of the questionnaire include low, unrepresentative return rates (especially for mailed questionnaires), biased responses due to inadequate alternative responses or leading questions, and difficulty in coding open-ended questions. Often the questionnaires tend to incorporate cultural biases, especially in language use.

To guard against these problems, the following precautions should be taken during the construction of the questionnaire: (1) The respondent's identity should be anonymous, (2) items included should be free of bias, and (3) there should be only one way to interpret the question asked in each item.

The Interview

The interview ". . . is the most powerful and useful tool of social scientific society research" (Kerlinger, 1973, p. 412). Essentially, the interview is "a form of oral communication involving two parties, at least one of whom has a preconceived and serious purpose, and both of whom speak and listen from time to time" (Goyer, Redding & Rickey, 1968, p. 6). Although many authors make little distinction between the questionnaire and the interview, there are some important differences.

The interview is much more versatile than the questionnaire. In addition to serving as the main instrument of the research, the interview also functions as an explanatory device as well as a supplemental aid to other research methods. Moreover, the interview has the distinct advantage of being an immediate and direct communication exchange between the parties involved. While this format enables the interviewee to explain his answers more fully, it gives the interviewer insight into both the conscious and preconscious attitudes, beliefs, and perceptions of the respondent.

Besides having certain advantages over the questionnaires, the interview also possesses some disadvantages not found in the questionnaire, specifically (1) it requires a great deal of time and money; and (2) bias can result from the interaction between the parties and/or subjective interpretation of the informant's responses by the interviewer. An auditor experienced in the various approaches and techniques of interviewing can eliminate (or at least minimize) some of the interview's weaknesses.

Observation Methodology

The third overall methodology useful in the communication audit is observation. It is "collecting information-in-society first-hand by maintaining alert attention, with maximum use of the observer's complement of perceptual abilities and sensitivities, to all the accessible and relevant interpersonal and intrapersonal events going on in the immediate field situation through a period of time" (Junker, 1960, p. 14). The phases of the observation technique are: (1) observing, (2) recording, and (3) analyzing.

In the observational phase, achieving and adapting to the situation are crucial to the methodology. The establishment of rapport is important throughout the course of the audit, first to enter the organization, and second to maintain cooperation from its members. Rapport between the observer and the observed influences the quality of data which are obtained, since the person observed will not behave in his usual manner unless he trusts the observer. Achieving rapport is an ongoing process that necessitates the observer's concern with dress, nonverbal symbols, intimacy of relations, conformity, eavesdropping, and revealing information about the audit to be observed.

Adaptations are essential to the maintenance of rapport and by extension to the success of the study, i.e., characteristics of the person being observed who would assure the success or failure of gathering observation data. Adaptation to the environment discourages contamination of observation and encourages social interaction. Cues given by the observed guide the observations of the observer and prepare him for role adjustments or unanticipated events.

Such flexibility in approach is a major advantage of observation methodology. Another advantage is that the auditor not only observes the actual communication patterns of specific individuals, but also has the opportunity to question them about their behavior as soon as it occurs.

The major disadvantage of this methodology is that it tends to disrupt the normal activities and functions of the individuals being observed. Thus, the observed behaviors are not necessarily routine behaviors, but possibly reactions to the presence of the observer, a form of the Hawthorne effect. A further disadvantage of observation is that the observer is limited to the number of places in which he can be at one time to observe, and by the number of detailed observations he can make. The technique is also time consuming and the accuracy of observations is contingent upon rapport establishment. In addition, lack of attention to the situation and subjectivity in data interpretation are problems inherent to observation methodology.

Application of Techniques

Once selected, the auditor has to decide how he wants to employ the research instruments. This decision requires the auditor to examine the operational factors or procedures inherent in the use of a particular research method. The term *operational factors* refers to the mechanics involved in using each instrument. Since each instrument has its own operational factors, attention is focused here on the three principal information gathering categories: the questionnaire, the interview, and observation.

If a questionnaire is going to be included as part of the audit, some operational procedures to be considered are administration, time, and collection. *Administration* consists of determining: (1) whether the questionnaire is self-administering, (2) whether the directions are easy to follow, (3) if the items apply to all respondents, (4) whether the respondents have to take the test at the same time or location, and (5) if special instruments such as lead pencils are needed to complete the form. *Time* encompasses both the completion and scoring of the questionnaire. Finally, the auditor investigates the procedures involved in *collecting* the questionnaire. One method of collection requires the auditor to retrieve each form personally. While assuring a high return rate, it is also very time consuming. An alternative method permits the respondents to return the questionnaire to stations conveniently located. Unfortunately, the percentage rate of return declines sharply when this procedure is employed.

Treatment of the Data

Beyond the cursory discussion of data treatment specifically designed for each instrument, the auditor should be aware of the general steps in data treatment while maintaining alertness to his purpose: he is seeking a frequency of occurrence, percentage of the total, difference between groups, average of time or number, pictorial representation of a process, or illustrative details. This, in turn, will determine if the data he gathered must be qualitative—such as flow-chart, nondirective interview, or sociometric technique analyses— or quantitative—such as a highly structured questionnaire elicits.

The auditor must also determine if his data are categorical: can they be portioned into appropriate classes? Often qualitative data can be converted into quantitative units for analysis through such categorization. Generally, the more highly structured the research instruments, the more easily classifiable are the data obtained.

In constructing categories, the auditor should keep the following rules in mind: (1) Categories are set up according to the research problem; (2) the categories are exhaustive; (3) the categories are mutually exclusive and independent; (4) each category is derived from one classification principle; (5) any categorization scheme must be one level of discourse (Kerlinger, 1973, p. 137). Another rule which might be added is that it is usually better to have too many separate categories which can be combined at a later date, than too few (Madge, 1953, p. 259).

Similar procedural decisions have to be made when the interview is used in the communication audit; the auditor again analyzes the administrative and time factors involved, deciding what approach he will use—directive or nondirective. He also selects his informants and determines the sequence in which they will be interviewed. Depending on whom he interviews, the auditor also decides if he needs to modify his appearance or language so that it will be more compatible with that of the interviewee. Finally, the auditor must also determine the best physical location for the interview.

If the auditor selects observation methodology to supplement other data gathering techniques, he still has to make some decisions before taking on the role of an observer: (1) He decides at which sub-unit in the organization he will begin; (2) he selects the type of observation best suited to his purpose—be it participant observation, observer as participant, or complete participant; (3) he finds the most subtle and effective way of recording the observed behavior; and, (4) he considers how much time needs to be spent in collecting information.

Having evaluated the operational factors of the instrument he intends to use, the auditor has to examine the environmental factors particular to the organization under study. Upon completion of this task, the auditor applies his instrument, gathers his data, and treats it using the appropriate analytical method.

Once the data have been categorized, the form of statistical presentation is determined. The simplest and most commonly used type of statistical presentation is frequency distribution, or the number of cases or distribution of cases falling into different categories. Primary presentation is descriptive, while secondary analysis consists of comparing frequencies and percentages.

Often the auditor may wish to present a visual representation of the data gathered. Graphs, tables, and figures are especially helpful here. For information on their construction and uses, one may refer to available style manuals.

Evaluation of Communication Effectiveness

Determine Present State of the Organization

Having analyzed the data, the auditor looks for patterns, familiar elements, relationships, and trends which they show, making inferences about the state of the organization at the present time. The second step is to determine the optimal state of the organization.

Optimal State of the Organization

Information about the optimal state of the organization is derived from the organization's statements of its objectives (regarding the ideal or desired state of the organization's communication and obtained in the initial and secondary contact interviews).

Is Present State Optimal?

The third step in audit evaluation is the actual comparison of the present state of the organization as determined by the audit, with the optimal state as determined in the pre-audit inquiries. This phase requires the auditor to compare the data he has collected and the conclusions he has drawn from them with the statements made by his organizational contact persons regarding its desired state or standard of communication. If the auditor determines that the present state of the organization is in line with the organization's optimal state, then no further work is necessary.

Making Recommendations

If the auditor determines that the present state of the organization fails to meet the communication standards of the client, then he may make recommendations proposing ways that the organization can achieve its goals and objectives through corrective action of communicative behavior.

Expertise of the Auditor

In making recommendations, the auditor draws on his own knowledge, training and experience. He is, for example, aware of specific techniques that may be employed to alleviate certain communication problems. He knows of communication and organizational models whose application may prove helpful to the client. Furthermore, he has acquired experience in applying certain methods in real life situations, and is expected to know how well or to what extent those methods have worked in the past. The auditor should bring to bear on the problem the sum total of his knowledge and experience.

Conclusion

The auditor must be thoroughly trained and experienced in understanding the communication characteristics of organizations. He must develop an understanding of the organizational characteristics of the firm being considered for an audit. Repeated contacts, primarily of a face-to-face nature between audit personnel and top management representatives, are mandatory to establish the foundations for thorough and mutual understanding. Optimum planning must be an objective of both parties. Data must be evaluated against communication standards previously set by the organization and not the audit team. Top management's support of the audit and announcement interest must be evident from the initial contact through completion.

The communication audit is relatively new to the management environment. While any given audit will be tailored to fit a particular organization, there will be universalities which lend themselves to all organizations.

Notes

[1] This paper is based on a research report submitted in partial fulfillment of the requirements in the course Interpersonal Communication 746: "Communication Process in Organizations" conducted during the Winter Quarter, 1975, School of Interpersonal Communication, Ohio University, Athens, Ohio. Participants in the research were: Robert Edmunds, Craig Harter, R. A. Iglowski, Craig Inabnet, John Nolan, Jean Rahrig, C. E. Tapie Rohm, Jr., William Rossiter, Geraldine Simone, Leah Vaughan, Holly Ann Wellstead, Dudley A. Williams, and James W. Wright.

References

Bavelas, A., and Barrett, D. "An Experimental Approach to Organizational Communication." *Personnel* 27 (March 1951): 366–371.

Becker, H. S. "Problems of Interference and Proof in Participant Observation." In *Issues in Participant Observation,* edited by G. McCall and J. L. Simmons. Reading, Mass.: Addison-Wesley Publishing Company, 1961.

Bogdan, R. *Participant Observation in Organizational Settings.* Syracuse: Syracuse University Press, 1972.

Chase, A. "How to Make Downward Communication Work." *Personnel Journal* 48 (1970): 478–483.

Davis, K. "The Organization That's Not on the Chart." *Supervisory Management* 6 (1961): 2–7.

Dennis, H. "A Theoretical and Empirical Study of Managerial Communication Climate in Complex Organizations." Unpublished doctoral dissertation, Purdue University, 1974.

Drucker, P. F. *Management.* New York: Harper & Row, Publishers, 1974.

Goldhaber, G. M. *Organizational Communication.* Dubuque, Iowa: Wm. C. Brown Company, 1974.

Goyer, R.; Redding, W. C.; and Rickey, J. *Interviewing Principles and Techniques.* Rev. ed. Dubuque, Iowa: Wm. C. Brown Company, 1968.

Haimann, T., and Scott, W. G. *Management*

in the *Modern Organization.* New York: Houghton-Mifflin, 1970.

Haney, W. V. *Communication and Organizational Behavior.* Homewood, Illinois: Richard D. Irwin, Inc., 1967.

Hulbert, J., and Capon, N. "Interpersonal Communication Marketing." *Journal of Marketing Research* 9 (February 1972): 27–34.

Hunt, G. T. "Communication, Satisfaction and Decision-Making at Three American Colleges." Unpublished doctoral dissertation, Purdue University, 1972.

Junker, B. *Field Work.* Chicago: University of Chicago Press, 1960.

Kerlinger, F. *Foundations of Behavioral Research.* 2nd ed. New York: Holt, Rinehart & Winston, Inc., 1973.

Madge, J. *The Tools of Social Science.* New York: Doubleday & Company, 1953.

Miner, J. B. *The Management Process.* New York: Macmillan Company, 1973.

Redding, W. C., and Sanborn, G. A. *Business and Industrial Communication: A Source Book.* New York: Harper & Row, 1964.

Redding, W. C. *Communication Within the Organization.* New York: Industrial Communication Council, Inc., 1972.

Redding, W. C. "The Empirical Study of Human Communication in Business and Industry." In *The Frontiers in Experimental Speech-Communication Research,* edited by P. E. Reid, pp. 47–81. Syracuse, New York: Syracuse University Press, 1966.

Sincoff, M. Z. "An Experimental Study of the Effects of Three 'Interviewing Styles' upon Judgment of Interviewees and Observer Judges." Unpublished doctoral dissertation, Purdue University, 1969.

Townsend, L. A. "A Corporate President's View of the Internal Communication Function." *Journal of Communication* 15 (December 1965): 208–15.

Weisman, W. "Management's Toughest Job—Organizational Communication." *Defense Management Journal* 6 (1969): 33–37.

Weisman, W. *Wall-to-Wall Organizational Communication.* Third rev. ed. Huntsville, Alabama: Walter Weisman, 1974.

Wren, D. A. *Evolution of Management Thought.* New York: Ronald Press Company, 1972.

7

In Search of an MIS

JOHN T. SMALL *and* WILLIAM B. LEE

The first computer was installed for a business application in 1954; and in the slightly over twenty years since that time, more than 100,000 computers have been installed in the United States alone. The term *management information systems* (MIS) has evolved in application and popularity to describe many of the activities associated with computers. Unfortunately, the present state of MIS is one of much confusion. The term itself has become so all-pervasive that it is used to mean almost anything anyone chooses it to mean. To many, MIS appears to be a concept that is ill-defined, promises much, but delivers little. Nevertheless, it also appears to be a concept in which much hope is retained for the future.

A considerable amount of debate in the academic literature over the past several years has been focused on MIS. As a result, a variety of definitions have been proposed by those pushing particular points of view. The practicing manager, on the other hand, frequently lacks both the time and the inclination to join this academic debate. Since the term has developed a certain aura of mysticism, managers simply have accepted and used the term regardless of its applicability. This unfortunate cycle is completed when the academician considers the jumble of applications and misapplications and concludes that the whole idea lacks a conceptual scheme and is in need of another definition. This resulting confusion has left the practicing manager with little useful empirical criteria and data on which to evaluate an organization's relative degree of success using MIS.

The purpose of this article is to put MIS into perspective by clarifying some of the concepts and current writings for the practicing manager. Due to the central role that computers usually play, the evolution of computers and their application will be outlined briefly. Areas of agreement and disagreement will be presented on just what constitutes an MIS, what were its promises, and why it has failed in many cases. Finally, some comments on the developing trends of MIS will be considered along with some implications for management.

Playing an ever-expanding role in business activities for more than two decades, computers and their applications have passed through three "generations" and are entering a fourth.[1]

The first generation can be dated approximately from 1953 to 1958, and has been considered the "gee whiz" era. During this period, few firms had cost-effective reasons for their acquisition, and a company simply had to have one to appear progressive. For most, initial applications involved such well-defined and formalized systems as payroll, billing, and accounting. As a result of these applications, computers typically were assigned to the controller's organization.

The second generation lasted roughly from 1958 to 1966 and has been termed the era of the "paper pushers." The technology remained oriented toward well-understood tasks and was designed to support batch processing. Computers were used in most areas that involved processing large quantities of data in a routine manner. This era also saw the innovation of on-line inquiry systems by airlines and the securities industry as more rapid access to information was demanded. As the number of applications proliferated, a great debate ensued about who was to control the "total information system."

The third generation ran approximately from 1966 to 1974 and saw the development of remote terminals that enabled geographically dispersed users to communicate with centrally located computers. Large organizations were able to tie their operations together with a centralized computer. However, this increased degree of communication entailed much overhead including complicated software which was developed to perform the necessary housekeeping functions. Organizationally, this centralization of computing activities resulted frequently in users losing control of their computer applications.

At the present time, the development of large-scale, application-independent data bases is enabling firms to make more effective use of their organizational data.[2] During the next few years, traditional cycles of chained, independent batch runs will remain the rule. However, on-line communication is becoming increasingly easier to use. Users are developing data bases that will permit more efficient use of operational resources. A fourth generation of hardware and software is being designed to facilitate data base applications. Eventually, much of a company's data is expected to be contained in a computerized data base system. Frederic G. Withington believes that the evolution of this technology is heading toward a single ultimate objective: "the machine that can collect, organize, and store all existing data."[3] The data will be accessible in a variety of ways by a variety of people for a variety of purposes. Use of the data would range from conducting routine operations to supporting high-level managerial decisions.

What Is an MIS?

An exact, universally acceptable definition for an MIS does not exist. Authors vary widely in the specificity of their definitions. For example, J. W. Konvalinka and H. G. Trentin consider an MIS as a system of reports designed to help management plan, execute, and control.[4] However, Hope T.

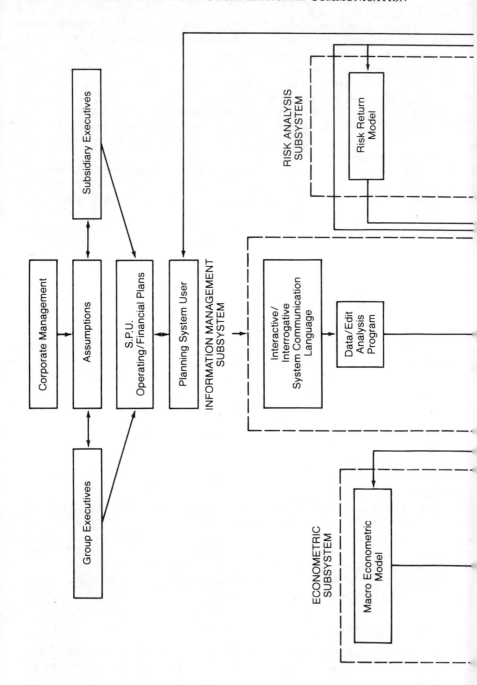

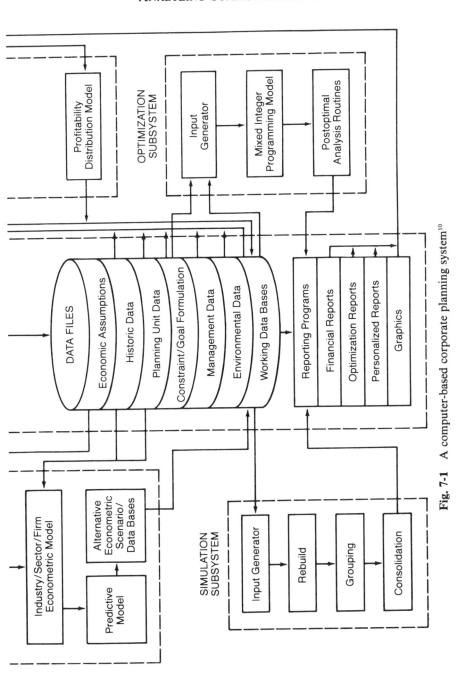

Fig. 7-1 A computer-based corporate planning system[10]

Ludlow is a bit more general in applying a definition which identifies an MIS as any "specially designed method to provide management with needed information on a regular basis. It may be manual or computer based."[5] To be even more general, A. T. Spaulding states that an MIS is "a system which provides . . . the right information for the right people at the right time."[6] Furthermore, Stanley J. PoKempner referred to an MIS as the "most highly formalized of the many procedures in business and government by which data are transformed into information."[7]

In a recent article, Richard O. Mason and Ian I. Mitroff propose a definition which shows promise as a guideline for research:

> An information system consists of at least one PERSON of a certain PSYCHOLOGICAL TYPE who faces a PROBLEM within some ORGANIZATIONAL CONTEXT for which he needs EVIDENCE to arrive at a solution (that is, to select some course of action) and that the evidence is made available to him through some MODE OF PRESENTATION.[8]

This definition identifies some of the key variables that comprise an MIS. It is sufficiently general and comprehensive to allow for a myriad of activities, yet it also is sufficiently definitive to provide guidelines for research.

These definitions serve to suggest, however, that the MIS concept still is somewhat nebulous. This lack of agreement as to exactly what constitutes an MIS has led to many activities generally being referred to as management information systems. For example, Gary W. Dickson, John J. Mauriel, and John C. Anderson argue that modeling should be included under MIS.[9] Often considered also as MIS are automatic data processing (ADP), electronic data processing (EDP), and even corporate planning systems as illustrated in Fig. 7-1. This system performs many of the functions generally referred to under the heading of management information systems.

The practicing manager, however, has little time or inclination to participate in such definitional activities. Many authors have proposed definitions and, although they may provide an intuitive understanding and perhaps the "flavor" of the concept, they are lacking in precision. Thus, a useful and practical definition of MIS must include all the important aspects of MIS and must be specific enough to provide guidelines for action to the practicing manager. The elusiveness of most MIS definitions leads naturally to vague understandings and to elusive promises.

A simplified and yet comprehensive way to look at this array of definitions is to consider MIS as a *system* for providing *information* to *management.* Taking these terms one-at-a-time, the following notions are evident:

- A *system* implies order, arrangement, and purpose. It is not ad hoc.[11]
- *Information* should be distinguished from *data.* Data are raw facts in isolation and do not become information until someone has a need to know and utilizes the data to become informed.
- *Managerial activities* that require information can be considered as performing routine operations, allocating and controlling resources, and planning the future strategy of the firm.

Along these same lines, James C. Emery feels that a growing consensus exists regarding some of the important characteristics of management information systems: MIS is an integral part of the organization's activities; it is more than just a computer; it is composed of a collection of interrelated and interdependent subsystems; it utilizes and is dependent upon a data base; and it is responsive to the organization's changing needs.[12]

What Were Its Promises?

The computer, as a central component of an MIS, can be an extremely useful element in the process of transforming data into useful information. However, visions like the following:

> radar-like screens constantly scanning the business horizon, pushbutton consoles for instantaneous pulse-taking of every corporate artery, and immediate communication with every decision and action center of the business.[13]

have led both managers and designers to expect more than an MIS can deliver. Although such statements as "radar-like screens" seem incredulous, authors have persisted in fostering these expectations. For example, consider the following passages:

> By 1970 we shall see the commercial perfection of man-computer communications. Programming languages by then will be more like everyday language, and man will use voice communication and visual communication to direct computers.[14]
>
> One information system will feed the entire business. This system will be the arteries through which will flow the life stream of the business: market intelligence, control information, strategy decision, feedback for change.[15]

Perhaps one of the most persistent pictures of the future MIS is that of the top executive sitting at his terminal, interacting with the computer. In fact, some experts go so far as to predict a sizable staff reduction resulting from these advances. John Dearden satirizes on this notion:

> A manager in the year 1985 or so will sit in his paperless, peopleless office with his computer terminal and make decisions based on information and analysis displayed on a screen in his office.[16]

Fortunately, other authors have attempted to consider rationally the possible benefits to a business in applying the MIS concept. Among those benefits mentioned most often are the following:

- Experts schooled in MIS can more effectively analyze and define a company's information needs than those traditionally responsible for this task;

- MIS is better coordinated and more consistent than a number of separate systems;
- MIS can provide answers rapidly and at a lower cost than traditional methods;
- The system can be readily kept up to date;
- MIS will provide a communication link throughout the company enabling the functional areas to work together better;
- MIS will make for better management of resources;
- MIS will reduce clerical work and errors.

In view of today's rapidly changing and complex business environment, it is easy to understand why such promises would attract the attention of management; unfortunately, not all of these promises have been fulfilled.

Why Has It Failed?

The potential benefits of a successful MIS are indeed impressive. However, there is a general consensus that the reality has so far fallen short of expectations. The original enchantment with the possibility of quickly achieving a large-scale and all encompassing MIS has been replaced with a pragmatic acceptance by both management and designers of the long, hard road ahead. The literature confirms that the idealized concept of the total computer-based system has not been achieved by any company. In fact, some feel that this may be an impossible attainment.[17]

Numerous reasons have been cited for the failure of MIS to fulfill its promise. Some of these pertain to difficulties with management and some to difficulties with design of MIS. To be sure, such a division is somewhat artificial; however, it does serve to facilitate discussion.

Management Difficulties

Perhaps one of the more interesting fundamental assumptions that has been questioned is that a manager's decisions will improve if he is given the relevant information. Russell L. Ackoff doubts this assumption.[18] In his opinion, managers often perform poorly under complex situations involving several decision variables. This conclusion is predicated on the belief that managers often fail to understand the delicate cause and effect relationships between relevant variables.

A second misconception, according to Ackoff, is that "better interdepartmental communication enables managers to coordinate their decisions more effectively and hence improve the organization's overall performance."[19] This is not the case because functional areas often work at each other's expense in a competitive atmosphere. Thus, improved communication often can hurt overall performance.

A third management difficulty is that virtually no place exists in most organizational structures for the MIS group. Originally, the MIS mission generally was assigned to the controller. Gradually, as the hardware and procedures became increasingly complex, a separate function was formed for this mission. However, this new entity often was grafted awkwardly onto the traditional functional organization structure. Usually, the new MIS function also lacked power. The MIS mission was ". . . often viewed with suspicion or hostility by managers whose role potentially could be changed adversely by the MIS."[20]

A fourth failing often cited is that managers have selected the wrong people to plan the installations. The MIS teams frequently are composed mostly of technical specialists who fail to appreciate the manager's task. Some writers feel that the MIS "expert" simply cannot exist because no one person can possess a broad enough set of special skills to apply to even a small proportion of the problems encountered in constructing a total MIS.[21]

Finally, John T. Garrity feels that management does not become sufficiently involved in the process: "Only infrequently, in my experience, do top executives take the time to work on this problem."[22] If this difficulty, in fact, does exist, then it quite readily explains some of the problems found in design of MIS.

Design Difficulties

A common theme throughout much of the critical literature is that designers have not adequately planned their systems with the manager in mind.[23] This is a very general criticism, but it does indicate, perhaps, that fault in the MIS difficulties lies equally heavy with those responsible for its design.

Another area of common agreement is the faulty assumption that a manager need not understand how the MIS works, but only how to use it. The logic is simple: a manager must know how the MIS works if he is to evaluate adequately its performance and, if necessary, exercise control over it. Otherwise, he will be controlled by it.

Authors also have taken opposition to some fundamental assumptions which are usually implicitly made by system designers.[24] First, most managers operate under a lack of relevant information. Instead, the argument goes, managers suffer from an overabundance of irrelevant information. Hence, they spend a great amount of time searching for the appropriate information for their particular problem. Adding stacks of computer output does little to lighten a manager's already heavy load.

A second objection is the assumption that managers know what information they need to perform their job. The contention is that only when an explanatory model for the particular decision process has been constructed can managers know precisely what information is required. Therefore, basing an MIS design on asking managers what information they *need* may be an exercise in futility. Rather than simply taking "potshots" at information requirements, a more fruitful approach would be to model the decision process. It is interesting to note that Xerox recently has claimed success in implementing an MIS in which emphasis was placed on "modeling" the manager's thinking process.[25]

Other criticisms have been advanced which conflict with the promises of MIS previously discussed. Consider the opinion by Dearden that centralization of the company's information system creates insolvable problems.[26] This occurs because the MIS technicians are not sufficiently familiar with all the company's information requirements. Dearden goes on to comment that the "total systems concept" has failed because individual systems change at different rates. This creates problems at the interfaces which offset the efforts of designers and improvements in the technology.

Others argue that the systems so far developed are not cost-effective. In this regard the literature lacks extensive documentation to draw firm conclusions. However, in view of the cost of hardware and the man-years required to make many of the subsystems operational, this argument may be valid.

Also encountered are problems with extensive and often unrealistic data requirements. For example, the Sun Oil Company's corporate model reportedly required some 1,500 items of input.[27] All too often, these data are assembled ad hoc for particular applications. The data subsequently become "locked into" these particular programs. This causes much duplication and large amounts of overhead for housekeeping chores such as updating. This, in turn, causes the already cumbersome "corporate" models to be even more inflexible.

Finally, some authors have noted that MIS technicians tend to be over-concerned with computer hardware to the detriment of the overall system design. Although a thorough knowledge of hardware is essential for most MIS designs, "computeritis" certainly may tend to interfere with the objective of developing an information system for the management's benefit.

Clearly, the MIS concept as originally envisioned has not been successfully implemented. Some of the more commonly cited explanations are summarized as follows:

1. A manager's decisions may not improve if he is given the relevant information.
2. Improved interdepartmental communication may often hurt overall performance.
3. No place exists in the organization for the MIS group.
4. The wrong people are selected to plan the installation of the MIS.
5. There has been insufficient involvement by top management.
6. Designers have not adequately planned their systems with the manager in mind.
7. Managers are not instructed as to how their systems really work.
8. Managers may not operate with a lack of relevant information.
9. Managers may not know what information they need; therefore, asking them may be of little value.
10. Centralization of the company's MIS may create insolvable problems.
11. The cost-effectiveness of many systems has not been demonstrated.
12. Extensive and often unrealistic data requirements are encountered.
13. "Computeritis" may interfere with the overall objective.

The Outlook

In spite of the apparent lack of success in developing a "total" MIS, companies continue to feel that eventually the concept will be achieved.[28] In a 1969 survey, George W. Gershefski found that only 20 percent of those surveyed were using or developing a corporate model.[29] Of this group, very few had started development prior to 1966. Approximately six years later, another survey indicated a 73 percent usage or development of corporate planning models. This survey indicated that "Companies increasingly are turning to the computer for help in assessing the impact of dozens of constantly changing variables on their business."[30] For example, one consulting firm was reported to be helping seventy-six corporations computerize their planning process at the present time.

Taking a broad definition of MIS, another recent survey found that 98 percent of those with sales greater than $50 million used some form of MIS.[31] This implies the use of some form of MIS by a large population of corporations since the 500th company on the 1974 *Fortune* industrial survey has a sales volume of $243 million.[32] Furthermore, it is likely that pressure for further development may come as a result of an increasing concern with the productivity disparity between present labor-intensive methods and the capital-intensive (computer) methods. Additionally, we may see reduced managerial resistance due to the new generation of managers who have been exposed extensively to computer-oriented techniques.

Given that management retains much interest and continued optimism in the eventual development of a computer-based total MIS, what directions might efforts take in the near future? Four likely new directions emerge from various attempts to answer this question.

Data bases

Users are becoming aware of the inefficiencies that result from the traditional ad hoc development of data bases. More advanced users are moving toward the development of one central data base, to be accessed by each program as necessary.[33] In this approach, a data base is viewed as shared random-access files to be used for periodic programs and ad hoc management requests. The economics of flexible data bases for use in multiple programs are becoming increasingly apparent to large-scale users. Data should be considered as a valuable resource, not to be locked into a number of separate files, often duplicated, for specific applications. The technology for building these data bases is available now.

Functional Design

A recent survey noted that work is now being centered on the subsystems, or major functional areas of a corporation as opposed to the previous "total MIS" objective.[34] This renewed concern with the functional areas of the business is partly because of the difficulty of one central group acquiring the expertise necessary to fully design and implement the "total" system.

Additionally, many believe that a specialists' group does not deliver the information management needs most because they are usually only responsible for that part of the system which interfaces directly with the computer. Possibly, a more practical approach would be to teach functional experts the new information technology rather than to teach information experts the functional specialties.

Traditionally, the functional areas most affected by MIS have been accounting and production/logistics. These are relatively well-defined areas that require the processing of large amounts of data to maintain basic operations. The transactions-processing applications (for example, inventory, accounts receivable, and so forth) now have been in place in most companies for many years and concern is now shifting to the building of models to assist in managerial decision making.

Modeling

Modeling appears to be the second step taken by most corporations in developing their MIS. Ludlow's survey found that in 1973 approximately 60 percent of corporations with more than $50 million in sales were using or developing decision models.[35] The literature contains numerous articles describing various models—mostly simulation.

Decision models typically are developed to assist management with resource-allocation or planning decisions. Modeling is the result of "MIS moving up the organization." That is, decision models are utilized typically by higher level management. Financial decisions, marketing strategy, and capacity planning are areas where models have been implemented successfully and show promise for further development. The financial functions seem destined to play a leading role in model building because this is such an important concern to top management.

Approximately 94 percent of all models in 1970 were simulation.[36] Differing opinions exist as to whether simulation or some form of optimization modeling is to be preferred. With some form of optimizing model, the best financial choices would be identified for a given set of assumptions. This holds the number of alternatives to a minimum and serves to encourage management to explore each alternative more carefully. William F. Hamilton and Michael A. Moses advocate some form of optimization rather than simulation.[37] They suggest a mixed integer programming approach that maximizes earnings per share over a multi-period planning horizon. Willard T. Carleton, Charles L. Dick, Jr., and David H. Downes,[38] and also Stewart C. Myers and Gerald A. Pogue[39] recommend a linear programming approach that maximizes the firm's present market value.

Additionally, past work has dealt mostly with deterministic simulation models. Gershefski's survey found that 88 percent of the models then in use were deterministic.[40] Unfortunately, the present treatment of uncertainty is not sufficiently robust and is difficult to apply to observed phenomena. However, much work is progressing in this area and the outlook is for increased use of stochastic models, particularly in the financial area.

Behavioral Approaches

A recent development has advanced the possible use of management myth-information systems (MMIS). An MMIS presents information to management by means of stories. Ian I. Mitroff, John Nelson, and Richard O. Mason posit that information is most readily conveyed when it is tied to an appropriate story or myth with meaning to the individual who needs the information.[41] However, the approach is new and the authors suggest the need for future research to determine what types of stories best convey the required information.

A recent study claims support for the general belief that the presentation of information by use of descriptive statistics improves managerial decision making.[42] However, Mitroff argues that the best way to present information is not in summary statistics but rather by listening to debate between two "experts."[43] Developments along these lines are progressing rapidly.

Conclusions

In an attempt to bring the MIS concept into perspective for the practicing manager, the authors discovered that MIS is still ill defined after ten years, of experimentation. However, research is continuing on a large scale, in both the academic and business community, and the practicing manager is well-advised to keep up-to-date in this area.[44]

Notes

[1] Frederic G. Withington, "Five Generations of Computers," *Harvard Business Review* (July–August 1974): 99–108.

[2] Richard L. Nolan, "Computer Data Bases: The Future Is Now," *Harvard Business Review* (September–October 1973): 98–114.

[3] Withington, "Five Generations of Computers," p. 105.

[4] J. W. Konvalinka and H. G. Trentin, "Management Information Systems," *Management Services* (September–October 1965): 27–39.

[5] Hope T. Ludlow, "Management Techniques in the Management Marketplace," *The Conference Board Record* (May 1973): 55–60.

[6] A. T. Spaulding, Jr., "Is the Total Systems Concept Practical?" *Systems and Procedures Journal* (January–February 1964): 29–32.

[7] Stanley J. PoKempner, "Management Information Systems—A Pragmatic Survey," *The Conference Board Record* (May 1973): 49–54.

[8] Richard O. Mason and Ian I. Mitroff, "A Program for Research on Management Information Systems," *Management Science* (January 1973): 475–87.

[9] Gary W. Dickson, John J. Mauriel, and John C. Anderson, "Computer Assisted Planning Models: A Functional Analysis," ed. A. N. Schrieber, *Corporate Simulation Models* (Seattle, Wash.: University of Washington, 1970), pp. 43–70.

[10] From William F. Hamilton and Michael A. Moses, "A Computer-Based Corporate Planning System," *Management Science*, October 1974. Reprinted with permission of The Institute of Management Sciences.

[11] For a comprehensive set of definitions of the systems concepts, see: Russell L. Ackoff, "Towards a System of Systems Concepts," *Management Science* (July 1971): 661–71.

[12] James C. Emery, "Overview of Management

Information Systems," *Management Review* (July 1974): 44–47.

[13] Stanley J. PoKempner, "Management Information Systems—A Pragmatic Survey," *The Conference Board Record* (May 1973): 49. PoKempner calls this the "Hollywood portrayal.

[14] John Diebold, "ADP—The Still-Sleeping Giant," *Harvard Business Review* (September–October 1964): 60–65.

[15] Ibid.

[16] John Dearden, "Myth of Real-Time Management Information," *Harvard Business Review* (May–June 1966): 123–32.

[17] John Dearden, "MIS Is A Mirage," *Harvard Business Review* (January–February 1972): 90–99.

[18] Russell L. Ackoff, "Management Misinformation Systems," *Management Science* (December 1967): B145–B156.

[19] Ibid, p. B150.

[20] Emery, "Overview of Management Information Systems," p. 46.

[21] Dearden, "MIS Is A Mirage."

[22] John T. Garrity, "The Management Information Dream: The End or a New Beginning," *Financial Executive* (September 1964): 11–16.

[23] William M. Zani, "Blueprint for MIS," *Harvard Business Review* (November–December 1970): 95–100.

[24] Ida R. Hoos, "Information Systems and Public Planning," *Management Science* (June 1971): B658–B671.

[25] Ronald A. Seaberg and Charlotte Seaberg, "Computer Based Decision Systems in Xerox Corporate Planning," *Management Science* (December 1973, part II): 575–84.

[26] Dearden, "MIS Is A Mirage."

[27] George W. Gershefski, "Building a Corporate Financial Model," *Harvard Business Review* (July–August 1969): 61–72.

[28] PoKempner, "Management Information Systems—A Pragmatic Survey."

[29] George W. Gershefski, "Corporate Models—The State of the Art," ed. A. N. Schrieber, *Corporate Simulation Models* (Seattle, Wash.: University of Washington, 1970), pp. 26–42.

[30] "Corporate Planning: Piercing Future Fog in the Executive Suite," *Business Week* (28 April 1975): 46–54.

[31] Ludlow, "Management Techniques in the Management Market Place."

[32] "Directory of the 500 Largest Industrial Corporations," *Fortune,* (May 1974): 230–51.

[33] Nolan, "Computer Data Bases: The Future is Now."

[34] PoKempner, "Management Information Systems—A Pragmatic Survey."

[35] Ludlow, "Management Techniques in the Management Market Place."

[36] Gershefski, "Corporate Models—The State of the Art."

[37] William F. Hamilton and Michael A. Moses, "A Computer-Based Corporate Planning System," *Management Science* (October 1974): 148–59.

[38] Willard T. Carlton, Charles L. Dick, Jr., and David H. Downes, "Financial Policy Models: Theory and Practice," *Journal of Financial and Quantitative Analysis* (8 December 1973): 691–709.

[39] Stewart C. Myers and Gerald A. Pogue, "A Programming Approach to Corporate Financial Planning," *Journal of Finance* (May 1974): 579–99.

[40] Gershefski, "Corporate Models—The State of the Art."

[41] Ian I. Mitroff, John Nelson, and Richard O. Mason, "On Management Myth-Information Systems," *Management Science* (December 1974): 371–82.

[42] Norman L. Chervany and Gary W. Dickson, "An Experimental Evaluation of Information Overload in a Production Environment," *Management Science* (June 1974): 1335–44.

[43] Ian I. Mitroff, "A Communication Model of Dialectical Inquiring Systems—A Strategy for Strategic Planning," *Management Science* (June 1971): B634–B648.

[44] For a more in-depth treatment, one of the better textbooks in the field is Gordon B. Davis, *Management Information Systems* (New York: McGraw-Hill, 1974). Also see the special section "The Office of the Future," *Business Week* (30 June 1975): 48 +, esp. 80–84.

Part Four

The Open Organization

8

The Physical Environment and Communication

STEWART FERGUSON *and* SHERRY DEVEREAUX
FERGUSON

Physical systems create a context within which social interaction takes place, influencing the nature and frequency of the interaction. Fred Steele has coined the term "environmental competence" to refer to awareness of one's physical environment and its impact and "the ability to use or change that environment to suit one's ends."[1]

Too often management has failed to recognize the relevance of setting; and when it has acknowledged the influence of the physical environment on workers, it has looked for a single "right" solution to the arrangement of the setting. This attitude on the part of management results in fashion trends in office design, such as are evidenced in the move from private cubicles to bull pen to office landscape systems.[2] More often than not, no one researches the effects of these settings on the individuals who must operate within them.[3]

Lack of Control of Employees over Setting

Advisers to management are plant location and layout experts (primarily concerned with cost factors in building design) and space-planning firms (skilled in the areas of economic analysis, engineering, and interior design, but with little training in the social sciences).[4]

The architect who designs a building that "stands out" is frequently rewarded over the one who creates a structure that "fits in."[5] The bold impressive building will often be a hard monumental one. Frequently the basis of architectural awards will be the presumed *lack* of popular appeal of the design. Boards of specialists acting on behalf of the public, but not necessarily in their interests, make the awards. An example in point is Paul Rudolph's Art Architecture building at Yale,[6] a building that won a citation for good design but was described in the following way:

> It is . . . not an easy building to live with. Physically it is often uncomfortable. It gets hot when the sun pours in. Security controls are difficult. Offices are cramped. The spaces are not perfect for twenty-foot high paintings or intimate conversation or classroom study. The lighting is inadequate. There are great difficulties in manipulating one's personal environment.[7]

Some architects specify in their contracts that their written permission is required to make any changes to the building, including such minor adjustments as moving partitions and changing the drapes. In many public buildings, long lists of regulations governing employees' behavior may include prohibitions against hanging pictures on the walls, rearranging furniture, bringing live plants into the building, and even placing a family portrait on one's desk.[8] In many such buildings, where the architects do not hold such rigid control, the office furnishings will still be standard ones, selected by business agents out of catalogues.

Typically, in such hard office buildings, employees do not control the temperatures of their own work areas; rather they must adjust to that preferred by the building custodians.[9] Similarly, janitors make most decisions on day-to-day spatial arrangements, placing chairs and tables in accordance with their own norms and expectations and for ease of maintenance.[10] In some institutional settings, furnishings are bolted to the floor.

From the point of view of the organization, many see the company's physical facilities as the most visible and concrete representation of the organization, and they see these facilities as the most direct way of projecting an image to the public. This concern with appearances may override the issue of suitability of a structure for what is to happen within its walls. Using sociologist Edgar Friedenberg's analogy, Sommer stated the problem in this way: "Institutional architecture is like the pet food business—the consumer is not the purchaser and unless the consumer becomes ill or bites the purchaser, there isn't going to be much change."[11]

It is difficult to complain about a building. It is existent, often at great cost or for long periods of time. If the building falls into the category of hard architecture, change is expensive. Sommer uses the term "hard architecture" to refer to structures that are designed to be "strong and resistant to human imprint."[12] The most accessible persons, the custodians and one's co-workers, may have the least interest or the least power to effect changes. The administration has other priorities.

Buildings Communicate

Some buildings are designed to make people feel their own unimportance. The Kramberg building in West Germany is a 12-tiered structure, broadest at the base, where the lowest-echelon workers are housed, and visibly narrowing in stairstep fashion at each additional floor level until finally at the highest level the top administrators occupy only a fraction of the floor space used at the lower levels. The building is a strong symbolic representation of the very limited numbers of employees who will realize their aspirations to reach the highest echelons of the organization.[13] The Kramberg building typifies the tendency of management to set aside the top floors of its buildings for the president of the company, the chairman of the board, and other top line executives.[14]

In older buildings, the location of the offices will reflect the dominance of the hierarchy, with corner offices with windows housing senior executives and heads of departments. The most powerful executive will have the office with the greatest square footage and the most windows. Also the higher-status offices will be less accessible, with secretaries and receptionists acting as gatekeepers.[15]

Buildings and their furnishings can tell the prospective employee much about the organization, its values, and how open the organization is to the newcomer. Extremes of office decoration may point to the fact that no power is available to the outsider.[16] The following has been cited as exemplary of such a case:

> One company I know of has its senior executives segregated on the top floor of the building, in a kind of garden-penthouse overlooking New York's harbor, reached by a small private elevator which is simply but expensively decorated by a Renoir landscape. The floors below look like any other office, the usual mixture of shabby and modern. The penthouse is full of English wood paneling, French eighteenth-century furniture, enormous hunt tables, breakfront libraries, chinoiserie commodes, paintings, and furniture gathered from every salesroom and antiques shop in Paris and London. Adams fireplaces have been hacked out of ancestral walls to be recessed into offices without chimneys. Regency wine coolers which once held bottles of champagne now serve as telephone tables. At one corner of the office stands a carved and gilded horse from an old fairground carrousel, the rest of which, together with its machinery, is packed away in crates somewhere below. An office like this as good as warns you that you aren't going to get any power until you get the key to that private elevator, and the people up there in the penthouse are not likely to want to see you have one. Indeed, sharp divisions like this one are partly *intended* to keep the lower echelons in their places, and to make the access to power mysterious, difficult, and impressive.[17]

It has been said that where the offices of senior executives are located at the upper levels of a building, a tight control and supervision of day-to-day activities of the organization is implied. The residence of senior executives on the ground floor, on the other hand, implies an abdication of responsibility for the routine functioning of the organization.[18]

The size of offices, the quality and color of the carpets, even the floor on which an employee works speak of a person's place in the hierarchy and of the options available to him. The lower his position, the more limited will be his range of choices.

Relationship of Setting to Communication

The physical environment, inside which communication takes place, has a profound effect on the nature of the communication. We speak of some places having a warm, friendly atmosphere and of other places being cold and oppressive. These kinds of folksy observations are far from being superficial. Indeed there is abundant evidence that the psychological impact of setting can be extremely powerful. The history of urban planning in London offers one such example. A great deal of original work in city planning and development took place in London following the Second World War. This was so for several reasons. London was one of the largest cities in the world. England had been involved in a war for seven years, during which time normal ongoing construction projects had been stopped. The older slum sections of the city had further deteriorated, and added to this natural decay was a considerable amount of bomb damage.

The London County Council built up a team of young, competent, and enthusiastic architects and town planners, many of whom had grown up in the areas where new concentrated development was proposed. In many regards, these men understood the problem; in other regards, they only thought they understood the problem. People living in overcrowded conditions in slum areas tend to regard the problems of development as being largely a matter of providing adequate, sanitary accommodation with a high level of privacy. In the case of the London city planning project, these objectives were met by well-constructed high rise developments. Care was taken in the design of the projects to ensure that the apartment windows did not overlook other apartments and that the occupants of each apartment had direct access to the apartments from the elevators.

What had been conceived to be utopian apartments for the working class turned out to be isolation cells where people became so depressed after a few months that many gave up their new residences to return to slum areas in other parts of the city. The chief cultural characteristic of the lifestyle of the east-end Londoner, by necessity, was gregariousness. To remove such a man from virtually all social intercourse was to guarantee neurosis.

In fairness to the early designers, they learned by their mistakes and built subsequent complexes so that there were clusters of families who did share common space in the hallways and whose balconies overlooked each other. The planners also brought back some of the street culture to the antiseptic lots on which the apartments were set. They did so by accommodating street vendor stalls, which played in important part in the traditional lifestyle of the Londoners.[19] In many ways, the London development story is similar to the old children's story of the rich man who built a castle with a high wall surrounding his garden to ensure his privacy. After a time he found himself to be poor company and knocked a hole in the wall so that the children and the wildlife could come back into the garden.

In an organizational communication context, the physical environment has for some time been recognized as an important factor. The classic Hawthorne studies examined different aspects of the effects of the work environment on employees and production. Humphrey Osmond identified the "sociopetal" and "sociofugal" functions of settings and the tendency for the physical setting to bring people together or to push them apart.[20] He proposed that the arrangement of chairs, desks, and sofas directly influence the quality and quantity of interaction. For example, placing chairs in straight rows, back to back, as is common in airports and institutional waiting rooms, discourages communication between those occupying the chairs. People will respond more to those seated across from them, as in across-table and across-corner seating arrangements.[21]

The nature and size of rooms will also influence the degree to which people tend to be drawn together and to interact. Studies by Maslow and Mintz suggest that more positive exchanges between people will occur in "beautiful" rooms, surroundings that are visually and aesthetically pleasing to the eye.[22]

The design and furnishing of some meeting rooms may serve to discourage rather than encourage interaction. Comparing some corporate headquarters to cold and unresponsive airports, Sommer discusses the fact that the hard architecture used in such settings tends to limit severely the interaction that goes on there:

> The board room contains a long rectangular table with twelve to twenty chairs on each side and the chairman's place at the head. Everything is dark brown, royal blue or black to suggest dignity and responsibility. Common sense dictates that meetings in these rooms are largely ceremonial. All the real work of the company is done beforehand. . . . The hard conference room is designed to restrict interaction to prescribed patterns. Most often this means statements from the chair followed by brief requests for clarification from the wings and by replies from the chair. Robert's Rules of Order or frequent votes do little to enhance discussion. Except for the person at the head of the table who addresses everyone, the other people talk only to the Chair. At a long conference table, side-by-side interaction would be impolite and distracting. Most votes taken at this kind of meeting are unanimous. Interaction within this type of room can be made polite, superficial, and restricted to prearranged channels. Older hard furniture was wood-stiff and straight-backed. Modern hard wood is steel, plastic, and glass but still cold, stiff, and unresponsive and if not permanently fixed, at least pseudo-fixed.[23]

In the office situation, people will be more responsive to those whom they can easily see.[24] Those whose desks are in close proximity will probably interact more frequently. On the other hand, those who wish to maintain social distance may use desks to do so. Business and social discourse conducted at seven to twelve feet has a more formal character than that which occurs at four to seven feet.[25]

The relative location of facilities and people will affect the level of contact. The best meeting places are those centrally located with resting places that allow people to stop and converse without obstructing the way.[26]

Some studies indicate that degree of contact is correlated negatively with the amount of difficulty encountered "by way of corners to be turned, indirect paths to be followed, etc.,"[27] explaining why people who live near mailboxes, entrance ways, and stairways have a much more active social life.[28] Other typical studies reveal that people in departments that share space on the same floor know each other better than those who have offices on different floors.[29] The Hawthorne studies have been interpreted as demonstrating how a single room can increase group interaction and influence the appearance of cliques.[30]

Bureaucratic buildings are often sociofugal in design, operating so as to keep people apart, separating those who work in different departments and at different levels of the organization. Persons isolated by floors and buildings will have very restricted communication patterns.[31]

Bürolandschaft

The justification for open-office landscaping has been the assumption that lowering of physical barriers will increase interaction between task partners. Office landscaping, or bürolandschaft, was developed in Germany and brought to the U.S. by the Quickborner team in 1964. Bürolandschaft involves mapping out the already existing communication and work flow patterns in a system and then attempting to facilitate those exchanges through appropriate spatial arrangements. Shoulder-level partitions, file cabinets, bookcases, and greenery replace fixed walls and allow employees to designate individual and group territories.[32]

The Chicago headquarters of the MacDonald Corporation has been cited as an example of successful office landscaping. It is said that staff efficiency improved 35 percent after bürolandschaft was introduced. Turnover rates, which had been averaging 100 percent every two years in the old offices, dropped to 25 to 30 percent.[33]

Even where offices are completely landscaped, some degree of privacy is still required for certain office functions such as the personnel one. Private offices and small meeting rooms are provided to meet these needs. For example, the MacDonald Corporation headquarters has set aside one room with a giant waterbed as a "think tank."[34]

The rationale for the office landscaping approach is that it encourages greater communication between work teams, gives increased opportunity to supervise employees,[35] and reduces the cost of renovating. The low cost of change means the organization will more readily change.[36] Kleinschrod suggests that the open plan is most efficient under conditions of changing work patterns.[37]

Those critical of the office landscaping method claim that (1) few studies have demonstrated improvements in morale, efficiency, or work habits attributable to bürolandschaft,[38] (2) it can be distracting and dysfunctional for upper management to be drawn into the details of day-to-day functioning of the organization when their main tasks necessitate making judgments based on a larger view of the system,[39] (3) some studies indicate that while increasing general interaction, open office landscaping decreases intimate contacts that may be important in completing work tasks,[40] (4) workers are frequently interrupted while engaged in work-related activities,[41] and (5) this approach assumes that the existing communication patterns are the most appropriate ones. Taking a different approach could mean setting up goals aimed at bringing the system up to what it should and potentially *could* be, with physical change as facilitator.[42]

Also cynics note that the few studies done of open offices have shown that top management rarely relinquishes its private offices. Secretaries and lower echelon workers generally like the landscaping arrangements, which they find colorful and appealing. Those who most resent the open plan and who experience the keenest sense of loss of privacy are the middle-level employees, the supervisors and administrators who have been forced from their closed offices.[43]

Employees resistant to bürolandschaft also cite noise[44] and untidiness[45] as major problems. Organizations initiating such a system use carpeting and acoustically-treated ceilings to lower the noise level.

Overconcentration

On the other end of the spectrum from those concerned about placing employees in quarters close enough to facilitate communication are those anxious about the possibility of overcrowding. Rather than increasing communication or social contact, they say that crowding may "strengthen a social order that discourages communication in order to prevent overstimulation from too many people in too little space."[46] The concept of territoriality is an important one as relates to crowding.[47] Animals and people mark out spaces that they defend against trespassers. Among humans, a potted plant or a storage cabinet or an ashtray may mark "home" territory.

The employee who feels that his territory has been violated may well attempt to defend it.[48] For the same reasons, a worker may flee a bureaucratic environment over which he has no personal control and take his work to the more private territory of his home.[49] Bureaucratic organizations that attempt to insure that no one can designate personal space, forbidding members of the organization to bring personal furnishing or effects to their work environments, are acting against very strong (albeit culturally-influenced) employee needs.

When people complain of not having privacy, they are saying that they cannot control their relation to their social surroundings, for privacy is a relative term.[50] As Steele points out, crowding is in large part a psychological and social phenomenon, not an engineering measure. Whether a layout *seems* crowded will depend on the norms and needs of the people who use it. For instance, it has been found in Canadian university dormitories that room densities preferred by French-speaking students seem too crowded to English-speaking students.[51] Conversational distances will vary from culture to culture, with Arabs preferring much closer physical proximity than Americans. By the same token, the Americans set physical barriers, whereas the English set psychic barriers.[52]

The same principles apply to organizational settings. Sommer prefers, however, to differentiate between the term *overcrowding* and the term *overconcentration*. He says that when we talk about high rise office buildings, the problem to which we are making reference is more one of overconcentration than overcrowding. *Overconcentration* refers to too many people in one place, regardless of size.[53] An example could be two advertising executives sharing the same office. While the office floor space may be sufficient for two people, ringing telephones and client visits would make the situation an untenable one for both parties. Similarly, our personal space requirements, which are for the most part culturally based, make some spatial arrangements intolerable. For that reason, standard office settings are not appropriate for international companies who must house people of many cultural origins.[54]

Overconcentration can occur easily in any organization that attempts to base its space layout calculation on "purely mechanistic notions of the amount of space taken up by bodies and movement."[55]

Conclusions

Buildings should not be ones in which office workers must "live up" to an environment and change their behavior to fit the architecture. Rather physical structures should accommodate as well as possible the people they were designed to house. The focus should not be upon novelty and private expression on the part of the architect. Office buildings, airport terminals, and banks should not be evaluated by the same sculptural standards as national monuments; and prisons should not be a model for schools, housing projects, or commercial buildings.[56] The emphasis should be on the comfort and satisfaction of the occupants and upon encouraging the kind of communication patterns most appropriate to the activities going on inside the structure. As Latham has noted, utilitarian aspects of design cannot be separated from the aesthetic, for we experience the total.[57] Sommer made this same point when he said:

> There can be no dichotomy between good design and usable design or between beauty and function in architecture. To look beyond the physical structure of a building to its social consequences, to the sorts of activity it will contain, and to its effect upon the surrounding community is a necessary aspect of good design.[58]

Hard architecture is expensive and difficult to change, has no connection with the surrounding environment, clearly differentiates status levels, and restricts activities and people to specified locations. If Churchill was right when he said that the buildings we shape will eventually shape us, then "the inevitable result of hard buildings will be withdrawn, callous, and indifferent people."[59]

In recent years many banks and nightclubs have attempted to humanize and soften their settings in an effort to make their customers feel less out of place and less intimidated by a hard, cold environment.[60]

Organizations should place as much importance on the image that they project to their employees as on the one they project to the public. The "backstage" areas where members of social systems carry out their "performances" should rank in importance with the "front stage" areas.[61] The offices of lower echelon workers and of personnel departments no more belong in underground quarters or in windowless buildings or in drab out-of-the-way locations than do those of the administrators; and ugly, depersonalized buildings and rooms cannot be justified on the basis of economy. An environment that contains inadequate stimuli will produce bored, apathetic, and disinterested employees who eventually "tune out" their environment or who flee to their homes in an effort to get something accomplished.[62]

Studies have found that companies placing employees in underground facilities have higher turnover rates and lower employee morale than do those with more agreeable settings.[63] Where placement of computers and other technology necessitates that workers be housed in underground facilities, management should look for ways to relieve the dullness of such an environment. An atrium from the higher to the lower floors, surrogate windows in the form of tropical fish tanks, posters, and profusion of plants and flowers have been used by some firms to counteract the negative features of basement quarters. Astute management will make every effort to try to counter the numbness that people may develop toward disagreeable surroundings:

> To survive he [man] accepts very quickly, almost subserviently, the pressures of his environment. His brain is apparently designed so that when intolerable signals come in over the circuits, the perceptive systems themselves shut down and do not perceive. A man can live and even be happy in the environment of a garbage heap. This is demonstrated (in the extreme) during wartime, when the human mind and perceptive system survives massive continuous shock. Most of man's ability to use his brain for emotional and aesthetic purposes must be cut off, and in some cases it is never regained.[64]

Settings should serve to reinforce a sense of the value of the individual in the organization, rather than to underscore and point to his insignificance, as does the Kramberg building of Germany. Offices and conference rooms should be flexible and capable of being personalized, humane and attractive, giving occupants the feeling that they have an investment in their surroundings and that modification of the undesirable is possible.[65] Settings should draw out the creativity that resides in the individual. Variety in color, lighting, humidity, and temperature will help to eliminate the feelings of boredom and restlessness that are created by a homogeneous environment.[66] It has been proposed that the best situation is "*some* novel stimuli in a *familiar* setting."[67]

Organizations need to realize that universal solutions applied to all settings will be inappropriate as often as not and that settings must vary with the people and activities that go on inside them.[68] Schweitzer's hospital at Lambarene is said to represent such an attempt to take into account the cultural and individual identities of the people who were to be accommodated within its walls. Schweitzer made modifications in the design of the hospital, changes that would not be acceptable to modern Western institutions, in order not to frighten away the bush people whom he was serving.[69]

There is no single best arrangement of furniture or artifacts. The work task may demand increased or decreased social contact, or the employee may prefer to work in private or in cooperation with others. There are certain kinds of work activity that traditionally have involved open plan interaction, and it is difficult to see how some of these work tasks could be performed in any environment other than an open arena. The newsroom with its frequent and rapid communication exchanges would slow to a costly halt if its reporters and editors were segregated in private offices with secretaries to act as gatekeepers. In the same way, the stock exchange is an open activity, and it is appropriately called the stock *market*.

Design offices of highly complex technologies such as aircraft manufacturing are usually very large open areas, with rows of draftsmen and designers working at and walking around drawing boards. So many different skills must come together in the design of anything so complex as an aircraft that the work environment must reflect and stimulate easy interaction.

Other instances where a "cabbage-patch" arrangement may be most appropriate involve what Mehrabian terms "low-load" tasks, jobs that do not demand high levels of concentration and mental input.[70] In such cases, the open office or work area can provide stimulation and allow the work experience to be enhanced by the social overtones. The high degree of interpersonal contact can compensate for other environmental inadequacies. It has been observed that "high density makes other people a more important stimulus."[71] In general terms, Mehrabian states that "the lower the load of a task, the more it requires a high-load setting for optimum performance."[72] He does also note, however, that certain complex jobs can become so familiar as to reduce their loads to moderate or low and allow the parties to benefit from an open work environment.[73]

On the other hand, some kinds of work would be difficult, if not impossible, in an open arena. This would be the case where the work is of a contemplative nature or where too intimate a level of contact with processes could impair the capacity to understand or to administer systems as a whole. The top level policy maker of the aircraft company or the newspaper will not choose an open office in which to carry out his duties. Decisions on spatial arrangements should be made in accord with the need to bring people together (sociopetal) or to keep them apart (sociofugal).

If the open plan is considered to be the appropriate one for a particular person or business (and new experiences are sometimes needed to make employees aware of their range of alternatives), it should also be remembered that man is a territorial being. Not only walls, but also furniture and artifacts may be used to designate personal and group territory. Allowing employees to bring personal belongings to their work environments recognizes the very real nature of these socio-psychological needs.

Out of the open plan room was born the room divider, the function of which was to return the open plan to a more psychologically closed one. The outside environment and adjacent inside environments can be distracting, and movable partitions and dividers may be highly practical, not only for the individual but also for the organization. The worker who can give his total attention to a task when a high level of concentration is required will contribute more than the frustrated employee who attempts to engage in problem-solving in an atmosphere that he finds distracting and disorienting. Even the lowest level clerk should have access to a closed facility when he feels the need for such a setting. Overcrowding, or overconcentration, can be as serious a problem as that of inadequate contact between members of an organization.

The ideal situation would probably be one where an employee, whether low level or top line, had easy access to both open and closed work environments. While performing pleasant and easy or pleasant and complex (but very familiar) tasks, a worker could select to be with others and to discuss as he worked. When under pressure to meet a deadline or working on a project demanding high concentration, the same worker could retreat behind closed doors.[74]

While not all office buildings can afford the same space for individual options, most buildings can incorporate central lounge areas and coffee shops. Such areas can be especially effective when placed in the center of a cluster of offices and can serve a function not filled by conference rooms placed "deep in executive territory."[75] The coffee shop or the lounge is neutral territory and encourages cross-status exchanges important to the vitality of any system.

Such common lounging areas are especially important in academic settings and business settings involving information transfer. Faculty members and administrators need the opportunity to exchange ideas and to merge the findings of their different disciplines. Similarly, office buildings shared by different companies can benefit from such central socializing areas where cross-fertilization occurs.

Mehrabian proposes a design for such a social area that departs from the traditional coffee-shop format and uses limited numbers of "conversation pits." Strangers are forced into the same pit, thus enriching the "impersonal, alien, and sterile atmosphere of many office buildings, especially the new high-rise variety."[76]

To speak of most organizations as bureaucracies is to speak pejoratively of them. Yet as Sommer points out, it need not be so, for political scientists consider bureaucracy to be the most rational system of decision making for a complex society:

> Max Weber, the father of bureaucratic studies, maintained that a bureaucratic system increased efficiency to the extent that it *depersonalized* the performance of official tasks. . . . But the impersonality that was the antidote to favoritism, nepotism, and arbitrariness, when transferred to the area of design, resulted in faceless buildings in which no one feels at home.[77]

For this reason, numerous social scientists are today urging that "the people who study human behavior and the people who plan the human environment should join forces."[78] Environmental consultants should work in collaboration with architects and space planners, and management in general should seek to become more environmentally "competent."

Notes

1 *Physical Settings and Organization Development* (Reading, Mass.: Addison-Wesley Publishing Company, 1973), p. 8.

2 Ibid., p. 15.

3 Norman W. Heimstra and Leslie H. McFarling, *Environmental Psychology* (Monterey, Calif.: Brooks/Cole Publishing Company, 1974), p. 63.

4 Steele, p. 17.

5 Francis D. Lethbridge, "The Honors Awards Program in Retrospect," *A.I.A. Journal* (May 1973): 22. Cited in Robert Sommer, *Tight Spaces: Hard Architecture and How to Humanize It* (Englewood Cliffs, N.J.: Prentice-Hall, Inc., 1974), p. 129.

6 Sommer, pp. 129–30.

7 Henry Wollman, "Calendar for the Yale School of Architecture," 1971. Cited in Sommer, p. 130.

8 Ibid., p. 104. Also see Albert Mehrabian, *Public Places and Private Spaces* (New York: Basic Books, Inc., 1976), p. 145.

9 Sommer, pp. 104–105, also p. 112.

10 Ibid.

11 Robert Sommer, *Design Awareness* (San Francisco: Rinehart Press, 1972), p. 85.

12 Sommer, *Tight Spaces*, p. 2.

13 Steele, p. 49.

14 Mehrabian, p. 141.

15 Ibid.

16 Michael Korda, "Office Power—You Are Where You Sit," in Lawrence B. Rosenfeld and Jean M. Civikly, *With Words Unspoken: The Nonverbal Experience* (New York: Holt, Rinehart and Winston, 1976), p. 183.

17 Ibid., pp. 183–84.

18 Ibid., p. 183.

19 Numerous other examples of city planning efforts that failed in the same way and for the same reasons exist. Some of these examples are discussed by William H. Ittelson, Harold M. Proshansky, Leanne G. Rivlin, and Gary H. Winkel, *An Introduction to Environmental Psychology* (New York: Holt, Rinehart and Winston, Inc., 1974), pp. 267–84; also by Heimstra and McFarling, pp. 87–114.

20 Humphrey Osmond, "Function as a Basis of Psychiatric Ward Design," *Mental Hospitals* 8 (1957): 23–29.

21 Some of the most often cited studies supporting these conclusions were by Robert Sommer. According to Edward Hall, "The Anthropology of Space: An Organizing Model," in Harold M. Proshansky, William H. Ittelson, and Leanne G. Rivlin, eds., *Environmental Psychology: Man and His Physical Setting* (New York: Holt, Rinehart and Winston, Inc., 1970), p. 19, Osmond was the person responsible for Sommer's initial interest in the relationship of furniture to conversation. Sommer has published this research in numerous articles and books; one of his earliest was "Studies in Personal Space," *Sociometry* 22 (1959): 247–60.

22 Abraham H. Maslow and Norbett L. Mintz, "Effects of Esthetic Surroundings: I. Initial Effects of Three Esthetic Conditions Upon Perceiving 'Energy' and 'Well-Being' in Faces," *Journal of Psychology* 41 (1956): 253. Also Norbett L. Mintz, "Effects of Esthetic Surroundings: II. Prolonged and Repeated Experience in a 'Beautiful' and 'Ugly' Room," *Journal of Psychology* 41 (1956): 465–66.

23 Sommer, *Tight Spaces*, p. 108.

24 Steele, p. 36.

25 Edward T. Hall, *The Hidden Dimension* (Garden City, N.Y.: Doubleday, 1966), p. 115.

26 Steele, p. 38.

27 T. Allen, "Meeting the Technical Information Needs of Research and Development Projects," MIT Industrial Liaison Program Report, no. 13–314, November 1969. Cited in Steele, p. 65.

28 Leon Festinger, Stanley Schacter, and Kurt Back, *Social Pressures in Informal Groups: A Study of Human Factors in Housing* (Stanford, Calif.: Stanford University Press, 1950).

29 Sommer, *Tight Spaces*, p. 12.

30 George C. Homans, *The Human Group* (New York: Harcourt Brace & World, 1950), pp. 88–89.

31 Sommer, *Tight Spaces*, p. 102.

32 Phillip Howard, "Office Landscaping Revisited," *Design and Environment* (Fall 1972): 40–47.

33 Everett M. Rogers and Rekha Agarwala-Rogers, *Communication in Organizations* (New York: The Free Press, 1976), p. 104.

34 Ibid.

35 Mehrabian, p. 142.

36 Howard, p. 43.

37 Walter A. Kleinschrod, "The Case for Office Landscape," *Administrative Management* (October 1966): 19–20.

38 Sommer, *Tight Spaces*, p. 109, is one of many who point to the gaps in research in this area.

39 Sommer, p. 110.

40 Steele, p. 37.

[41] Jan Nemecek and Etienne Grandjean, "Results of an Ergonomic Investigation of Large-Space Offices," *Human Factors* 15 (1973): 123.

[42] Steele, p. 17.

[43] Sommer, *Tight Spaces,* p. 109.

[44] Malcolm J. Brookes and Archie Kaplan, "The Office Environment: Space Planning and Affective Behavior," *Human Factors* 14 (1972): 388–389.

[45] John Pile, "Clearing the Mystery of the 'Office Landscape' or 'Bürolandschaft,'" *Interiors* (1968): 94–103.

[46] Sommer, *Tight Spaces,* p. 122.

[47] Jonathan L. Freedman, *Crowding and Behavior* (New York: The Viking Press, 1975), pp. 24–40.

[48] Proshansky, Ittelson, and Rivlin, "Freedom of Choice and Behavior in a Physical Setting," in *Environmental Psychology,* p. 179.

[49] Hall, *Hidden Dimension,* p. 31.

[50] Proshansky, Ittelson, and Rivlin, "Freedom of Choice," pp. 175–83.

[51] Steele, p. 29.

[52] Hall, *Hidden Dimension,* p. 131.

[53] *Tight Spaces,* p. 122. Also see Proshansky, Ittelson, and Rivlin, pp. 181–83.

[54] Hall, p. 32.

[55] Steele, p. 29.

[56] Sommer, *Tight Spaces.*

[57] Richard S. Latham, "The Artifact as a Cultural Cipher," in Laurence B. Holland ed., *Who Designs America?* (Garden City, N.Y.: Doubleday Anchor, 1966), p. 262.

[58] Sommer, *Design Awareness,* p. 4.

[59] Sommer, *Tight Spaces,* pp. 24–26.

[60] Mark L. Knapp, *Nonverbal Communication in Human Interaction* (New York: Holt, Rinehart and Winston, Inc., 1972), p. 30.

[61] Erving Goffman used these terms in *The Presentation of Self in Everyday Life* (Garden City, N.Y.: Doubleday Anchor, 1959).

[62] John Platt, "Beauty, Pattern and Change," in Donald W. Fiske and Salvatore R. Maddi eds., *Functions of Varied Experience* (Homewood, Ill.: Dorsey Press, 1961), pp. 402–30.

[63] Sommer, *Tight Spaces,* pp. 114–19.

[64] Latham, p. 264.

[65] Sommer, *Tight Spaces,* p. 107.

[66] Heimstra and McFarling, p. 67. Also Civikly, p. 178.

[67] Civikly, p. 179.

[68] Steele, p. 15.

[69] Sommer, *Tight Spaces,* p. 105.

[70] Mehrabian, pp. 143–45.

[71] Freedman, p. 105.

[72] Mehrabian, p. 143.

[73] Ibid.

[74] Ibid., p. 146.

[75] Ibid.

[76] Ibid., pp. 147–48.

[77] Sommer, *Tight Spaces.*

[78] Sommer, *Tight Spaces,* pp. 106–107, and Sommer, *Design Awareness,* pp. 86–87. Other persons supporting this view include Steele, p. 17, and C. M. Deasy, "When Architects Consult People," *Psychology Today* 3 (1970): 54–57, 78–79.

9

Mutual Trust Is the Key to Open Communications

WILL LOREY

Giant industrial companies do it boldly; banks do it coyly; automotive companies do it brashly. Sooner or later it seems that they all develop a slogan, or at least advertisement copy that proclaims in one way or another: "People are what we are all about." This pitch, at one time directed toward the consumer (as in: "Service Is Our Most Important Product") is now slanted toward employees. The message is simple and basic—*trust us,* do what we say is needed in the way of direction, orders, loyalty, and we will take care of our employees in the way of pay, rewards, and fringe benefits.

They seem to overlook that *trust* is a two-way street, as are all effective communications. If workers are bombarded with statements that they are supposed to trust the organization while they have first-hand evidence that the organization doesn't trust them, then they soon learn that they are being used. And no one wants to be used.

The need for open communications, which is dependent upon the degree of trust between worker and boss, is so common that it has become a truism. The proof of our desire to have the employee "understand," if any proof were needed, is merely to look at the number of articles printed on communications in a wide range of publications. Not only does the *Harvard Business Review* consistently deal with the topic, but practically every issue of other management magazines contains one or more articles on communications. And yet readers looking for ways to improve their personal communications technique are not aware that many of their daily actions demonstrate a lack of trust in their subordinates. This lack of trust will negate any pointers picked up in reading because if employees know that they are not trusted then they will communicate upwards only what the boss wants to hear.

We Are the Enemy

Since each of us thinks of ourselves as an enlightened boss, there is a natural tendency to reject any statement that implies that *we* don't trust our workers and that *we* don't demonstrate that trust every day. If there is distrust then it is the organization's fault, not ours. But as Pogo so aptly put it, "We have met the enemy and he is us." We are the organization and we are guilty of the symptoms of distrust.

People oriented formal controls are the best way that an organization can graphically demonstrate to employees that they can be, and are in fact, trusted to work in an adult fashion. To insist on a formal dress code for employees who never see a customer, to use time clocks when the company isn't on flextime, to insist on a physician's certificate when workers are absent more than two days, to have workers lose bonus leave if they are a minute late from lunch, to have supervisors sit facing the work force (like in school), and to have a detailed rule book for every occasion is not the way to show employees that they are trusted!

Formal rules can get to be so stiff that they actually impede the work itself. At one time I worked for a firm that would not permit a manager to sign a memo that went to all others in his peer group, some 30 people. It made no difference whether the memo was information only or a policy directive. The formal rules stated that this type of memo had to be released by a vice president, which either slowed it down tremendously or the memo had to be rewritten several times as it went up the channels. I found the solution was to send out two identical memos, but each one multi-addressed to 15 managers, or one half the total group. The organization found that acceptable although my secretary protested a bit at having to type the same memo twice.

Formal rules can become so fixed that they end up being ridiculous. In one case a manager responsible for more than 80 workers, with an annual budget of $1.5 million, had to obtain a vice president's signature for a $15 bill to join a local professional society related to the job she held. The cost in discussing this item was more than the $15 charge itself.

After working for 25 years I moved to a different organization, one that prized itself on excellent employee relations. I was amused to find that one of the formal rules was that no one, except at the senior vice-presidential level, was permitted to have coffee at his or her desk. The reason given was that coffee might be spilled on important papers. When I replied that in 25 years I hadn't had this kind of spastic difficulty, I was told "a rule is a rule." Five years later the company management made an announcement that coffee would be allowed, but only during the mornings. Which means that the firm, in my opinion, is still 30 years behind the times.

Just as all of us in our personal life want to know what is going on and want the information we have to be up to date, the same is true of our working life. Most students of management know and nearly every book of management states that the cardinal rule of good communications is: *Keep Employees Informed.*

Knowing good management principles and applying them seem to be two mutually exclusive matters for some organizations. One company I know of was experiencing steady employee growth and found itself forced to put clerical workers' desks as close as 12 inches apart. This overcrowding became objectionable and the noise levels and confusion got to everyone, workers and supervisors.

This condition became a constant employee gripe and came up at every opportunity: section meetings with supervisors; merit reviews; questions in the company magazine; special meetings with managers and vice presidents; and exit questionnaires.

From the very first higher management was aware of the overcrowded conditions and undertook an active search for more space. But management didn't see fit to inform employees of this search, rather it permitted the honest grumbling to go on. When space was finally found and contracted, that information was released. I know that this company's managers are well aware of all the research that has been done and published on keeping employees informed and involved, of letting them participate in a new move. But when it comes to their own company, many senior executives revert to the role of autocratic boss, paying only lip service to all those excellent theories on open communications.

In another company when there was a reduction in force, either because of the economy or a shifting work load, the policy was for management to inform released workers at the last possible moment that they were being let go. The reason was if employees knew any earlier that they were being released they would not work at all during their last week, and worse yet, they would become a disruptive element.

This outdated attitude created the feeling of a sword hanging over all employees' heads and even the excellent workers resented the idea that they could be dumped without an opportunity to prepare for a change. The end result was distrust in the organization and a high turnover rate as workers left as soon as they could find another job.

Status Symbols

During six years of participation in management development courses I used Maslow's Hierarchy of Needs as a discussion topic. In some 47 different classes with some 550 participants it never failed that the class members could quickly identify all the status symbols (or privileges) their bosses had. But they had difficulty in listing the status they had. In order to satisfy my own curiosity I then worked with several groups of subordinates of these class members. And once again the workers could quickly identify the status privileges of their superiors but had trouble in listing their own. They did have some, but precious few.

We should ask ourselves the question: Are organizational status symbols used to enhance productivity of the holder or are they only a reflection of the pecking order? Or worse, do they mask the inefficiency of the holder? If the workers are in an open bay without any dividers, plants, or module furniture and are under the visual control of a supervisor while the boss sits in a closed office with a secretary to guard him or her from interruptions, then workers get the impression that they can't be trusted to work on their own.

Based on first-hand knowledge, I know that in one company employees resented that there was a separate dining room for senior managers. These privileged individuals had to walk through the open cafeteria to reach their secluded area. This walk couldn't have been calculated more deliberately to convince the workers that there was a definite caste system, of which they were at the bottom. All the workers believed (wrongly) that separate and better food was served in this executive dining room and nothing would convince them that it was the same food at the same price.

The justification for such a status symbol was that business was frequently discussed at lunch and to require senior managers to eat in the open bay would inhibit conversation. Most workers found this answer a cop-out as it was the same reason given for why managers needed private closed offices. They felt it would help communications if once in a while an executive sat down and broke bread with the troops and listened to some straight talk. It was also interesting to note that when guests were on the premises, lunch would frequently be taken at outside restaurants.

If you want to stir up a hornet's nest or test your organization's formal rules at the next meeting, recommend doing away with all the reserved parking spaces. As Robert Townsend in *Up the Organization* (Alfred A. Knopf, 1970) put it: "If you're so bloody important, you better be the first one in the office. Besides, you'll meet a nice class of people in the employees' parking lot."

If modern life within the past 10 to 15 years has been responsible for eliminating unnecessary social distance between people, then the working place has not kept pace. Of course, there are laws against social discrimination in the public sector, but social distinction within the organization is still with us, and just as hard to take as it ever was.

In another firm I know of *all* employees are on a first name basis, including all senior officers. Yet when it comes to signing internal correspondence, only those above a certain grade level are permitted to use their initials, such as J. V. Jones instead of John Jones. This is carried even into the internal telephone book where a glance at who has initials before his or her surname provides one with a quick index of the pecking order.

I once used this social distance to cut off a relationship, to my later shame and regret. I had been eating lunch with a group of young workers and the general conversation usually centered on some of the "whys" of company policy and actions (Why does it still come as a surprise to some senior executives that the younger worker is also interested in the company?). Since I was better acquainted with the answers, I used this time for a dual purpose: to promote the idea that the organization did operate in a rational way once one understood the problems and possible alternatives, and as a developmental process for some promising employees. But one of the individuals ate with his mouth open and it finally got to a point that I was having trouble eating my own lunch. So I dropped out of these gatherings and started eating lunch with my peer group which was both older and senior in grade to the young workers. They ate with their mouths closed but many of them also had closed minds!

If you wonder if your organization really has a social distance problem watch the behavior of all of the company people at the next picnic. It has been my experience that at any type of company outing one sees the workers and supervisors generally mingling but the senior management staff will stay together in a tight group. The impression given out is that they don't want to meet the workers in this once-a-year event. Or is it that they are afraid that out of the protected office environment they will be discovered as humans who drip mustard on their sport shirts like the rest of us?

The refusal by organizations to allow employees at all levels to make decisions, or at least participate in decision making, is pernicious. We all know that the person closest to the problem often has the best data available and organizations do go to considerable pains to urge the employee to communicate such information upwards. More often than we care to admit, the decision based on this data is reserved for a much higher level and frequently the decision comes too late, in insufficient magnitude to eliminate the problem, or a wrong alternative is selected.

I doubt that there is a reader who hasn't one personal example of when he or she should have made the decision but the boss made it instead. There are hundreds of examples of organizational life in which competitively-priced office typewriters are chosen by the office service director, the shade of paint in the word processing office is selected by a vice president, or the chief executive announces a surprise decision to buy a subsidiary.

Effective decision-making must rest on open, full communications. As long as one does not become overwhelmed with data, the more information the better. Yet it is constantly demonstrated to employees who furnish such data that they can't be trusted to make the right decision. Worse, management doesn't even allow them to practice by making small decisions. It doesn't take any worker long to get the message and begin to lose all interest in the organization's extensive and expensive communications effort.

Everyone in an organization wants good, open communications. Supervisors and managers spend a lot of time and effort in keeping the channels open and the organization spends effort and money in developing ways of communicating with employees.

But management must have faith that employees can be "turned on" about work, can be trusted, and will, as Douglas McGregor's Theory notes in *The Human Side of Enterprise* (McGraw-Hill, 1960):

- Be interested in and come to enjoy the work.
- Commit themselves to mutually agreed upon objectives.
- Not only accept but seek responsibility.
- Exercise a higher degree of imagination, ingenuity, and creativity in the solution of organizational problems than bosses credit them for.
- Commit themselves to the extent that they can see rewards that satisfy their egos and needs.

And that end can best be accomplished in the following manner:

- Eliminate outdated formal controls that no longer serve a useful purpose.

The examination of formal rules should be made by a committee of workers and supervisors, not by the personnel officer or president.

- Realize that the withholding of only certain proprietary information from employees makes sense. Otherwise information will circulate on the grapevine and either be incorrect and damaging, or correct and faster-moving than the formal communications medium.
- Conclude that status symbols and social distance no longer deserve a sanctum sanctorum in organizational life. If it can be demonstrated that the social/status privilege is helpful to increased productivity it should remain. If not, get rid of it.
- Realize that the lack of decision-making ability is a major frustration to motivated employees. Most workers want to grow, be better in their jobs, and help the organization reach its goals. Reserving the decision-making ability to top level management stunts the growth of excellent workers and kills any potential in promising workers.

Open communications must include messages up from employees. If you haven't asked, haven't taken into account their aspirations, hopes, desires to grow, and to have a useful productive work life, then you have one-way communications. And you will end up with an employee who will write on his exit interview as one I know of wrote: "You wouldn't listen to me when I was here, so I ain't got nothing to say now."

10

Developing a Facilitation System for Horizontal and Diagonal Communications in Organizations

M. BLAINE LEE *and* WILLIAM L. ZWERMAN

The modern view of organizations sees them as information exchange systems as well as mechanisms for control. A frequent question in organizations in the past was, "Who has the power and why?" Today an appropriate question might be, "Who has the information and how did they get it?" In a rapidly changing environment it is imperative that decision-makers have the appropriate information upon which to base their decisions. In a complex organization within a changing environment it is unlikely that any decision-maker can depend solely upon information provided by his subordinates or superior to make critical decisions. Much of the information required for effective decision-making in an organization is held by peers and/or by people in diagonal positions within the organization. Success in organizations today is dependent upon effective horizontal and diagonal communications systems, as well as the traditional vertical communications.

While it is acknowledged that information held horizontally or diagonally could eventually be acquired through the vertical communication system: *some decisions require prompt action, and reliance upon the vertical communication system may be too slow and, as a result, costly.*

Some Results of Inadequate Information

A classic example of reliance on the vertical communication system for information leading to costly error was the United States experience of Pearl Harbor. The information on the Japanese attack on Pearl Harbor was held by people within the United States government service; however, since vertical communication was emphasized, and the horizontal and diagonal communication system was not effective, the Pearl Harbor disaster occurred.

An example from within industry is the situation in which the marketing division of a corporation finally convinces the production department to make modifications on a product to meet customers specifications so that they can conclude a major order. The production department goes to considerable expense to retool and make modifications in a basic product, only to discover after it has started production of the items that the customer has cancelled the order. The marketing department chose to use the vertical communication system to inform them.

The vertical system was too slow.

Effective horizontal and diagonal communication would have eliminated or reduced the two problems discussed. It should be noted that horizontal and diagonal communications are not the same as grapevine communication. Horizontal and diagonal communication is formalized communication, while the grapevine is informal. Since horizontal and diagonal information exchange is so important, why doesn't it take place naturally?

Natural Social Barriers to Horizontal and Diagonal Communication

Most complex organizations have gone to specialization and departmentalization to capitalize on the efficiency that can come from specialization and the coordination and control that can come from departmentalization. While there may well be advantages to specialization and departmentalization, a natural consequence is a reduction of information exchange. The reduction of information exchange is partly determined by personal self-interest and interdepartmental conflict.

Personal Self-Interest

Progress in the traditional organization is partly determined by a person's performance relative to peers. A man who has information vital to peers may not want to provide them with that information, since this new knowledge would improve their relative performance. The aggressive, upwardly motivated man may therefore withhold information, unless an incentive system for information exchange is installed in the organization.

Interdepartmental Conflict

The satisfaction people experience in organizations is frequently associated with individual status. Personal status in an organization is partly determined by the status of one's division or department.

Departmental status can be increased if other divisions or departments are dependent upon you. One way to create dependency is to withhold voluntary information and force the division or department to come to you for that information. While information hoarding may be functional to departmental status, it is dysfunctional to organizational effectiveness.

Although personal self-interest and interdepartmental competition are examples of natural barriers to communication, they are not intended as an exhaustive list. *The natural barriers to horizontal and diagonal must be overcome if information exchange is to be improved. One approach to overcome the barriers is to develop a facilitating system.*

Facilitating Communication Systems

Although problems in vertical communication are frequent, there is some concern with a formal facilitating system for vertical communication. The facilitating system is tied to the reward system of the organization. In most organizations formal rewards and sanctions are levied through the hierarchy of the formal organization structure. The formal organization structure in most organizations is a vertical one. In recent years different organization structures, such as the Matrix Organization, have appeared, but the vast majority of organizations are vertical hierarchies. In most organizations within our society, at this time, the superior rewards and punishes his subordinate, partially on the basis of the information that the subordinate has provided to the superior, and on how the subordinate has performed as a link in the vertical communication, at least on an annual review basis. If there have been blocks in vertical communication channels, and these have been demonstrated to be dysfunctional, they may well be picked up and partially rectified through the vehicle of the annual appraisal.

While there seems to be only a partial facilitation system for vertical communication, a comparable facilitation system for lateral and diagonal communication does not seem to exist at all in most organizations.

A Proposal to Facilitate Lateral and Diagonal Communication

The first element in developing a facilitating system for horizontal and diagonal communication is to use an input-output approach to analyze the position that an individual occupies. The input-output approach consists of determining what inputs are required for effective performance in the position, and the outputs required for effective performance of the organization.

1. *The inputs required for effective performance in the job.* A determination of the inputs would be arrived at by asking: what information does this individual require in order to be effective in his job? Secondly, where does that information come from, or who has that information in the organization? If the individual is not getting the information he requires to be effective in his position, it is not appropriate to hold him responsible for the failure to reach the objectives assigned for that position.
2. *The outputs, which include attainment of objectives; also, the information that an individual provides to others so that they can reach their objectives.*

A determination of the output can be arrived at by asking: what information is required from this position by others? Secondly, who are the individuals that require the information?

Once the information input-output is determined, the organization has the data necessary to chart the information flow system for the entire organization. With this information, they are also prepared to go to the next step of the facilitation system, which is the information appraisal system.

The Information Appraisal System

The information appraisal system is an integral part of the employee appraisal system. However, a separate section on information appraisal would be developed for each employee. The information appraisal on an employee would be done by the individuals who require information coming from this position. Thus, an information appraisal system would be conducted by superiors, peers, subordinates and people in diagonal positions. The two sections to the information appraisal system are:

1. Assess the quality and accuracy of the information provided by employee X as it relates to the attainment of objectives for your position;
2. Assess the timeliness of the information provided by employee X as it relates to the attainment of objectives for your position.

Once the information appraisal has been completed, the organization can take the appraisal information and tie that information into a reward system that will facilitate horizontal and diagonal communications. One way to do this would be to load or weight the information appraisal system as part of the employee merit system. If the organization has had difficulty with success in the organization as a result of inadequate information due to deficiencies of lateral and diagonal communication, then a heavy weighting or loading would be placed on the information appraisal component of the employee appraisal. If the information element within the organization has been reasonably adequate in the past and other areas of employee appraisal may be more important, then the loading would be adjusted to a relatively lighter weight. With an information appraisal system tied in with the reward system, we now have a facilitating system for lateral and diagonal communication within an organization. This will lead to improved organization success and more effective interpersonal relationships within the organization.

An organization's success is a total performance success, not an individual member performance success within an organization. The facilitating system for vertical communication, although essential, and in need of improvement, is inadequate to insure total organization success. The addition of the facilitating system for lateral and diagonal communication will increase organization effectiveness and improve interpersonal relations within our organizations.

This will provide a beginning toward better general understanding of the two most mysterious subsystems in an organization—information and decision systems.

Part Five

Barriers to Effective Interpersonal Communication

11

Macrobarriers to Successful Communication

DAVID S. BROWN

Communication is a part of all human endeavor. It is always with us, always related to whatever we do. An improvement in communication, while not the universal cure-all many seem to expect from it, will usually help with the problems we face. Certainly poor communication distorts and aggravates them.

We have learned much about the communication process, but most of us continue to be frustrated by it. We communicate easily, enthusiastically, and copiously—but often mechanically and negligently as well. Most of us are rich in communicative experience but poor in performance. We do not use what we know. Despite all the new knowledge, techniques, and tools available to us, our ability to communicate is not even keeping pace with the demands we face.

Understandably, we are eager for help. Understandably, also, we are ready to try any new nostrum—from TA (transactional analysis) to TV—that is available to us. Alas, poor communication, like the common cold, seems to be impervious to all our efforts to remedy it, and the situation will undoubtedly get worse.

Communication does not occur unless a message is received and understood in basically the form the sender intended—and acknowledged. A person who speaks to another in language unknown to him is, of course, not communicating with him. And even if the words are understood, if the concepts are beyond the receiver's grasp, communication has not occurred. So, the sender must have evidence that the message has gotten through; thus the importance of feedback.

The reasons why messages are not received, not understood, and not acknowledged involve macro- and microbarriers. Macrobarriers concern the environment, the larger world in which communication takes place. Microbarriers are those of the immediate situation, Mr. A talking to Mr. B. Each enormously affects the communication process.

There are more macrobarriers than most of us realize, and, unfortunately, they seem to be increasing. They affect not only what we communicate but how, when, how much, and why. The most important include:

- The role of information as a "currency"
- The increasing need for more information
- The escalating number of messages
- The increasing complexity of the subject matter
- The imprecision of the communication process
- The variety of languages
- The variety of media
- The amount and nature of interference
- The problem of the generalized message
- The pressure of time
- Self-defense systems

Information As a "Currency"

Information has great value. Those who possess it have something others do not have and, presumably, need or want. And whether a person possesses information or not also indicates his status and role.

When something has high value, people try to acquire it. Many of them use extraordinary means to do so. Once acquired, it is used to influence others. It may even be hoarded. Those with access to inside information have both prestige and power. They know what others do not. When we whisper, it is not so much to convey information as to insure that the "wrong" persons do not gain it without our permission. People who are not in the know are nonequals. Small wonder that we get so uptight about communications. Small wonder that we give our own needs high priority and so often neglect the needs of others.

The Increasing Need for More Information

The amount of information a peasant might require in the Middle Ages was limited, but the information needed today is boundless. Our time is one in which, willy-nilly, we must have information, vast amounts of it. Our jobs change, our needs change, our lifestyles change rapidly and greatly. No sooner have we accommodated to one situation than we are faced with another. Each of us learns new things daily. In fact, we must learn if we are to survive. We are trained to search for more and better information, and so we place new and greater burdens on our already overloaded communication systems.

The Escalating Number of Messages

Such needs and desires lead inescapably to an increasing number of communications. We are bombarded with messages from morning until night. And we bombard others. This results in a frightful cacophony. That the Adam-and-Eve model of the human receiving set—which is all we are—may not be equal to the new demands should surprise no one. In fact, the majority of the messages beamed at us—the specific as well as the general—pass by us. There are just too many of them for us to handle, despite the selective listening all of us practice.

The Increasing Complexity of the Subject Matter

English has become the language of science, commerce, diplomacy, and profanity largely because of its flexibility. But the demands placed upon it have in fact outstripped even its great capabilities.

We devise more than we can describe—and often more than we can name. This applies not only to physical things but to ideas as well. While many of us are still wrestling with such basic concepts as gravity and space, others are already into curved light, magnetic pull, and black-holes. We are involved with abstractions, contractions, and distractions. "What with the tendency of one thing to lead to another," E. B. White has noted, "I predict a bright future for complexity." His future has already arrived, but most of us are still not prepared to cope with it.

The Imprecision of the Communication Process

Communication as a process is not precise. Neither is language. One does not need to be a lawyer to note the extent to which the Supreme Court labors to discover the intent of those who have put the law into words. "Yes" has many meanings, depending upon the tone or emphasis one gives it, including "no." The word "difficulty," used earlier in this piece, has 107 synonyms—including scrape, stew, and pickle, which have other more specific meanings—in my thesaurus. ("Thesaurus" has 25 synonyms itself.) The task of both sender and receiver is to agree on common meanings, not an easy assignment when they are often not on speaking—to say nothing of listening—terms.

The Variety of Languages

The world has thousands of languages—tongues, dialects, and patois—of which English is only the second most popular. But these are dwarfed by the vocabularies of subjects and professions that one must know to understand what is being communicated. We learn also, thanks to the study of chimpanzees, dolphins, and dogs, that other creatures have their own communication systems, some of which man may be able to master. All of us speak several languages and some of us speak many, but we need to understand that the language must be a shared one if we are to communicate fully. We must, in short, get on the same wave length.

The Variety of Media

So far we have been concerned with the spoken or written language. There are also sign languages, as deaf-mutes remind us; the language of gestures and inflections, which all of us use without ever having taken a course in it; the so-called "body language"—what we use besides our lips and hands; and, most recently, "skin talk," which is what our skin says by way of heat or conductivity. McLuhan has reminded us that "the medium is the message." Said another way, what is conveyed is greatly influenced by the medium or conveyance. Our choices are many. We can rent a billboard to tell our enamored what we think of him/her; we can convey the same idea in a letter; or we may say it by telephone, by our looks, or, more feelingly, by touch. (The pun is intentional.) This, of course, does not exhaust the possibilities. "The media" is the name given to newspapers, magazines, TV, and radio, but it is really a broader term that can and should be aplied to *all* means of communicating. The receiver as well as the sender must have at least a working familiarity with most of these.

The Amount and Nature of Interference

To be successful, a communication must overcome—or at least escape—many kinds of interference. Some of this is within the sender, some within the receiver, some in the process itself, and some is from the outside. Outside interference is easiest to identify: It is, as with your radio, the background noise that keeps you from getting the signal as clearly as it was sent. It may derive from other (and competing) messages, such as tuning in Baltimore and getting San Juan; or it may be sun spots, a passing thunderstorm, or the like. Interference may be due to a defective tube in the sending or receiving apparatus or someone standing too near or too far from the transmitter. Or—insidious thought—it may also be because you have a number of messages to send and get them mixed up. We will say more about this kind of interference later.

The Generalized Message

To compensate for some of the problems we know we face, we try to make one message serve a number of purposes. We send "to whom it may concern" and "box holder" messages because we do not know who all our targets are, or we may not be able to address each of them individually. This, of course, takes something from the message. Good sense suggests that we should not address an adult as we would a child, and yet because we often have no really good alternative, we do this a greal deal of the time. Nor should we address a Spanish-speaking audience in English or advertise women's clothing in a publication aimed at men—not until recently, at least. We face additional problems when, to avoid naming the addressee, we use the imperative verb form. To generalize is often to overgeneralize, yet this is what we consistently do. And so our messages go undelivered.

The Pressure of Time

All of us feel the pressure of time. We may live longer than our forebears, but we seem to have much less time than they had to do the things we like.

Our communications must fit time demands, and even when time pressure is not rigorous, we find we have developed a habit about it and make it so anyway. We cram our communications with information, whether needed or not. We compete with each other to talk. We set arbitrary deadlines and unneeded requirements. Talk is cheap, so we spend it recklessly, overloading our message systems and thereby depreciating their contents. With so much garbage in the system, much of it will inevitably be sent out.

Self-Defense Systems

Ultimately the germ becomes impervious to the drug, and so also do we become impervious to the battering we get from the innumerable communicative thrusts addressed to us. It is not enough to say "No Smoking"; we must now say "POSITIVELY No Smoking" to get the message through—and then we must be prepared to police it as well. We build barriers to protect ourselves against radiation, and also against communication. These take a variety of forms. The individual *assumes* what others are intending to say and then turns off his hearing aid. He *hurdles* to get to the ending ahead of the communicator. He *interprets,* he *interpolates,* he *fills in,* he *selects out* as he thinks— at the moment—is appropriate. And he *prejudges.* *Pre*-judicial, incidentally, is the root of the word "prejudice."

The mind is a restless receiver. We talk at the rate of two- or three-hundred words a minute, but our mind is capable of thinking in the thousands. In fact, we think in terms of scenarios—to use a popular word—rather than dialogue. We use the time we "save" to think of other things: whether what is being said is true or not; whether we agree with it; what effect it will have on us; how we should respond to it. We appear to listen, and sometimes we do, but we become preoccupied with other, if not unrelated, matters. And in doing so, we receive less than we might of what is being sent us.

These are some of the macrobarriers to communication.

12

Communication—An Essential of Reality

CHARLES B. SMITH

Some years ago the Reader's Digest told about a man driving alone in a remote area of the West when one of his tires went flat. His search produced no jack to change the tire; so he set out walking to find a farmhouse and help. As he walked on into darkness, thinking of every possible reason why someone wouldn't want to help him, he saw a light in the distance—a farmhouse. Then the light went out, suggesting the farmer had gone to bed. By this time our man had worked himself into such a mental state that when, after knocking on the door and a man answered from an upstairs window, our man said, "Keep your damned jack! I didn't want it anyway."

This story reflects the relationship of communication to reality—a relationship involving each of us every day. If we are to understand this relationship, we must know the nature of *reality*, the nature of *communication*, and how the two relate.

The Nature of Reality

We may interpret reality as consisting of two elements—tangible factors and intangible factors. Tangible factors are those things that are the same for all people. They're objective and verifiable; they're facts concerning time, distance, space, weight, and movement. You and I can measure these things with available instruments and arrive at reasonably the same answer. In reality, though, you and I accept some of these facts on faith; we don't measure to reaffirm. We accept on faith such facts as the number of miles to the moon, the speed of light, and the number of pounds to a bushel of wheat.

The intangible factors are things relating to our subjective world. They are subject to our individual perception, so I have to see through your eyes to agree with you. These are our beliefs, attitudes, and values. These factors include such things as what we believe about dress, respect for people, tolerance, morality, and the like. They are the things that interact inside of us when we react to a situation.

Thus, we live in a real world in which things exist—a world of things we can see, touch, and measure. But when we try to talk about these things, we're in a social world—a world that is one of language, both spoken and unspoken, in which attitudes, beliefs, and values prevail. Our problem is to connect the *real* world and the *social* world through communication.

The Nature of Communication

Communication is a process; it happens. The moment a person attaches meaning to something, communication is going on. But the extent to which the process happens depends on how we use and interpret the communication vehicles—both verbal and nonverbal. The verbal vehicles for communication are speaking and listening; the non-verbal include time, place, space, and body language. To understand the nature of communication, we need to examine each of these.

Verbal Communication

Successful communication through speaking and listening requires a language containing words and symbols. And if you and I are to communicate, we must attach the same meaning to these words and symbols. Here, then, is one of the barriers to our successful communication: meaning. The meaning given to a word can come from three sources: you, me, and a dictionary. With these three possibilities existing for meanings of words, we can understand why communication is never perfect. We can only approximate the meanings from one mind to another.

To convey meaning through language involves speaking and listening, and each requires a separate skill. If a person speaks before he knows clearly in his own mind what he wants to say, he will blame any resulting communication problem on the listener's stupidity. And the listener will blame the speaker for the failure. The fact is, people just aren't completely rational; yet, each of us thinks he is and that the other fellow ought to be. We are constantly deceiving ourselves about reality.

A listener, like the speaker, needs skill. As listeners, we must do more than just hear; we must participate actively with the speaker. A reality, though, is that most of us *hear* a lot of things, but we don't really *listen*. We can hear background music and conversation while we're working. But we're not actively participating. We can tell Dick to turn off TV and start his homework. He says "yes," but takes no action. Effective listening happens when the listener can repeat what was said, when the listener participates actively with the speaker by evaluating what was said, and when the listener furnishes feedback. It's a give-and-take process. The effect that speaking and listening have upon what we do or don't do is *reality.*

Although we're prone to concentrate on improving verbal skills, non-verbal communication, too, is an essential of reality and needs to be understood. These are the ideas communicated through body movements and contacts and through the physical realities of time, place, and space.

Non-Verbal Communication

We can convey a great many of our ideas through body language. Think what a smile, a frown, a raised eyebrow or a manner of walking can convey. A nod or shake of the head, a clenched fist, or closed eyes give us a message. And each of us attaches the same general meaning to these body movements in our culture—our silent language.

So, too, does physical contact provide a basis for communication. The handshake, a pat on the shoulder, a kiss, a spanking, a shove, a caress, or a slap all carry rather standardized meanings in our culture. And when these body movements are used in conjunction with our verbal language, they may add to or subtract from our intended message. The speaker who shows no enthusiasm about his subject as emphasized by his body carriage and facial expression can only detract from his message. The person who sneaks glances at his wrist watch or wall clock suggests that it's time to leave, or that his day is being interrupted.

These body movements and contacts may speak as loud as words, but again they must be interpreted in terms of the realities of time and place. The handshake does not mean the same in all cultures. To the older generation in this country, a man's position on the curb side when walking with a woman conveys respect and a carryover idea of protecting the woman. The same is true of opening doors. Yet, today—in a new time—we find a trend away from such actions in many of our young people. It may be, however, that those who no longer walk curbside or open doors still respect women, but show it in a manner not yet fully understood by another age group.

The physical realities such as time, place, and space are mediums of communication, again as related to customs in our culture. Time, for example, is significant when company news is released to the press before it is to the employees. It is also significant when an employee is kept waiting outside his boss's office and has always been told "My office is always open to you; come in anytime." Time is important when a person is late for an appointment. Being on time conveys respect; lateness connotes disrespect. So time does talk, in a silent language. The significance of what is communicated through time is no less important than that of word of mouth.

Place in our society can reflect our values and carry a message. Where a person's desk is located can show status. In the days when air conditioning consisted of opening windows, the desks nearest the windows were preferential spots, with a carryover in today's offices. Some administrators like to keep visitors' chairs positioned so the visitors must be across the desk, with the desk to serve as a barrier. Some like to have the visitor facing the light from a window to put the visitor at a disadvantage.

Place is important, too, because it establishes territories for both humans and animals. When someone invades these territories, that person's or animal's status is threatened. Invasion by a "rival" of such territories as: mother's kitchen or sewing room; father's shop or den; the children's room or playhouse can create problems. Animals' territories are sacrosanct, too. A dog's or cat's bed is an established territory. On wildlife TV programs we're shown how lions, bears, and birds establish territories. All these represent the place element in non-verbal communication. Again on TV we see the importance of place as reflected when someone occupies Archie Bunker's own chair in "All In The Family."

Place can also connote status from the standpoint of an address. Compare the connotation of a Park Avenue address with one in a ghetto; one shopping center with another; and note how some communities carry more status than others. Some businessmen rent an office at a status address to convey an image of the stature of their business.

Like the reality of place, space, too, is a non-verbal symbol in communication. The size of an office, the size of a building (which is the tallest, which covers the most space), convey status. We are susceptible to advertisers' claims of "family size," " giant," and "jumbo." Thus, communication is a part of reality—both the tangible and intangible; it's how we relate one to the other.

Relationships of Communication to Reality

Communication connects our two worlds—the physical world of things and the social world of attitudes, values, and perception. We're immersed in a world of impressions, and we are trying to transform them into symbols and then ideas. But we see and hear and understand only those things within our realm of experience. Under such limitations, we attempt to express in speech and writing these ideas connecting two worlds. Three elements of the relationships of communication to reality are:

1. What We Don't Clearly Understand, We Can't Clearly Communicate.

From the standpoint of one who is being communicated with, I'm ready to say to you "What do you mean?" or "I don't know." We can call this approach either the "joy of ignorance" or "the power of negative thinking." What we're likely to find out is that our communicator doesn't really know or understand either. He was bluffing. Too many people speak or write in fuzzy terms only to impress others. Then we may really say communication is a means of finding out what a person *doesn't* know.

What we should do more often, of course, is to avoid nodding in agreement and avoid thinking "I don't know what you said, but, gosh, you must be smart." The power of negative thinking will put the burden of being understood on the speaker or writer. We don't necessarily need to accept some idea because no one has challenged it. If a person can't communicate clearly, he is likely to be a nuisance to his profession as is shown in this prize piece of bureaucratic gobbledygook from an executive order to employees on state salary increases:

> "Employees may determine their new salary rate from the attached chart by following the steps outlined below: Locate your current salary on the chart. Determine the range and subrange of your current salary rate by adding the whole number on the same line as your minimum step of range and the decimal subrange number at the top of the same column as your current salary. Identify the percentage increase for your civil service class. Add 1.0 to your range-subrange number for each one-half per cent salary increase.

If that one hasn't left your head swimming, try your hand at interpreting this art review from a newspaper: "The assemblages of John Doe are superb examples of the relatively new art of 'waste orchestration.' Their art lies in the uncanny, evocative mood of the 'total ensemble' rather than in the highly refined assembling and mounting of diverse materials. John Doe is apparently preoccupied with the mind-expanding properties of solitude, with the poignancy of remembrances of things past, self-experienced or vicarious, and with a certain crazed malevolence below the surface of the conduct of our daily lives."

In spite of the humor we may see in retrospect in the foregoing examples, our problem sometimes may also be that we don't really recognize we are baffling our readers. One may not detect his own use of generalities and meaningless words to his audience when surrounded by them any more than fish discover water. We are our own worst critics; we can see problems in other people's writing and speaking, not our own.

2. *Words Are Both Carriers of and Barriers to Meaning, and They May Be Both at the Same Time.*

Words carry meaning in communication when they are in our listener's or reader's vocabulary. And when they are, the meaning he attaches to these words depends upon his years of living, his depth of experience, and his culture. Recently in a store I overheard a customer asking a clerk where the "light globes" were. The clerk looked puzzled, and said he thought the store didn't have any. It wasn't until after a few more verbal exchanges, when the customer happened to say he wanted 60-watt globes, that communication took place. With depth of experience, the clerk would have recognized that "globes," "lamps," and "bulbs" have the same general meaning.

When a man filling out a credit application blank came to the words: "length of residence" he wrote "35 feet." What was wanted, of course, was "how long have you lived at this address." We can see, then, that words can be both carriers and barriers to meaning.

3. We Communicate As We Perceive Reality—Not from the Facts of Reality.

How we perceive our world at any given moment is based upon our memory of our previous experiences, and these perceptions are cumulative. One major drawback, however, is that the meaning we put to these perceptions may be wrong. We misperceive. We ignore the facts of reality.

We misperceive reality when we believe detergents must make suds to be effective; that blenders must be noisy to be working properly; or that merchandise must be expensive to be top quality. We misperceive reality when we put all people or acts into one class. We create a communication barrier when we say all doctors are mercenary; all professors are forgetful; all nurses are callous; all college students are radicals; all store clerks are lazy and indifferent. We tend to abstract an unpleasant experience with a person in a particular classification and apply it to the entire class of people.

When I, for example, see a student dozing in class, I may perceive his actions as meaning he isn't interested in what I have to say, or that he likely was out most of the night having fun to the detriment of his class work. Were I to see reality, however, I may find he is working 40 hours a week on a midnight to 8:00 a.m. shift and then coming to a 10:30 a.m. class. I have misperceived. My cumulative perception has led me to believe anyone sleeping in class is bored, lazy, or uninterested. But student 3 is not the same as student 2, is not the same as student 1.

These misperceptions, then, are reflected in our communication as evidenced by our word choices and actions involving such things as two-valued orientation and the use of euphemisms and prepossessives.

We depart from reality both social and physical when we perceive only two values in our world. Physical reality consists of ranges of values—more than just hot or cold, fast or slow, hard or soft. In social reality, too, we have more than right or wrong, friendly or hostile, pro or con, competent or incompetent. We must recognize all values in between if we are to improve communication. Recognition of only two values can lead one to morbidity and depression. One who sees only the two values of success or failure, and recognizes no middle ground, can be susceptible to mental breakdown.

We reflect how we perceive reality by the words we choose to circumvent or change the unpleasant in our social and physical world. We choose words to make the sour sound sweet. One city's garbagemen asked to be called "public works combustible fieldmen." Janitors are now called custodians, so library custodians are now using a new title—archivist. Once we called brain paralysis a "stroke"; now we may hear "cardiovascular accidents." Even our toilets are called restrooms or lounges. And we neither rest nor lounge in them. We carry the unreal world to such an extreme that when we are hiking or camping in the forest we may say we are going to the bathroom. But neither do we intend to take a bath nor is there a bathroom out there. We're really trying to keep the truth invisible; we're avoiding reality.

Prepossessives are words used to impress people favorably. Some people may be impressed by terms such as French wine, English wool, Irish linen,

German cameras, or Japanese electronics. Our perceptions ascribe favorable meanings to "homemade, handmade, from the kitchen of . . ., original recipe, imported, and established in 1890." The point is, however, the impressions these words give may have some basis in fact, but they're no longer wholly sound.

What do these ideas about communication and reality have to do with "keep your damned jack; I didn't want it anyway"? The man with the flat tire was overreacting to his social and physical realities. He was misperceiving based upon his cumulative perceptions from his years of living and his experience. We recognize he is like all of us—not completely rational; that we sometimes behave in an irrational manner. If we are to do a good job of communicating, we must recognize communication happens when you affect yourself as you want to affect others—when you are sincere, friendly, factual, and aware of reality.

13

Seeing Eye to Eye: Practical Problems of Perception

JOHN SENGER

Byron Cartwright, plant superintendent, ran his fingers worriedly through his thick, greying hair. He had a tough decision on his hands. With Frank Bauer's retirement he was faced with the problem of selecting a new foreman for the machine shop. But instead of the usual problem of a dearth of qualified people to promote, Byron felt that he had two equally well qualified men to take over. Pete Petroni and Sam Johansen were both highly skilled machinists, conscientious workers, liked and respected by the other men in the department.

To help make up his mind, Byron called Pete and Sam into his office separately to talk to them about how they thought the shop should be run. He didn't actually say to either of them that he was considering them for the foremanship, but they knew why they were there. In fact the other men in the shop had been talking for some time about which one of them would succeed "Mr. Bauer." Both Pete and Sam were aware of these discussions and their own obvious qualifications for the job.

Byron even felt that either man had so much potential talent that one of them could succeed him as superintendent some day. With the new equipment orders in, it looked like a bright future for the machine shop—a great opportunity for the man he selected. That's what was bothering him so much. Which man?

But this was Byron's perception of the matter: opportunity, advancement, achievement, getting-ahead. He didn't know what was going on inside Pete's head. Pete, as a matter of fact, was very upset by the prospect. He recognized the "opportunity" and the extra hundred bucks every month. A chance to get his wife, Marge, a car of her own and additionally, put some-

138

thing away in the bank. But Pete just doesn't like to tell other people what to do, he doesn't want the responsibility for planning the shop's work and keeping everyone busy. He doesn't want to be involved in paperwork—he doesn't even do that at home. Marge pays all the bills and figures the taxes and does the family planning.

What Pete loves is being a machinist. He likes the odor of the hot metal as it curls, shining away from the cutting edge of the turning tool. He likes the "feel" of the calipers as he slips them over the surface of a finished part, checking dimensions. He likes the precision, the craftsmanship, the sense of productiveness of his occupation. Pete likes to use his long, strong fingers for something besides shuffling papers. He doesn't want to tell other guys what to do. He doesn't want the responsibility for somebody else's work.

Byron Cartwright finally does make the decision to promote Sam, and he feels guilty every time he passes Pete hunched over his lathe. But, boy, is Pete relieved! He tells Byron how pleased he is that Sam is going to be the new foreman. But Byron doesn't really believe him. Pete, however, could take a deep breath for the first time in weeks without the worried tightness across his chest. Marge, his wife, is a little disappointed. She thought he deserved the promotion—he'd been there longer than Sam. But she had also been aware of Pete's edginess the past several weeks, and his noticeable relief since the announcement.

People's actions, emotions, thoughts and feelings are triggered by their perceptions of their surrounding situations. In the instance above, Byron Cartwright perceived the shop foremanship situation in one way—as a reward, a chance to get ahead, an opportunity to exercise authority, an achievement. Pete Petroni perceived it in quite a different way—as a threat, taking responsibility for others' mistakes, forcing his will on others, being separated from his lathe. Pete, while friendly and well-liked, preferred doing his own thing—alone.

Pete's perception is somewhat unusual in our "achieving society," but by no means rare. Even at that, Pete would have probably accepted the promotion. He was expected to, and Pete is enough of a child of his culture not to question that it is important to accept promotions and "get ahead," much as he might dislike it. That, after all, was his conflict.

But the point here is not about attitudes toward achievement, but about kinds of perception. The same set of circumstances can result in widely divergent perceptions. And differences in perception between managers and their subordinates make managing a tougher job.

We sense that people do see things differently. But we are at times so much a captive of our own perceptual sets that it becomes virtually impossible to see things as others see them. Part of the difference in what people perceive can be explained by the fact that they do see *different* things. Some of what is there to be seen may be physically obscured or unavailable knowledge to one perceiver. After all, Pete had never supervised and couldn't really accurately assess the situation. It might not be as bad as he thinks. But the important thing is that this information was not available to him, and this affected his perception.

Even greater differences in perception are the result of selectivity. One's senses are so overwhelmed by the mass of stimuli vying for attention that in order to carry on any directed activity we must somehow decide what we want most to attend to and block out or sublimate perceptual inputs that aren't related to that activity. If we go too far with selectivity, however, we block out some useful information and make it much more difficult to understand, or even be aware of, another's perception. Cartwright is an achiever, and to be an achiever he has to block out and sublimate distracting non-achievement oriented stimuli. In the process, he blocks out a perception of how someone like Pete Petroni sees things.

Organization of Perception

Selectivity is an important means of handling the perceptual overload. We further attempt to handle the myriad of perceptual inputs by various manners of organizing perceptions. A group of German psychologists, identified with the organization of perceptions, called themselves Gestalt psychologists, and placed great emphasis upon the organization and inter-relationship of perceptions. No, Virginia, there was no one named Wolfgang Gestalt. Gestalt is a German word essentially meaning to organize.

Common methods of organizing perceptions include grouping, figure-ground and closure. These techniques which we unconsciously utilize in an effort to cope with the mass of stimuli were first identified in connection with visual perception, but they help explain nearly as well much of social perception, as will be seen in the following illustrations.

Figure-Ground

When Doris Graham started to work as secretary to Myron Green in the accounting department, the whole place and the people in it were a kind of amorphous blur in her mind. Slowly, it seemed, features of her new environment began to emerge. At first she was only really aware of chief accountant Myron Green's name and face, and employment manager Dave Brigg's name and face. As she began taking dictation and typing, she began to realize Mr. Portley was an important figure to Myron Green and, therefore, to her. Otto Kowalski seemed helpful and Bill Crandell nice, but she didn't really define them against the background of the rest of the accounting department at first. Then, after a couple weeks or so, they began to emerge as people as well as important contacts in her job as secretary.

Here we see the figure-ground phenomenon at work. Certain "figures," Myron Green, Dave Briggs, Mr. Portley, Otto Kowalski and Bill Crandell emerge from the "ground" represented by the people and things that make up the rest of the Accounting Department and the company. Then, slowly, the entire department begins to emerge as a "figure" against the "ground" of the entire company. Dave Briggs was the person to emerge as a "figure." (She had memorized his name from the slip of paper given her at White Collar Employment Agency before she ever got out to the company.) He had made her feel comfortable and a little as if she belonged. But now, only several weeks later, because of lack of contact, he was fading into the general company "ground" as the Accounting Department became a more distinct entity. Here we see the phenomenon of figure-ground reversal, not unlike the visual eye trick which occurs when silhouetted designs can be seen to reverse themselves, so that when, for example, the design is looked at one way, a white vase (the figure) appears against a dark background, and when the white portion of the design is perceived as the ground, the dark portions appear to represent a new figure, two faces.

This reversal was also seen by Doris, back when she was identified by the rest of the office as attached to Mr. Green, and she herself identified with Myron Green more than she did with the others. As time went on, she and the rest of the office got to know one another better. Sometimes when she knew Mr. Green and Mr. Portley were going to be away from the office for a certain period of time, she would pass the information along to the gang and they could all relax a little. A mutual trust developed and the office group began to emerge as the figure, while Myron Green and Mr. Portley tended to become a part of the general company background.

Figure-ground, a phenomenon long known as a visual parlor stunt, is a useful means of organizing our perceptions. It is a helpful way to think about what we see and experience and why we happen to perceive some things the way we do.

Grouping

Stan Menke eased the Mustang to a stop in one of the lines of traffic funneling out of the South Parking Lot, and half turned to address Allyn White in the back seat. "Whaddya think the raise is going to be this time, Allyn?" "Gee, I dunno," replied Allyn. But Allyn, by now, wasn't surprised that Stan should ask him about details of important company decisions. So did Pete Petroni and Juan Fernandez, the other guys in the pool. All were older and had been with the company much longer than Allyn. Stan was a foreman and Allyn just a clerk. Juan was active in the union and knew a lot about how the wage negotiations were going. But Stan asked Allyn. Why?

Because Allyn worked in the accounting department, and the accounting department was on the second floor with the executive offices. Allyn wore a coat and tie, as did Mr. Portley and the rest of the executives. So Allyn was being "grouped" with the seat of the power in the company and was thought to be privy to important information. The fact that this was not the case didn't prevent the grouping from taking place.

This tendency to group persons or things that appear to be similar in certain ways, but not in all, is a common means of organizing our perceptions. Because these persons and things are similar in certain ways, but not all, distortion of perception can take place, as was the case with Allyn. Grouping helps us learn, it helps us remember, it is a valuable cognitive device, but it does carry with it the not infrequent cost of perceptual distortion.

A common example of grouping in the organization: The design engineers, the industrial engineers, the production engineers, the cost people, the production control group, who may be every bit as realistic and shop-problem oriented as the people on the shop floor, are viewed by the shop as "unrealistic," "too theoretical," "head-in-the-clouds," "ivory tower" and generally unconcerned with the shop. Why? Because they operate out of the second floor, don't wear blue collars (though some wear sport shirts and no ties) and are educated differently. They are up there with the sales people, the administrative people, the office girls and others less involved with production. They are *grouped* with those less involved with the factory floor. Proximity and similarity contribute stongly to grouping. Some lack of awareness of shop problems among the engineers, cost accountants and production control people is perhaps justified, but certainly not to the degree the grouping indicates.

It should be re-emphasized, on the other hand, that *grouping, like figure-ground,* helps us organize and cope with our environment. Without such aids we would be overwhelmed by detail, forced to make too many decisions. When the guys in the shop see somebody wandering around in a coat and tie and assume he's somebody pretty important, they are *usually* right. It's just that more than occasionally such generalizations can be misleading if followed blindly.

Closure

Otto Kowalski is big and broad shouldered. He has a thick neck and a jutting jaw. He never wears a coat in the office, and works with his sleeves rolled up, his tie pulled down and his collar open. He walks like a bear with a slight charley horse. His voice is very deep and coarse. He looks tough, although he's not tough at all. Otto is not a stevedore, but an accountant. On Saturday afternoons he listens to the symphony on FM, not the excited voice of a television sports announcer. Or he tends his roses. People who know Otto only casually find this all very confusing. Why? Because Otto's appearance, voice and bearing send out certain perceptual signals from which the observer begins building a perceptual image of Otto. Big, loud guys with rolling gaits are "jocks," right? Tough, right? Aggressive, insensitive, kinda dumb, right? Wrong. Otto isn't any of these things. He is sensitive, intelligent, not particularly athletic, and gentle. Then why is almost everyone wrong about Otto on first impression?

Because of the perceptual phenomenon of "closure." Big, muscular guys are frequently stereotyped as athletic, aggressive, tough, insensitive, and, often, not too smart. It doesn't make any difference if this is the case or not. It's a common belief and when we meet someone who looks like Otto, we start with those parts of his apparent behavior we observe, and then fill in the gaps left by those parts we don't observe; that is, we "close." It is just like seeing a line that curves around until it almost meets itself. We see it as a circle with a gap in it, not a curved line. We meet someone and like several things about him. So we go right ahead and close and assume that we also like the many other characteristics of this person. The tendency to assume that because we like someone, almost everything about him is good, is referred to as a "halo effect," a special case of closure.

And then there's Myron Green. He has a sallow complexion, round shoulders, a bald head, wears rimless glasses, terribly conservative clothes and a perpetual scowl. Myron Green is, therefore, cold, aloof, over-meticulous, inhibited, unathletic, has a "Friden for a brain," and is kind of sneaky, right? Right! You see we don't miss them all. But it's seductively easy to fill in an image based upon incomplete evidence and come up with the *wrong* answer.

Organization of our perceptions helps us cope with an overabundance of perceptual information, but it also misleads us sometimes, and we should be aware of this possibility, both in ourselves and others. We don't react equally to all stimuli that bombard us, but select or attend to certain of them.

Attention: External Factors

Industrial engineer Eldon Peavey's clothes are *not* conservative. Some people refer to them as "far out," some say "flashy," some say "too much." But no one can really ignore them—or Eldon. And that's Eldon's intent. He wants to attract attention to himself, and we do find ourselves attending to guys like Eldon. The biggest, brightest, loudest things clamor for our attention. Over in accounting, Otto Kowalski attracts our attention because he is so big. Like six feet four, and two hundred and thirty-five. We therefore will perceive Otto and Eldon before we perceive others less large or more mousey. If two objects are competing for our attention at the same time we shall perceive the more intense first. The Safety Department was thinking about this when they painted the exposed moving parts of machines red, in contrast to the drab grey of the rest of the machine. Size and intensity are important attention-getters.

Why did the Peabody Company finally close a deal with Harry Balou, even though Harry's price on the pumps was higher than that of the competition? Largely because Harry kept beating away at them about the superiority of "his" pumps. Monthly, sometimes weekly visits. Brochures. Telephone calls. Personal letters. He constantly reiterated the advantage of the pumps. Peabody finally had to pay attention. *Repetition* has been known for a long time by salesmen, and particularly advertisers, as an excellent means of attracting attention. When the company was big on the "Zero Defects" campaign in an attempt to cut down on scrap costs and improve quality, the term was seen everywhere. Taped to machines, on every bulletin board, in the company magazine, under windshield wipers in the parking lot, on the sign board in front of the factory, over the loud speaker system, in the cafeteria. Repeated and repeated and repeated. And it did appear to have an effect on quality and scrap. Certainly everyone was aware of the campaign.

The noticeability of coats and ties in the shop was previously mentioned. And the men who go up to the office from the shop are just as noticeable because of their clothes. Contrast also attracts attention. Byron Cartwright is usually pretty subdued and quiet-spoken at the weekly foreman's meetings, so when he's upset about something and raises his voice a little, everyone snaps to. If he shouted all the time, his change of tone wouldn't be as effective. Contrast again. And it works the other way. Myron Green keeps a very close eye on everything and everyone in the accounting office, and when he steps into Mr. Portley's office or is preoccupied with someone or something else, his subordinates immediately sense it. The termination of a stimulus can be nearly as attention-provoking as its onset.

Attention: Internal Factors

"Bleeding us! Taking what rightfully belongs to us workers. How can Portley have that big fat smile on his face with his right hand stuffed so deep into my wallet? Look at this picture in the paper. Look at him! Proud that he's taking 18% profit out of the company. Bragging about it. Look at my hands. Look at your own hands. That's what makes the pumps—and the money—for this company! Not Portley sitting around on his big fat chair in his big fancy office! Not the stockholders. What have they ever done to turn out one single pump? Little old ladies doing nothing but pampering their dogs are the ones who get all that profit. Doing nothing. And their dogs eat better than I do!"

Sean O'Flaretty, fiery old unreconstructed Trotskyite, was very upset by Mr. Portley's announcement in the company paper that profits were up for the year. Holding forth to the luncheon crowd lounging on the castings pile outside the foundry, as orange peels, egg shells and "baggies" were gathered up and stuffed back into lunch boxes, Sean continued, "I ask you guys, why is it we do all the work around here and Portley and the little old ladies take all the money out of the place? It's not fair, never been fair, and one of these days you guys will quit sitting around and demand your rightful share."

Obviously Sean—and maybe several others—was upset by the increased profit announcement. Why? Because the word "profit" to Sean is like a red flag to a bull. The word to him is filtered through a set of values which perceive profits as money taken away from the workers. Mr. Portley doesn't see it that way at all. He has a different set of filters. And he sees profits as evidence of a healthy organization, a feedback as to how well he is running the company, a source of income to those persons who had risked their savings in his enterprise, the generation of new wealth which can cause the company to expand and flourish.

The values, interests, beliefs and motivations that people have, tend to distort their perceptions. It is little wonder people have difficulty understanding one another when the values they hold cause them to perceive the same word quite differently. To Mr. Portley, "profit" is a very satisfying term; to Sean O'Flaretty, a threat.

Postman, Bruner and McGinnies tested people to find what their major value orientations were. Then for a brief millisecond they flashed the words representing these values on a screen. The time the word remained on the screen was gradually increased until it was there long enough to be recognized by all the participants in the experiment. It was found, for example, that those persons with a strong religious value orientation were able to see the word "religion" when it was on the screen for a very brief instant. Others, less religiously oriented, required that the word be on the screen for a longer period before they recognized it. Things that are important to us, those which we value, are the ones we perceive.

Set

Sam Johansen looked up from the schedule board to see Pete Petroni bending over his lathe, while beside him the tote pan for finished parts contained only a dozen of the counter-shafts Pete was making up for a special order, No. 5008. Sam stood beside Pete and watched for a while. "Say, Pete," he asked, "what's wrong with this job that it's taking you so long to get it out?" "Long?" from Pete, "I only got started on this job this morning." "Well, then you oughta be half done. I only see twelve in the tote pan. Are the rest of them someplace else?" Sam wanted to know. "Ye gods, no, Sam," replied Pete, "whaddaya mean? It takes a little while to make all these double-oh-one-cuts." ".001? Are you holding those things to a .001 tolerance?" blurts Sam. "Lemme see the print. Yeah, see here, it says. .01. Right there. See?" "Oh, my pet cow!" grumbled Pete, "you mean all these little deals are only supposed to be held to .01. How could I have done that? I'll tell you how I did it. I haven't done anything to that loose a tolerance in five years. I just simply read another 'oh' in there. Oh, my pet cow!" "Yeah, that's probably it, Pete," replied Sam. "The new guys who normally do this kind of work were tied up on long runs, so I simply scheduled it over here." "I sure didn't see there was just one 'oh' behind that point. Well, yah got a dozen nice expensive counter-shafts, Sam. I'm awful sorry," said Pete dejectedly. Pete had a *preparatory set,* an expectancy, to see what he saw: one more order for highly skilled, close tolerance work of the kind he was accustomed to doing. We go through life having our perceptions influenced by such preparatory sets. Our previous experience prepares us to see something such as we have seen before, and it's not just a matter of past experience, either. What we need and want to see also causes a perceptual set.

We all have sets, as the result of previous experiences and as the result of personal needs and interests. What might simply look like an old letter to you or me may be an object of intense interest to a stamp collector. An automobile enthusiast may pick out the exhaust tone of a Ferrari which is lost in the cacophony of traffic noises, to someone else. To see Juan Fernandez take a couple of quick steps from his turret lathe to deposit a finished part in a tote pan and then move briskly back to start work on the next piece appears to be efficient performance, to most people. But the fellows in industrial engineering immediately identify the action as evidence of an inefficient job layout. The way they see it, *no* steps should be taken, and better yet, the part should come out of the chuck and drop immediately into a tote pan untouched by Juan. The industrial engineers have a set to perceive wasted motion, which most of us miss. We are set to perceive what we value, what we're interested in, what we are trained to see, and what we've seen before.

Projection

Allyn White turned into the accounting office and was just about to close the door behind him when the tail of his eye caught a glimpse of Eldon Peavey coming down the hall behind him. He didn't close the door all the way, but left it slightly ajar. Now Eldon was quite obviously not coming into the accounting department, but was headed for his desk in the industrial engineering department two doors down. But Allyn just couldn't shut the door in his face. Why? Because Allyn felt that Eldon would perceive the act as a personal rejection. Eldon probably wouldn't even have noticed, and had he noticed, he wouldn't look upon a closing door as an act of rejection. You had to get a lot more blunt than that before Eldon felt rejected. But Allyn, in the same situation, would have felt rejected. So what Allyn was doing was *projecting* his own feelings.

We can misinterpret others' actions and motives rather markedly, as a result of projection. Our perceptions are distorted in the direction of our own needs and attitudes, which we tend to assume are needs and attitudes shared by others. If one tends to be insincere, he perceives others as being insincere. Sears and Frenkel-Brunswick found that to be true in experimentation with both American and Austrian students.

Myron Green tends to be a sneaky sort and, sure enough, he distrusts everyone else a good deal. We saw Byron Cartwright assuming that because he liked achieving, directing and taking responsibility, Pete Petroni did, too. Otto Kowalski likes to help people, and so assumes that nearly everyone else does, also, to his frequent disillusionment. Projection is a very common, internalized perception distorter. An acute form of perceptual distortion, through over-simplification, is stereotyping.

Stereotype

Dave Briggs, employment manager, was working his way down through the pile of recently received application letters, when he came to a resume that caused him to emit a low whistle and reach for the telephone. Dialing quickly, Dave got Ed Yamamoto, chief engineer, on the phone. "Ed," enthused Dave, "I have the group leader for the bi-valve pump section." The bi-valve pump design section had been getting along without a direct supervisor since last February, when Hal Coombs had left the company. Herb Borgfeldt, senior man in the section, had twice refused the job, saying he was a designer, not a straw boss, and no one among the rest of the men in the section was experienced enough to take over as supervisor. The job really needed an expert pump designer, preferably with some supervisory experience.

"Graduated from Cal Tech, honors, three years with Livermore Radiation Lab, seven years with Cleveland Pump, last two and a half as supervisor of the bi-valve section. Lessee, two patents in own name, paper in 'Hydraulic Occlusion' at last year's SME meeting—" "Wow!" from Ed. "—and her letter says she wants to relocate to be close to her mother, and since we are the only pump manufacturer in town, I can't see why we can't get her." "Wait one minute," Ed burst forth, "you said 'her'?" "Yeah," replied Dave, "Ann

Farmer. She apparently grew up here. Lessee, went to Horace Mann High School, where she was salutatorian and editor of the yearbook." "A woman!" snorted Ed. "Look, I'm no male chauvinist, you understand, but this is no job for a girl! There's lots of pressure. She'll be too emotional to run things, too illogical to think through design problems, too absorbed with details to see the big picture, too—" "W-a-i-t," protested Dave. "I'm not insisting you hire this engineer, but you did sound enthusiastic when I read her qualifications." "Well, *sure,* who wouldn't be? Cal Tech, supervisory experience, patents, papers, honors. But you hadn't told me he's a her!"

Ed is going through a form of perceptual distortion known as *stereotyping,* a form of categorization. Categorization is, of course, an extremely useful cognitive device, permitting us to handle and understand large bodies of complex information. Used restrictively, however, it causes the observer to draw conclusions from too narrow a range of information, and to generalize too many other traits from this minimal data, usually relating to the categorization of people. The way it works is for the perceiver to have established several ready-made, oversimplified categories of people who he thinks possess a few distinctive characteristics. Then he classifies the people he meets into one of these categories. The classification is made on the basis of one or a very few characteristics. The person so classified is then assumed to have all the characteristics thought to represent the category. Ed classified Ann Farmer as a woman, not as an engineer. Under Ed's "woman" classification are the characteristics of emotionalism, illogic, detail-mindedness, etc. Ed's prejudiced, but then there are those who would stereotype Ed as an engineer, which to them would tend to mean that he is unemotional, socially inept and so on. Stereotypes are usually learned young and go unquestioned. The learning usually takes place out of intimate contact with those assigned to the stereotyped category; therefore, the resulting attributed characteristics cannot help but be distorted.

Selective Perception and Behavioral Reversal

Mabel Lindsey, typing pool supervisor, is aware that the girls in the typing pool don't like the clatter and din of working together in one big, noisy room, she knows they prefer doing work for one or a few people rather than typing whatever is parceled out to them, that they dislike the lack of individuality being a member of the pool implies. She is aware that Charlotte Bettendorf's loudness and exhibitionism irritates the rest of the girls in the pool, and that her own perfectionism is often hard to live with. She is aware of all these irritants *at the subconscious level.* To protect her own sanity, she has sublimated her awareness of these irritants and does not really perceive them anymore at the conscious level. If she were to consciously perceive and be sensitive to all the needs of her girls, she wouldn't have time to do anything else. In order to get on with her work, she must selectively stifle those perceptions of disturbing stimuli which don't contribute to what she perceives as important to her job as typing pool supervisor. This phenomenon has been described by Harold Leavitt as a self-imposed psychological blindness which helps persons maintain their equilibrium as they pursue their goals.

If, on the other hand, all in the same week, first Betty, and then Claudine and then Hope were to complain about the noise, the irritation might break through Mabel's selective defense. She might then immediately burst in upon office manager Clyde Ferguson and demand that the ceiling be insulated. Selective perception, with its blackout of mild disturbances, can suddenly change to acute perception when the irritant exceeds a certain threshold. At this point, the individual shifts his attention sharply and fully to the irritant. As Leavitt puts it, "The distant irritation increases to a point at which it becomes so real, so imminent, and so threatening that we reverse our course, discard the blindfold and preoccupy ourselves completely with the thing we previously ignored." The phenomenon is a complex one, because if things are threatening, they must be fended off, but in order to fend them off they must first be seen. Therefore, in order for one to protect himself from threat, he must first perceive the threat and then manage to deny to himself that he has seen it. This combination of selective perception and defensive behavior helps explain some actions on the part of others that would otherwise be extremely puzzling.

Self-Perception

Bill Crandell, senior accountant, doesn't really think much of Bill Crandell. The company's personnel records show Bill's intelligence to be in the upper 98th percentile of the general population. He has clear-eyed good looks, with an open, ingenuous expression appealing to everyone. He moves with an easy grace. No one else can put others at their ease as readily as Bill does. His MBA is from a prestigious business school. He is vice president of Midwestern division of the CPA Association. He has an adoring wife and two happy kids doing well in Lakeside Heights Elementary School. Everyone likes Bill. But Bill doesn't like himself very much.

He doesn't feel that he's doing nearly as well as he should, professionally. He doesn't feel that he is providing adequately for his family. He can't afford household help, nor the riding lessons his daughter wants so much, and he can only just manage to rent a place at the lake for the family during the summer.

If only he had the ability to concentrate like Otto Kowalski. If he only had Myron Green's coldly efficient approach. If he could only speak in public like Eldon Peavey. If he could acquire Mr. Portley's ability to see the big picture.

So, bright, charming Bill Crandell sees himself as plodding, ineffectual Bill Crandell. He has a self-percept that is not at all realistic, but realistic or not it's the one he has. It causes him to be depressed a lot of the time, and it seems to be developing into a self-fulfilling prophecy. Bill sees himself as pleasant but ineffectual, and as a result, he is becoming pleasant but ineffectual. He doesn't extend himself much anymore. He just takes orders from Myron Green. His intelligence and training permit him to do an adequate job, but he shows very little initiative. He loves being with people because it takes his mind off his own problems. But even this tends to be self-defeating. He spends more and more time talking, and less time working. A low self-percept is a difficult cross to bear.

Low self-percept? Not so with Gordon Green. Although no brighter than Bill Crandell and not nearly as charming, Gordon thinks of himself as a real winner. He chose industrial engineering in college because he figured this would be the place he could learn more about the operation of a company faster than from any other starting point. As he saw it, he could quickly move up to chief, then shift over into line management as superintendent, then VP of production and right on up. Gordon thinks he's good and he is, though probably not *that* good. But as a result, he probes every opportunity to see where he can make his impact. Gordon's self-percept is high, but not excessively high. He *may* accomplish many of his goals. In the case where one's perception is too high, the accompanying lack of realism can often cause a poor social adjustment. It can also result in a series of too-ambitious undertakings that can't end up anywhere but in failure. Still, society probably has more to gain from those with high self-percepts than from those with low ones. The high self-perceivers will at least *try* many things, and some are bound to be successful.

Part Six

Leadership in the Organization

14

Leadership: A Beleaguered Species?

WARREN BENNIS

Something's happened—something that bewilders, something turbulent, convulsive, and spastic. What appears is a panorama going in and out of focus like a faulty TV tube; its flickering bluish images, pulsing to a strobe-light cadence, express the chaos of our times. Although our technology is so advanced and precise that it brings together in New York—at 600 m.p.h. speeds—people who left Los Angeles, San Francisco, Denver, Chicago, and Atlanta shortly before, it delivers them just in time to be blown to smithereens by a bomb in a baggage locker.

It's as if mankind, to paraphrase Teilhard de Chardin, is *falling suddenly out of control of its own destiny*. Perhaps only a new Homer or Herodotus would be able, later on, to show us its patterns and designs, its coherences and contours. What we hear and discern now is not one voice or signal, but a jim-jangle of chords: an *a capella* choir here, a closely harmonized brass quintet there, a raucous, atonal gang in the balcony blowing on kazoos and holding up placards.

All we know for sure is that we cannot wait a generation for the historian to tell us what happened; we have to try to make sense out of the jumble of voices, dare to order the dissonant chorus of kazoos. Indeed we must try, for the first test of any leader today is to discover just what he or she *does* confront; only then will it be possible to devise the best ways of making that reality—the multiple realities—potentially manageable.

The Erosion of Institutional Autonomy

The most serious threat to our institutions and the cause of our diminishing sense of able leadership is the steady erosion of institutional autonomy. This erosion results from forces in both the external and the internal environment.

The External Environment: Multiple Dependencies

Time was when the leader could decide—period. A Henry Ford, an Andrew Carnegie, a Nicholas Murray Butler could issue a ukase—and all would automatically obey. Their successors' hands are now tied in innumerable ways—by governmental requirements, by various agencies, by union rules, by the moral and sometimes legal pressures of organized consumers and environmentalists. When David Mathews was president of the University of Alabama, before he became Secretary of Health, Education and Welfare, he characterized federal regulations (in *Science,* Vol. 190, 1975, p. 445) as threatening to

> . . . bind the body of higher education in a Lilliputian nightmare of forms and formulas. The constraints emanate from various accrediting agencies, federal bureaucracies, and state boards, but their effects are the same . . . a loss of institutional autonomy, and a serious threat to diversity, creativity, and reform. Most seriously, that injection of more regulations may even work against the accountability it seeks to foster, because it so dangerously diffuses responsibility.

Dr. Mathews will often be reminded of those words and the deadly hidden costs of compliance.

The external forces that impinge and impose upon the perimeter of our institutions—the incessant concatenation of often contrary requirements—are the basic reasons for the loss of their self-determination. Fifty years ago this external environment was fairly placid, like an ocean on a calm day. Now that ocean is turbulent and highly interdependent—and it makes tidal waves. In my own institution right now, the key people for me to reckon with are not only the students, the faculty, and my own management group, but people external to the university—the city manager, city council members, state legislature, accrediting and professional associations, federal government, alumni, alumnae, and parents. There is an incessant, dissonant clamor out there. The institution that proliferates its dependence on these "external patronage structures" blunts and diffuses its main purposes. A brilliant example of such an institution is the university; indeed, the boundaries of its autonomy resemble Swiss cheese. To cope with these pressures, every leader must create a department of "external affairs"—a secretary of state, as it were, to deal with external constituencies. (Ironically, our real Secretary of State Kissinger often found foreign affairs thwarted by *internal* constituencies that undid his long, laborious, and precarious negotiations.)

In an analysis of my own time allocation, a research analyst determined that "50 percent of the university president's contacts were with external people, 43 percent with internal constituents, 4 percent with trustees, and 3 percent with personal or undetermined contacts. Sixty-seven percent of phone calls, 43.7 percent of mail, and 38.9 percent of meetings were with external groups." (Drea Zigarmi, "The Role of the University President as a Boundary Person," Dissertation at the University of Massachusetts, Amherst, 1974.) The study was done in the second year of my incumbency; I suspect that my involuntary orientation toward external audiences has increased year by year since then.

The Internal Environment: Multiple Advocacies

Accompanying all this is a new kind of populism—not the "free silver" of Bryanism, but the fragmentation of constituencies. On my own campus, which is typical, we have over 500 organized pressure groups. We have a coalition of women's groups, a gay society, black organizations for both students and faculty, a veterans' group, a continuing education group for women (late returnees to the university), a handicapped group, a Jewish faculty caucus, a faculty union organized by the American Association of University Professors, an organization for staff members who are neither faculty nor administrators, an organization of middle-management staff members, an association of women administrators, and a small, elite group of graduate fellows.

This fragmentation, which exists more or less in all organizations, marks the end not only of community, a sense of shared values, and symbols, but of consensus, an agreement reached despite differences. It was Lyndon Johnson's tragedy to plead, "Come, let us reason together," at a time when all these groups scarcely wanted to *be* together, much less reason together.

These pressure groups are intentionally fragmented. Going their separate and often conflicting ways, they say: "No, we don't want to be part of the mainstream of America—we just want to be us," whether they're blacks, Chicanos, women, the third sex, or Menominee Indians seizing an empty Catholic monastery. They tell us that the old dream of "the melting pot," of assimilation, does not work. They have never been "*beyond* the melting pot" (as Glazer and Moynihan wrote about it); they have been *behind* it.

So what we have now is a new form of politics—King Caucus, who has more heads than Cerberus, and Contending Queens who cry, "Off with their heads!" as they play croquet with flamingos. It is *the politics of multiple advocacies*. They represent people who are fed up with being ignored, neglected, excluded, denied, subordinated. No longer, however, do they march on cities, on bureaus, or on organizations that they view as sexist, racist, anti-Semitic, and so on. Now, they file suit. The law has suddenly emerged as the court of first resort.

A Litigious Society: "Is the Wool Worth the Cry?"

And so we have become a litigious society in which individuals and groups—in spectacularly increasing numbers—bring suit to resolve issues that previously might have been settled privately. An injured hockey player bypasses institutional procedures to bring formal suit. The club owners are outraged that "one of their own" took the case "outside." College students, too, unhappy with what they are learning on campus, are turning to the courts. A lawsuit against the University of Bridgeport may produce the first clear legal precedent. It was filed last spring by a woman seeking $150 in tuition, the cost of her books, and legal fees because a course required of secondary education majors was "worthless" and she "didn't learn anything." My own university faces a suit from a black woman because she lost the administrative position I had mistakenly thought she could fill. A law review has been sued for rejecting an article. In New Jersey, a federal judge has ordered 28 state Senators to stand trial for violating the constitutional rights of the 29th member, a woman, by excluding her from their party caucus. They did so, they claimed, because she was "leaking" their deliberations to the press. In a test case in Columbus, Ohio, the U.S. Supreme Court recently ruled that secondary-school students may not be suspended, disciplinarily, without formal charges and a hearing—that the loss of a single day's education is a deprivation of property. A federal court in Washington has just awarded $10,000 to each of the thousands of May 1970 antiwar demonstrators who, it found, had been illegally arrested and confined at the behest of former Attorney General Mitchell.

Aside from the merits of any particular case, the overriding fact is clear: The hands of all administrators are increasingly tied by real or potential legal issues. I must consult our lawyers in advance before making trivial decisions. The university has so many suits against it (40 at last count) that my mother now calls me "My son, the defendant."

The courts and the law are, of course, necessary to protect individual rights and to provide recourse for negligence, breach of contract, and fraud. But a "litigious society" presents consequences that no one foresaw, not least of which are the visible expense of legal preparation and the invisible cost of wasted time.

Far more serious than the expense, however, are the confusion, ambiguity, and lack of subtlety of the law and what that does to institutional autonomy and leadership. To take the example of consumer protection, we see that lawsuits are forcing universities to insert a railroad-timetable disclaimer in their catalogues—for example, "Courses in this catalogue are subject to change without notice"—in order to head off possible lawsuits. At the same time, the Federal Trade Commission is putting pressure on doctors, architects, lawyers, and other professionals to revise their codes of ethics forbidding advertising. The Buckley Amendment, which permits any student to examine his own file, tends to exclude from it any qualitative judgments that could provide even the flimsiest basis for a suit. (Ironically, Senator Buckley himself refuses to make a "full financial disclosure" of his personal wealth because he finds "the mood of suspicion . . . has created almost a presumption that public officials are corrupt or corruptible unless proven innocent.")

The confusion, ambiguity, and complexity of the law—augmented by conflicting court interpretations—tend toward institutional paralysis. Equally forbidding is the fact that the courts are substituting their judgments for the expertise of the institution. Justice may prevail, but at a price to institutional leadership so expensive, as we shall see later on, that one has to ask if the "wool is worth the cry."

A Cat's Cradle

Many of our institutions are careening (or catatonic) because of an invasion and overstimulation by external forces. We know what that does to an individual: A total reliance on external cues, stimuli, rewards, and punishments leads to an inability to control one's own destiny. People in this state tend to avoid any behavior for which there is no external cue. Without signals, they vegetate. With contrary signals, either they become catatonic—literally too paralyzed by fear of risk to choose, let alone *act* on a choice—or, conversely, they lunge at anything and everything.

The same is true of organizations and their leadership; under the influence of coercive political and legal regulations, they exhibit the same effects. Although these regulations are more pronounced in the public sector than in the private sector, in the latter area the market mechanism has heretofore been the linking pin between firm and environment—providing feedback in terms of rewards and punishments and reflecting the success or failure of decisions. Whether the organization is private or public, whether the controls are legitimate or not, there is only one natural conclusion: An excess of (even well-intended) controls will lead inexorably to lobotomized institutions.

What neither lawmakers nor politicians seem to realize is that laws and regulations deal primarily with sins of commission. Sins of omission are more difficult to deal with—partly, as Kenneth Boulding points out, because it is just damned hard in practice to distinguish between honest mistakes and deliberate evil. Legitimate risk-taking can land you in jail. On the other hand, by "playing it safe," by living up to the inverted expression, "Don't just do something, sit there," an institution, a leader, a person can avoid error; and if they keep it up long enough, they can *almost* avoid living.

As legal and political systems become increasingly concerned with sins of commission—an event exemplified in the dramatic switch from *caveat emptor* to *caveat vendor,* in the deluge of consumer protection legislation, in malpractice suits, in the environmental protection movement, in the court decisions awarding damages to purchasers of faulty products—we can get to a point where, like the California surgeons who quit operating on any but emergency patients, no producer or organization will do anything at all. Why should they? The costs of uncertainty and honest mistakes are now far too costly to bear.

At my own and many other universities, for example, we are now in the process of rewriting our catalogues so carefully that it will be virtually impossible for any student (read: *consumer*) to claim that we haven't fulfilled our end of the bargain. At the same time, because we have to be so careful, we can never express our hopes, our dreams, and our bold ideas of what a university experience could provide for the prospective student. I suspect that in ten years or so, college catalogues (rarely a publication that faculty, students, or administrators are wild about in any case) will devolve into statements that resemble nothing more than the finely printed cautions and disclaimers on the back of airline tickets—just the opposite of what education is all about: an adventurous odyssey of the mind.

All this—all the litigation, legislation, and *caveat vendor*—not only diminishes the potency of our institutions, but leads to something more pernicious and possibly irrecoverable. We seek comfort in the delusion that all our troubles—our failures, our losses, our insecurities, our "hang-ups," our missed opportunities, our incompetence—can be blamed on "someone else," can be relegated to the seamless, suffocating, and invisible "system." How convenient, dear Brutus.

Just think: At a certain point, following our current practices and national mood, all sense of individual responsibility will rapidly erode. And along with that, the volume of "belly-aching" and vacuous preaching about "the system" will grow more strident. The result: Leaders who *are* around either will be too weak or will avoid the inevitable risks involved in doing *anything*—whether good, bad, or indifferent.

I am *not* arguing the case against all regulations and controls; I am painfully conscious that some have been too long in coming—that, indeed, some are imperative for the great body of citizens and necessary if we are to realize our nation's values (for example, equality of opportunity for all); without them, I fear, our basic heritage would long ago have become indelibly corrupted. (And, of course, it is not hard to understand why campaign finances have come under control recently. How do we excuse or deal with Gulf's $12 million bribes?)

All the same, when it comes to protecting people from their exploiters, we have an extra responsibility to be so vigilant that we don't end up in a situation where everyone is enmeshed in a cat's cradle of regulations erratically intertwined with the filaments of "good intentions."

As Justice Brandeis put it many years ago:

> Experience should teach us to be most on guard to protect liberty when the governments' purposes are beneficent. Men born to freedom are naturally alert to repel invasion of their liberty by evil minded rulers. The greatest dangers to liberty lurk in insidious encroachments by men of zeal, well-meaning, but without understanding.

Variations on a Theme

The basic problem is that leaders are facing a set of conditions that seemed to take shape suddenly, like an unscheduled express train looming out of the night. Who would ever have forecast the post-Depression development in the public sector of welfare, social service, health, and education? Who, save a Lord Keynes, could have predicted the scale and range of the multinational corporations? Prophetically, he wrote:

Progress lies in the growth and the recognition of semi-autonomous bodies within the states. Large business corporations, when they have reached a certain age and size, approximate the status of public corporations rather than that of the individualistic private enterprise.

The Keynesian prophecy is upon us. When David Rockefeller goes to London, he is greeted as if he were a chief of state (and some of his empires *are* bigger than many states). But in addition to the growth of semi-autonomous, often global corporations that rival governments, we have public-sector institutions that Keynes could not have imagined. Our society's biggest employer, and the one with the fastest growth rate, is local and state govern-

---

MEMORANDUM OF THE PEOPLE OF OHIO'S
13TH CONGRESSIONAL DISTRICT:

Summary: Being the Congressman is rigorous servitude, ceaseless enslavement to a peculiar mix of everyone else's needs, demands and whims, plus one's own sense of duty, ambition or vanity. It is that from which Mrs. Mosher and I now declare our personal independence, to seek our freedom, as of January 3, 1977. . . .

It is a Congressman's inescapable lot, his or her enslavement, to be never alone, never free from incessant buffeting by people, events, problems, decisions. . . . It is a grueling experience, often frustrating, discouraging, sometimes very disillusioning. . . . House debates, caucuses, briefings, working breakfasts, working lunches, receptions, dinners, homework study, and even midnight collect calls from drunks . . . you name it!

I am for opting out. I shall not be a candidate for reelection in 1976.

CHARLES A. MOSHER
Representative
13th Congressional District
State of Ohio
December 19, 1975

Memorandum of the people of Ohio's 13th congressional district

ment. Higher education, which less than twenty years ago was 50 percent private and 50 percent public, is now about 85 percent public and is expected to be 90 percent public by 1980. And whereas a century ago 90 percent of all Americans were self-employed, today 90 percent work in what I would call bureaucracies, as members of some kind of corporate family. They might be called "juristic" persons who work for a legal entity called a corporation or agency. Being juristic persons, they are not masters of their own actions; they cannot place the same faith in themselves that self-employed persons can.

These are the problems of leadership today. We have the important emergence of a Roosevelt-Keynes revolution, the new politics of multiple advocacy, new dependencies, new constituencies, new regulatory controls, new values. And how does our endangered species, the leaders, cope with these new complications and entanglements?

Managing, Not Leading

For the most part, the leaders are neither coping nor leading. One reason, I fear, is that many of us misconceive what leadership is all about. *Leading* does not mean *managing:* The difference between the two is crucial. I am acquainted with many institutions that are very well *managed* and very poorly *led.* They may excel in the ability to handle daily routines and yet never ask whether the particular routines should exist at all. To lead, so the dictionary tells us, is to go in advance of, to show the way, to influence or induce, to guide in direction, course, action, opinion. To manage means to bring about, to accomplish, to have charge of or responsibility for, to conduct. The difference may be summarized as activities of vision and judgment versus activities of efficiency.

In his decision making, the leader today is a multidirectional broker who must deal with four estates—his immediate management team, constituencies within his organization, forces outside his organization, and the media. While his decisions and actions affect the people of these four estates, their decisions and actions, too, affect him. The fact is that the concept of "movers and shakers"—a leadership elite that determines the major decisions—is an outdated notion. Leaders are as much the "shook" as the shakers. Whether the four estates force too many problems on the leader or whether the leader takes on too much in an attempt to prove himself, the result is what I call "Bennis's First Law of Pseudodynamics," which is that routine work will always drive out the innovational.

Securing the certainty of routine can be detected in the following example:

> I noticed that frequently my most enthusiastic deputies were unwittingly keeping me from working any fundamental change in our institution. My own moment of truth came toward the end of my first ten months as head of the university. It was one of those nights in the office. The clock was moving toward three in the morning, and still I was not through with the incredible mass of paper stacked before me. Bone weary and

soul weary, I found myself muttering, "Either I can't manage this place or it is unmanageable." I reached for my daily appointments calendar and ran my eye down each hour, each half-hour, each quarter-hour, to see where my time had gone that day, the day before, the month before.

I had become the victim of an amorphous, unintentional conspiracy to prevent me from *doing anything whatever to change the university's status quo.* Even those of my associates who fully shared my hopes to set new goals and work toward creative change were unconsciously doing the most to ensure that I would never find the time to begin. People play the old army game. They do not want to take responsibility for or bear the consequences of decisions that they should properly make. Everybody dumps his "wet babies" (as old hands in the State Department call them) on my desk even though I have neither the diapers nor the information to take care of them.

"Copping Out"

Today's leader is often baffled and frustrated by a new kind of politics—not following traditional party lines, but arising from significant interaction with various governmental agencies, the courts, the consumers, and other factions. It is the politics of maintaining institutional self-determination and mastery in times of environmental turbulence. Many leaders do not want to recognize these forces, let alone face the new politics. In 1974, the director of the New York Health Corporation resigned, saying, "I already see indications that the corporation and its cause are being made a political football in the current campaign. I'm not a politician. I do not wish to become involved in the political issues here." Yet he had earlier said that he found himself "at the center of a series of ferocious struggles for money, power, and jobs among the combatants, political leaders, labor leaders, minority groups, medical militants, medical school deans, doctors and nurses, and many of my own administrative subordinates." His corporation had an $800 million budget, was responsible for capital construction of more than $1 billion, and employed 40,000 people, including 7,500 doctors and almost 15,000 nurses and nurses' aides. It embraced 19 hospitals which, with 15,000 beds, numerous out-patient clinics, and emergency rooms, treated 2,000,000 New Yorkers a year. And he was *surprised* that he was into politics—and didn't like it.

Leading Through Limits

We are now experiencing a transition period that may aptly be called an "era of limits." After the Club of Rome warned us of this in *The Limits of Growth,* the Arab petroleum boycott, soaring fuel costs, and the continuing energy crisis confirmed the brutal fact that our national goals have outrun our current means. Some political and institutional leaders exploit the situation by turning the public's disenchantment with growth into a political asset. They want to follow the popular mood rather than lead it.

The National Observer (November 29, 1975, pp. 1 and 16) calls California's young Governor Edmund G. Brown "the hottest politician in America," and quotes him thus: "Growth in California has slowed down . . . the feeling is strongly antigrowth. Once, people seemed to think there were no limits to the growth of California. Now Californians are moving to Oregon and Colorado. . . . There are limits to everything—limits to this planet, limits to government mechanisms, limits to any philosophy or idea. And that's a concept we have to get used to. Someone called it the Europeanization of America. That's part right. You take an empty piece of land and you fill it up with houses and soon the land is more scarce and the air is more polluted and things are more complicated. That's where we are today. . . ." *The National Observer* says his rhetoric works: "Over 90 percent of the people in California applaud his performance."

Leading by Diminuendo

Compared with the grandiose rhetoric of the past quarter-century about the ability of size and scale plus technological "know-how" to solve all of society's basic problems, the management of decline sounds at least respectably sane—especially when compared with a pronunciamento by a leader of the European Economic Community, Dr. Sicco Mansholt: "*More, further, quicker, richer* are the watchwords of present-day society. We must adapt to this for there is no alternative." *That* kind of rhetoric, especially when at brutal odds with current reality, denies the very nature of the human condition.

Thus it is understandable that a new movement, growing in popularity and becoming more sophisticated in its approach, has arisen. I call it "cameo leadership," which aspires to carve things well, but smaller. It preaches a less complicated time, a communal life, a radical decentralization of organizational life—a return to Walden before the Pond was polluted, before the Coke stand made its appearance, before *Walden* itself was required reading . . . when most things were compassable.

A chief spokesman for this counter-technology movement is E. F. Schumacher, a former top economist and planner for England's National Coal Board. In his book, *Small Is Beautiful,* Schumacher writes that:

- We are poor, not demigods.
- We have plenty to be sorrowful about, and are not emerging into a golden age.
- We need a gentle approach, a nonviolent spirit, and small is beautiful. . . .

Governor Brown of California is an avid disciple of Dr. Schumacher's "Buddhist economics." Small *is* beautiful. Sometimes. Perhaps it is beautiful more often than big is beautiful. When big gets ugly, we see human waste, depersonalization, alienation, possibly disruption. When small gets ugly, something that never crosses Schumacher's mind, it leads to a decentralization bordering on anarchy—and to poverty, famine, and disease as well.

Small is beautiful. The era of limits is upon us. Who can argue? Nevertheless, these slogans are as empty as they are appealing and timely. Because they are appealing, we fail to see that they represent no specific programs for change. In fact, instead of opening up possibilities for solutions, they close them. Basically, they reflect the symptoms now afflicting us by setting rhetorical opposites against each other. Small is beautiful, so big must be ugly. A grain of sand may be more beautiful than a pane of glass. But must we trade the glass for the sand?

The real point is not one of beauty. The real point is whether leaders can face up to and cope with our present crises, worries, and imperatives. The real problem is how we can lead institutions in a world of over two billion people, millions of whom will starve while other millions can't find work. Even those whose work is exciting and meaningful often live with quiet desperation in fear of "the others." The real question: How do we provide the needed jobs and, after that, how do we learn to lead so that people can work more cooperatively, more sensibly, more humanely with one another? How can we lead in such a way that the requisite interdependence—so crucial for human survival and economic resilience—can be realized in a humane and gentle spirit?

Sweeping and Dusting

They won't provide the answers, either, the leaders who are custodians and bookkeepers. And they don't use slogans, they positively hate them—as they do poetry, or beauty, or politics. But then, they're not running for office; instead, they run offices.

T. S. Eliot was right; the world does end with a whimper. How else, when we have bookkeepers and custodians silently tidying things up, when we have input/output without even a throughput?

Recently, an acting president of one of our most august private universities was appointed its president. He had been "acting" for about eighteen months. One of the local newspapers, in an editorial written after he was made the official president, rhapsodized about the "acting's" performance. "Dr. (X)," the editor wrote, "put the budget first in his message (*State of the University*). He acknowledged that 'a budget is merely a means to an end,' but he also knows that budgetary success is required 'to enable the continued existence of a university with ends that have characterized this University from its beginning.' "

I can no more argue with that—of course we must live within our means!—than I can with the aesthetics of size. "Small is beautiful" and "balanced budgets" somehow emerge as epochally captivating phrases. Shortly before his appointment, the acting president wrote a *State of the University* report in which he said, "I do not have a personal academic agenda to propose, nor one against which progress might be assessed. That must await the new president." After eighteen months, no "personal academic agenda. . . . "

Coda

Where have all the leaders gone? They're consulting, pleading, trotting here and there, temporizing, putting out fires, either avoiding or (more often) taking too much heat, and spending too much energy in doing both. They are peering at a landscape of "bottom lines" and ostentatiously taking the bus to work (with four bodyguards rather than the one chauffeur they might need if they drove) to demonstrate their commitment to energy conservation. They are money changers lost in a narrow orbit. They resign. They burn out. They decide not to run or serve. They read Buddhist economics, listen to prophets of decentralization, and then proceed to create new bureaucracies to stamp out old ones. (Nixon's "Anti-Big Government" one was bigger than Johnson's.) They are motivating people through fear or by cautiously following the "trends" or adopting a "Let's face it" cynicism. They are all characters set in a dreamless society—groping in the dark and learning how to "retrench," as if that were an art like playing the violin. And they are all scared.

And who can blame them? Sweaty palms are understandable. That is the final irony. Precisely at the time when the credibility of our leaders is at an all-time low, and when the surviving leaders feel most inhibited in realizing the potentiality of power, we most need individuals who can lead. We need people who can shape the future, not just barely manage to get through the day.

There is no simple solution. But there are things we must recognize:

- *Leaders must develop the vision and strength to call the shots.* There are risks in taking the initiative—but the greater risk is to wait for orders. We need leaders at every level who can lead, not just manage. This means that institutions (and followers) have to recognize that they *need* leadership, that their need is for vision, energy, and drive rather than blandness and safety.
- *The leader must be a "conceptualist" (not just someone to tinker with the "nuts and bolts").* A conceptualist is more than an "idea man"; he must have an entrepreneurial vision, a sense of perspective, the time and the inclination to think about the forces and raise the fundamental questions that will affect the destiny of both the institution and the society within which it is embedded.
- *He must have a sense of continuity and significance in order, to paraphrase the words of Shelley, to see the present in the past and the future in the present.* He must, in the compelling moments of the present, be able to clarify problems—elevate them into understandable choices for the constituents—rather than exploit them; to define issues, not aggravate them. In this respect, leaders are essentially educators. Our great political leaders, such as Jefferson, Lincoln, and Wilson, tried to educate the people about problems by studying the messy existential groaning of the people and transforming murky problems into understandable issues. A leader who responds to a drought by attacking the lack of rainfall is not likely to inspire a great deal of confidence. What we see today is sometimes worse: leaving the problem as a problem (for example, "the economy" or "the energy crisis") or allowing the problem to stay out of control until it becomes a "crisis." What is essential, instead, are leaders who will get at the underlying issues and present a clear alternative. Dr. Martin Luther King, Jr. provided this perspective for black people. We sorely need the same leadership for the whole nation.

- *Leaders must get their heads above the grass and risk the possibility, famil-iar to any rooster, of getting hit by a rock.* If a leader has the vision, takes the time, and makes the effort to lead the way by presenting a perspec-tive, an alternative, a choice, he will need courage. He must be allowed to take risks, to embrace error, to "create dangerously" (as Camus put it in his last formal lecture—before a university audience), to use his creativity to the hilt and encourage others to do the same.

- *The leader must get at the truth and learn how to filter the unwieldy flow of information into coherent patterns.* He must prevent the distortion of that information by overeager aides who will tailor it to satisfy what they consider to be his prejudices or vanities. The biggest problem of a lead-er—any leader—is getting at the truth. Pierre du Pont put it well in a long-ago note to his brother Iréné, "One cannot expect to know what will happen, one can only consider himself fortunate if he can know what *has* happened." The politics of bureaucracy tend to interfere with rather than facilitate truth gathering.

  That's mainly true because the huge size of our organizations and the enormous overload burdening every leader make it impossible for him to verify all his own information, analyze all his own problems, or always decide who should or should not have his ear or time. Since he must rely for much of this upon his key assistants and officers, he would not feel comfortable in so close and vital a relationship with men (women, unfor-tunately, would not even be considered!) who were not at least of kindred minds and compatible personalities.

  Of course, this is perfectly human and, up to a point, understandable. But the consequences can be devastating because the leader is likely to see only that highly selective information or those carefully screened peo-ple that his key assistants decide he should see. And he may discover too late that he acted on information that was inadequate or inaccurate, or that he has been shielded from "troublesome" visitors who wanted to tell him what he should have known, or that he has been protected from some problem that should have been his primary concern.

  In too many institutions, a very few people are filtering the facts—im-plicitly skewing reality and selecting information that provides an inaccu-rate picture on which decisions may be based. Such skewing can affect history: Barbara Tuchman in her recent book on China tells how, in the 1940s, Mao Tse-tung wanted very much to visit Roosevelt, but Roosevelt cancelled the proposed meeting on the basis of incredibly biased informa-tion from Ambassador Pat Hurley. It was nearly thirty years later that another President sought out the meeting with Mao that, earlier, could conceivably have averted many subsequent disasters.

  So the leader cannot rely exclusively on his palace guards for informa-tion. Hard as it is to do, he must have multiple information sources and must remain accessible—despite the fact that accessibility in modern times seems one of the most underrated political virtues. The Romans, who were the greatest politicians of antiquity and probably also the busi-est men, valued that quality highly in their leaders. Cicero, in praising

Pompey, commented on his ready availability not only to his subordinates, but also to the ordinary soldiers in his command.

A later Roman historian recounted this even more telling anecdote about the Emperor Hadrian. The emperor, who at that time ruled almost the entire civilized world, was riding into Rome in his chariot when an old woman blocked his path and asked him to hear a grievance. Hadrian brushed her aside, saying he was too busy. "Then you're too busy to be emperor," she called after him. Whereupon he halted his chariot and heard her out.

• *The leader must be a social architect who studies and shapes what is called the "culture of work"—those intangibles that are so hard to discern but are so terribly important in governing the way people act, the values and norms that are subtly transmitted to individuals and groups and that tend to create binding and bonding.* Whatever goals and values the leader pursues, he must proceed toward their implementation by designing a social architecture that encourages understanding, participation, and ownership of the goals. He must, of course, learn about and be influenced by those who will be affected by the decisions that permit the day-to-day realization of goals. At the very least, he must be forever conscious that the culture can facilitate or subvert "the best laid plans . . ."

The culture of an organization dictates the mechanisms by which conflict can be resolved and the degree to which the outcomes will be costly, humane, fair, and reasonable. It can influence whether, on the one hand, there is a "zero-sum" mentality that insists upon an absolute winner or an absolute loser or, on the other, there is a climate of hope. There can be no progress without hope, and there can be no hope if our organizations view conflict as a football game, a win-lose (or possibly tie) situation. While zero-sum situations are extremely rare, most leaders, (and followers) tend to respond to most conflicts as if there can be only one winner and only one loser. In reality, organizations and nations are involved in a much different kind of contest, resembling not so much football as the remarkable Swedish game, Vasa Run; in the latter many take part, some reaching the finish line earlier than others and being rewarded for it, but all get there in the end.

Lots of things go into producing a culture: the particular technology of the institution, its peculiar history and geography, the characteristics of its people, and its social architecture. The leader must understand these things. He must have the capacities of an amateur social anthropologist so that he can understand the culture within which he works and which he himself can have some part in creating and maintaining.

• *To lead others, the leader must first know himself.* His ultimate test is the wise use of power. As Sophocles says in *Antigone:* "But it is hard to learn the mind of any mortal, or the heart, till he be tried in chief authority. Power shows the man."

He must learn to listen to himself. He must integrate his ideals with his actions and, even when a crackling discrepancy exists, learn to tolerate ambiguity between the desirable and the necessary—not, however, with so much tolerance that the margins between them become undiscernible. When that happens, the leader can unwittingly substitute an evasion of convenience for an authentic ideal. Soon he'll forget about the goal—and even feel "comfortable" with an illusion of progress. He must learn how to listen to understand, not to evaluate. He must learn to play, to live with ambiguity and inconsistency. Most of all, the test of any leader is whether he can ride and direct the process of change and, in the process, build new strengths.

Finale

The virtues I have just discussed may strike the reader as majestically useless—like textbook moralities, unconscionably demanding—and, worse, far too abstract to help the leader execute the complex political decisions he confronts. Moreover, the concepts of leadership I have emphasized diverge somewhat from the conventional roles assigned to the leader. Leadership has appeared in an array of more familiar metaphoric guises: the leader as judge (he pronounces verdicts and metes out punishments and rewards), the leader as manager (he conducts the routine), the leader as negotiator (he facilitates agreement or compromise), the leader as communal delegate (he presides over a town meeting), the leader as ruler (he governs despotically or democratically).

None of these appears to be the right metaphoric embodiment for organizational leadership. "Politics" might do it, if we think of the term as the arrangement of human life, relationships, and organizations in comfortable and rational modes. The leader engaged in such politics will need all the skills—of vision, conceptualization, issue definition, social architecture, and more—necessary to clarify and arrange the conduct of organized human endeavor.

All formulations of leadership, including those I have set forth here, can be dangerously misleading. For the world changes and the particulars change, and the most serious reader should apply my counsel with great caution. More important than the right metaphor in the years ahead is the capacity to be open to the unprecedented, not to get ready for *some*thing, but for *any*thing. We must learn nothing more than the value of examining—of focusing attention on the conditions of life, the particular circumstances that emerge unexpectedly—and develop an alertness in adapting to them.

We inevitably impose the order or disorder that seems inherent in things, both natural and social. Once we find the right metaphor for articulating leadership, the right conceptual framework—and as long as we realize that the metaphor must be altered as the world is altered—then we may begin to lead.

Selected References

Douglas McGregor's *The Professional Manager* (McGraw-Hill, 1967) summarizes the views on a variety of subjects, including leadership, of Bennis's mentor. Robert Tannenbaum and Warren Schmidt's "How to Choose a

Leadership Pattern" (*Harvard Business Review,* March 1958, pp. 95–101) is a by now classic statement of the normative and pragmatic issues surrounding participation in decision making, while Victor Vroom and Philip Yetton's *Leadership and Decision Making* (University of Pittsburgh Press, 1973) is a full-length treatment of the same issue, participation in decision making from a similar perspective.

An article by Chris Argyris, "The CEO's Behavior: Key to Organizational Development" (*Harvard Business Review,* March–April 1973, pp. 54–64), suggests that most CEO's are autocratic leaders who tend to block or subvert most of what comes under the heading of organizational development. Anyone interested in a complete bibliography of the current literature on the subject should consult Ralph Stogdill's *Handbook of Leadership* (The Free Press, 1974).

A summary of the contrasting approaches to leadership held by three of the best-known authorities on the subject—Fred Fiedler, Victor Vroom, and Chris Argyris—appeared in "Leadership Symposium" (*Organizational Dynamics,* Winter 1976, pp. 2–43). Last, Bennis's own recent book, *The Unconscious Conspiracy: Why Leaders Can't Lead* (AMACOM, 1976), elaborates on many of the points mentioned in this article.

15

Managers and Leaders: Are They Different?

ABRAHAM ZALEZNIK

What is the ideal way to develop leadership? Every society provides its own answer to this question, and each, in groping for answers, defines its deepest concerns about the purposes, distributions, and uses of power. Business has contributed its answer to the leadership question by evolving a new breed called the manager. Simultaneously, business has established a new power ethic that favors collective over individual leadership, the cult of the group over that of personality. While ensuring the competence, control, and the balance of power relations among groups with the potential for rivalry, managerial leadership unfortunately does not necessarily ensure imagination, creativity, or ethical behavior in guiding the destinies of corporate enterprises.

Leadership inevitably requires using power to influence the thoughts and actions of other people. Power in the hands of an individual entails human risks: first, the risk of equating power with the ability to get immediate results; second, the risk of ignoring the many different ways people can legitimately accumulate power; and third, the risk of losing self-control in the desire for power. The need to hedge these risks accounts in part for the development of collective leadership and the managerial ethic. Consequently, an inherent conservatism dominates the culture of large organizations. In *The Second American Revolution,* John D. Rockefeller, III describes the conservatism of organizations:

> An organization is a system, with a logic of its own, and all the weight of tradition and inertia. The deck is stacked in favor of the tried and proven way of doing things and against the taking of risks and striking out in new directions.[1]

Out of this conservatism and inertia organizations provide succession to power through the development of managers rather than individual leaders. And the irony of the managerial ethic is that it fosters a bureaucratic culture in business, supposedly the last bastion protecting us from the encroachments and controls of bureaucracy in government and education. Perhaps the risks associated with power in the hands of an individual may be necessary ones for business to take if organizations are to break free of their inertia and bureaucratic conservatism.

Manager vs. Leader Personality

Theodore Levitt has described the essential features of a managerial culture with its emphasis on rationality and control:

Management consists of the rational assessment of a situation and the systematic selection of goals and purposes (what is to be done?); the systematic development of strategies to achieve these goals; the marshalling of the required resources; the rational design, organization, direction, and control of the activities required to attain the selected purposes; and, finally, the motivating and rewarding of people to do the work.[2]

In other words, whether his or her energies are directed toward goals, resources, organization structures, or people, a manager is a problem solver. The manager asks himself, "What problems have to be solved, and what are the best ways to achieve results so that people will continue to contribute to this organization?" In this conception, leadership is a practical effort to direct affairs; and to fulfill his task, a manager requires that many people operate at different levels of status and responsibility. Our democratic society is, in fact, unique in having solved the problem of providing well-trained managers for business. The same solution stands ready to be applied to government, education, health care, and other institutions. It takes neither genius nor heroism to be a manager, but rather persistence, tough-mindedness, hard work, intelligence, analytical ability and, perhaps most important, tolerance and good will.

Another conception, however, attaches almost mystical beliefs to what leadership is and assumes that only great people are worthy of the drama of power and politics. Here, leadership is a psychodrama in which, as a precondition for control of a political structure, a lonely person must gain control of him or herself. Such an expectation of leadership contrasts sharply with the mundane, practical, and yet important conception that leadership is really managing work that other people do.

Two questions come to mind. Is this mystique of leadership merely a holdover from our collective childhood of dependency and our longing for good and heroic parents? Or, is there a basic truth lurking behind the need for leaders that no matter how competent managers are, their leadership stagnates because of their limitations in visualizing purposes and generating value in work? Without this imaginative capacity and the ability to communicate, managers, driven by their narrow purposes, perpetuate group conflicts instead of reforming them into broader desires and goals.

If indeed problems demand greatness, then, judging by past performance, the selection and development of leaders leave a great deal to chance. There are no known ways to train "great" leaders. Furthermore, beyond what we leave to chance, there is a deeper issue in the relationship between the need for competent managers and the longing for great leaders.

What it takes to ensure the supply of people who will assume practical responsibility may inhibit the development of great leaders. Conversely, the presence of great leaders may undermine the development of managers who become very anxious in the relative disorder that leaders seem to generate. The antagonism in aim (to have many competent managers as well as great leaders) often remains obscure in stable and well-developed societies. But the antagonism surfaces during periods of stress and change, as it did in the Western countries during both the Great Depression and World War II. The tension also appears in the struggle for power between theorists and professional managers in revolutionary societies.

It is easy enough to dismiss the dilemma I pose (of training managers while we may need new leaders, or leaders at the expense of managers) by saying that the need is for people who can be *both* managers and leaders. The truth of the matter as I see it, however, is that just as a managerial culture is different from the entrepreneurial culture that develops when leaders appear in organizations, managers and leaders are very different kinds of people. They differ in motivation, personal history, and in how they think and act.

A technologically oriented and economically successful society tends to depreciate the need for great leaders. Such societies hold a deep and abiding faith in rational methods of solving problems, including problems of value, economics, and justice. Once rational methods of solving problems are broken down into elements, organized, and taught as skills, then society's faith in technique over personal qualities in leadership remains the guiding conception for a democratic society contemplating its leadership requirements. But there are times when tinkering and trial and error prove inadequate to the emerging problems of selecting goals, allocating resources, and distributing wealth and opportunity. During such times, the democratic society needs to find leaders who use themselves as the instruments of learning and acting, instead of managers who use their accumulation of collective experience to get where they are going.

The most impressive spokesman, as well as exemplar of the managerial viewpoint, was Alfred P. Sloan, Jr. who, along with Pierre du Pont, designed the modern corporate structure. Reflecting on what makes one management successful while another fails, Sloan suggested that "good management rests on a reconciliation of centralization and decentralization, or 'decentralization with coordinated control.' "[3]

Sloan's conception of management, as well as his practice, developed by trial and error, and by the accumulation of experience. Sloan wrote:

> There is no hard and fast rule for sorting out the various responsibilities and the best way to assign them. The balance which is struck ... varies according to what is being decided, the circumstances of the time, past experience, and the temperaments and skills of the executive involved.[4]

In other words, in much the same way that the inventors of the late nine-teenth century tried, failed, and fitted until they hit on a product or method, managers who innovate in developing organizations are "tinkerers." They do not have a grand design or experience the intuitive flash of insight that, bor-rowing from modern science, we have come to call the "breakthrough."

Managers and leaders differ fundamentally in their world views. The di-mensions for assessing these differences include managers' and leaders' orien-tations toward their goals, their work, their human relations, and their selves.

Attitudes toward Goals

Managers tend to adopt impersonal, if not passive, attitudes toward goals. Managerial goals arise out of necessities rather than desires, and there-fore, are deeply embedded in the history and culture of the organization.

Frederic G. Donner, chairman and chief executive officer of General Mo-tors from 1958 to 1967, expressed this impersonal and passive attitude toward goals in defining GM's position on product development:

> . . . To meet the challenge of the marketplace, we must recognize changes in customer needs and desires far enough ahead to have the right prod-ucts in the right places at the right time and in the right quantity.
>
> We must balance trends in preference against the many compromises that are necessary to make a final product that is both reliable and good looking, that performs well and that sells at a competitive price in the necessary volume. We must design, not just the cars we would like to build, but more importantly, the cars that our customers want to buy.[5]

Nowhere in this formulation of how a product comes into being is there a notion that consumer tastes and preferences arise in part as a result of what manufacturers do. In reality, through product design, advertising, and pro-motion, consumers learn to like what they then say they need. Few would ar-gue that people who enjoy taking snapshots *need* a camera that also develops pictures. But in response to novelty, convenience, a shorter interval between acting (taking the snap) and gaining pleasure (seeing the shot), the Polaroid camera succeeded in the marketplace. But it is inconceivable that Edwin Land responded to impressions of consumer need. Instead, he translated a technology (polarization of light) into a product, which proliferated and stim-ulated consumers' desires.

The example of Polaroid and Land suggests how leaders think about goals. They are active instead of reactive, shaping ideas instead of responding to them. Leaders adopt a personal and active attitude toward goals. The influ-ence a leader exerts in altering moods, evoking images and expectations, and in establishing specific desires and objectives determines the direction a busi-ness takes. The net result of this influence is to change the way people think about what is desirable, possible, and necessary.

Conceptions of Work

What do managers and leaders do? What is the nature of their respective work?

Leaders and managers differ in their conceptions. Managers tend to view work as an enabling process involving some combination of people and ideas interacting to establish strategies and make decisions. Managers help the process along by a range of skills, including calculating the interests in opposition, staging and timing the surfacing of controversial issues, and reducing tensions. In this enabling process, managers appear flexible in the use of tactics: they negotiate and bargain, on the one hand, and use rewards and punishments, and other forms of coercion, on the other. Machiavelli wrote for managers and not necessarily for leaders.

Alfred Sloan illustrated how this enabling process works in situations of conflict. The time was the early 1920s when the Ford Motor Co. still dominated the automobile industry using, as did General Motors, the conventional water-cooled engine. With the full backing of Pierre du Pont, Charles Kettering dedicated himself to the design of an air-cooled engine, which, if successful, would have been a great technical and market coup for GM. Kettering believed in his product, but the manufacturing division heads at GM remained skeptical and later opposed the new design on two grounds: first, that it was technically unreliable, and second, that the corporation was putting all its eggs in one basket by investing in a new product instead of attending to the current marketing situation.

In the summer of 1923 after a series of false starts and after its decision to recall the copper-cooled Chevrolets from dealers and customers, GM management reorganized and finally scrapped the project. When it dawned on Kettering that the company had rejected the engine, he was deeply discouraged and wrote to Sloan that without the "organized resistance" against the project it would succeed and that unless the project were saved, he would leave the company.

Alfred Sloan was all too aware of the fact that Kettering was unhappy and indeed intended to leave General Motors. Sloan was also aware of the fact that, while the manufacturing divisions strongly opposed the new engine, Pierre du Pont supported Kettering. Furthermore, Sloan had himself gone on record in a letter to Kettering less than two years earlier expressing full confidence in him. The problem Sloan now had was to make his decision stick, keep Kettering in the organization (he was much too valuable to lose), avoid alienating du Pont, and encourage the division heads to move speedily in developing product lines using conventional water-cooled engines.

The actions that Sloan took in the face of this conflict reveal much about how managers work. First, he tried to reassure Kettering by presenting the problem in a very ambiguous fashion, suggesting that he and the Executive Committee sided with Kettering, but that it would not be practical to force the divisions to do what they were opposed to. He presented the problem as being a question of the people, not the product. Second, he proposed to reorganize around the problem by consolidating all functions in a new division that would be responsible for the design, production, and marketing of the new car. This solution, however, appeared as ambiguous as his efforts to placate and keep Kettering in General Motors. Sloan wrote: "My plan was to create an independent pilot operation under the sole jurisdiction of Mr. Kettering, a kind of copper-cooled-car division. Mr. Kettering would designate his own chief engineer and his production staff to solve the technical problems of manufacture."[6]

While Sloan did not discuss the practical value of this solution, which included saddling an inventor with management responsibility, he in effect used this plan to limit his conflict with Pierre du Pont.

In effect, the managerial solution that Sloan arranged and pressed for adoption limited the options available to others. The structural solution narrowed choices, even limiting emotional reactions to the point where the key people could do nothing but go along, and even allowed Sloan to say in his memorandum to du Pont, "We have discussed the matter with Mr. Kettering at some length this morning and he agrees with us absolutely on every point we made. He appears to receive the suggestion enthusiastically and has every confidence that it can be put across along these lines."[7]

Having placated people who opposed his views by developing a structural solution that appeared to give something but in reality only limited options, Sloan could then authorize the car division's general manager, with whom he basically agreed, to move quickly in designing water-cooled cars for the immediate market demand.

Years later Sloan wrote, evidently with tongue in cheek, "The copper-cooled car never came up again in a big way. It just died out, I don't know why."[8]

In order to get people to accept solutions to problems, managers need to coordinate and balance continually. Interestingly enough, this managerial work has much in common with what diplomats and mediators do, with Henry Kissinger apparently an outstanding practitioner. The manager aims at shifting balances of power toward solutions acceptable as a compromise among conflicting values.

What about leaders, what do they do? Where managers act to limit choices, leaders work in the opposite direction, to develop fresh approaches to long-standing problems and to open issues for new options. Stanley and Inge Hoffmann, the political scientists, liken the leader's work to that of the artist. But unlike most artists, the leader himself is an integral part of the aesthetic product. One cannot look at a leader's art without looking at the artist. On Charles de Gaulle as a political artist, they wrote: "And each of his major political acts, however tortuous the means or the details, has been whole, indivisible and unmistakably his own, like an artistic act."[9]

The closest one can get to a product apart from the artist is the ideas that occupy, indeed at times obsess, the leader's mental life. To be effective, however, the leader needs to project his ideas into images that excite people, and only then develop choices that give the projected images substance. Consequently, leaders create excitement in work.

John F. Kennedy's brief presidency shows both the strengths and weaknesses connected with the excitement leaders generate in their work. In his inaugural address he said, "Let every nation know, whether it wishes us well or ill, that we shall pay any price, bear any burden, meet any hardship, support any friend, oppose any foe, in order to assure the survival and the success of liberty."

This much-quoted statement forced people to react beyond immediate concerns and to identify with Kennedy and with important shared ideals. But upon closer scrutiny the statement must be seen as absurd because it promises a position which if in fact adopted, as in the Viet Nam War, could produce disastrous results. Yet unless expectations are aroused and mobilized, with all the dangers of frustration inherent in heightened desire, new thinking and new choice can never come to light.

Leaders work from high-risk positions, indeed often are temperamentally disposed to seek out risk and danger, especially where opportunity and reward appear high. From my observations, why one individual seeks risks while another approaches problems conservatively depends more on his or her personality and less on conscious choice. For some, especially those who become managers, the instinct for survival dominates their need for risk, and their ability to tolerate mundane, practical work assists their survival. The same cannot be said for leaders who sometimes react to mundane work as to an affliction.

Relations with Others

Managers prefer to work with people; they avoid solitary activity because it makes them anxious. Several years ago, I directed studies on the psychological aspects of career. The need to seek out others with whom to work and collaborate seemed to stand out as important characteristics of managers. When asked, for example, to write imaginative stories in response to a picture showing a single figure (a boy contemplating a violin, or a man silhouetted in a state of reflection), managers populated their stories with people. The following is an example of a manager's imaginative story about the young boy contemplating a violin:

> Mom and Dad insisted that junior take music lessons so that someday he can become a concert musician. His instrument was ordered and had just arrived. Junior is weighing the alternatives of playing football with the other kids or playing with the squeak box. He can't understand how his parents could think a violin is better than a touchdown.
>
> After four months of practicing the violin, junior has had more than enough, Daddy is going out of his mind, and Mommy is willing to give in reluctantly to the men's wishes. Football season is now over, but a good third baseman will take the field next spring.[10]

This story illustrates two themes that clarify managerial attitudes toward human relations. The first, as I have suggested, is to seek out activity with other people (i.e. the football team), and the second is to maintain a low level of emotional involvement in these relationships. The low emotional involvement appears in the writer's use of conventional metaphors, even clichés, and in the depiction of the ready transformation of potential conflict into harmonious decisions. In this case, Junior, Mommy, and Daddy agree to give up the violin for manly sports.

These two themes may seem paradoxical, but their coexistence supports what a manager does, including reconciling differences, seeking compromises, and establishing a balance of power. A further idea demonstrated by how the manager wrote the story is that managers may lack empathy, or the capacity to sense intuitively the thoughts and feelings of others. To illustrate attempts to be empathic, here is another story written to the same stimulus picture by someone considered by his peers to be a leader:

> This little boy has the appearance of being a sincere artist, one who is deeply affected by the violin, and has an intense desire to master the instrument.
>
> He seems to have just completed his normal practice session and appears to be somewhat crestfallen at his inability to produce the sounds which he is sure lie within the violin.
>
> He appears to be in the process of making a vow to himself to expend the necessary time and effort to play this instrument until he satisfies himself that he is able to bring forth the qualities of music which he feels within himself.
>
> With this type of determination and carry through, this boy became one of the great violinists of his day.[11]

Empathy is not simply a matter of paying attention to other people. It is also the capacity to take in emotional signals and to make them mean something in a relationship with an individual. People who describe another person as "deeply affected" with "intense desire," as capable of feeling "crestfallen" and as one who can "vow to himself," would seem to have an inner perceptiveness that they can use in their relationships with others.

Managers relate to people according to the role they play in a sequence of events or in a decision-making *process,* while leaders, who are concerned with ideas, relate in more intuitive and empathetic ways. The manager's orientation to people, as actors in a sequence of events, deflects his or her attention away from the substance of people's concerns and toward their roles in a process. The distinction is simply between a manager's attention to *how* things get done and a leader's to *what* the events and decisions mean to participants.

In recent years, managers have taken over from game theory the notion that decision-making events can be one of two types: the win-lose situation (or zero-sum game) or the win-win situation in which everybody in the action comes out ahead. As part of the process of reconciling differences among people and maintaining balances of power, managers strive to convert win-lose into win-win situations.

As an illustration, take the decision of how to allocate capital resources among operating divisions in a large, decentralized organization. On the face of it, the dollars available for distribution are limited at any given time. Presumably, therefore, the more one division gets, the less is available for other divisions.

Managers tend to view this situation (as it affects human relations) as a conversion issue: how to make what seems like a win-lose problem into a win-win problem. Several solutions to this situation come to mind. First, the manager focuses others' attention on procedure and not on substance. Here the actors become engrossed in the bigger problem of *how* to make decisions, not *what* decisions to make. Once committed to the bigger problem, the actors have to support the outcome since they were involved in formulating decision rules. Because the actors believe in the rules they formulated, they will accept present losses in the expectation that next time they will win.

Second, the manager communicates to his subordinates indirectly, using "signals" instead of "messages." A signal has a number of possible implicit positions in it while a message clearly states a position. Signals are inconclusive and subject to reinterpretation should people become upset and angry, while messages involve the direct consequence that some people will indeed not like what they hear. The nature of messages heightens emotional response, and, as I have indicated, emotionally makes managers anxious. With signals, the question of who wins and who loses often becomes obscured.

Third, the manager plays for time. Managers seem to recognize that with the passage of time and the delay of major decisions, compromises emerge that take the sting out of win-lose situations; and the original "game" will be superseded by additional ones. Therefore, compromises may mean that one wins and loses simultaneously, depending on which of the games one evaluates.

There are undoubtedly many other tactical moves managers use to change human situations from win-lose to win-win. But the point to be made is that such tactics focus on the decision-making process itself and interest managers rather than leaders. The interest in tactics involves costs as well as benefits, including making organizations fatter in bureaucratic and political intrigue and leaner in direct, hard activity and warm human relationships. Consequently, one often hears subordinates characterize managers as inscrutable, detached, and manipulative. These adjectives arise from the subordinates' perception that they are linked together in a process whose purpose, beyond simply making decisions, is to maintain a controlled as well as rational and equitable structure. These adjectives suggest that managers need order in the face of the potential chaos that many fear in human relationships.

In contrast, one often hears leaders referred to in adjectives rich in emotional content. Leaders attract strong feelings of identity and difference, or of love and hate. Human relations in leader-dominated structures often appear turbulent, intense, and at times even disorganized. Such an atmosphere intensifies individual motivation and often produces unanticipated outcomes. Does this intense motivation lead to innovation and high performance, or does it represent wasted energy?

Senses of Self

In *The Varieties of Religious Experience,* William James describes two basic personality types, "once-born" and "twice-born."[12] People of the former

personality type are those for whom adjustments to life have been straightforward and whose lives have been more or less a peaceful flow from the moment of their births. The twice-borns, on the other hand, have not had an
easy time of it. Their lives are marked by a continual struggle to attain some
sense of order. Unlike the once-borns they cannot take things for granted. According to James, these personalities have equally different world views. For
a once-born personality, the sense of self, as a guide to conduct and attitude,
derives from a feeling of being at home and in harmony with one's environment. For a twice-born, the sense of self derives from a feeling of profound
separateness.

A sense of belonging or of being separate has a practical significance for
the kinds of investments managers and leaders make in their careers. Managers see themselves as conservators and regulators of an existing order of affairs with which they personally identify and from which they gain rewards.
Perpetuating and strengthening existing institutions enhances a manager's
sense of self-worth: he or she is performing in a role that harmonizes with the
ideals of duty and responsibility. William James had this harmony in mind—
this sense of self as flowing easily to and from the outer world—in defining a
once-born personality. If one feels oneself as a member of institutions, contributing to their well-being, then one fulfills a mission in life and feels rewarded for having measured up to ideals. This reward transcends material
gains and answers the more fundamental desire for personal integrity which
is achieved by identifying with existing institutions.

Leaders tend to be twice-born personalities, people who feel separate
from their environment, including other people. They may work in organizations, but they never belong to them. Their sense of who they are does not depend upon memberships, work roles, or other social indicators of identity.
What seems to follow from this idea about separateness is some theoretical
basis for explaining why certain individuals search out opportunities for
change. The methods to bring about change may be technological, political,
or ideological, but the object is the same: to profoundly alter human, economic, and political relationships.

Sociologists refer to the preparation individuals undergo to perform in
roles as the socialization process. Where individuals experience themselves as
an integral part of the social structure (their self-esteem gains strength
through participation and conformity), social standards exert powerful effects
in maintaining the individual's personal sense of continuity, even beyond the
early years in the family. The line of development from the family to schools,
then to career is cumulative and reinforcing. When the line of development is
not reinforcing because of significant disruptions in relationships or other
problems experienced in the family or other social institutions, the individual
turns inward and struggles to establish self-esteem, identity, and order. Here
the psychological dynamics center on the experience with loss and the efforts
at recovery.

In considering the development of leadership, we have to examine two
different courses of life history: (1) development through socialization, which
prepares the individual to guide institutions and to maintain the existing bal-

ance of social relations; and (2) development through personal mastery, which impels an individual to struggle for psychological and social change. Society produces its managerial talent through the first line of development, while through the second leaders emerge.

Development of Leadership

The development of every person begins in the family. Each person experiences the traumas associated with separating from his or her parents, as well as the pain that follows such frustration. In the same vein, all individuals face the difficulties of achieving self-regulation and self-control. But for some, perhaps a majority, the fortunes of childhood provide adequate gratifications and sufficient opportunities to find substitutes for rewards no longer available. Such individuals, the "once-borns," make moderate identifications with parents and find a harmony between what they expect and what they are able to realize from life.

But suppose the pains of separation are amplified by a combination of parental demands and the individual's needs to the degree that a sense of isolation, of being special, and of wariness disrupts the bonds that attach children to parents and other authority figures? Under such conditions, and given a special aptitude, the origins of which remain mysterious, the person becomes deeply involved in his or her inner world at the expense of interest in the outer world. For such a person, self-esteem no longer depends solely upon positive attachments and real rewards. A form a self-reliance takes hold along with expectations of performance and achievement, and perhaps even the desire to do great works.

Such self-perceptions can come to nothing if the individual's talents are negligible. Even with strong talents, there are no guarantees that achievement will follow, let alone that the end result will be for good rather than evil. Other factors enter into development. For one thing, leaders are like artists and other gifted people who often struggle with neuroses; their ability to function varies considerably even over the short run, and some potential leaders may lose the struggle altogether. Also, beyond early childhood, the patterns of development that affect managers and leaders involve the selective influence of particular people. Just as they appear flexible and evenly distributed in the types of talents available for development, managers form moderate and widely distributed attachments. Leaders, on the other hand, establish, and also break off, intensive one-to-one relationships.

It is a common observation that people with great talents are often only indifferent students. No one, for example, could have predicted Einstein's great achievements on the basis of his mediocre record in school. The reason for mediocrity is obviously not the absence of ability. It may result, instead, from self-absorption and the inability to pay attention to the ordinary tasks at hand. The only sure way an individual can interrupt reverie-like preoccupation and self-absorption is to form a deep attachment to a great teacher or other benevolent person who understands and has the ability to communicate with the gifted individual.

Whether gifted individuals find what they need in one-to-one relationships depends on the availability of sensitive and intuitive mentors who have a vocation in cultivating talent. Fortunately, when the generations do meet and the self-selections occur, we learn more about how to develop leaders and how talented people of different generations influence each other.

While apparently destined for a mediocre career, people who form important one-to-one relationships are able to accelerate and intensify their development through an apprenticeship. The background for such apprenticeships, or the psychological readiness of an individual to benefit from an intensive relationship, depends upon some experience in life that forces the individual to turn inward. A case example will make this point clearer. This example comes from the life of Dwight David Eisenhower, and illustrates the transformation of a career from competent to outstanding.[13]

Dwight Eisenhower's early career in the Army foreshadowed very little about his future development. During World War I, while some of his West Point classmates were already experiencing the war first-hand in France, Eisenhower felt "embedded in the monotony and unsought safety of the Zone of the Interior . . . that was intolerable punishment."[14]

Shortly after World War I, Eisenhower, then a young officer somewhat pessimistic about his career chances, asked for a transfer to Panama to work under General Fox Connor, a senior officer whom Eisenhower admired. The army turned down Eisenhower's request. This setback was very much on Eisenhower's mind when Ikey, his first-born son, succumbed to influenza. By some sense of responsibility for its own, the army transferred Eisenhower to Panama, where he took up his duties under General Connor with the shadow of his lost son very much upon him.

In a relationship with the kind of father he would have wanted to be, Eisenhower reverted to being the son he lost. In this highly charged situation, Eisenhower began to learn from his mentor. General Connor offered, and Eisenhower gladly took, a magnificent tutorial on the military. The effects of this relationship on Eisenhower cannot be measured quantitatively, but, in Eisenhower's own reflections and the unfolding of his career, one cannot overestimate its significance in the reintegration of a person shattered by grief.

As Eisenhower wrote later about Connor, "Life with General Connor was a sort of graduate school in military affairs and the humanities, leavened by a man who was experienced in his knowledge of men and their conduct. I can never adequately express my gratitude to this one gentleman. . . . In a lifetime of association with great and good men, he is the one more or less invisible figure to whom I owe an incalculable debt."[15]

Some time after his tour of duty with General Connor, Eisenhower's breakthrough occurred. He received orders to attend the Command and General Staff School at Fort Leavenworth, one of the most competitive schools in the army. It was a coveted appointment, and Eisenhower took advantage of the opportunity. Unlike his performance in high school and West Point, his work at the Command School was excellent; he was graduated first in his class.

Psychological biographies of gifted people repeatedly demonstrate the important part a mentor plays in developing an individual. Andrew Carnegie owed much to his senior, Thomas A. Scott. As head of the Western Division of the Pennsylvania Railroad, Scott recognized talent and the desire to learn in the young telegrapher assigned to him. By giving Carnegie increasing responsibility and by providing him with the opportunity to learn through close personal observation, Scott added to Carnegie's self-confidence and sense of achievement. Because of his own personal strength and achievement, Scott did not fear Carnegie's aggressiveness. Rather, he gave it full play in encouraging Carnegie's initiative.

Mentors take risks with people. They bet initially on talent they perceive in younger people. Mentors also risk emotional involvement in working closely with their juniors. The risks do not always pay off, but the willingness to take them appears crucial in developing leaders.

Can Organizations Develop Leaders?

The examples I have given of how leaders develop suggest the importance of personal influence and the one-to-one relationship. For organizations to encourage consciously the development of leaders as compared with managers would mean developing one-to-one relationships between junior and senior executives and, more important, fostering a culture of individualism and possibly elitism. The elitism arises out of the desire to identify talent and other qualities suggestive of the ability to lead and not simply to manage.

The Jewel Companies Inc. enjoy a reputation for developing talented people. The chairman and chief executive officer, Donald S. Perkins, is perhaps a good example of a person brought along through the mentor approach. Franklin J. Lunding, who was Perkins's mentor, expressed the philosophy of taking risks with young people this way:

> Young people today want in on the action. They don't want to sit around for six months trimming lettuce.[16]

This statement runs counter to the culture that attaches primary importance to slow progression based on experience and proved competence. It is a high-risk philosophy, one that requires time for the attachment between senior and junior people to grow and be meaningful, and one that is bound to produce more failures than successes.

The elitism is an especially sensitive issue. At Jewel the MBA degree symbolized the elite. Lunding attracted Perkins to Jewel at a time when business school graduates had little interest in retailing in general, and food distribution in particular. Yet the elitism seemed to pay off: not only did Perkins become the president at age 37, but also under the leadership of young executives recruited into Jewel with the promise of opportunity for growth and advancement, Jewel managed to diversify into discount and drug chains and still remain strong in food retailing. By assigning each recruit to a vice president who acted as sponsor, Jewel evidently tried to build a structure around the mentor approach to developing leaders. To counteract the elitism implied in such an approach, the company also introduced an "equalizer" in what Perkins described as "the first assistant philosophy." Perkins stated:

> Being a good first assistant means that each management person thinks of himself not as the order-giving, domineering boss, but as the first assistant to those who 'report' to him in a more typical organizational sense. Thus we mentally turn our organizational charts upside-down and challenge ourselves to seek ways in which we can lead . . . by helping . . . by teaching . . . by listening . . . and by managing in the true democratic sense . . . that is, with the consent of the managed. Thus the satisfactions of leadership come from helping others to get things done and changed—and not from getting credit for doing and changing things ourselves.[17]

While this statement would seem to be more egalitarian than elitist, it does reinforce a youth-oriented culture since it defines the senior officer's job as primarily helping the junior person.

A myth about how people learn and develop that seems to have taken hold in the American culture also dominates thinking in business. The myth is that people learn best from their peers. Supposedly, the threat of evaluation and even humiliation recedes in peer relations because of the tendency for mutual identification and the social restraints on authoritarian behavior among equals. Peer training in organizations occurs in various forms. The use, for example, of task forces made up of peers from several interested occupational groups (sales, production, research, and finance) supposedly removes the restraints of authority on the individual's willingness to assert and exchange ideas. As a result, so the theory goes, people interact more freely, listen more objectively to criticism and other points of view and, finally, learn from this healthy interchange.

Another application of peer training exists in some large corporations, such as Philips, N.V. in Holland, where organization structure is built on the principle of joint responsibility of two peers, one representing the commercial end of the business and the other the technical. Formally, both hold equal responsibility for geographic operations or product groups, as the case may be. As a practical matter, it may turn out that one or the other of the peers dominates the management. Nevertheless, the main interaction is between two or more equals.

The principal question I would raise about such arrangements is whether they perpetuate the managerial orientation, and preclude the formation of one-to-one relationships between senior people and potential leaders.

Aware of the possible stifling effects of peer relationships on aggressiveness and individual initiative, another company, much smaller than Philips, utilizes joint responsibility of peers for operating units, with one important difference. The chief executive of this company encourages competition and rivalry among peers, ultimately appointing the one who comes out on top for increased responsibility. These hybrid arrangements produce some unintended consequences that can be disastrous. There is no easy way to limit rivalry. Instead, it permeates all levels of the operation and opens the way for the formation of cliques in an atmosphere of intrigue.

A large, integrated oil company has accepted the importance of developing leaders through the direct influence of senior on junior executives. One chairman and chief executive officer regularly selected one talented university graduate whom he appointed his special assistant, and with whom he would work closely for a year. At the end of the year, the junior executive would become available for assignment to one of the operating divisions, where he would be assigned to a responsible post rather than a training position. The mentor relationship had acquainted the junior executive firsthand with the use of power, and with the important antidotes to the power disease called *hubris*—performance and integrity.

Working in one-to-one relationships, where there is a formal and recognized difference in the power of the actors, takes a great deal of tolerance for emotional interchange. This interchange, inevitable in close working arrangements, probably accounts for the reluctance of many executives to become involved in such relationships. *Fortune* carried an interesting story on the departure of a key executive, John W. Hanley, from the top management of Procter & Gamble, for the chief executive officer position at Monsanto.[18] According to this account, the chief executive and chairman of P&G passed over Hanley for appointment to the presidency and named another executive vice president to this post instead.

The chairman evidently felt he could not work well with Hanley who, by his own acknowledgement, was aggressive, eager to experiment and change practices, and constantly challenged his superior. A chief executive officer naturally has the right to select people with whom he feels congenial. But I wonder whether a greater capacity on the part of senior officers to tolerate the competitive impulses and behavior of their subordinates might not be healthy for corporations. At least a greater tolerance for interchange would not favor the managerial team player at the expense of the individual who might become a leader.

I am constantly surprised at the frequency with which chief executives feel threatened by open challenges to their ideas, as though the source of their authority, rather than their specific ideas, were at issue. In one case a chief executive officer, who was troubled by the aggressiveness and sometimes outright rudeness of one of his talented vice presidents, used various indirect methods such as group meetings and hints from outside directors to avoid dealing with his subordinate. I advised the executive to deal head-on with what irritated him. I suggested that by direct, face-to-face confrontation, both he and his subordinate would learn to validate the distinction between the authority to be preserved and the issues to be debated.

To confront is also to tolerate aggressive interchange, and has the net effect of stripping away the veils of ambiguity and signaling so characteristic of managerial cultures, as well as encouraging the emotional relationship leaders need if they are to survive.

Notes

1 John D. Rockefeller, III, *The Second American Revolution* (New York: Harper-Row, 1973), p. 72.

2 Theodore Levitt, "Management and the Post Industrial Society," *The Public Interest* (Summer 1976): 73.

3 Alfred P. Sloan, Jr., *My Years with General Motors* (New York: Doubleday & Co. 1964), p. 429.

4 Ibid., p. 429.

5 Ibid. p. 440.

7 Ibid. p. 91.

8 Ibid. p. 93.

9 Stanley and Inge Hoffmann, "The Will for Grandeur: de Gaulle as Political Artist," *Daedalus* (Summer 1968): 849.

10 Abraham Zaleznik, Gene W. Dalton, and Louis B. Barnes, *Orientation and Conflict in Career* (Boston: Division of Research, Harvard Business School, 1970), p. 316.

11 Ibid. p. 294.

12 William James, *Varieties of Religious Experience* (New York: Mentor Books, 1958).

13 This example is included in Abraham Zaleznik and Manfred F. R. Kets de Vries, *Power and the Corporate Mind* (Boston: Houghton Mifflin, 1975).

14 Dwight D. Eisenhower, *At Ease: Stories I Tell to Friends* (New York: Doubleday, 1967).

15 Ibid. p. 187.

16 "Jewel Lets Young Men Make Mistakes," *Business Week* (January 17, 1970): 90.

17 "What Makes Jewel Shine so Bright," *Progressive Grocer* (September, 1973): 76.

18 "Jack Hanley Got There by Selling Harder," *Fortune* (November, 1976).

16

Style or Circumstance: The Leadership Enigma

FRED E. FIEDLER*

What is it that makes a person an effective leader?

We take it for granted that good leadership is essential to business, to government and to all the myriad groups and organizations that shape the way we live, work and play.

We spend at least several billions of dollars a year on leadership development and executive recruitment in the United States. Leaders are paid 10, 20 and 30 times the salary of ordinary workers. Thousands of books and articles on leadership have been published. Yet, we still know relatively little about the factors that determine a leader's success or failure.

Psychologists have been concerned with two major questions in their research on leadership: How does a man become a leader? What kind of personality traits or behavior makes a person an *effective* leader? For the past 15 years, my own work at the University of Illinois Group-Effectiveness Research Laboratory has concentrated on the latter question.

Psychologists used to think that special personality traits would distinguish leaders from followers. Several hundred research studies have been conducted to identify these special traits. But the search has been futile.

People who become leaders tend to be somewhat more intelligent, bigger, more assertive, more talkative than other members of their group. But these traits are far less important than most people think. What most frequently distinguishes the leader from his co-workers is that he knows more about the group task or that he can do it better. A bowling team is likely to choose its

*Reprinted from *Psychology Today* magazine, Copyright © 1969, Ziff-Davis Publishing Company.

captain from good rather than poor bowlers, and the foreman of a machine shop is more likely to be a good machinist than a poor one.

In many organizations, one only has to live long in order to gain experience and seniority, and with these a position of leadership.

In business and industry today, the men who attain a leadership position must have the requisite education and talent. Of course, as W. Lloyd Warner and James C. Abegglen of the University of Chicago have shown, it has been most useful to come from or marry into a family that owns a large slice of the company's stock.

Becoming a leader, then, depends on personality only to a limited extent. A person can become a leader by happenstance, simply by being in the right place at the right time, or because of such various factors as age, education, experience, family background and wealth.

Almost any person in a group may be capable of rising to a leadership position if he is rewarded for actively participating in the group discussion, as Alex Bavelas and his colleagues at Stanford University have demonstrated. They used light signals to reward low-status group members for supposedly "doing the right thing." However, unknown to the people being encouraged, the light signal was turned on and off at random. Rewarded in this unspecified, undefined manner, the low-status member came to regard himself as a leader and the rest of the group accepted him in his new position.

It is commonly observed that personality and circumstances interact to determine whether a person will become a leader. While this statement is undoubtedly true, its usefulness is rather limited unless one also can specify how a personality trait will interact with a specific situation. We are as yet unable to make such predictions.

Having become a leader, how does one get to be an effective leader? Given a dozen or more similar groups and tasks, what makes one leader succeed and another fail? The answer to this question is likely to determine the philosophy of leader-training programs and the way in which men are selected for executive positions.

There are a limited number of ways in which one person can influence others to work together toward a common goal. He can coerce them or he can coax them. He can tell people what to do and how to do it, or he can share the decision-making and concentrate on his relationship with his men rather than on the execution of the job.

Of course, these two types of leadership behavior are gross oversimplifications. Most research by psychologists on leadership has focused on two clusters of behavior and attitudes, one labeled autocratic, authoritarian and task-oriented, and the other as democratic, equalitarian, and group-oriented.

The first type of leadership behavior, frequently advocated in conventional supervisory and military systems, has its philosophical roots in Frank W. Taylor's *Principles of Scientific Management* and other early 20th Century industrial engineering studies. The authoritarian, task-oriented leader takes all responsibility for making decisions and directing the group members. His rationale is simple: "I do the thinking and you carry out the orders."

The second type of leadership is typical of the "New Look" method of management advocated by men like Douglas McGregor of M.I.T. and Rensis

Likert of the University of Michigan. The democratic, group-oriented leader provides general rather than close supervision and his concern is the effective use of human resources through participation. In the late 1940s, a related method of leadership training was developed based on confrontation in unstructured group situations where each participant can explore his own motivations and reactions. Some excellent studies on this method, called T-group, sensitivity or laboratory training, have been made by Chris Argyris of Yale, Warren Bennis of State University of New York at Buffalo and Edgar Schein of M.I.T.

Experiments comparing the performance of both types of leaders have shown that each is successful in some situations and not in others. No one has been able to show that one kind of leader is always superior or more effective.

A number of researchers point out that different tasks require different kinds of leadership. But what kind of situation requires what kind of leader? To answer this question, I shall present a theory of leadership effectiveness that spells out the specific circumstances under which various leadership styles are most effective.

We must first of all distinguish between leadership style and leader behavior. Leader behavior refers to the specific acts in which a leader engages while directing or coordinating the work of his group. For example, the leader can praise or criticize, make helpful suggestions, show consideration for the welfare and feelings of members of his group.

Leadership style refers to the underlying needs of the leader that motivate his behavior. In other words, in addition to performing the task, what personal needs is the leader attempting to satisfy? We have found that a leader's actions or behavior sometimes does change as the situation or group changes, but his basic needs appear to remain constant.

To classify leadership styles, my colleagues and I have developed a simple questionnaire that asks the leader to describe the person with whom he can work least well:

LPC—Least-Preferred Co-worker

Think of the person with whom you can work least well. He may be someone you work with now, or he may be someone you knew in the past. Use an X to describe this person as he appears to you.

helpful	:___:___:___:___:___:___:___:___:	frustrating
	8 7 6 5 4 3 2 1	
unenthusiastic	:___:___:___:___:___:___:___:___:	enthusiastic
	1 2 3 4 5 6 7 8	
efficient	:___:___:___:___:___:___:___:___:	inefficient
	8 7 6 5 4 3 2 1	

From the replies, a Least-Preferred-Co-worker (LPC) score is obtained by simply summing the item scores. The LPC score does not measure perceptual accuracy, but rather reveals a person's emotional reaction to the people with whom he cannot work well.

In general, the high-scoring leader describes his least-preferred co-worker in favorable terms. The high-LPC leader tends to be "relationship-oriented." He gets his major satisfaction from establishing close personal relations with his group members. He uses the group task to gain the position of prominence he seeks.

The leader with a low score describes his least-preferred co-worker in unfavorable terms. The low-LPC leader is primarily "task-oriented." He obtains his major satisfaction by successfully completing the task, even at the risk of poor interpersonal relations with his workers.

Since a leader cannot function without a group, we must also know something about the group that the leader directs. There are many types of groups, for example, social groups which promote the enjoyment of individuals and "counteracting" groups such as labor and management at the negotiating table. But here we shall concentrate on groups that exist for the purpose of performing a task.

From our research, my associates and I have identified three major factors that can be used to classify group situations: (1) position power of the leader, (2) task structure, and (3) leader-member personal relationships. Basically, these classifications measure the kind of power and influence the group gives its leader.

We ranked group situations according to their favorableness for the leader. Favorableness here is defined as the degree to which the situation enables the leader to exert influence over the group.

Based on several studies, leader-member relations emerged as the most important factor in determining the leader's influence over the group. Task structure is rated as second in importance, and position power as third. (See Fig. 16-1.)

Under most circumstances, the leader who is liked by his group and has a clear-cut task and high position power obviously has everything in his favor. The leader who has poor relationships with his group members, an unstructured task and weak position power likely will be unable to exert much influence over the group.

The personal relationships that the leader establishes with his group members depend at least in part upon the leader's personality. The leader who is loved, admired and trusted can influence the group regardless of his position power. The leader who is not liked or trusted cannot influence the group except through his vested authority. It should be noted that a leader's assessment of how much he is liked often differs markedly from the group's evaluation.

Task structure refers to the degree the group's assignment can be programmed and specified in a step-by-step fashion. A highly structured task does not need a leader with much position power because the leader's role is detailed by the job specifications. With a highly structured task, the leader clearly knows what to do and how to do it, and the organization can back him up at each step. Unstructured tasks tend to have more than one correct solution that may be reached by any of a variety of methods. Since there is no step-by-step method that can be programmed in advance, the leader cannot influence the group's success by ordering them to vote "right" or be creative. Tasks of committees, creative groups and policy-making groups are typically unstructured.

Position power is the authority vested in the leader's position. It can be readily measured in most situations. An army general obviously has more power than a lieutenant, just as a department head has more power than an office manager. But our concern here is the effect this position power has on group performance. Although one would think that a leader with great power will get better performance from his group, our studies do not bear out this assumption.

However, it must be emphasized that in some situations position power may supersede task structure (the military). Or a very highly structured task (launching a moon probe) may outweigh the effects of interpersonal relations. The organization determines both the task structure and the position power of the leader.

In our search for the most effective leadership style, we went back to the studies that we had been conducting for more than a decade. These studies investigated a wide variety of groups and leadership situations, including basketball teams, business management, military units, boards of directors, creative groups and scientists engaged in pure research. In all of these studies, we could determine the groups that had performed their tasks successfully or unsuccessfully and then correlated the effectiveness of group performance with leadership style.

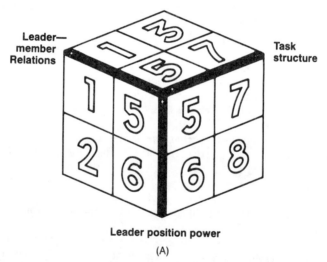

Leader position power

(A)

Fig. 16-1 (a) Group situation model—task-oriented groups are classified in a three-dimensional model using the three major factors affecting group performance; and (b) the effective leader—directive leaders perform best in very favorable or in unfavorable situations. Permissive leaders are best in mixed situations (graph is based on studies of over 800 groups).

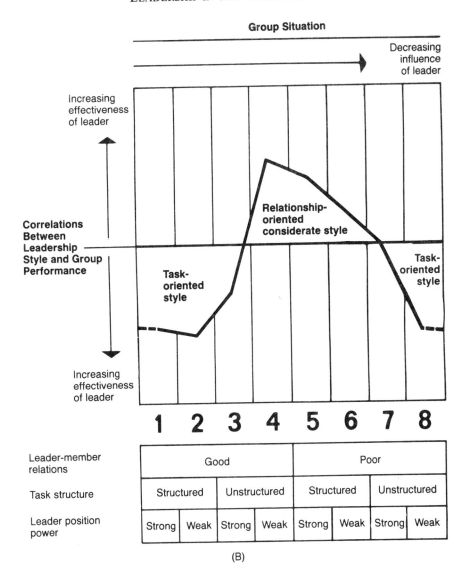

Group Situation

Decreasing influence of leader

Increasing effectiveness of leader

Correlations Between Leadership Style and Group Performance

Relationship-oriented considerate style

Task-oriented style

Task-oriented style

Increasing effectiveness of leader

	1	2	3	4	5	6	7	8
Leader-member relations	Good				Poor			
Task structure	Structured		Unstructured		Structured		Unstructured	
Leader position power	Strong	Weak	Strong	Weak	Strong	Weak	Strong	Weak

(B)

Now by plotting these correlations of leadership style against our scale of group situations, we could, for the first time, find what leadership style works best in each situation. When we connected the median points on each column, the result was a bell-shaped curve [Fig. 16-1(b)].

The results show that a task-oriented leader performs best in situations at both extremes—those in which he has a great deal of influence and power, and also in situations where he has no influence and power over the group members.

Relationship-oriented leaders tend to perform best in mixed situations where they have only moderate influence over the group. A number of subsequent studies by us and others have confirmed these findings.

The results show that we cannot talk about simply good leaders or poor leaders. A leader who is effective in one situation may or may not be effective in another. Therefore, we must specify the situations in which a leader performs well or badly.

This theory of leadership effectiveness by and large fits our everyday experience. Group situations in which the leader is liked, where he has a clearly defined task and a powerful position, may make attempts at nondirective, democratic leadership detrimental or superfluous. For example, the captain of an airliner can hardly call a committee meeting of the crew to share in the decision-making during a difficult landing approach. On the other hand, the chairman of a voluntary committee cannot ask with impunity that the group members vote or act according to his instructions.

Our studies also have shown that factors such as group-member abilities, cultural heterogeneity and stressfulness of the task affect the degree to which the leader can influence members of the group. But the important finding and the consistent finding in these studies has been that mixed situations require relationship-oriented leadership while very favorable and very unfavorable job situations require task-oriented leaders.

Perhaps the most important implication of this theory of leadership is that the organization for which the leader works is as responsible for his success or failure as is the leader himself.

The chances are that *anyone* who wants to become a leader can become one if he carefully chooses the situations that are favorable to his leadership style.

The notion that man is a "born" leader, capable of leading in all circumstances, appears to be nothing more than a myth. If there are leaders who excel under all conditions, I have not found them in my 18 years of research.

When we think of improving leadership performance, we tend to think first of training the leader. Personnel psychologists and managers typically view the executive's position as fixed and unchangeable and the applicant as highly plastic and trainable. A man's basic style of leadership depends upon his personality. Changing a man's leadership style means trying to change his personality. As we know from experiences in psychotherapy, it may take from one to several years to effect lasting changes in a personality structure. A leader's personality is not likely to change because of a few lectures or even a few weeks of intensive training.

It is doubtful that intensive training techniques can change an individual's style of leadership. However, training programs could be designed to provide the opportunity for a leader to learn in which situations he can perform well and in which he is likely to fail. Laboratory training also may provide the leader with some insights into his personal relationships with group members.

Our theory of leadership effectiveness predicts that a leader's performance can be improved by engineering or fitting the job to the leader. This is based, at least in part, on the belief that it is almost always easier to change a leader's work environment than to change his personality. The leader's authority, his task and even his interpersonal relations with his group members can be altered, sometimes without making the leader aware that this has been done.

For example, we can change the leader's position power in either direction. He can be given a higher rank if this seems necessary. Or he can be given subordinates who are equal or nearly equal to him in rank. His assistants can be two or three ranks below him, or we can assign him men who are expert in their specialties. The leader can have sole authority for a job, or he may be required to consult with his group. All communications to group members may be channeled through the leader, making him the source of all the inside information, or all members of the group can be given the information directly, thus reducing the leader's influence.

The task structure also can be changed to suit the leader's style. Depending upon the group situation, we can give the leader explicit instructions or we can deliberately give him a vague and nebulous goal.

Finally, we can change the leader-member relations. In some situations it may be desirable to improve leader-member relations by making the group homogeneous in culture and language or in technical and educational background. Interdisciplinary groups are notoriously difficult to handle, and it is even more difficult to lead a group that is racially or culturally mixed. Likewise, we can affect leader-member relations by giving a leader subordinates who get along well with their supervisor or assign a leader to a group with a history of trouble or conflict.

It may seem that often we are proposing the sabotaging of the leader's influence over his group. Although common sense might make it seem that weakening the leader's influence will lower performance, in actuality our studies show that this rarely happens. The average group performance (in other words, the leader's effectiveness) correlates poorly with the degree of the leader's influence over the group.

In fact, the findings from several studies suggest that a particular leader's effectiveness may be improved even though the situation is made less favorable for him.

The leader himself can be taught to recognize the situations that best fit his style. A man who is able to avoid situations in which he is likely to fail, and seek out situations that fit his leadership style, will probably become a highly successful and effective leader. Also, if he is aware of his strengths and weaknesses, the leader can try to change his group situation to match his leadership style.

However, we must remember that good leadership performance depends as much upon the organization as it does upon the leader. This means that we must learn not only how to train men to be leaders, but how to build organizations in which specific types of leaders can perform well.

In view of the increasing scarcity of competent executives, it is to an organization's advantage to design jobs to fit leaders instead of attempting merely to fit a leader to the job.

17

An Overview of the Grid ®

ROBERT R. BLAKE *and* JANE SRYGLEY MOUTON

Dramatic changes are occurring in the way Americans handle their affairs. This is true across the spectrum, from commercial firms to government agencies, to schools and universities. What these are, and how they can be met and brought under management is discussed below.

Breakdown of Authority and Obedience

In the past, bosses could exercise work-or-starve authority over their subordinates. They expected and got obedience from them. Authority-obedience was the basis for supervision that built pyramids, big ships, great armies and that made Prussia famous.

But authority-obedience as a way of life has been under greater and greater attack for the past hundred years. Though wars tended to bring it back, during peacetime it became more and more objectionable as a basis for getting people to cooperate. But today, in an environment of vastly improved education and of relative affluence, many are rejecting traditional authority and trying to set up and act upon their own.

The year 1968 might be taken as the beginning of the end for authority-obedience as the control mechanism of American society. That was the year when Detroit and Watts burned. It was when young people were burning their draft cards and dodging the draft by heading for Canada, Sweden and elsewhere. And it was when several universities' presidents were held as hostages in their offices. Furthermore, truancy, runaways and drug problems tell us that the old family pattern where father was boss and the children complied with his authority has crumbled too.

The 1964 Civil Rights Act put society on notice that equality, not authority and obedience, was to be the basis for race relations in the future. Other federal legislation established standards for organizations to be more responsible for the safety of their employees, for their customers and for the everyday citizen as well. Understanding all this new-found and partly enforced equality and social justice and the motivations that underlie it is important for comprehending the new day that is emerging.

These many influences tell us as far as bosses and subordinates are concerned that authority and obedience is no longer the name of the game.

The new relationship between a "boss" and a "subordinate" is such that they seek to reach mutual understanding and agreement as to the course of action to be taken, as well as how to go about it. Before coming to any conclusion on the "how," though, the *main* alternative ways of managing will be presented. First examined is how management occurs under an authority-obedience system and its strengths and weaknesses. Then the "love conquers all" proposition will be considered. This is where the boss says, "If my subordinates love me, they'll do what I want without my having to tell them."

Then those hard-to-notice managers who are doing the least amount to get by on a "see no evil, speak no evil, hear no evil" basis will be viewed. Next to be described is the "halfway is far enough" manager who deals with problems by compromise, adjustment, and accommodation of differences, by being willing to do what's "practical." Finally the possibility already introduced, seeking for excellence through getting the highest possible involvement-participation-commitment to organization purpose up and down the line, is evaluated.

The Grid®

The Grid is a way of sorting out all these possibilities and seeing how each compares with the others. What is involved is this:

The Grid, shown in Fig. 17-1, clarifies and crystallizes many of the different possible ways of supervision. Here is the basis of it. Any person who is working has some assigned responsibilities. This is true whether he or she works very low on the job ladder or high up in the organization. There are two matters on his or her mind whenever acting as a manager. One is *production*—getting results, or accomplishing the mission. How intensely he or she thinks about results can be described as a degree of concern for production. On the Grid, the horizontal axis stands for concern for production. It is a nine-point scale where 9 shows high concern for production and 1, low concern.

A manager is also thinking about those whose work he or she directs, because he or she has to get results through people. The Grid's vertical axis represents this concern for people. This, too, is on a nine-point scale with 9 a high degree and 1 a low degree.

The Grid identifies these two concerns. It does so in a way that enables a person to see how the two concerns interact. Various "theories" are found at points of intersection of the two scales. Whether he or she realizes it or not, these are theories that different managers use when they think about how to get results through people. Five of the many possible theories or styles of

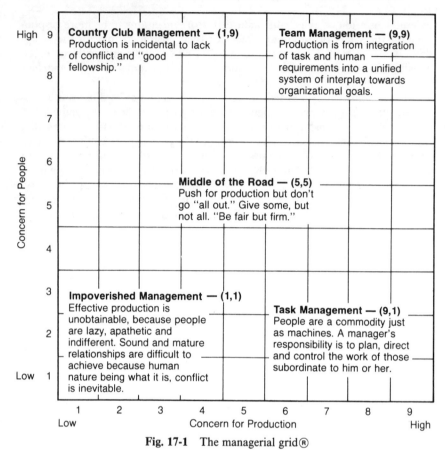

Fig. 17-1　The managerial grid®

management mentioned earlier stand out clearly. They appear in the four corners and in the center of the Grid.

Going Around the Grid

As can be seen from the Grid figure, in the lower right corner, 9,1 represents a great deal of concern for output but little for the people who are expected to produce. 9,1 is the authority-obedience theory. At the opposite corner of the Grid, the top left, is the 1,9 theory. It's the "love conquers all" approach. In the lower left Grid corner is 1,1. It might seem odd that a manager could have almost no concern for either production or people. He or she goes through the motions of being part of the organization but is not really contributing to it. But such managers do exist, even though they may not be easy to notice until you know their theory. They are not doers but freeloaders, getting by on a "speak no, hear no, see no evil" basis. They have not physically quit the firm, but they walked out mentally, perhaps years ago.

In the center is the 5,5 style. The manager with this approach is going up the middle of the road. His or her attitude is, "Get results but don't kill yourself! Don't push too much or you will be seen as a 'hard nose.' Don't let people off too easily or they will think you are soft. Be fair but firm. Do the job but find a comfortable tempo." The 5,5 manager is an "organization man."

The upper right corner, the 9,9 position, is high concern for production united with high concern for people. A person who manages according to this theory stresses understanding and agreement through involvement-participation-commitment as the key to solving boss-subordinate problems. Whenever disagreements arise, he or she sees to it that facts are examined. The problem is thrashed through to solution in an open and aboveboard way that can result in mutual understanding with full commitment to conclusions reached. People working together in a 9,9 manner know that they have a common stake in the outcome of their endeavors. They mesh effort in an interdependent way. The 9,9 theory doesn't abide by the laws of simple arithmetic. On the joining of contributions, "one" plus "one" can add up to "three."

You may have figured out that there are 81 combinations of concerns represented on the Grid. Adjacent to 9,1 are 8,2 and 7,3. And 1,9 has 2,8 and 3,7 near it. There are 3,3, 4,4, 6,6, 7,7 along the diagonal between 1,1 and 9,9 and so on. But our main emphasis is on the theories in the corners and at the middle of the Grid. These are the most distinct styles. They're the ones you see most often. But you might think of a Grid style as you do shades of hair—black, brown, red, blond and white.

Within each hair shade there's a variety—for example, twenty-seven different ways to be blond—yet on your driver's license the outstanding feature is enough for identification. The five main Grid styles, too, are broadly descriptive. We'll use them in much the same way. While talking about 9,1, remember it's just a tinge away to 8,2 or 7,3, or a halftone or so to 6,4, but all these neighboring combinations describe behavior in broadly similar ways.

Basic Assumptions

Grid theories describe sets of basic assumptions under which people deal with one another. An *assumption* is what you take for granted as being true or reliable. Maybe you learned most of your present-day assumptions as you grew up. "I have to be . . . (a tough character or nice person) . . . to get what I want," illustrates some assumptions from childhood that persist. In supervision they lay down the pathway of the boss's everyday approach. Managers act on the assumptions they hold even though it may be rare for you to put them into words. The same set of assumptions usually underlies a whole range of attitudes and activities.

For example, a 1,9-oriented boss who wants to please subordinates may be quite inventive in finding all sorts of ways to show personal warmth. His or her behavior may not be so simple as to say "I appreciate you and everything you do" 25 times a day, but, nonetheless, the subordinate dominates his or her thoughts and concerns. His or her subordinate might say, "I never know what nice surprise the boss will think up next," and yet the manager's core assumptions are remarkably consistent—to please his or her subordinate and win their appreciation.

Were persons to act without assumptions, their behavior would be random, purposeless; it would make no sense in any predictable way. Even so, it is not enough just to have a set of assumptions—any old set. Faulty assumptions can ruin a manager. More reliable ones can enhance his or her work and enrich his or her life on the job, not to mention elsewhere. When a person acting under any set of assumptions understands them, this Grid knowledge can aid him or her to predict what the impact of his or her behavior will be on colleagues and subordinates. Thus, learning the Grid framework will help you understand what kinds of actions are likely to lead to what kind of results.

"Dominants" and "Backups"

Does a manager have just one Grid style strategy or does he or she skip over the surface of the Grid, shifting and adapting according to how he or she sees the situation?

All but a very few do have characteristic styles which, presently, they are using most of the time. Let's call this the manager's *dominant* style. Each boss's basic approach resembles one that is founded on either 9,1; 1,9; 5,5; 1,1; or 9,9 assumptions. How can the idea that a person has a dominant Grid style be squared with the fact that people observably do shift and change? It can be understood in the following way. Not only does a supervisor have a dominant style, he or she also has a back-up strategy, and sometimes a third strategy to fall back on even beyond the second way of operating.

The back-up strategy is likely to show when a manager runs up against difficulty in using the dominant strategy. A back-up Grid strategy is the one he or she falls back on, particularly when feeling the strain of tension, frustration or conflict. This can happen when initial efforts meet nothing but resistance or when, at the point of getting down to working on a project the subordinate's enthusiasm turns to stubborn reluctance.

Apparent complexity, when you first encounter it, can be confusing. Maybe you have played with a kaleidoscope. It contains bits of glass, not many, of different shapes and colors, and these can arrange themselves in an endless variety of patterns that you see reflected from its mirrors. Children are fascinated yet bewildered by this. When the key to understanding has been found, however, what previously appeared bewildering now makes sense.

Any Grid style can be a back-up to any other. For example, even a 1,9-oriented manager, when sharply challenged, might turn stubborn and go 9,1. Again, a person who normally deals in a 9,9 way may meet continued resistance from a subordinate. Unable to find a way of getting on to an action basis with him or her, he or she may shift to a 5,5 approach, negotiating for some kind of compromise where both boss and subordinate will be partially satisfied.

There are no natural links between one particular Grid style and another in terms of dominant-to-back-up. It all depends on the individual and his or her situation. You may sometimes see a person who habitually comes on in a 9,1 way, pressing hard for a time, then breaking off, crestfallen. He or she has switched to a different set of assumptions and moved back to a 1,1 state of resignation, feeling a sense of powerlessness, feeling that he or she is a victim of hostile fate. Who knows, had he or she used a different style from the beginning, or another set of back-up assumptions, and continued talking with the subordinate, he or she might have gotten the reaction desired.

The 9,9 approach is acknowledged by managers as the soundest way to achieve excellence. This conclusion has been verified from studies throughout the U.S. and around the world. The 9,9 theory defines a model that people say with conviction they want, not only for a guide to their own conduct but also as a model of what they want their organization and agencies to become.

That's what the Grid is. The Grid can be used to investigate how a boss supervises in everyday work. There are many boss-subordinate issues that can be looked at in this way. How boss and subordinate communicate is one. Another is the manner in which the boss gives work directions. Others involve managing mistakes, dealing with complaints, and how the boss reacts to hostile feelings.

Change

There are many approaches to change and development, but two are of particular importance in business, industry and government. One critical development step involves the matter of performance evaluation, i.e., how the boss talks with a subordinate to help him or her increase effectiveness. This is individual development. The other, to be treated later, involves *organization development.*

Individual Development

A special word needs to be said about person-to-person individual development. One of the major approaches used today to help people develop involves having bosses interview their subordinates, usually once a year but with the option of doing so more frequently, to help each subordinate see how he or she is performing and how he or she might do better.

This performance review and evaluation involves a more or less prescribed procedure. It starts with the boss and (in principle) the subordinate mutually setting up performance standards and measures of results. The second step, perhaps a year later, or at the end of a briefer period, is for the boss and subordinate to hold another session to review how well the subordinate did in meeting specific and agreed performance standards.

Then, whether simultaneously at annual performance rating time or not, the boss, working alone, also calibrates subordinate performance in terms of standard categories on a rating for such as "responsibility" and "initiative," which apply to all jobs. These evaluations are intended to be used for several purposes. One is for aiding a subordinate to see how he or she can improve performance. Another is to identify special training and development opportunities. Most generally they are used as the basis for pay raises, promotion and termination.

A boss can do any one of these things in a 9,1, 1,9, 1,1, 5,5, or 9,9 way, and, as you can well appreciate, the quality of individual development, if any, hangs in the balance.

Organization Development

Sound management can only meet the challenge of change by seeing the deeper issue: organization development. But a blueprint of an excellent organization is needed to describe an organization so well managed that it can grasp opportunity from the challenge of change. What would such an organization be like?

1. *Its objectives would be sound, strong and clear.* Its leaders would know where it was headed and how to get there. Its objectives would also be understood and embraced by all members of the management body. These persons would strive to contribute because the organization's objectives and their own goals would be consistent. There would be a high level of commitment to organization goals as well as to personal goals. Commitment would be based on understanding. To be understood, goals would be quite specific.

   Every business has an objective "profit." But this is too vague to motivate persons to greater effectiveness. Profit needs to be converted into concrete objectives. One might be, "To develop a position in the plastic industry which will service 20 percent of this market within the next five years." In a government organization, a specific objective might be "To establish six urban renewal demonstration projects distributed by regions and by city size within 10 months." Government objectives would be implemented through program planning and budgeting rather than the profit motive.

2. *Standards of excellence would be high.* Managers would be thoroughly acquainted with their areas of operation. A premium would be placed on knowledge and thorough analysis rather than on opinion and casual thought.

3. *The work culture would support the work.* It would be an organization culture in which the members would be highly committed to achieving the goals of the organization, with accomplishment the source of individual gratification.

4. *Teamwork would increase individual initiative.* There would be close cooperation within a work team, each supporting the others to get a job done. Teamwork would cut across department lines.

5. *Technical business knowledge is needed.* This is critical for valid decision-making and problem-solving and would come through coaching, developmental assignments, on-the-job training and special courses.

6. *Leadership would be evident.* With sound objectives, high standards of excellence, a culture characterized by high commitment, sound teamwork and technical know-how, productivity would increase.

The way of life or culture of an organization can be a barrier to effectiveness. Barriers may stem from such elements of culture as the attitudes or traditions present in any unit of the organization. Culture both limits and guides the actions of the persons in the organization. Because of traditional ways and fear of change, an organization's leaders may be reluctant to apply modern management science. Yet, the need for change may be quite evident.

Criteria for Change

A sound approach to introducing change and improvement is a *Grid Organization Development* effort. It should:

1. *Involve the widest possible participation of executives, managers and supervisors* to obtain a common set of concepts about how management can be improved.
2. *Be carried out by the organization itself.* The development of subordinates is recognized as part of the manager's job. When organization members from the line become the instructors, higher management's commitment, understanding and support for on-the-job application and change are ensured.
3. *Aim to improve the skills of executives and supervisors who must work together to improve management.* This means the skills of drawing on each other's knowledge and capacities, of making constructive use of disagreement and of making sound decisions to which members become committed.
4. *Aim to improve the ability of all managers to communicate better* so that genuine understanding can prevail.
5. *Clarify styles of management* so that managers learn how the elements of a formal management program (e.g., planned objectives, defined responsibilities, established policies) can be used without the organization's becoming overly formal and complex or unduly restricting personal freedom and needed individual initiative.
6. *Aid each manager to investigate managerial style* to understand its impact and learn to make changes to improve it.
7. *Provide for examination of the organization's culture* to develop managers' understanding of the cultural barriers to effectiveness and how to eliminate them.
8. *Constantly encourage managers to plan and introduce improvements* based on their learnings and analysis of the organization.

How to Get There

Grid Organization Development is one way of increasing the effectiveness of an organization, whether it is a company, a public institution or a government agency. The behavioral science concepts on which organization development is based reach back more than 50 years. Because organization development itself is only a decade or so old, those unfamiliar with its rationale may look upon it with doubt or skepticism, see it as a mystery or a package, a gimmick or a fad. Experience pinpoints which behavioral science concepts are tied to the struggle for a more effective organization. This has done much to help managers apply the pertinent concepts to everyday work.

There are several questions preceding the definition of organization development as it is applied to raise an organization's capacity to operate by using behavioral science concepts. One question is, "What is an organization?" Another is, "What is meant by development?" Finally, "What is it that organization development adds to the organization, that it lacks without it?" The goal of organization development is to increase operational effectiveness by increasing the degree of integration of the organization around its profit/production/or service purpose.

It seems almost self-evident that everyone in an organization would have a clear idea of the *purpose* toward which its efforts were being directed. Yet this is seldom true. For many persons, an organization's purpose is fuzzy, unrealistic and with little force as a motivator. A major organization development contribution is to clarify organization purposes and identify individual goals with them to increase efforts toward their attainment.

As for the *human interaction* process, some styles of managing may decrease a person's desire to contribute to the organization's purpose. The kind of supervision exercised not only fails to make a subordinate feel "in" but even serves to make him or her feel "out." His or her efforts are alienated rather than integrated. This may hold true in the coordination of efforts between organized units. Relationships between divisions, for example, may deteriorate into the kind of disputes that can be reconciled only through arbitration by higher levels of management. At best, they are likely to encourage attitudes of appeasement and compromise.

The organization's *culture,* its history, its traditions, its customs and habits which have evolved from earlier interaction and have become norms regulating human actions and conduct may be responsible for many of the organization's difficulties and a low degree of integration within it.

Organization development deliberately shifts the emphasis away from the organization's structure, from human technical skill, from wherewithal and results *per se* as it diagnoses the organization's ills. Focusing on organization purpose, the human interaction process and organization culture, it accepts these as the areas in which problems are preventing the fullest possible integration within the organization. Once an organization has moved to the point of which the three key properties are fully developed, the problems that originally seemed to be related to the others are more easily corrected.

Six Phase Approach

How, specifically, does one go about organization development? The Managerial Grid is one way of achieving it. The six-phase approach provides the various methods and activities for doing so.

Phase 1 of the six-phase approach involves study of *The Managerial Grid.* Managers learn the Grid concepts in seminars of a week's length.

These seminars are conducted both on a "public" and on an internal basis. They involve hard work. The program requires 30 or more hours of guided study before the beginning of the seminar week. A seminar usually begins Sunday evening, and participants work morning, afternoon and evening through the following Friday.

The sessions include investigation by each person of his or her own managerial approach and alternative ways of managing which he or she is able to learn, experiment with and apply. He or she measures and evaluates team effectiveness in solving problems with others. He or she also studies methods of team action. A high point of Grid Seminar learning is when he or she receives a critique of style of managerial thoughts and performance from other members of his or her team. The emphasis is on personal style of managing, not on character or personality traits. Another high point of the Grid Seminar is when the manager critiques the style of his or her organization's culture, its traditions, precedents and past practices, and begins to consider steps for increasing the effectiveness of the whole organization.

Participants in a Grid Seminar can expect to gain insight into their own and other managerial approaches and develop new ways to solve managerial problems. They can expect to improve team effectiveness skills. They will on completion of Phase 1 have new standards of candor to bring to work activities and a greater awareness of the effects of his company's culture upon the regulation of work.

Comments are often heard to the effect, "The Grid has helped me to better understanding and is useful in many aspects of my life." But the vital question is in the use made of Phase 1 learning. The test for the manager is usefulness on the job. To direct this usefulness to the work situation, and incidentally to enhance it from a personal point of view, one must proceed to Phase 2.

Work Team Development

Phase 2 is Work Team Development. As the title suggests, work team development is concerned with development of the individual and the work team. Phases 1 and 2 are often viewed as *management* development, while Phases 3 through 6 move into true *organization development.* The purpose of Phase 2 is to aid work team members to apply their Phase 1 learning directly to the operation of their team.

Individual effort is the raw material out of which sound teamwork is built! It cannot be had just for the asking. Barriers that prevent people from talking out their problems need to be overcome before their full potential can be realized.

Work team development starts with the key executive and those who report to him or her. It then moves down through the organization. Each supervisor sits down with subordinates as a team. They study their barriers to work effectiveness and plan ways to overcome them.

An important result to be expected from the Phase 2 effort is teamwide agreement on ground rules for team operation. The team may also be expected to learn to use critique to improve teamwork on the job. Teamwork is increased through improving communication, control and problem-solving. Getting greater objectivity into work behavior is vital to improved teamwork.

A team analysis of the team culture and operating practices precedes the setting of goals for improvement of the team operation along with a time schedule for achieving these goals. Tied into the goal-setting for the team is personal goal-setting by team members. This might be a goal for trying to change aspects of behavior so as to increase a member's contribution to teamwork. Setting standards for achieving excellence are involved throughout the process.

Intergroup Development

Phase 3 is Intergroup Development. It represents the first step in Grid OD that is applied to organization components rather than to individuals. Its purpose is to achieve *better problem-solving between groups through a closer integration of units that have working interrelationships!*

Managers examine and analyze these working relationships to strengthen and unify the organization across the board. Some dramatic examples of successful Phase 3 applications between labor and management groups are on record. Other units that might appropriately be involved in Phase 3 would be a field unit and the headquarters group to whom it reports, or two sections within a division, or a region and its reporting parent group. It is the matter of coordination between such units that is the target of Phase 3. Problems of integration may be problems of function or merely problems in terms of level.

Management is inclined to solve the problem of functional coordination by setting up systems of reporting and centralized planning. Misunderstandings or disagreements between levels are often viewed as "a communications problem." Phase 3, in recognition that many problems are relationship problems, seeks closer integration of units through the exchange and comparison of group images as set forth by the members of two groups.

Areas of misunderstandings are identified while conditions are created to reduce such intergroup problems and plan steps of operational coordination between the groups. Only groups that stand in a direct, problem-solving relationship with one another and share a need for improved coordination participate in Phase 3 intergroup development. And only those members with key responsibilities for solving the coordination problem are participants.

The activities of Phase 3 naturally follow Phase 2 because when there is conflict between working teams, if the teams themselves have already had the opportunity to solve their internal problems, they are prepared to engage in activities designed to solve their problem of working together. Phase 3 also can be expected to clear the decks for Phases 4 and 5. Any past intergroup problems that were barriers to coordinated effort are solved before the total organization development effort is launched in the latter phases.

A successful Phase 3 will link groups vertically and horizontally and reduce intergroup blockages. This increases the problem-solving between departments, divisions and other segments wherever coordination of effort is a vital necessity. Persons who have participated in Phase 3 report improved intergroup relationships and express appreciation of the team management concept, pointing out that it reverses the traditional procedure in which criticism flows from one level of management down to the next.

Organization Blueprint

Phase 4 calls for the Production of an Organization Blueprint. If Phases 1, 2 and 3 represent pruning the branches, Phase 4 gets at the *root structure.* A long-range blueprint is developed to ensure that the basic strategies of the organization are "right." The immediate goal is to set up a model that is both realistic and obtainable for an organization's system for the future. How is this done? The existing corporate entity is momentarily set aside while an ideal concept is drawn up representing how it would be organized and operated if it were truly effective. The optimal organization blueprint is produced as a result of a policy diagnosis based on study of a model organization culture. The blueprint is drawn up by the top team and moves down through lower levels. The outcome is organization-wide understanding of the blueprint for the future.

It can be expected that as a result of Phase 4, the top team will have set a direction of performance goals to be achieved. Individuals and work teams will have developed understanding and commitment to both general and specific goals to be achieved.

Blueprint Implementation

Phase 5 is Blueprint Implementation. That is, Phase 5 is designed for the carrying out of the organizational plan through activities that change the organization from what it "is" to what it "should be." A Phase 5 may spread over several years, but as a result there comes about the effective realization of the goals that have been set in Phase 4 and specific accomplishments, depending on concrete issues facing the organization. During Phase 5, the members who are responsible for the organization achieve agreement and commitment to courses of action that represent steps to implement the Phase 4 blueprint for the future.

Stabilization

Phase 6 is stabilization. It is for reinforcing and making habitual the new patterns of management achieved in Phases 1 through 5. Organization members identify tendencies to slip back into the older and less effective patterns of work and take corrective action. Phase 6 involves an overall critique of the state of the OD effort for the purpose of replanning for even greater effectiveness. It is not only to support and strengthen the changes achieved through earlier activities, but also to identify weaknesses and plan ways of eliminating them.

By the time Phase 6 is under way, the stabilization of new communication, control and problem-solving approaches should be evident. Moreover, there should be complete managerial confidence and competence in resisting the pressures to revert to old managerial habits.

As we see our business, government and educational institutions facing crisis after crisis, we realize the need for change becomes more imperative with each passing day. Behavioral science ideas and technology now provide a way through which need can become actuality.

"Organizations *can* change!" The issue is *will* they? Problems are inherent in every organization. What is needed is the will, determination and effort to solve them.

Notes

[1] Robert R. Blake and Jane Srygley Mouton, *The Managerial Grid Laboratory-Seminar Materials* (Austin, Texas: Scientific Methods, Inc., 1962).

18

Leadership Models

THOMAS J. FREEMAN

Leadership Types

Types of leadership are called by many different names. One writer proposed twenty-one types of educational leadership: autocrat, cooperator, elder statesman, eager beaver, pontifical, muddled, loyal staff man, prophet, scientist, mystic, dogmatist, open-minded, philosopher, business expert, benevolent despot, child protector, laissez-faire, community-minded, cynic, optimistic, and democrat.[1] Plato proposed three types of leadership: philosopher-statesman, military commander, and businessman.[2] Weber proposed three types of leaders: bureaucratic, patrimonial, and charismatic.[3] Getzels and Guba proposed the nomothetic, ideographic, and transactional.[4] Cattell and Stice identified persistent momentary problem solvers, salient, sociometric, and elected.[5] Blake and Mouton identified country club management, middle of the road, impoverished management, team management, and task management as leadership types.[6] Bogardus identified mental, social, prestige, and democratic.[7] Sixteen authors, publishing between 1915 and 1951, recognized most frequently the following types of leadership: authoritative (dominator), persuasive (crowd arouser), democratic (group developer), intellectual (eminent man), executive (administrator), and representative (spokesman).[8] Lewin, Lippitt and White, in their classic studies, identified laissez-faire, autocratic, and democratic.[9] In much of the current literature these latter three are the designations used to describe the styles of leadership being exercised.

The study of leadership and what makes good leaders has apparently not produced a definitive description of just what does do so. Studies have focused on the trait approach, the situational approach, the behavioral approach, the styles-of-leadership approach, and the functional leadership approach.[10]

Model Types

Some of the models of organization within which leadership of various types operate are presented below. That a particular organization is graphically represented in a certain manner does not necessarily indicate that is the leadership style of the organization. Organization charts, or organigrams, are the formal structure. The real leadership may be in the informal structure. The model in Fig. 18-1 is more a stereotype than a living structure.

The scalar chain or pyramid indicates that authority should flow from top to bottom and responsibility from bottom to top. The stereotype of the leader in this model is the authoritarian or autocratic leader.

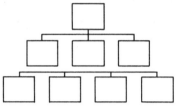

Fig. 18-1   Scalar chain or pyramid

Proponents

A Biblical example of pyramidal leadership is Moses' organization of people with leaders over thousands, hundreds, fifties, and tens.[11] In the management literature, one of the early advocates of the scalar chain was Henri Fayol. Fayol defined the scalar chain in the following way:

> . . . the chain of superiors ranging from the ultimate authority to the lowest ranks. The line of authority is the route followed—via every link in the chain—by all communications which start from or go to the ultimate authority. This path is dictated both by the need for some transmission and by the principle of unity of command.[12]

The usage of the pyramidal form of organization for leadership is implicit in Frederick Taylor's writings. His contention that the foreman should tell the worker exactly how to do, when to do, and how much to do on a job is authoritarian in the ultimate. A further illustration of Taylor's attitudes can be seen in his "functional foremanship" principle. This principle says in effect that a foreman should be put in charge of a job. Men moving from job to job will be under the supervision and direction of different foremen when working on different jobs.[13]

The exercise of authority as implied in the pyramidal form was advocated by Mooney, Reiley, Urwick, and most other writers before 1940. These men defined authority as the legitimate right to direct or influence the performance of others and the power to exact performance from other persons.[14]

When to Use

As previously stated, leadership in the pyramidal organization is stereotyped as being authoritarian in style. The authoritarian style should be used only when all other forms either have not succeeded or cannot succeed. It is to be used when people are dependent. Some people need and are highly dependent upon the authoritative guidance of leaders. Characteristically, the authoritarian style is used when decisions have already been made. When policies and procedures for a specific action have previously been determined and formulated, it is assumed that the actions to be accomplished are binding on an organization and the members. The mission then is to communicate and enforce the policies and the procedures; therefore, the authoritarian style is appropriate.

The authoritarian style is perhaps justified when satisfactory work specifications and routines exist. When quality control standards are such that products meet specifications, the authoritarian style of leadership can be utilized to maintain the standards. In this instance, the organization's guidelines become the authoritative source for management.

The authoritarian style may be used when positional or expert leverage is primary. This is exemplified in organizations where technical or highly skilled persons or groups operate.

The authoritarian style is frequently used in emergencies. When quick and decisive action must be taken, a leader must exert authority and initiate appropriate action in order to respond to the emergency situation.

A final occasion when authority must be exercised is in breaking ties in a deadlocked situation. Whenever the democratic process ends in a tie that stalemates a situation, someone must exercise authority to break the tie and move the activity to some conclusion. This act of tie-breaking is in effect authoritarian.[15]

Strengths and Weaknesses

The effectiveness of the authoritarian style is dependent in part upon the type of followers a leader is leading and the size of the work group. Medalia found in his studies that men scoring high on the F Scale (an indication that they were themselves highly authoritarian) accepted authoritarian leaders.[16] Vroom and Mann found that workers exhibited more positive attitudes toward authoritarian leaders when located in large groups where they interacted less frequently with each other and with the leader.[17] There is a common belief that the authoritarian style of leadership accomplishes more and with greater accuracy than the democratic, and examples cited to support this belief are Hitler in Germany, Napoleon in France, and Mao Tse-tung in China.[18] The Hawthorne studies, which are discussed below, indicated that workers under a democratic arrangement were more productive.[19] The Coch and French studies in the pajama factory tended to support this same conclusion.[20]

The Continuum

Experiments, beginning in 1927, at the Hawthorne plant of the Western Electric Company in Cicero, Illinois, caused some major changes in the concept of relations between workers and leaders. These studies, which became known as the "Hawthorne studies," were conducted by Elton Mayo, F. J. Roethlisberger, and William J. Dickson. The implications of the outcome of the studies were that the organization should be built around the workers and that more consideration should be given to the feelings and attitudes of the workers.[21] Additional studies by Coch and French and by others[22] led to an increased concern for, and extension of participation by workers in, the managerial functions of the organization.

The participation of employees may be on a variety of levels. Robert Tannenbaum and Warren H. Schmidt depicted their view of the leadership process, as it relates to participation of the workers, on a continuum (Fig. 18-2) moving from complete leader domination to complete group domination or laissez-faire leadership.[23]

Proponents

Proponents of this model use it to illustrate the degree of authority exercised by the leader and the degree of participation left available for subordinates to participate in work design, time of work, and other actions consistent with the overall purpose and mission of the organization.

When to Use

The continuum is a graph that explains levels that exist and varieties of styles exercised by leaders. It is not a model of advocacy.

Strengths and Weaknesses

This model can be used to illustrate a relationship with variations between domination and laissez-faire. The weakness is that it shows this relationship on one plane only. It does not have the capacity to depict the leader who is task-oriented but who also exhibits concern for the workers.

The Grids

Some attempts have been made to construct models that depict both concern for the task and for the workers. In the early studies by the Survey Research Center at the University of Michigan, there was an attempt to approach the study of leadership by locating clusters of characteristics that seemed to be related to each other and to tests of effectiveness. The studies identified two concepts that came to be called *employee orientation* and *production orientation*.[24] Several studies at the Research Center for Group Dynamics indicated that leader and group objectives fall into two categories: (1)

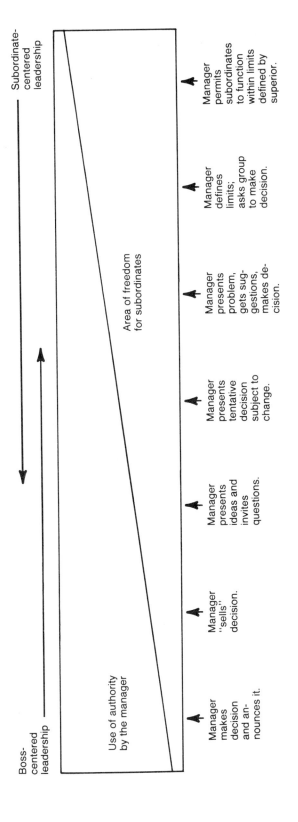

Fig. 18-2 Continuum of leadership behavior

the achievement of some specific group goal, or (2) the maintenance or strengthening of the group itself.[25] Leadership studies at the Bureau of Business Research at Ohio State University narrowed the description of leader behavior to two dimensions: *Initiating Structures* and *Consideration*. Initiating structure was defined as the leader's behavior in delineating the relationship between himself and the members of the work group in endeavoring to establish well-defined patterns of organization, channels of communication, and methods. Consideration was defined as behavior indicative of friendship, mutual trust, respect and warmth in the relationship between the leader and the members of his staff.[26]

In connection with the Ohio State studies a grid was constructed on which leader behavior was plotted on both axes rather than on a continuum. On the Ohio State grid the vertical axis was labeled "Consideration" and the horizontal axis was labeled "Initiating Structure" to indicate the concepts defined above.[27]

Robert R. Blake and Jane S. Mouton, working independently, also developed a two axis grid which they called the managerial grid.® On the Blake and Mouton managerial grid the vertical axis is labeled "Concern for People" and the horizontal axis is labeled "Concern for Production." On the managerial grid, five different types of leadership based on concern for production and concern for people are located in the four quadrants and at their intersection. The five leadership styles are Impoverished, Country Club, Task, Middle-of-the Road, and Team. The impoverished leadership has little concern for production and little concern for people. Country club leadership gives great concern for people with little to moderate concern for production. Task leadership gives great concern to production but little to the human element. Middle-of-the-road leadership balances concern for production with concern for maintaining the morale of the people. Team leadership is achieved through committed people having a common stake in organization purposes.[28]

Proponents

Robert R. Blake and Jane S. Mouton popularized the two-axis grid shown in Fig. 18-3. The preface to the 1964 edition of their book indicated that people associated with Humble Oil Refining Company and people associated with Scientific Methods, Inc., participated with them in the development of the grid.[29]

When to Use

Then 1,1 or impoverished management is the laissez-faire style of management. The person marked by this style exerts only the minimum effort required to get the minimal required work done to sustain organization membership.

The 1,9 or country club managerial style is one in which thoughtful attention to the needs of people to have satisfying relationships leads to a comfortable friendly organization. This seems to be an appropriate style for the business that is being operated as a tax writeoff.

The 9,1 or task managerial style suggests that the conditions of work are so arranged that the human elements interfere to a minimum degree. The authoritarian style of management is almost the same as the task managerial style, and the same terms that apply to usage of the authoritarian style are appropriate for the task situation.[30]

The 5,5 or middle-of-the-road managerial style is one where it is possible to balance getting the work out with maintaining the morale of people at a satisfactory level. Management is by persuasion. The manager explains how observance of standard practice is for the good of all.[31]

The 9,9 or team managerial style implies that there is a relationship of trust and respect between the manager and the workers. Work is accomplished by committed people who have a common stake in fulfilling the organization's purpose. As the name suggests, the 9,9 style is appropriate for an athletic team.[32]

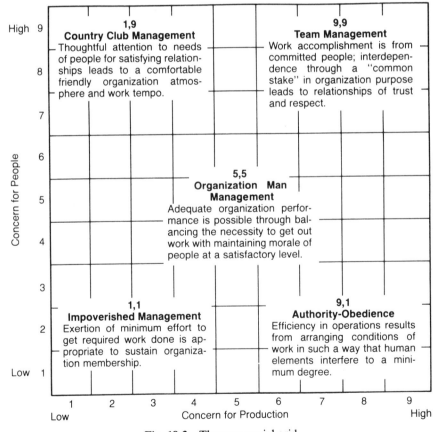

Fig. 18-3   The managerial grid

Strengths and Weaknesses

The managerial grid permits one to graph concern for people and concern for tasks in the 81 different positions that the two-axis nine-positions-per-side indicate. The weakness of the grid is that it measures only two dimensions. Proposed extensions to make the grid three, four, or more dimensioned to permit graphing teamwork, effectiveness, etc., were being investigated at the time of the writing of this article.[33] These proposals have not been sufficiently developed to make their usage widespread.

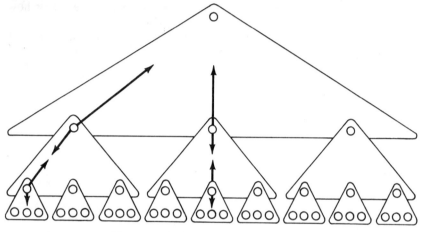

(The arrows indicate the linking pin function)

Fig. 18-4   The linking pin

Linking Pin

A leadership model that makes the leader the linking pin between his work group and the next higher group in the organization has been proposed (see Fig. 18-4).[34] The plan would have organizations form work groups with overlapping group membership. The leader in each work group is also a member of the next higher work group and functions in both groups.

Proponents

The linking-pin model of organizational leadership was proposed by Rensis Likert.[35] Likert advocated holding occasional meetings over two hierarchical levels so that coordination of purpose could be discussed and understood by all members of groups on both levels.[36]

When to Use

The work groups connected by linking pin key members who are also members of other groups may be an appropriate model for leadership people with a high level of education who tend to be capable of mature and independent behavior.[37]

Strengths and Weaknesses

The strength of the linking pin organization for leadership is that it is a loosely controlled flexible organization that utilizes the full potential of capable group members.[38] The weakness may be that this organization pattern is not appropriate for people who need authoritarian supervision in order to work effectively.

Contingency Model

Fred Fiedler and his associates at the University of Illinois devoted considerable study to determining whether task-oriented leadership or employee-related leadership is more effective. Their conclusions were that task-oriented leadership may be more effective under some conditions and employee-oriented leadership may be more effective under other conditions. Fiedler's leadership theory postulates that leadership style is determined by the needs the individual seeks to satisfy in the leadership situation. Individuals with different styles respond to different conditions in many ways. Performance of interacting groups and organizations is contingent upon the favorableness of the leadership situation, as well as upon the individual leader's style. Leadership performance depends as much on the organization as upon the attributes of the leader. Leaders are not effective or ineffective; they are effective in one situation and ineffective in other situations.[39]

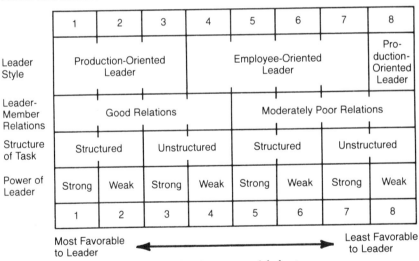

Fig. 18-5 Contingency model chart

Proponents

Fred E. Fiedler and his associates at the Group Effectiveness Research Laboratory at the University of Illinois supplied the information on which the model in Fig. 18-5 was based.[40] Dale S. Beach translated the information from one of Fiedler's tables to the model.

When to Use

The contingency model depicts eight different combinations of leader style, member relations, and task structures that lead to strong or weak power for the leader. Reading the chart from bottom to top indicates what may be the best type of leadership to exercise. For example, reading number 3, a leader with strong power by reason of position or other factors, working in an unstructured situation and enjoying good relations with members, could employ a production-oriented leadership style.

Strengths and Weaknesses

This model can be used, perhaps better than any other, to indicate to personnel directors and others who must build organizations, the type of match that should be made between individuals and the different positions in the organization.[41]

The Circle

Robert Townsend did not think very highly of organizational charts with people's names in small boxes arranged in hierarchical order. He said that in the best organizations people like to think of themselves as working in a circle, as around a table. One of the positions at the table is designated the chief executive officer (see Fig. 18-6) because someone must make the tactical decisions; but leadership passes from one to the other as the situation changes and as tasks are completed.[42]

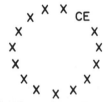

Fig. 18-6   The circle

Proponents

The concept is essentially the same as the democratic system of leadership. Seifert and Clinebell described this system as one in which the leader functions as a participant, alongside the other members of the group. He reaches out to people rather than down to them. Decision-making resides in the group, with each member having an equal opportunity to participate.[43]

When to Use

The circular model, or democratic system, is used when the group size is small enough to have each member participate in discussion and when members have developed their abilities and self-concept to an extent that they can be comfortable in their role.

Strengths and Weaknesses

The strength of this system of organization is that it develops leaders. Townsend indicated that this technique worked in his company to this effect. When Townsend became head of Avis, he was assured that no one at headquarters had any leadership potential. Three years later it was recognized that there was an abundance of management ability in the company. The people were the same people who had been there when he arrived, but subsequently their potential had been more fully realized.[44]

The weakness of the system may be that it takes time to train others to act efficiently.[45] Democracy in organizations necessarily demands that everyone have the chance to develop and contribute according to his ability, aiming for the greatest good for the greatest number.

Notes

[1] L.W. Harding, "Twenty-one Varieties of Educational Leadership," *Educational Leadership* 6 (February 1949): 299–302.

[2] Plato, *The Republic*, translated by G.M.A. Grube (Indianapolis: Hackett Publishing Co.), Books 5 and 8.

[3] Max Weber, *The Theory of Social and Economic Organization*, translated by A.M. Henderson and Talcott Parsons (New York: Oxford University Press, 1947), p. 329.

[4] J.W. Getzels and E.G. Guba, "Social Behavior and the Administrative Process," *School Review* 65 (Winter 1957): 423–441.

[5] R.B. Cattell and G.F. Stice, "Four Formulae for Selecting Leaders on the Basis of Personality," *Human Relations* 7 (1954): 493–507.

[6] Robert R. Blake and Jane S. Mouton, *The Managerial Grid* (Houston, Texas: Gulf Publishing Company, 1964).

[7] Emory S. Bogardus, *Fundamentals of Social Psychology* (New York: The Century Company, 1924), pp. 409–445.

[8] Ralph M. Stogdill, *Handbook of Leadership: A Survey of Theory and Research* (New York: The Free Press, 1974), p. 27.

[9] Ralph K. White and Ronald Lippitt, *Autocracy and Democracy: An Experimental Inquiry* (New York: Harper and Brothers, 1960), p. 61.

[10] Gordon L. Lippitt, "What Do We Know About Leadership?" in *The Planning of Change*, ed. by Warren G. Bennis, Kenneth D. Benne, and Robert Chin (New York: Holt,

Rinehart and Winston, 1962), pp. 431–434.

[11] *Exodus* 18: 17–27.

[12] Henri Fayol, *General and Industrial Management*, trans. Constance Storrs (London: Pitman, 1949), p. 34.

[13] Frederick W. Taylor, *The Principles of Scientific Management* (New York: Harper and Brothers, 1911).

[14] Dale S. Beach, *Personnel: The Management of People at Work*, 3rd edition (New York: Macmillan Publishing Company, 1975), p. 518.

[15] George T. Vardaman, *Dynamics of Managerial Leadership* (Philadelphia: Auerbach Publishers, Inc., 1973), pp. 36–40.

[16] N.Z. Medalia, "Authoritarianism, Leader Acceptance, and Group Cohesion," *Journal of Abnormal Social Psychology* 51 (Sept. 1955): 207–213.

[17] V.H. Vroom and C.F. Mann, "Leader Authoritarianism and Employee Attitudes," *Personnel Psychology* 13 (Summer 1960): 125–140.

[18] Ralph K. White and Ronald Lippitt, *Autocracy and Democracy: An Experimental Inquiry* (New York: Harper & Brothers, 1960), p. 275.

[19] Elton Mayo, *The Social Problems of an Industrial Civilization* (Boston: Graduate School of Business Administration, Harvard University, 1945), pp. 68–86.

[20] L. Coch and J.R.P. French, "Overcoming Resistance to Change," *Human Relations* 1 (1948): 512–532.

[21] Elton Mayo, pp. 68–86.

22 Several studies are cited in Ralph M. Stogdill, *Handbook of Leadership: A Survey of Theory and Research* (New York: The Free Press, 1974), pp. 106–111.

23 From Robert Tannenbaum and Warren H. Schmidt, "How to Choose a Leadership Pattern," *Harvard Business Review,* March–April 1958, Copyright © 1958 by the President and Fellows of Harvard College; all rights reserved. Reprinted with permission of the publisher.

24 D. Katz, N. Maccoby, and Nancy C. Morse, *Productivity, Supervision, and Morale in an Office Situation* (Ann Arbor: Survey Research Center, 1950), as quoted in Paul Hersey and Kenneth H. Blanchard, *Management of Organizational Behavior: Utilizing Human Resources,* 2nd ed. (Englewood Cliffs: Prentice Hall, 1972), p. 72.

25 Dorwin Cartwright and Alvin Zander, eds. *Group Dynamics: Research and Theory,* 2nd ed. (Evanston, Ill.: Row, Peterson and Company, 1960).

26 Andrew W. Halpin, *The Leadership of School Superintendents* (Columbus, Ohio: College of Education, Ohio State University, 1956), p. 4.

27 Hersey and Blanchard, pp. 73–74.

28 Ibid., pp. 75–76.

29 Robert R. Blake and Jane S. Mouton, *The Managerial Grid* (Houston, Texas: Gulf Publishing Company, 1964), p. xi. The grid is reprinted with permission of Robert R. Blake and Jane S. Mouton, from *The New Managerial Grid* (Houston: Gulf Publishing Company, 1978), p. 11.

30 Ibid., pp. 22–37.

31 Ibid., p. 115.

32 Ibid., p. 145.

33 Hersey and Blanchard, pp. 83–87.

34 From *New Patterns of Management* by Rensis Likert. Copyright © 1961 McGraw-Hill Book Company. Used with permission of McGraw-Hill Book Company.

35 Rensis Likert, *New Patterns of Management* (New York: McGraw-Hill, 1961), pp. 109–115.

36 Ibid., p. 115.

37 Ibid., p. 114.

38 Hersey and Blanchard, p. 147.

39 Fred E. Fiedler, *A Theory of Leadership Effectiveness* (New York: McGraw-Hill Book Company, 1967), p. 261.

40 The chart is based upon data in Fiedler, *A Theory of Leadership Effectiveness,* chapter 9, as interpreted and illustrated in Dale S. Beach, *Personnel: the Management of People,* p. 527. Copyright © 1970 by Macmillan Company of New York. Reprinted with permission of the publisher.

41 Beach, pp. 527–528.

42 Robert Townsend, *Up the Organization: How to Stop the Corporation from Stifling People and Strangling Profits* (Greenwich, Conn.: Fawcett Publications, Inc., 1970), pp. 116–117.

43 Harvey Seifert and Howard J. Clinebell, Jr., *Personal Growth and Social Change: A Guide for Ministers and Laymen as Change Agents* (Philadelphia: The Westminster Press, 1969), p. 143.

44 Townsend, p. 123.

45 Emory S. Bogardus, *Fundamentals of Social Psychology* (New York: The Century Company, 1924), p. 443.

Part Seven

Psychology of Motivating and Communicating

19

A Model of Managerial Motivation

STEVEN H. APPELBAUM

How can the manager of an organizational department, division, component, unit, etc., motivate subordinates to achieve the common purposes of need satisfaction and goal attainment?

This problem may appear to be either pedestrian or overly abstract, but a solution does not always encompass classical behavioral science theories and programmed interventions. Also, how does the organizational leader create and utilize a sophisticated motivational system capable of channeling the stratified and varied drives of subordinates into team efforts yielding an effective team resultant and not individual, isolated victories?

While motivation is a critical determinant of behavior, it is often believed to be a panacea. Motivation is a most complex process since subordinates expect it and managers find the behavioral science theories to be enigmatic. In essence, individuals have basic and secondary needs which must be satisfied. We have a network of *complex needs* beginning with innate needs such as hunger, thirst, sex and curiosity; *acquired needs* which are dependent upon experience such as the coffee break in industrial organizations which is actually a real need; and, finally, *social needs* focusing upon belongingness to a group.

A *Model of Managerial Motivation* (Fig. 19-1) has been developed for the purpose of conceptualizing this enigmatic phenomenon. The least significant approach is "Motivation By Theory." Another method, considered to be somewhat more successful, but by no means growth oriented is "Motivation By Fear." "Motivation By Development" is the third motivational method employed by managers. The process of goal setting is quite rational and deserves the fourth most effective approach, "Motivation By Objectives." Next, in the hierarchical model of managerial motivation is "Motivation By Intrinsic Need Satisfaction" which is concerned with individual development and most successful. The broadest and most pervasive method is "Motivation By Management" which is the essence of the model and blueprint of how to motivate the human resources of an organization.

Fig. 19-1   Model of managerial motivation

Motivation by Theory

Abraham Maslow hypothesized that needs are ordered from low to high and as each need level is satisfied, the needs at the next level begin to determine the individual's behavior. When each level is satisfied and fulfilled, the individual then is motivated to achieve the next level of needs since an unfulfilled need is a motivator. The sequence of needs is as follows:

1. *Physiological needs:* hunger, thirst, sex, shelter
2. *Safety needs:* health, security
3. *Belonging and love needs:* identification, affection, affiliation
4. *Ego needs:* esteem, success, prestige, self-respect
5. *Self-Actualization needs:* self-fulfillment, personal growth

We quote Maslow repeatedly without really knowing whether or not his hierarchy has organizational applicability since managers adopt models without testing their validity or reliability. While most progressive managers review the psychological and management literature proposed by Likert, Argyris, McGregor, Myers, Herzberg and their major contributions to managerial motivation, the most significant prerequisite of the manager's job is to actually know *how to motivate!*

Organizations can only achieve their goals of perpetuation by revitalizing their human resources. While McGregor's *Theory Y* appears to be more rational than his *Theory X* philosophy, Argyris' proposal that organizations are incompatible with the mental health of employees and Herzberg's satisfiers of achievement, recognition and the work itself as motivators to make a job challenging are guides to motivation theory, a real pragmatic-action based model for managers is needed. Theory must now be transformed into a practical, pragmatic, workable blueprint for immediate implementation. In essence, theory is only as valuable as its contribution to viable situations in need of direction.

Motivation by Fear

We know that individual motivational patterns are altered as environmental conditions and personal experiences change and as the individual becomes more sophisticated. When the new employee becomes part of the organization, he or she is surrounded by positive and negative factors which will influence behavior. Managers must be able to use varied organizational channels positively and not rely on punitive systems and fear as deterrents.

Fear is a motivator since it connotes reprimand, discharge or even worse, ostracism. The innovative manager uses fear only as an irresponsible extreme exercise. It appears to be uncertain as to how far a manager can exploit his or her subordinates via fear threats to induce favorable results. Organizations suffer from the byproducts of fear and the uncertainty it brings.

If fear and uncertainty do not develop motivated employees and effective organizations, is the reverse, an emphasis on security, an efficient method? The problem is how to take high security and make it a reward and motivational goal! Security systems are developed in organizations via group membership when employees seek to attain protection. But, with proper organization and leadership, productivity increases as well, which is a prime objective of an employing firm.

An employee's security is affected by the manner in which his or her organization balances corporate risk with individual contribution. Security is often used as the motivator/reward for this achievement. While productivity, higher income and greater security are obvious tools used by managers in motivating subordinates, they fall short in visualizing the totality of complex motivations which drive employees to greater performance. The emphasis placed upon security connotes leadership by criticism rather than by praise.

Motivation by Development

The key objective of the manager is to enhance motivation in the employee and not highlight and quantify inadequacies. Managers must be cognizant of the fact that subordinates want praise in order to succeed because of personal efforts. If they fail, the manager must now enhance their self-respect. Managers must motivate individuals as they are and not try to recreate them in a different image.

Many managers dispute and even reject some ideas about motivating employees because they contradict personal experience, while others have tried to implement techniques of behavioral scientists in a mechanical, "cookbook" style without adapting them personally to their own unique situations. Other managers do not feel a commitment to human resource management should necessitate a greater change in their new roles and relationships than in those of their employees.

Managerial motivation does not necessarily mean doing things to or for subordinates. The manager must redirect and channel the drives of employees toward a synthesis of individual and organizational satisfactions. Managers, in order to strike the proper motivational climate, must accept the concept of individual differences since people are not Pavlovian dogs, to be stimulated in the quest of controlled results.

It appears that the most effective and rational motivator is the job itself. A person must know his or her job contributes to organizational success and fulfills personal aspirations, as well. Managers must also be willing to restructure closed organizational systems and prehistoric attitudinal values to allow employees to grow and achieve. Imposing and forcing motivational gimmicks upon individuals deters growth and achievement since both parties lose as a result of coercive manipulation.

In order for employees to grow, motivation must assume experimental forms. Managers must test varied techniques to ascertain those considered effective from inefficient ones. The manager must also support an open climate and a feedback system in which he or she encourages subordinates to motivate him or her, since to actually motivate is to develop subordinates and people through the vehicle of influence. This is what managerial motivation is about.

Motivation by Objectives

Managers fail and illuminate human resource malfunctions due to their inability to cope and live with change. Individuals, in addition to need satisfaction must develop and follow their own blueprints or goals and when these goals are obscured or destroyed, motivation is destroyed as well. This problem is evident in organizations when lip service is given to an unrealistic need to motivate employees. The traditional pattern for applying theories and techniques of motivation is to evaluate the individual and list his or her drives, needs, aspirations and desires. This analysis does not consider the most significant event which is the goal itself as a motivational influence.

One misconception perceived by managers suggests that it is not important to define goals for subordinates but to prescribe a required action. When managers stereotype individuals rather than support individual differences and individual identification with organizational goals, the resultant is action-oriented employees who are not intrinsically motivated but are stereotyped and perceived as instruments or tools on an assembly line.

In a similar vein, paternalistic leaders perceive subordinates as children who are dependent, motivated by basic needs only, and not capable of actualizing potentialities. This was one of Chris Argyris' organizational inequities. Research findings presented by Likert, Maslow, Herzberg and McClelland reveal a relationship existing between motivation and goal development. Some of the data suggest:

1. Motivation begins with goal setting.
2. Motivation is possessed by individuals who seek to achieve future goals.

3. Motivation is learned and goal-directed. When action is substituted for goals, motivation declines.
4. Motivation changes as goals are achieved and evolves throughout the life of an individual.
5. Motivation improves if the goal setting event is declared significant via organization objectives and individual need fulfillment. Both must be congruent and energized.

However, management must be willing to remove all obstacles to goal achievement in order to ensure a healthy and open motivational climate. Supportive leadership occurs when these obstacles which appear to be deterrents to subordinates are removed. This act is one of commitment by management for individual goal achievement. The supportive leadership model actually permits and encourages positive motivation to surface within the organization since all of the highest echelons of managerial motivation require objectives to which the individual employee can openly commit him or herself and for which he or she experiences intrinsic-personal responsibility. Unless these criteria are endorsed and practiced by management, motivation is not possible unless punitive and coercive techniques are negatively employed.

Motivation by Intrinsic Need Satisfaction

The final proposal for managers endorsing commitment to satisfying the needs of workers while achieving organizational objectives focuses upon intrinsic systems of motivation. There have been archaic assumptions about the nature of individuals and work that are seldom put to scrutiny since they appear to be self-evident. Maslow, Argyris, McGregor and Herzberg developed the philosophy intended to reverse the historic attitudinal trend. Their success is still open for discussion since worker psychology changes constantly under the constraints of technology, politics, environment, etc., but management has not been over-sensitized to perceive and recognize these changes. Therefore, it is not inconceivable that obsolete "old wives' tales," or revolutionary laboratory discoveries of how people should be managed and motivated continue to be implemented with apprehension.

Organizations develop motivational systems based upon external rewards that subordinates receive in exchange for work performed which include security, salary, compensation and prestige. However, it is those internal rewards that an individual experiences during work that enhance motivation. These rewards include perfection of skills, discovering new data or techniques, solving problems and achieving high quantity and quality. Internal rewards have not been actually envisioned as rewards but have been perceived as job requirements imposed upon the employee which do not yield satisfaction.

The concept that work should be intrinsically satisfying and not a negativistic experience is a recent method of managerial philosophizing. In actual practice, it is external rewards which attract candidates to organizations and it is a deficiency of these rewards which causes his defection to another organization, employing intrinsic motivational symbols as an attractor. The behavioral scientists reject this premise totally, but empirical research has yielded nebulous conclusions. But, a deficiency of internal rewards will not motivate an employee to quit an employer; it will also not motivate him or her to exceed production requirements and standards. The balance of external-internal rewards is the organizational problem affecting motivational systems.

As an example, corporations employing high security and low challenge eliminate creative, innovative candidates, while attracting maintenance motivated types. But corporations attracting low security and high challenge types cannot control turnover. To solve this problem and maintain an effective motivational mix suggests corporations provide employees with as much security as needed and as much challenge as they feel they want.

Motivation by Management

Motivation is not the simplistic resultant of actions that a manager does to other subordinates since to be motivated is to guide an individual's drives toward specific goals and to have the individual commit him or herself to achieving these goals. To motivate employees, the manager must redesign a great number of stimuli or signals these individuals receive from the internal and external environment so that the world begins to look different to them. Valid motivational changes only happen when the employee learns that his or her environment has changed or that his or her previous conceptions of it were inaccurate. This process of motivation is affected by the slow process of emotional growth and development and it is only an incidental event when a manager directly affects changes in subordinates.

An accurate conceptualization of the role of the manager begins with an understanding that his or her influence is quite indirect. Managers can only influence subordinate behavior if their leadership style is consistent with what the employee already believes about managerial behavior and its effect upon him or her. Effective managers are catalysts, not drill sergeants; they coach and not command, and finally motivate their employees by reality-centered management and an open climate which makes work an intrinsically rewarding experience for employees.

20

Transactional Analysis for Managers, or How to Be More OK with OK Organizations

V. P. LUCHSINGER *and* L. L. LUCHSINGER

A contribution from current nonfiction literature and psychoanalysis that will have a great impact on the management profession is Transactional Analysis. Introduced over a decade ago by Eric Berne, M.D., Transactional Analysis provides the manager with an analytical tool that can help him understand the most complex phenomena in management—the interactions between manager and employee.

Many managers have already been exposed to the principles of Transactional Analysis. The subject received much publicity in 1964 when the book *Games People Play* by Dr. Berne climbed to the top of the popular reading lists. A more current title on the best seller lists, *I'm OK—You're OK,* by Thomas A. Harris, M.D., explores the subject of Transactional Analysis in greater depth.

A possible reason for the delay in applying the principles of Transactional Analysis to management has been the fascination and popularity of games, perhaps to the extent of faddism. Dr. Berne wrote *Games People Play* in response to requests for more information about games. Games overshadowed the subject of Transactional Analysis. The more recent book by Dr. Harris is directed at the general public and has not been identified as a manual for managers. Practitioners and scholars of management are looking at the possible contributions of Transactional Analysis to the improved practice of management.

Harris describes Transactional Analysis as a method for examining a

224

transaction between two people "wherein 'I do something to you and you do something back' and determining which part of the multinatured individual is 'coming on.' "[1]

Transactional Analysis (this term will be capitalized when referring to the entire system) can be divided into four component parts: structural analysis, transactional analysis (the analysis of a specific transaction), games analysis, and script analysis. The four areas are briefly described to provide a reference for the language and terms of Transactional Analysis.

Structural Analysis

Structural Analysis is concerned with the "segregation and analysis of the ego states."[2] Berne identified the three ego states as the Parent, Adult, and Child. (When referred to as ego states these terms are capitalized.) They are represented in Fig. 20-1 and in the literature on Transactional Analysis as P-A-C.

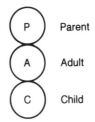

Fig. 20-1   The three ego states

The three ego states are not concepts like Freud's id, ego, and superego. They are phenomenological realities, based on real world behavior. Although lines separate the ego states, the lines are not barriers. A healthy person is able to move from ego state to ego state.

The Parent ego state is that body of recordings in the brain that reflects the unquestioned events or imposed external restraints perceived by a person during his early years of life. Characteristics of a person acting in the Parent include being overprotective, distant, dogmatic, indispensable, and upright. Physical and verbal clues that someone is acting in the Parent include the wagging finger to show displeasure, reference to laws and rules, and reliance on ways that were successful in the past. Parent inputs to behavior are taught.

The Adult, assuming the rationality of man, is the information seeker and processor. It functions as a computer processing new data, making decisions, and updating the data in the original recording of the Parent and Child. The Adult is characterized by logical thinking and reasoning. This ego state can be identified by verbal and physical signs which include thoughtful concentration and factual discussion. Adult inputs to behavior are reasoned.

The Child ego state is the body of data that is recorded in the brain as a result of experiences during the first five years of life. Characteristics of the Child include creativity, conformity, depression, anxiety, dependence, fear, and hate. Physical and verbal clues that a person is acting in the Child are silent compliance, attention seeking, temper tantrums, giggling, and coyness. The Child is also characterized by nonlogical and immediate actions which result in immediate satisfaction. Child inputs to behavior are laden with feeling and emotion.

Analysis of Transaction

Analysis of transactions (T.A.) is the technique for examining a transaction or interaction between two people and the ego states involved. Recognizing the ego states of the two people involved in the transaction can help a person communicate and interact more effectively.

Transactions can be classified as complementary or noncomplementary. Transactions are complementary when the lines of communication between the two people are parallel. For example, a person in the Parent state interacting with the Child of another person would be involved in a complementary transaction if the response from the second person originates from the Child and is directed to the Parent (see Fig. 20-2). Both are acting in the perceived and expected ego states. Complementary transactions are important because they indicate completed communications or interaction between the two people.

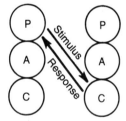

Fig. 20-2   Complementary transaction

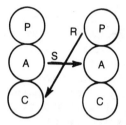

Fig. 20-3   Noncomplementary transaction

A noncomplementary or crossed transaction occurs when the interactions do not have common origination and terminal ego states. Figure 20-3 shows the stimulus directed from the Adult to the Adult being crossed with a response from the Parent to the Child. In this situation the communication is crossed and ineffective.

It is possible for the stimulus to originate in any of the three ego states and be directed to any of the three ego states. This produces nine possible types of complementary transactions.

The number of noncomplementary transactions varies depending upon how one describes the ego states and the forms of contamination-mixed ego states that might appear in an ego state. At this point we turn the subject of noncomplementary transactions back to the psychoanalyst and consider only complementary transactions.

Games Analysis

Berne defines a game as an ongoing series of complementary ulterior transactions progressing to a well-defined, predictable outcome.[3] Games are basically dishonest and self-defeating as the interactions are not honest requests but gambits or moves in a game.

Some of the games managers play include "You're a Professional Now" and "The Man at the Bench." Articles about the games managers play have been written by Ronald J. Burke (1968),[4] Joe Kelly (1968),[5] and Curtis J. Potter (1969).[6] However, a more serious pragmatic approach has been offered by J.V.D. Meininger (1973).[7] The purpose of this article is to avoid the popularity of games and focus upon the analysis of transactions.

Script Analysis

Script analysis is an examination of transactions and interactions to determine the nature of one's life script. It is a method for uncovering early decisions on how life should be lived. When confronted with a situation, a person acts according to his script which is based on what he expects or how he views his life position. In a sense, man's behavior becomes quasi-programed by the script which emerges out of life experience.

Life Positions

Transactional Analysis uses the four following classifications to describe the life positions that a person holds for himself and others:

I'm not OK, You're OK
I'm not OK, You're not OK
I'm OK, You're not OK
I'm OK, You're OK[8]

A person lives his life in one of these life positions. Such a life position or view of himself and others affects how he will interact with them. Only the "I'm OK, You're OK" position is considered healthy.

Manager—Employee Interaction

Managers and employees continually interact with each other. Accepting the idea that the manager initiates most of the interactions and transactions, examples of the nine complementary transactions are used to illustrate manager-employee interactions.

Manager in the Parent Ego State

The manager in the Parent is typified by the "I'm OK, You're not OK" life style. He will be a source of admonitions, rewards, rules, criticisms, and praise. He can be expected to thrive on power and use personal successes or the failures of others as justification for a course of action.

Parent-Parent Transaction (Fig. 20-4)

The Parent-Parent transaction can be beneficial in cases where the employee joins forces with the manager and supports the manager. An executive secretary who dictates orders in the absence of the manager provides an excellent example of the cooperative or supportive Parent-Parent transaction. There are disadvantages to this type of transaction. Consider the situation in which the manager and employee are competing for the position of "Best" Parent. In such a situation the employee will promote his own ideas and orders rather than those of the manager.

If the manager and employee have opposing recordings in the Parent, they will work against each other.

Another disadvantage can be found when the employee communicates with the manager. In the example below the employee is agreeing with the Parent in the manager without really engaging in a meaningful dialogue.

MANAGER: "An effective maintenance repair program always reduces costs."

EMPLOYEE: "I always say that a stitch in time saves nine."

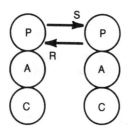

Fig. 20-4   Parent-parent transaction

Both the manager and employee agree on a basic philosophical issue that a maintenance program can save money. No facts were mentioned or introduced in this transaction.

Parent-Adult Transaction (Fig. 20-5)

The manager in the Parent ego state will have difficulty with the employee in the Adult ego state. In such transactions the manager will be frustrated because the employee will not perform as directed. The manager may consider the employee an incorrigible smart aleck. The employee will be condemned for not respecting the voice of authority and experience.

The employee will be frustrated by the manager's failure to act in the Adult.

The dialogue below provides an example of this transaction:

MANAGER: "An effective maintenance repair program always reduces costs."
EMPLOYEE: "The problem is the new supplier. Maintenance and production records show that his parts don't last as do the parts from Acme Company."

The manager, using the standard cliche about effective maintenance, finds himself confronted with facts. In the Parent he is not able to accept this "smart alecky" reply and the idea that his successful method from the past may be wrong. The employee will not be able to accept a slogan in place of facts and records. Due to the mutual frustration, such a relationship will not be productive or long lasting.

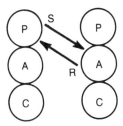

Fig. 20-5   Parent-adult transaction

Parent-Child Transaction (Fig. 20-6)

Perhaps the ideal situation when the manager is in the Parent is for the employee to be in the Child. The manager will find this advantageous in that he will have a loyal and dutiful employee who will respect him and follow his orders.

This ideal situation has disadvantages. The manager may feel that his employees are incapable of assuming responsibility. The manager continually

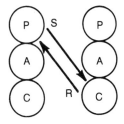

Fig. 20-6   Parent-child transaction

lives with the possibility that someday one or more of the employees in the Child will change from compliance to tantrums.

The employee finds such a transaction advantageous in that it eliminates much responsibility and pressure. Acting in the Child prevents much conflict and provides for ease in operation. The employee suffers from this interaction in that he must surrender his Adult. He doesn't think and his job must be routine so he performs only as directed. The example below uses the same stimulus used in the previous example:

> MANAGER: "An effective maintenance repair program always reduces costs."
> EMPLOYEE: "Yes, sir."

In this transaction there is no meaningful feedback for the manager except that he has a loyal employee who agrees. Although a real problem may exist, the employee finds it easier to perform as directed than to bring the factual information to the attention of the manager.

A closing note on the Parent: The Parent is not the best ego state for the manager to exercise in his daily interactions with employees. The limitations outweigh the advantages. Although it may be useful and required in some situations, it limits effectiveness and denies the use of current facts.

Manager in the Adult Ego State

The manager in the Adult tries to reason out issues, clarifies and informs employees of issues, and has concern for facts, figures, and human needs. His life style generally is the "I'm OK, You're OK" position.

Adult-Parent Transaction (Fig. 20-7)

While the manager attempts to use the information he has processed, the employee in the Parent prefers to use cliches and rules of the past. Citing past successes or proven methods, the employee will not favor change or progress even when it is based on facts, figures, and logic.

In such a transaction the employee will try to control and dominate the manager by using the Parent ego state. This transaction style can be effective only on a temporary basis. It can be used to help a new manager understand the rules and guidance under which the employees operate. The employee in the Parent can be accepted for the facts that he can provide.

There are many disadvantages to this transaction style. The classic example is the Parent's resentment of the young college graduate in a managerial position. The older and experienced employees who know what is to be done and how to do it do not want the newcomers to change the ways of old. The manager in this situation must remain in the Adult. He must not compete by entering his Parent nor retreat by entering the Child. The manager must remind the employee who is the manager and who is the employee.

The employee in the Parent can create other difficulties for the manager if other employees in the Child recognize and accept the employee in the Parent. The employee in the Parent may have better interaction with the other employees. Acting in the Parent the employee may discount all of the benefits that management attempts to use while introducing change. An employee in the Parent can create hostile feelings toward managers in the Adult.

A typical Adult-Parent transaction is provided below:

> MANAGER: "The new supplier's parts will last if we make the adjustments as directed in his technical instructions."
> EMPLOYEE: "We never had this problem with the old supplier. You just can't beat the old reliable supplier."

In this example the manager is attempting to communicate with facts and logic. The employee is not concerned with facts or instructions but with past success. Although there may be valid reasons for changing suppliers, the employee in the Parent refuses to accept facts or technical instruction.

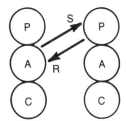

Fig. 20-7 Adult-parent transaction

Adult-Adult Transaction (Fig. 20-8)

An ideal manager-employee relationship exists in the Adult-Adult. Complementary transactions in these states are very effective because both persons are acting in a rational and businesslike manner. Data is processed, decisions are made, and both parties are working toward the solution. Satisfaction is gained from the solution rather than the manager having a dutiful employee or the employee only trying to please her boss.

There are some inherent disadvantages to the Adult-Adult transactions. The elimination of the Child can make the transactions dull due to the lack of stimulation that the Child can provide. The Adult-Adult level may prevent decisions from being reached due to the rational data-processing procedures. This may prevent the manager and employee from meeting deadlines. When a decision has to be made but cannot be reached because of lengthy discussions, the manager may have to make the decision in the Parent.

An example of the manager in the Adult directing a stimulus to an employee who responds in the Adult demonstrates the exchange of facts.

> MANAGER: "The new supplier's parts will last if we make the adjustments as directed in his technical instructions."
> EMPLOYEE: "We found that using his recommended tension level reduced our product acceptance by 6 percent."

Such a transaction, based on facts and figures, may help the manager and the employee identify the real problem. Both the manager and the employee want a solution based on facts.

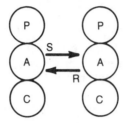

Fig. 20-8   Adult-adult transaction

Adult-Child Transaction (Fig. 20-9)

The Adult-Child interaction can be effective if the manager is aware of the ego state of the employee. In such interactions the manager can allow the employee in the Child to be creative.

The manager in the Adult often assumes that his employees are also in the Adult. Very often this assumption prevents the manager from recognizing that the employee is in the Child ego state. This creates a situation that will be frustrating to the manager and the employee. The manager will find himself assigning more responsibility than the employee can handle. The manager becomes frustrated when the work is not done and the employee becomes discouraged because he cannot do the work.

Another disadvantage is the irrational responses that an employee in the Child will give to the manager in the Adult. An example is provided.

MANAGER: "The new supplier's parts will last if we make the adjustments as directed in his technical instructions."

EMPLOYEE: "I hate to make that darn adjustment. I get my hands dirty."

In this example we can see the Child rebelling against the factual Adult.

A closing note on the Adult: The Adult is capable of providing efficient

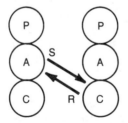

Fig. 20-9   Adult-child transaction

analysis of information. The efficiency of the Adult must be increased when it is supported by the strength of the Parent and the creativity of the Child.

Manager in the Child Ego State

The manager in the Child ego state will have very little to contribute in the form of effective management. Although creativity is one of the characteristics of the Child, the role of a manager requires more than just creativity. Creativity alone does not offset the disadvantages of being anxious, fearful, conforming, and acting on whims.

The manager in the Child is defensive. He assumes the basic "I'm not OK, You're OK" life position.

Child-Parent Transaction (Fig. 20-10)

An employee acting in the Parent will control the manager in the Child. The Parent will be strong and overbearing on the Child. The manager will yield to the employee. If the Child in the manager objects or does something that is not approved by the employee in the Parent, the manager is punished. The employee holds threats of punishment over the manager. The threats may be of ridicule, loss of popularity, or demotion.

An example of the manager and employee illustrates the Child-Parent transaction.

MANAGER: "I'll show them that we cannot operate with inferior parts. Stop the machines."

EMPLOYEE: "If you stop the machines the men don't get paid. The men will not like you if they stop getting paid."

The manager in the Child state, seeking an immediate solution, decides on an irrational course of action. The employee in the Parent condemns the manager. The Child in the manager might be expected to ask the employee, in the Parent, what to do. This results in the employee making the decisions.

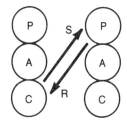

Fig. 20-10   Child-parent transaction

Child-Adult Transaction (Fig. 20-11)

Sometimes it is possible for an Adult employee to control the manager in the Child. More often, the employee will become discouraged by the manager. The manager who makes his decision on whims, fancies, and emotions will pose a threat to the employee who wants to interact with the manager in terms of facts. A major disadvantage of this transaction style is that the organization may lose many good employees.

The following example provides an Adult response to a Child stimulus.

MANAGER: "I'll show them that we cannot operate with inferior parts. Stop the machines."

EMPLOYEE: "Stopping the machines will not solve the problem. Our repair and production records should be shown to the purchasing department."

In this example the manager's Child has provided a solution to the problem. The employee, responding in the Adult, attempts to present a solution based on facts.

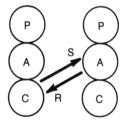

Fig. 20-11   Child-adult transaction

Child-Child Transaction (Fig. 20-12)

The manager in the Child interacting with an employee in the Child will not last very long in an organization that reviews performance. The manager is not capable of leading or directing and the employee is not able to follow. The manager will act on whim and fancy and the employee will be the same. The chances for effective transactions and performance are as great as might be observed with two small children building sand castles. All will go well as long as all is going well.

The effectiveness of the Child-Child transaction can be seen in the example below:

MANAGER: "I'll show them that we cannot operate with inferior parts. Stop the machines."

EMPLOYEE: "Good. We will have a good time with real long coffee breaks."

The manager is taking action that will halt production. In his Child he is having a tantrum. The employee, also in the Child, appreciates the immediate satisfaction.

A closing note on the Child: The manager in the Child ego state may prove to be a liability to the organization. In the Child a person cannot be ex-

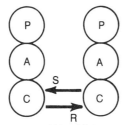

Fig. 20-12   Child-child transaction

pected to make decisions or provide the direction and guidance that is expected of a manager.

Hints for Managers

The effective manager should be able to analyze transactions with employees. Transaction Analysis provides him with a theoretical framework within which to examine the interactions with employees. The manager should be able to identify the ego states from which both parties are interacting. A better understanding of himself, employees, and interactions with others will make the manager more comfortable, confident, and effective. He will be aware of ego states and seek the proper ego states when interacting with employees.

Transactional Analysis is a managerial tool. It should help the manager in his daily transactions with employees.

Notes

[1] Thomas A. Harris, M.D., *I'm OK—You're OK* (New York: Harper & Row Publishers, Inc., 1967), pp. 12–13.

[2] Eric Berne, *Transactional Analysis in Psychotherapy* (New York: Grove Press, 1961), p. 22.

[3] Eric Berne, M.D., *Games People Play* (New York: Grove Press, 1964), p. 48.

[4] Ronald J. Burke, "Games Managers Play," *Personnel Administration* (September 1968): 52–57.

[5] Joe Kelly, "Executive Defense Mechanisms and Games," *Personnel Administration* (July 1968): 30–35.

[6] Curtis J. Potter, "Games Managers Play," *Supervisory Management* (April 1969): 29–33.

[7] J.V.D. Meininger, *Success through Transactional Analysis* (New York: Grosset & Dunlap, Inc., 1973).

[8] Harris, *I'm OK—You're OK*, p. 43.

Part Eight

Techniques for Effective Interviewing

21

Transactional Interviewing

DAVID L. AUSTIN

Every year, millions of interpersonal transactions take place throughout the industrial community. While many of these transactions may be trivial, a great many are of a more serious nature, affecting the evaluation, employment, promotion, discharge, or treatment of one's fellow employees. In looking at the interview situation from the theoretical framework outlined by Harry Stack Sullivan in his *The Psychiatric Interview,* we can apply some insights to the specific behavior of interviewers. The basic issue will be: Could an Interviewer do a better job if he became more aware of, and sensitive to, the effects of his own behavior?

Interviews are very special occasions and have certain qualities that are not usually found in most other forms of interpersonal communication. For the purpose of this discussion they will be thought of as consisting of two people with one interviewing the other. An interview is a course of events, a dynamic, interactive process, a form of participative observation in which two people have come together for their mutual satisfaction. Usually one party is more expert in some area than the other, with the more expert person making inferences about the other, inferences based upon information provided, or not provided, during the interview. It is a constantly changing process, approached with caution by most, and can be disrupted fairly easily by the dysjunctive forces of the anxieties of either party. Structure of some sort should be one important difference between conversations, rap sessions, casual chatter, and interviews.

Each interview usually has an inception, a general form of inquiry, a detailed form of inquiry, and then a conclusion. Effective use of each stage identifies the skilled interviewer from the novice. Special alertness to the following phenomenon is essential: both clarity and obscurity are possible *because of* the interaction taking place in an interview. In other words, questions, like words, do not have meaning in and of themselves; they have meaning only as perceived in a particular setting by a particular person. You, the interviewer, may have as much to do with the answer as the interviewee! To illustrate this vital point, a department manager asks an employee how he likes his job. The reply depends on two things: one is the question. But the other equally important contributor to the reply is how well the employee knows the supervisor, how secure he feels, how sincere he feels the question is, and a host of other factors. If a personnel director asks a terminating employee why he is leaving the company, the answer he receives will depend greatly on the situation as perceived by the employee who is terminating. Special sensitivity to this process will help prevent an interviewer from placing too much faith in some of the replies received. Perception of the interview as a dynamic process, influenced by both participants, could help to avoid many of the misunderstandings and misinterpretations taking place every day throughout the industrial community.

Let's begin with you, the interviewer. Before you conduct another interview, reflect for a moment on just exactly what you are trying to achieve. It is truly astounding how few interviewers do this. Think back on your own experiences and upon how many times you clearly perceived and wrote down the aims of your discussion. And yet without some clearly understood objective, how can you verify your own performance? It seems to this writer that there are five general steps to be taken by every competent interviewer.

First, outline in some detail specific objectives. No capable supervisor would purchase a five, ten, or twenty thousand dollar piece of equipment for his company without first having a clear set of specifications to guide his selection. And yet how many potential employees are interviewed without those same clear criteria? When the interview has been completed, you should be able to review the results based upon your initial objectives.

Second, establish and then maintain a relationship with the interviewee which will help achieve the purposes of the interview. One of the chief reasons for failure is the inability or unwillingness to create the rapport, mutual trust and openness to share information and feelings that are so vital to successful interviews. The real danger here is that unless this basis for meaningful communication is created, a significant portion of the data you are receiving will not be valid, and, in fact, may actually be misleading. If your manner, for example, is threatening, you may be finding out how your interviewee behaves when he feels threatened, but you may not be finding out much more than that. If you are interviewing a candidate for a policeman's job, that of course is very useful data; if you are not, its relevance is questionable.

Third, the information you need must be obtained. While this seems obvious, many interviewers who have been asked what they know as a result of the many exchanges that just took place are not sure. If this happens to you, and it will if you are not alert to this phenomenon, it is probably because you didn't consistently pursue the data you needed. Many people are a lot of fun to talk with, and unless you make some attempt to influence the course of the conversation, you may have an enjoyable but unproductive time.

Fourth, an important goal of many interviewers is that of conveying information. Not only is this important because it is one of the functions of the occasion, but it is an invaluable method of increasing your understanding of the person to whom you are talking. Their responses, and lack of responses, are one of the most important clues as to what may be taking place between you, as well as inside the interviewee.

Fifth, when the interview has come to an end, review in your own mind what has just taken place. In a laboratory setting you would have the opportunity to tape your exchanges and then listen to your own performance. Since this can make many people uncomfortable, it is probably not advisable to do this in a work setting. The next best thing is to carefully and thoughtfully analyze what role you played, what responses you elicited, what effect the interviewee had on you, and how well you conducted the event. If you record some of your impressions of your performance for a series of interviews, you could probably learn more about yourself and your style.

In addition to clearly outlining your general goals, attention should be given to the development of the special skills required to be an effective interviewer. Several of them are worth mentioning.

1. Refine your ability to elicit, recognize, explore, explain, and resolve varied behavior patterns. Without real skill in these areas, the majority of the information and impressions you receive will remain unintegrated. In short, you will not understand the interviewee.

2. Make and test hypotheses concerning the patterns of behavior that you are witnessing. More than one educated guess should be made so that you are not limited by what appears to be correct. Once you have a few tentative conclusions about the person, then set out to verify your hunches with the remainder of your time. The result should be that one of your hypotheses appears to be the correct one. In many situations, particularly those in which the interviewee also wants clarification, a good method is to explain your tentative impressions and then listen to and interpret the responses. You should be playing a very active role in the process, and have to be very aware of how much your methods are influencing the data you are receiving.

3. Improve your use of speech in the achievement of your goals. Watch carefully your attempts to clarify rather than obscure, to expose rather than conceal, to stimulate rather than frighten, and to support rather than to undermine. In many situations, you may discover that either you or the applicant are using language to maintain a distance from one another, rather than using it to facilitate an approach. Alertness to this can help you overcome it.

4. Increase your awareness of your own and your interviewee's nonverbal behavior. If you are unwittingly generating anxiety, the defensive restlessness of your interviewee may be telling you about it. Hostility, anger, resentment, and embarrassment can all be displayed with body language. Conversely, assurance, comfort and composure can be clearly transmitted. The very structure of your interviewing arrangements may contain a nonverbal message. If, for example, you are always placing a 30-inch

desk between you and your interviewee, maybe you are indicating the respectful distance you prefer to maintain between you and other people. If you seldom smile or make an effort to put the other person at ease, this is clearly a nonverbal message of your lack of concern for their psychological well being.

5. Prepare the interviewee for topics that may create concern or that are personal in nature. Most of us are made uncomfortable by emotional surprises. Conversely, if he appears to be caught in a situation from which he is having trouble extricating himself, why not help him out? People appreciate that kind of insight into their dilemmas, as they appreciate a helping hand. Protection of the interviewee from loss of esteem, from embarrassment, or from appearing stupid is an obligation all good interviewers accept.

6. Improve your ability to make smooth conversational transitions from one topic to another, from one level of inquiry to another, and from one degree of significance to another. To switch a discussion from the unimportant to the serious without adequate preparation will tend to make most people anxious. A simple phrase such as "Could we now talk about your reasons for leaving some of these positions" is a better way than asking abruptly "Why did you leave these two positions?"

7. Learn to rapidly and accurately track the conversational, emotional, and factual changes taking place in your dialogues, in your relationship with the interviewee and in his behavior in relation to you. Because the interview is such a dynamic process, several changes may take place during the course of a few hours. The types of changes provide you with some of the best data you have concerning how the interviewee is feeling, how he handles himself, how your behavior may be influencing him, and how he may be attempting to influence you. A good interviewer becomes a behavioral tracking expert, in the sense that radar scans or tracks a series of objects.

8. Many people respond badly to a series of questions, or to interview situations in general. If you can improve your ability to interview people with this problem, you may locate an exceptional employee during a job interview, or you may help an employee solve a complex situation without losing him.

9. Increase your sensitivity to the needs you project. If, for example, you project the need to control the conversation, you may find out how the interviewee reacts to a controlled situation. If you project the need to have answers that agree with your own, those are the answers you are likely to receive. People being interviewed are quite often alert to an unwritten or hidden agenda, that is, the things you appear to want to hear. Remember, you get what you deserve. There is a good possibility that if you are relatively inexperienced at interviewing, you may be unaware of the many signs you make that encourage interviewees to behave in certain ways.

Interviews that do not work out well for you need study. Analysis of these disappointments might reveal moves which unwittingly contributed to the failure, and consequently help you improve.

Like you, the interviewee has specific goals in mind when he walks into your office. A few of these are:

1. To learn more about his situation. If employment is the goal, then information about what will be expected from him is of paramount importance. If performance appraisal is the goal, then past activities and future requirements are of major concern. If pending discipline or vocational counseling are the goals, other very specific data are required. Your special attention to the goals of interviewees can help you satisfy their needs.

2. To learn more about himself. This is not a goal that is usually stated and has not traditionally been addressed by many interviewers. And yet countless interviewees have left vocational counseling, employment, disciplinary or appraisal interviews without learning about themselves. People being interviewed frequently feel that the responsibility for determining the scope and direction of the conversation rests with the interviewer only. Consequently, unless the interviewer is willing to pursue this point, it will not be pursued.

3. To present himself in the best possible manner. Many people find that the interview situation is an anxiety producing event, one in which they are not at their best. When upset, their natural psychological defense systems start operating and protection of their self esteem becomes important. The obligation, therefore, of the interviewer becomes one of preventing such situations from occurring, or if they occur, of helping the interviewee extricate himself as gracefully as possible.

Most people bring to a situation a fairly well-defined set of expectations. If you, by your respect, support and active encouragement, can help a person gain insight into himself and provide you with insight into his behavior rationale, then you have become a fine interviewer. Increased awareness of, and sensitivity to, the vital role you play in every personal transaction will hopefully improve your effectiveness as an interviewer, and as a person.

22

Active Listening

CARL R. ROGERS *and* RICHARD E. FARSON

The Meaning of Active Listening

One basic responsibility of the supervisor or executive is the development, adjustment, and integration of individual employees. He tries to develop employee potential, delegate responsibility, and achieve cooperation. To do so, he must have, among other abilities, the ability to listen intelligently and carefully to those with whom he works.

There are, however, many kinds of listening skills. The lawyer, for example, when questioning a witness, listens for contradictions, irrelevancies, errors, and weaknesses. But this is not the kind of listening skill we are concerned with in this booklet. The lawyer usually is not listening in order to help the witness adjust or cooperate or produce. On the other hand, we will be concerned with listening skills which *will help* employees gain a clearer understanding of their situations, take responsibility, and cooperate with each other.

Two Examples

The kind of listening we have in mind is called "active listening." It is called "active" because the listener has a very definite responsibility. He does not passively absorb the words which are spoken to him. He actively tries to grasp the facts and the feelings in what he hears, and he tries, by his listening, to help the speaker work out his own problems.

To get a fuller picture of what is meant by active listening, let us consider two different approaches to the same work problem.

Example No. 1

> *Foreman:* Hey, Al, I don't get this production order. We can't handle this run today. What do they think we are?
>
> *Supervisor:* But that's the order. So get it out as soon as you can. We're under terrific pressure this week.
>
> *Foreman:* Don't they know we're behind schedule already because of that press breakdown?
>
> *Supervisor:* Look, Kelly, I don't decide what goes on upstairs. I just have to see that the work gets out and that's what I'm gonna do.
>
> *Foreman:* The guys aren't gonna like this.
>
> *Supervisor:* That's something you'll have to work out with them, not me.

Example No. 2

> *Foreman:* Hey, Ross, I don't get this production order. We can't handle this run today. What do they think we are?
>
> *Supervisor:* Sounds like you're pretty sore about it, Kelly.
>
> *Foreman:* I sure am. We were just about getting back to schedule after that press breakdown. Now this comes along.
>
> *Supervisor:* As if you didn't have enough work to do, huh?
>
> *Foreman:* Yeah. I don't know how I'm gonna tell the guys about this.
>
> *Supervisor:* Hate to face 'em with it now, is that it?
>
> *Foreman:* I really do. They're under a real strain today. Seems like everything we do around here is rush, rush.
>
> *Supervisor:* I guess you feel like it's unfair to load anything more on them.
>
> *Foreman:* Well, yeah. I know there must be plenty of pressure on everybody up the line, but—well, if that's the way it is . . . guess I'd better get the word to 'em.

There are obviously many differences between these two examples. The main one, however, is that Ross, the supervisor in the second example, is using the active-listening approach. He is listening and responding in a way that makes it clear that he appreciates both the meaning and the feeling behind what Kelly is saying.

Active listening does not necessarily mean long sessions spent listening to grievances, personal or otherwise. It is simply a way of approaching those problems which arise out of the usual day-to-day events of any job.

To be effective, active listening must be firmly grounded in the basic attitudes of the user. We cannot employ it as a technique if our fundamental attitudes are in conflict with its basic concepts. If we try, our behavior will be empty and sterile and our associates will be quick to recognize this. Until we can demonstrate a spirit which genuinely respects the potential worth of the individual, which considers his rights and trusts his capacity for self-direction, we cannot begin to be effective listeners.

What We Achieve by Listening

Active listening is an important way to bring about changes in people. Despite the popular notion that listening is a passive approach, clinical and research evidence clearly shows that sensitive listening is a most effective agent for individual personality change and group development. Listening brings about changes in people's attitudes toward themselves and others, and also brings about changes in their basic values and personal philosophy. People who have been listened to in this new and special way become more emotionally mature, more open to their experiences, less defensive, more democratic, and less authoritarian.

When people are listened to sensitively, they tend to listen to themselves with more care and make clear exactly what they are feeling and thinking. Group members tend to listen more to each other, become less argumentative, more ready to incorporate other points of view. Because listening reduces the threat of having one's ideas criticized, the person is better able to see them for what they are, and is more likely to feel that his contributions are worthwhile.

Not the least important result of listening is the change that takes place within the listener himself. Besides the fact that listening provides more information than any other activity, it builds deep, positive relationships and tends to alter constructively the attitudes of the listener. Listening is a growth experience.

These, then, are some of the worthwhile results we can expect from active listening. But how do we go about this kind of listening? How do we become active listeners?

How to Listen

Active listening aims to bring about changes in people. To achieve this end, it relies upon definite techniques—things to do and things to avoid doing. Before discussing these techniques, however, we should first understand why they are effective. To do so, we must understand how the individual personality develops.

The Growth of the Individual

Through all of our lives, from early childhood on, we have learned to think of ourselves in certain, very definite ways. We have built up pictures of ourselves. Sometimes these self-pictures are pretty realistic but at other times they are not. For example, an overage, overweight lady may fancy herself a youthful, ravishing siren, or an awkward teenager regard himself as a star athlete.

All of us have experiences which fit the way we need to think about ourselves. These we accept. But it is much harder to accept experiences which don't fit. And sometimes, if it is very important for us to hang on to this self-picture, we don't accept or admit these experiences at all.

These self-pictures are not necessarily attractive. A man, for example, may regard himself as incompetent and worthless. He may feel that he is doing his job poorly in spite of favorable appraisals by the company. As long as he has these feelings about himself he must deny any experiences which would seem not to fit this self-picture, in this case any that might indicate to him that he is competent. It is so necessary for him to maintain this self-picture that he is threatened by anything which would tend to change it. Thus, when the company raises his salary, it may seem to him only additional proof that he is a fraud. He must hold onto this self-picture, because, bad or good, it's the only thing he has by which he can identify himself.

This is why direct attempts to change this individual or change his self-picture are particularly threatening. He is forced to defend himself or to completely deny the experience. This denial of experience and defense of the self-picture tend to bring on rigidity of behavior and create difficulties in personal adjustment.

The active-listening approach, on the other hand, does not present a threat to the individual's self-picture. He does not have to defend it. He is able to explore it, see it for what it is, and make his own decision as to how realistic it is. And he is then in a position to change.

If I want to help a man reduce his defensiveness and become more adaptive, I must try to remove the threat of myself as his potential changer. As long as the atmosphere is threatening, there can be no effective communication. So I must create a climate which is neither critical, evaluative, nor moralizing. It must be an atmosphere of equality and freedom, permissiveness and understanding, acceptance and warmth. It is in this climate and this climate only that the individual feels safe enough to incorporate new experiences and new values into his concept of himself. Let's see how active listening helps to create this climate.

What to Avoid

When we encounter a person with a problem, our usual response is to try to change his way of looking at things—to get him to see his situation the way we see it, or would like him to see it. We plead, reason, scold, encourage, insult, prod—anything to bring about a change in the desired direction, that is, in the direction we want him to travel. What we seldom realize, however, is that, under these circumstances, we are usually responding to *our own* needs to see the world in certain ways. It is always difficult for us to tolerate and understand actions which are different from the ways in which we believe we should act. If, however, we can free ourselves from the need to influence and direct others in our own paths, we enable ourselves to listen with understanding, and thereby employ the most potent available agent of change.

One problem the listener faces is that of responding to demands for decisions, judgments, and evaluations. He is constantly called upon to agree or disagree with someone or something. Yet, as he well knows, the question or challenge frequently is a masked expression of feeling or needs which the speaker is far more anxious to communicate than he is to have the surface questions answered. Because he cannot speak these feelings openly, the speaker must disguise them to himself and to others in an acceptable form. To illustrate, let us examine some typical questions and the type of answers that might best elicit the feeling beneath it.

Employee's Question	*Listener's Answer*
Just whose responsibility is the tool room?	Do you feel that someone is challenging your authority in there?
Don't you think younger able people should be promoted before senior but less able ones?	It seems to you they should, I take it.
What does the super expect us to do about those broken-down machines?	You're pretty disgusted with those machines, aren't you?
Don't you think I've improved over the last review period?	Sounds as if you feel like you've really picked up lately.

These responses recognize the questions but leave the way open for the employee to say what is really bothering him. They allow the listener to participate in the problem or situation without shouldering all responsibility for decision-making or actions. This is a process of thinking *with* people instead of *for* or *about* them.

Passing judgment, whether critical or favorable, makes free expression difficult. Similarly, advice and information are almost always seen as efforts to change a person and thus serve as barriers to his self-expression and the development of a creative relationship. Moreover, advice is seldom taken and information hardly ever utilized. The eager young trainee probably will not become patient just because he is advised that, "The road to success in business is a long, difficult one, and you must be patient." And it is no more helpful for him to learn that "only one out of a hundred trainees reach top management positions."

Interestingly, it is a difficult lesson to learn that positive *evaluations* are sometimes as blocking as negative ones. It is almost as destructive to the freedom of a relationship to tell a person that he is good or capable or right, as to tell him otherwise. To evaluate him positively may make it more difficult for him to tell of the faults that distress him or the ways in which he believes he is not competent.

Encouragement also may be seen as an attempt to motivate the speaker in certain directions or hold him off rather than as support. "I'm sure everything will work out O.K." is not a helpful response to the person who is deeply discouraged about a problem.

In other words, most of the techniques and devices common to human relationships are found to be of little use in establishing the type of relationship we are seeking here.

What to Do

Just what does active listening entail, then? Basically, it requires that we get inside the speaker, that we grasp, *from his point of view,* just what it is he is communicating to us. More than that, we must convey to the speaker that we are seeing things from his point of view. To listen actively, then, means that there are several things we must do.

Listen for Total Meaning

Any message a person tries to get across usually has two components: the *content* of the message, and the *feeling* or attitude underlying this content. Both are important, both give the message *meaning.* It is this total meaning of the message that we try to understand. For example, a machinist comes to his foreman and says, "I've finished that lathe set-up." This message has obvious content and perhaps calls upon the foreman for another work assignment. Suppose, on the other hand, that he says, "Well, I'm finally finished with that damned lathe set-up." The content is the same but the total meaning of the message has changed—and changed in an important way for both the foreman and the worker. Here sensitive listening can facilitate the relationship. Suppose the foreman were to respond by simply giving another work assignment. Would the employee feel that he had gotten his total message across? Would he feel free to talk to his foreman? Will he feel better about his job, more anxious to do good work on the next assignment?

Now, on the other hand, suppose the foreman were to respond with, "Glad to have it over with, huh?" or "Had a pretty rough time of it?" or "Guess you don't feel like doing anything like that again," or anything else that tells the worker that he heard and understands. It doesn't necessarily mean that the next work assignment need be changed or that he must spend an hour listening to the worker complain about the set-up problems he encountered. He may do a number of things differently in the light of the new information he has from the worker—but not necessarily. It's just that extra sensitivity on the part of the foreman which can transform an average working climate into a good one.

Respond to Feelings

In some instances the content is far less important than the feeling which underlies it. To catch the full flavor or meaning of the message one must respond particularly to the feeling component, if, for instance, our machinist had said "I'd like to melt this lathe down and make paper clips out of it," responding to content would be obviously absurd. But to respond to his disgust or anger in trying to work with his lathe recognizes the meaning of this message. There are various shadings of these components in the meaning of any message. Each time the listener must try to remain sensitive to the total meaning the message has to the speaker. What is he trying to tell me? What does this mean to him? How does he see this situation?

Note All Cues

Not all communication is verbal. The speaker's words alone don't tell us everything he is communicating. And hence, truly sensitive listening requires that we become aware of several kinds of communication besides verbal. The way in which a speaker hesitates in his speech can tell us much about his feelings. So too can the inflection of his voice. He may stress certain points loudly and clearly, and may mumble others. We should also note such things as the person's facial expressions, body posture, hand movements, eye movements, and breathing. All of these help to convey his total message.

What We Communicate by Listening

The first reaction of most people when they consider listening as a possible method for dealing with human beings is that listening cannot be sufficient in itself. Because it is passive, they feel, listening does not communicate anything to the speaker. Actually, nothing could be farther from the truth.

By consistently listening to a speaker you are conveying the idea that: "I'm interested in you as a person, and I think that what you feel is important. I respect your thoughts, and even if I don't agree with them, I know that they are valid for you. I feel sure that you have a contribution to make. I'm not trying to change you or evaluate you. I just want to understand you. I think you're worth listening to, and I want you to know that I'm the kind of person you can talk to."

The subtle but most important aspect of this is that it is the *demonstration* of the message that works. While it is most difficult to convince someone that you respect him by *telling* him so, you are much more likely to get this message across by really *behaving* that way—by actually *having* and *demonstrating* respect for this person. Listening does this most effectively.

Like other behavior, listening behavior is contagious. This has implications for all communications problems, whether between two people, or within a large organization. To insure good communication between associates up and down the line, one must first take the responsibility for setting a pattern of listening. Just as one learns that anger is usually met with anger, argument with argument, and deception with deception, one can learn that listening can be met with listening. Every person who feels responsibility in a situation can set the tone of the interaction, and the important lesson in this is that any behavior exhibited by one person will eventually be responded to with similar behavior in the other person.

It is far more difficult to stimulate constructive behavior in another person but far more profitable. Listening is one of these constructive behaviors, but if one's attitude is to "wait out" the speaker rather than really listen to him, it will fail. The one who consistently listens with understanding, however, is the one who eventually is most likely to be listened to. If you really want to be heard and understood by another, you can develop him as a potential listener, ready for new ideas, provided you can first develop yourself in these ways and sincerely listen with understanding and respect.

Testing for Understanding

Because understanding another person is actually far more difficult than it at first seems, it is important to test constantly your ability to see the world in the way the speaker sees it. You can do this by reflecting in your own words what the speaker seems to mean by his words and actions. His response to this will tell you whether or not he feels understood. A good rule of thumb is to assume that one never really understands until he can communicate this understanding to the other's satisfaction.

Here is an experiment to test your skill in listening. The next time you become involved in a lively or controversial discussion with another person, stop for a moment and suggest that you adopt this ground rule for continued discussion: Before either participant in the discussion can make a point or express an opinion of his own, he must first restate aloud the previous point or position of the other person. This restatement must be accurate enough to satisfy the speaker before the listener can be allowed to speak for himself.

This is something you could try in your own discussion group. Have someone express himself on some topic of emotional concern to the group. Then, before another member expresses his own feelings and thought, he must rephrase the *meaning* expressed by the previous speaker to that individual's satisfaction. Note the changes in the emotional climate and the quality of the discussion when you try this.

Problems in Active Listening

Active listening is not an easy skill to acquire. It demands practice. Perhaps more important, it may require changes in our own basic attitudes. These changes come slowly and sometimes with considerable difficulty. Let us look at some of the major problems in active listening and what can be done to overcome them.

The Personal Risk

To be effective at all in active listening, one must have a sincere interest in the speaker. We all live in glass houses as far as our attitudes are concerned. They always show through. And if we are only making a pretense of interest in the speaker, he will quickly pick this up, either consciously or unconsciously. And once he does, he will no longer express himself freely.

Active listening carries a strong element of personal risk. If we manage to accomplish what we are describing here—to sense deeply the feelings of another person, to understand the meaning his experiences have for him, to see the world as he sees it—we risk being changed ourselves. For example, if we permit ourselves to listen our way into the psychological life of a labor leader or agitator—to get the meaning which life has for him—we risk coming to see the world as he sees it. It is threatening to give up, even momentarily, what we believe and start thinking in someone else's terms. It takes a great deal of inner security and courage to be able to risk one's self in understanding another.

For the supervisor, the courage to take another's point of view generally means that he must see *himself* through another's eyes—he must be able to see himself as others see him. To do this may sometimes be unpleasant, but it is far more *difficult* than unpleasant. We are so accustomed to viewing ourselves in certain ways—to seeing and hearing only what we want to see and hear—that it is extremely difficult for a person to free himself from his needs to see things these ways.

Developing an attitude of sincere interest in the speaker is thus no easy task. It can be developed only by being willing to risk seeing the world from the speaker's point of view. If we have a number of such experiences, however, they will shape an attitude which will allow us to be truly genuine in our interest in the speaker.

Hostile Expressions

The listener will often hear negative, hostile expressions directed at himself. Such expressions are always hard to listen to. No one likes to hear hostile action or words. And it is not easy to get to the point where one is strong enough to permit these attacks without finding it necessary to defend himself or retaliate.

Because we all fear that people will crumble under the attack of genuine negative feelings, we tend to perpetuate an attitude of pseudopeace. It is as if we cannot tolerate conflict at all for fear of the damage it could do to us, to the situation, to the others involved. But of course the real damage is done to all these by the denial and suppression of negative feelings.

Out-of-Place Expressions

There is also the problem of out-of-place expressions, expressions dealing with behavior which is not usually acceptable in our society. In the extreme forms that present themselves before psychotherapists, expressions of sexual perversity or homicidal fantasies are often found blocking to the listener because of their obvious threatening quality. At less extreme levels, we all find unnatural or inappropriate behavior difficult to handle. That is, anything from an "off-color" story told in mixed company to seeing a man weep is likely to produce a problem situation.

In any face-to-face situation, we will find instances of this type which will momentarily, if not permanently, block any communication. In business and industry any expressions of weakness or incompetency will generally be regarded as unacceptable and therefore will block good two-way communication. For example, it is difficult to listen to a supervisor tell of his feelings of failure in being able to "take charge" of a situation in his department because *all* administrators are supposed to be able to "take charge."

Accepting Positive Feelings

It is both interesting and perplexing to note that negative or hostile feelings or expressions are much easier to deal with in any face-to-face relationship than are truly and deeply positive feelings. This is especially true for the business man because the culture expects him to be independent, bold, clever, and aggressive and manifest no feelings of warmth, gentleness, and intimacy. He therefore comes to regard these feelings as soft and inappropriate. But no matter how they are regarded, they remain a human need. The denial of these feelings in himself and his associates does not get the executive out of the problem of dealing with them. They simply become veiled and confused. If recognized they would work for the total effort; unrecognized, they work against it.

Emotional Danger Signals

The listener's own emotions are sometimes a barrier to active listening. When emotions are at their height, when listening is most necessary, it is most difficult to set aside one's own concerns and be understanding. Our emotions are often our own worst enemies when we try to become listeners. The more involved and invested we are in a particular situation or problem, the less we are likely to be willing or able to listen to the feelings and attitudes of others. That is, the more we find it necessary to respond to our own needs, the less we are able to respond to the needs of another. Let us look at some of the main danger signals that warn us that our emotions may be interfering with our listening.

Defensiveness

The points about which one is most vocal and dogmatic, the points which one is most anxious to impose on others—these are always the points one is trying to talk oneself into believing. So one danger signal becomes apparent when you find yourself stressing a point or trying to convince another. It is at these times that you are likely to be less secure and thus less able to listen.

Resentment of Opposition

It is always easier to listen to an idea which is similar to one of your own than to an opposing view. Sometimes, in order to clear the air, it is helpful to pause for a moment when you feel your ideas and position being challenged, reflect on the situation, and express your concern to the speaker.

Clash of Personalities

Here again, our experience has consistently shown us that the genuine expression of feelings on the part of the listener will be more helpful in developing a sound relationship than the suppression of them. This is so whether the feelings be resentment, hostility, threat, or admiration. A basically honest relationship, whatever the nature of it, is the most productive of all. The other party becomes secure when he learns that the listener can express his feelings honestly and openly to him. We should keep this in mind when we begin to fear a clash of personalities in the listening relationship. Otherwise, fear of our own emotions will choke off full expression of feelings.

Listening to Ourselves

To listen to oneself is a prerequisite to listening to others. And it is often an effective means of dealing with the problems we have outlined above. When we are most aroused, excited, and demanding, we are least able to understand our own feelings and attitudes. Yet, in dealing with the problems of others, it becomes most important to be sure of one's own position, values, and needs.

The ability to recognize and understand the meaning which a particular episode has for you, with all the feelings which it stimulates in you, and the ability to express this meaning when you find it getting in the way of active listening, will clear the air and enable you once again to be free to listen. That is, if some person or situation touches off feelings within you which tend to block your attempts to listen with understanding, begin listening to yourself. It is much more helpful in developing effective relationships to avoid suppressing these feelings. Speak them out as clearly as you can, and try to enlist the other person as a listener to your feelings. A person's listening ability is limited by his ability to listen to himself.

Active Listening and Company Goals

"How can listening improve production?"

"We're in business, and it's a rugged, fast, competitive affair. How are we going to find time to counsel our employees?"

"We have to concern ourselves with organizational problems first."

"We can't afford to spend all day listening when there's a job to be done."

"What's morale got to do with production?"

"Sometimes we have to sacrifice an individual for the good of the rest of the people in the company."

Those of us who are trying to advance the listening approach in industry hear these comments frequently. And because they are so honest and legitimate, they pose a real problem. Unfortunately, the answers are not so clear-cut as the questions.

Individual Importance

One answer is based on an assumption that is central to the listening approach. That assumption is: the kind of behavior which helps the individual will eventually be the best thing that could be done for the group. Or saying it another way: the things that are best for the individual are best for the company. This is a conviction of ours, based on our experience in psychology and education. The research evidence from industry is only beginning to come in. We find that putting the group first, at the expense of the individual, besides being an uncomfortable individual experience, does *not* unify the group. In fact, it tends to make the group less a group. The members become anxious and suspicious.

We are not at all sure in just what ways the group does benefit from a concern demonstrated for an individual, but we have several strong leads. One is that the group feels more secure when an individual member is being listened to and provided for with concern and sensitivity. And we assume that a secure group will ultimately be a better group. When each individual feels that he need not fear exposing himself to the group, he is likely to contribute more freely and spontaneously. When the leader of a group responds to the individual, puts the individual first, the other members of the group will follow suit, and the group comes to act as a unit in recognizing and responding to the needs of a particular member. This positive, constructive action seems to be a much more satisfying experience for a group than the experience of dispensing with a member.

Listening and Production

As to whether or not listening or any other activity designed to better human relations in an industry actually raises production—whether morale has a definite relationship to production is not known for sure. There are some who frankly hold that there is no relationship to be expected between morale and production—that production often depends upon the social misfit, the eccentric, or the isolate. And there are some who simply choose to work in a climate of cooperation and harmony, in a high-morale group, quite aside from the question of increased production.

A report from the Survey Research Center[1] at the University of Michigan on research conducted at the Prudential Life Insurance Company lists seven findings relating to production and morale. First-line supervisors in high-production work groups were found to differ from those in low-production work groups in that they:

1. Are under less close supervision from their own supervisors.
2. Place less direct emphasis upon production as the goal.
3. Encourage employee participation in the making of decisions.
4. Are more employee-centered.
5. Spend more of their time in supervision and less in straight production work.
6. Have a greater feeling of confidence in their supervisory roles.
7. Feel that they know where they stand with the company.

After mentioning that other dimensions of morale, such as identification with the company, intrinsic job satisfaction, and satisfaction with job status, were not found significantly related to productivity, the report goes on to suggest the following psychological interpretation:

People are more effectively motivated when they are given some degree of freedom in the way in which they do their work than when every action is prescribed in advance. They do better when some degree of decision-making about their jobs is possible than when all decisions are made for them. They respond more adequately when they are treated as personalities than as cogs in a machine. In short if the ego motivations of self-determination, of self-expression, of a sense of personal worth can be tapped, the individual can be more effectively energized. The use of external sanctions, or pressuring for production may work to some degree, but not to the extent that the more internalized motives do. When the individual comes to identify himself with his job and with the work of his group, human resources are much more fully utilized in the production process.

The Survey Research Center has also conducted studies among workers in other industries. In discussing the results of these studies, Robert L. Kahn writes:

> In the studies of clerical workers, railroad workers, and workers in heavy industry, the supervisors with the better production records gave a larger proportion of their time to supervisory functions, especially to the interpersonal aspects of their jobs. The supervisors of the lower-producing sections were more likely to spend their time in tasks which the men themselves were performing, or in the paperwork aspects of their jobs.[2]

Maximum Creativeness

There may never be enough research evidence to satisfy everyone on this question. But speaking from a business point of view, in terms of the problems of developing resources for production, the maximum creativeness and productive effort of the human beings in the organization are the richest untapped source of power still existing. The difference between the maximum productive capacity of people and that output which industry is now realizing is immense. We simply suggest that this maximum capacity might be closer to realization if we sought to release the motivation that already exists within people rather than try to stimulate them externally.

This releasing of the individual is made possible first of all by sensitive listening, with respect and understanding. Listening is a beginning toward making the individual feel himself worthy of making contributions, and this could result in a very dynamic and productive organization. Competitive business is never too rugged or too busy to take time to procure the most efficient technological advances or to develop rich raw material resources. But these in comparison to the resources that are already within the people in the plant are paltry. This is industry's major procurement problem.

G. L. Clements, president of Jewel Tea Co., Inc., in talking about the collaborative approach to management says:

> We feel that this type of approach recognizes that there is a secret ballot going on at all times among the people in any business. They vote for or against their supervisors. A favorable vote for the supervisor shows up in the cooperation, teamwork, understanding, and production of the group. To win this secret ballot, each supervisor must share the problems of his group and work for them.[3]

The decision to spend time listening to his employees is a decision each supervisor or executive has to make for himself. Executives seldom have much to do with products or processes. They have to deal with people who must in turn deal with people who will deal with products or processes. The higher one goes up the line the more he will be concerned with human relations problems, simply because people are all he has to work with. The minute we take a man from his bench and make him a foreman he is removed from the basic production of goods and now must begin relating to individuals instead of nuts and bolts. People are different from things, and our foreman is called upon for a different line of skills completely. His new tasks call upon him to be a special kind of person. The development of himself as a listener is a first step in becoming this special person.

Notes

[1] "Productivity, Supervision, and Employee Morale," *Human Relations,* Series 1, Report 1 (Ann Arbor, Mich.: Survey Research Center, University of Michigan).

[2] Robert L. Kahn, "The Human Factors Underlying Industrial Productivity," *Michigan Business Review* (November 1952).

[3] G. L. Clements, "Time for 'Democracy in Action' at the Executive Level," the A.M.A. Personnel Conference (February 28, 1951).

23

The Hiring Interview

ROBERT L. MINTER

"She's a nice person, likes to ski, has good feelings about her father—I think she'd be a good addition to our staff."

Preposterous? Yes. But too often, employment interviews yield a lot of peripheral information about an applicant and fail to delve into such important areas as work background, experience, and career aspirations. Regardless of size, purpose, or function, all organizations use some type of interview-screening process in recruiting personnel. But despite its wide use, the hiring interview is one of the most misunderstood and misused methods of communication.

Too often, people responsible for hiring receive little or no formal training in interviewing job applicants and so are unaware of the ways in which their interviewing styles influence an applicant's behavior. Organizations that do train their interviewers may give them only general information on company manpower requirements and personnel-placement policies. Rarely is an interviewer trained in the specific communication skills he needs to be effective.

Some personnel interviewers apparently feel that communication skills go along with common sense. They refuse even to consider special training. "I don't need training! I've been interviewing for years and the company has been satisfied." Part of this statement may be true (i.e., he has been interviewing for years), but whether he has been successful depends on the criteria used.

When an organization has high turnover and absenteeism, or when it must give new employees more on-the-job training than initially contemplated, its interviewing success must be termed something less than successful. Of course, not all problems with absenteeism, turnover, and on-the-job training stem from ineffective interviewing, but a large portion of such problems *can* be traced back to improper use of interview-screening procedures. (Communication problems are frequently created by interviewers who lack dialogue training or who are insensitive to the communication sins listed in Table 1.)

If any bells are ringing or if you are wondering how you and your company shape up, compare your procedures with those outlined here. Most effective interviewing procedures can be broken down into three distinct sequences—each with specific goals and appropriate methods for achieving them.

Table 1 Common Sins of the Employment Interviewer

1. The interviewer talks a lot and listens only a little—so gets sketchy information from which to assess the applicant's potential.

2. The interviewer fails to tell the applicant the major aim of the interview.

3. The interviewer wastes time by asking irrelevant questions. He may, for example, request information that is already on the application form or ask questions that range far afield from the job skills and attitudes needed for the vacancy.

4. The interview is disorganized because the interviewer has vague interview objectives and talks about whatever he is in the mood to.

5. The interviewer biases applicant responses by providing job information too early in the interview.

6. The interviewer "plays" psychologist by attempting an in-depth personality assessment.

7. The interviewer believes that the best way to assess an applicant's potential is to observe his behavior under stress—and then provides the necessary stress.

8. The interviewer overreacts to body language, permitting first impressions to stereotype the applicant.

9. The interviewer doesn't have enough information about the problems of the particular job (e.g., reasons for turnover, absenteeism, low morale, specific job duties and responsibilities not covered in the job description).

10. Because he screens too many applicants within a short period of time, the interviewer falls prey to fatigue—fatigue that influences his assessment and attitude toward applicants.

11. The interviewer overemphasizes or otherwise misuses the applicant's test results.

12. The interviewer attempts to conduct a thorough interview in ten to fifteen minutes.

13. The interviewer misinterprets letters of reference.

14. The interviewer oversells the job and company—thus building false hopes and expectations that are very likely to end up in turnover statistics.

Screening Procedures

If an organization is interested in a particular applicant, he may be given a battery of selection tests to assess such things as skills, aptitudes, and achievement. Some organizations (and some jobs) require only that an application form be completed in this first sequence. If the applicant "passes" these initial tests, he usually moves on to a more thorough interview.

However, two basic facts should be established before thorough selection-interviewing techniques are used.

1. The applicant has met basic selection criteria (such as appropriate work experience, education, test scores, letters of reference, training, and skills) required for the position.
2. The interviewer is well informed about existing job requirements and demands of the vacant position.

If the interviewer believes the applicant is underqualified or overqualified for the position, or has questionable letters of reference, then conducting a lengthy interview could waste time and motion for all concerned.

In-Depth Interviewing

The second sequence, in-depth interviewing, is designed to get information about the applicant's work experience, work attitudes, and motivation for applying for a particular position. It is also used to clear up any hazy information the applicant gave on the application form and to fill in any omissions. Several interview stages could be involved in this sequence, depending on the recruitment policy and size of the organization. Here are the major interview stages of this second sequence:

First-Stage Interview

This interview is quite short if the applicant does not seem to meet the job requirements. The interviewer tries to tell the applicant, tactfully, why he does not qualify for the position. In some instances, the interviewer may briefly counsel the applicant on firms in the area that have openings appropriate for him.

But if the first-stage interviewer believes on the basis of general exploratory questioning that the applicant has the necessary qualifications, he will then recommend considering the applicant for a second-stage interview. Of course, if the first-stage interviewer may decide whether to hire or not, further interviews are not necessary.

Subsequent Interviews

The number of interviews scheduled for a particular applicant will often depend on the type of job in question. The interview schedule can usually be cancelled anywhere along the interview chain if an interviewer believes the applicant to be unqualified.

Before seeing applicants, interviewers who are not familiar with the vacant position must bone up on its requirements. Job descriptions help, but they do not provide all the information required to develop meaningful position-related questions. Most job descriptions do not and cannot include the many day-to-day duties and problems inherent in the job.

Suppose you are responsible for screening applicants for the position of administrative secretary, and you have several applicants to interview. You are given the following job description:

Position Title: Administrative Secretary
  Responsibilities: The administrative secretary supervises a secretarial pool of approximately ten stenographer-typists who are responsible for taking dictation, typing, filing, and general clerical work. The administrative secretary reports directly to the manager of the commercial office. On occasion, the administrative secretary will be asked to do personal secretarial work for the vice-president of the commercial office. The major responsibility of the incumbent is to be responsible for the entire clerical and secretarial function of the commercial office. The incumbent must have at least a high-school diploma along with several years of experience as a private secretary; must be a proficient typist; and must demonstrate the ability to supervise others.
  Salary: Salary will be commensurate with experience ($9,000 to $11,000).

What additional information would you need before interviewing the applicants?

First, you would want to know how many interviewers will be involved and who will cover what areas. Once you know this, you can begin planning the areas to cover and the questions to ask each applicant.

You should also know something about the history of the job you are trying to fill. The following are examples of the kinds of information you should have at hand before you begin interviewing:

1. The rate and reasons for employee turnover and/or absenteeism.
2. The difficulties, if any, that the manager or vice-president of the commercial office has had with past administrative secretaries.
3. The problems inherent in the secretarial pool that the administrative secretary will have to cope with.
4. Any unusual demands of the position that are not stated in the job description.

5. The current expectations of the manager and vice-president regarding the qualities they look for in the administrative secretary.

Now suppose you talk to the manager and vice-president of the commercial office and learn that:

1. Absenteeism and turnover are extremely high in the secretarial pool. Consequently, if a backlog of work builds up, the administrative secretary will be expected to pitch in and help with work normally done only by secretaries. Unexpected absences and turnover in the secretarial pool have frequently required the administrative secretary to work as much as ten to fifteen hours of overtime per week.
2. Within the past year and a half, three administrative secretaries have worked in the commercial department. The new administrative secretary will be the fourth. The average time on the job for each administrative secretary has been approximately six months. Some of the past incumbents have quit because of job pressure. The combination of serving as personal secretary for two administrators and shouldering supervisory responsibilities for the secretarial pool created most of the stress.
3. Because some of the former administrative secretaries did not have cars, they had to depend on public transportation. Working overtime often made it quite difficult for them to catch the last bus of the evening and created baby-sitting problems for some.

Based on what is known from the job analysis, the following position-related questions could be pursued with individual applicants during the interview:

1. What is the applicant's philosophy of supervision?
2. How does the applicant feel about assuming the many role responsibilities required of a supervisor in this position?
3. What type of on-the-job pressure does the applicant appear to dislike? Like?
4. What does the applicant consider to be the greatest number of employees he feels comfortable in supervising?
5. How does he feel about training new secretarial personnel and working with a relatively inexperienced staff caused by a high turnover rate?
6. What is the applicant's opinion on the way to manage a secretarial pool?
7. How does the applicant feel about having to work for more than one boss?
8. What is the applicant's attitude toward "pinch-hitting" for some of the secretaries when they are absent?
9. What would be the applicant's mode of transportation?
10. What is the applicant's attitude toward overtime? Even if he appears to be enthusiastic, it pays to probe a bit.

During each stage, interviewers should avoid playing psychologist. Employment interviewers are usually not professionally qualified to assess anything more than surface personality attributes and social skills. Samples of questions that should be avoided follow (notice that these questions are clinically oriented and would require psychological expertise in analyzing the applicant's responses):

"How do you feel about your family?"
"To what degree can you take instructions without feeling upset?"
"Which of your parents has had the most profound influence on you?"
"What is the most difficult personal decision you've had to make?"
"Tell me about your home life during the time you were growing up."
"Who are your best friends? Why?"
"Tell me a story."

Improving Procedures

Regardless of the number of stages involved in the interview-screening process, several guidelines can improve its overall effectiveness and efficiency. One is to make sure that each interviewer has specific responsibilities and objectives for his interview—without much overlap or duplication of effort among interviewers.

The role of the first-stage interviewer, for example, might be to assess the completed application form for omissions, vagueness, and innuendoes that require clarification. This interviewer might also explore the applicant's aspirations, job expectations, career objectives, and likes and dislikes for specific types of work. If the first-stage interviewer is impressed with the interviewee's credentials, he may recommend the applicant to someone else for a second-stage interview.

The responsibilities of the second-stage interviewer might be to assess the applicant's training and job experience and to explore his ability to apply these to problem solving. (This would assume that the second interviewer has more experience with the particular job vacancy and is able to develop more task-relevant questions than the previous interviewer.)

The responsibilities of the final-stage interviewer might be to discover questions the interviewee has but did not ask earlier interviewers. He could also explore information the applicant obtained from previous interviewers and try to clear up any misunderstandings for the applicant. Salary negotiations could also take place here.

Communication among interviewers before the interview process begins, as well as discussion before and after each interview, will enhance the planning and effectiveness of the over-all screening sequence. This kind of interaction can give interviewers insight into the questioning strategy each should emphasize.

However, interviewers should avoid communicating impressions and feelings that will bias those who have not yet interviewed the applicant. Po-

Table 2 Checklist for the Interviewing Process

1. What pre-interview selection criteria will be used?

2. How many interviewers will be involved in the interview chain for qualified applicants?

3. How knowledgeable are the interviewers about the job vacancy?

4. What are the reasons for turnover, absenteeism, low morale, and/or grievances for the job vacancy? Are the interviewers familiar with these reasons?

5. Do the interviewers know their specific roles in the interview chain?

6. Do the interviewers' roles overlap too much?

7. Should any interviewers be omitted or added to the interview chain to improve the efficiency and effectiveness of the process?

8. How are test results, letters of reference, and interview results to be weighed?

9. Have past employers and references been checked?

10. What minimum standards have to be met in the first interview stage to qualify an applicant for further interview stages?

11. What channels of communication have been established to transmit information from one interviewer to the next without biasing the latter?

12. How much job information is to be given to the applicant in various interview stages, and by whom is it to be given?

13. Do the interviewers know the restrictions placed upon them by job-discrimination and civil-rights laws?

14. How are the interviewers going to explore the job knowledge and work attitudes of applicants?

15. How are interviewers attempting to guard against in-depth personality assessment?

tential bias can be controlled if earlier interviewers limit comments to areas of information that require further exploration.

Specific job information should not be given to the applicant too early in the interview chain. Providing premature job information usually tempts the applicant to answer questions in terms of what he thinks the interviewer wants to hear. Interviewers should try to discover as much as possible about the applicant's background and work attitudes before filling him in on job specifics.

Recruiters in the interview chain should decide on the point at which to give the applicant job specifics. The deductive method (general to specific questioning) should be used to obtain applicant information as well as to give job information.

After each applicant has completed the interview chain, the interviewers can pool their information and make a decision on whether to hire. Often, however, the decision-making process is not simple. Interviewers may have mixed opinions about the applicants. And some will inevitably believe that additional information is required before a final decision can be made.

Each applicant should be informed as soon as possible on the final decision reached by the interviewers. If there will be a delay before they can make a final decision, they should let applicants know to avoid building false hopes.

Interview-screening techniques can be improved through careful analysis of present procedures, analysis of inefficient interviewing styles, and development of constructive personnel interview training programs. See how well you can answer the questions provided in Table 2. If you find some weaknesses in your procedures, it may be time for you and your company to brush up on interviewing procedures.

24

A Human-Factored Approach to Appraisals

JOHN COWAN

In making appraisals, a supervisor is only human. To expect the process to be handled mechanically is to commit the same error as asking an inchworm to measure a marigold.

Appraisals can be carried out only by human beings responding to feelings and intuition as well as facts. But many attempts at appraisal training and appraisal system design ignore the human factor. Supervisors, for example, often are urged to (1) be objective, (2) be consistent, and (3) follow the steps in the appraisal manual.

- A computer can be objective, but a supervisor cannot—especially when he has worked with an employee for some time. When the relationship is close, a supervisor develops strong feelings—both for and against the individual—that will affect his appraisal results.
- Being consistent is similarly difficult. As a human being, a supervisor, by definition, is inconsistent, valuing certain characteristics in some persons and disliking identical characteristics in others. For some individuals, the supervisor feels compassion; for others, a relentless desire to push them to their limits. In the face of such inconsistencies, the best a supervisor can do is to try to clarify them by exploring such questions as:

    Why does he feel compassion for one person? Is that employee already far over his head?

    Why push another to the limit? Is that worker a gifted loafer?

- Nor are the steps in the appraisal manual easily followed. Even supervisors with excellent interpersonal skills become wooden and awkward when they try to follow an imposed sequence they did not develop for themselves. Some automatically try to make employees comfortable before opening a conversation; others do not. What response is expected from an employee whose boss, for the first time in years, asks him about his family life in an obviously contrived attempt to induce warmth into the appraisal interview? Appraisal manuals that recommend acting supportive as Step 1 in the appraisal interview have not defined the supervisor's problem broadly enough. Supervisors who are cold fish must change their entire management style, not only their approach to appraisals.

Preparing for the Appraisal

Guidelines for appraisals should be based on the premise that the supervisor and employee are human organisms, not machines. In practice, this means that the appraisal process is facilitated by the development of a meaningful personal relationship between the supervisor and the employee. Here are some ways for a supervisor to lay the groundwork that is important for a good appraisal.

Hold a group discussion with the employees to be evaluated to determine the broad criteria for their appraisals. Talking things out in advance provides a better perspective on employee performance. You gain a clearer understanding of the reasons why they may not have been able to meet their general objectives. Or perhaps you may learn that circumstances have made working conditions so easy that only to have met objectives is to have done little.

Is promptness a serious criterion for judgment? Some jobs require it, others don't. Is delivery of a particular contract of overriding importance? Perhaps when you set yearly objectives it was, but maybe now the customer will tolerate, or even prefer, some delay.

At this kind of meeting, you can develop a list of key criteria that can be evaluated as appraisal tools. They probably cannot be applied inflexibly to each employee across the board, but at least both the supervisor and the employee will have some foreknowledge of what's coming up in the appraisal interview.

It is important for you, as supervisor, to state your opinions during this meeting. Such a discussion is not entirely a democratic process—the idea is to permit your opinions to be influenced, not to abandon them to the will of the majority. But state this ground rule clearly before, during, and after the group discussion. In asking for the opinions of employees, the supervisor steps aside from an authoritarian role. But if they misunderstand and view the proceedings as a highly democratic process in which they are allowed to vote, they will be disappointed and resentful when it does not work out that way.

Discussions of appraisal criteria should be held any time the supervisor or employees believe the criteria are becoming unclear. There is no need to wait for a specific date, even if you have finished your objective-setting cycle only a month before. When the criteria are no longer valid, the time for the meeting has come.

Discuss your employees with your own management and with two or three of your peers. Seeking the subjective judgments of others will help a supervisor clarify his own thinking and at times will alter his opinion.

Feelings of disapproval toward a particular worker may be based on that individual's failure to look troubled, worried, and bedeviled at every problem that bothers you. A more relaxed peer may discern that the employee really is a good performer, even if he or she avoids having an ulcer.

On the other hand, perhaps approval of an employee is based on a happy coincidence of personalities. And if high marks are not necessarily justified, a peer supervisor or other manager who does not participate in that coincidence can add a grain of salt to your optimistic judgment.

If your management and peers have no relationships with or knowledge of your subordinates, you have a different problem. Such isolation is dangerous. Your employees are then overly dependent on your opinion and your judgment. Unless you are an extraordinary person, they have every right to be concerned about the risks of the appraisal interview.

Clear up any differences that may develop between the language of the formal written appraisal and the language of the informal interview. What goes into the personnel file and what you say to the employee may vary. In some companies, to call an employee "average" effectively condemns him. In others, it simply indicates he is competent but not extraordinary.

In any event, explain to the employee any differences between how you spoke to him in the interview and how you expressed your views in the written formal appraisal. The law has made it possible for government employees to see their personnel files; corporations may be next. Your credibility will suffer seriously if the employee discovers on his own apparent discrepancies between what you said and what you wrote.

If you are angry with an employee, talk about it before, not during, the appraisal interview. If you need a blow-up, a shouting match, or some ventilation of feelings, do it before the appraisal. The employee deserves to have a relatively cool head on the other side of the desk during his performance evaluation.

Delaying the angry conversation until after the appraisal does not work either. Since you are not as clever at hiding wrath as you think you are, your employee already knows you are angry. Instead of listening, he will spend the entire appraisal waiting for the dam to break.

Consider your stance in judging other people. As a guideline, keep in mind the responses of three umpires who were asked to explain their philosophy on calling balls and strikes. The youngest said, "I call them as I see them." The middle-aged umpire said, "I call them as they are." The old veteran umpire said, "They are what I call them." The first and third of these statements contain much truth for the supervisor.

In appraising employees, you certainly do not call them "as they are." As a human being, you can call them only as you "see them." A supervisor's perceptions, ideals, and desires muddle his view of employees' strengths and weaknesses.

On the other hand, you *are* a supervisor. Human frailty aside, your employees' strengths and weaknesses are what you "call them." What you say will be entered in their personnel files. What you think will strongly influence their chances for future promotions.

Like it or not, management must place tremendous weight on the supervisor's subjective judgment. No number of mechanical props will change this subjectivity. Willingness to converse with others, remaining open to positive influence, and efforts to improve self-understanding will enhance one's ability to judge—but nothing will objectify it. Supervisors deserve and demand training in personal development as human beings because their judgment is crucial to the well-being of others and to the well-being of their organizations.

Compensation and appraisals are related. Review the employee's compensation plan before sitting down for the review. Be prepared to discuss pay if he or she brings it up.

Some companies try to compartmentalize compensation and appraisals. It is fair, even desirable, to discuss each in a separate interview. But the supervisor must be ready to answer the question "If I'm so good, why am I not paid more?" And he must answer on the spot. Evasive answers leave a sour taste. In our society, the ultimate appraisal is the paycheck. The employee knows it.

If you have given the same employee a number of negative appraisals, prepare to take action. If an employee is really that deficient or if you dislike him that much, it is time for a change (transfer, demotion, firing). Repeated attempts to remodel the reluctant individual are simply punitive. Also, the employee may get a better break in a different department or even a different company. After time, your judgment becomes fixed. Another supervisor without your history with the employee may evaluate him higher. And as time goes on, the employee's recalcitrance strengthens. The issue is no longer truth, but *machismo.*

The employee also may be beyond his level of competence. This can be a hard fact to face, but confronting it once and for all is better than picking away at it year after year.

The kind of employee-supervisor relationship that leads to meaningful appraisals is developed over the year, not at the moment of appraisal. Little can be said to help the supervisor who is habitually cold, distant, withdrawn, authoritarian, or punitive. No one enjoys being told his faults. Because people need to know where they stand and what they must do to improve, they will accept, even seek, feedback from supervisors they trust and respect. But trust and respect are not developed in the opening 15 minutes of the interview.

During the Appraisal Interview

Destroying an employee's self-respect is an unforgivable offense. Do what you honestly can to improve it. Here are some guidelines:

Tell an employee about his good points. Appraisals are not intended to be merely negative, but employees often will say that they are uninterested in their strengths and ask you to get on with the negatives. Don't buy that. It is important for them to hear about their valuable sides, that they do offer something of value to you and the company. Studies have indicated that individuals become more competent through understanding and developing their strengths than through focusing on their weaknesses.

Remember that strengths and weaknesses usually spring from the same set of characteristics. Consider the consequences of asking that a strength be maintained and a weakness eliminated. For example, Bill is highly aggressive and gets things done. Fred is friendly and makes people happy. Bill tends to leave a wake of angry people; Fred, a trail of half-finished jobs.

Asking Bill and Fred to change means you will lose some of their strengths. If you want aggressive Bill to make fewer enemies, you will have to check his compelling need to get the job done. If you want friendly Fred to become more task-oriented, prepare for the protests of surprised fellow workers Fred has thrown out of his office.

Admit to the employee that your judgment is subjective and suggest that he consult others for supplementary evaluations. Tell him that he can get a broader picture of himself by talking to other supervisors and to his peers. Their appraisals cannot replace yours, but they can augment, supplement, and usefully contradict it. An employee who has not yet discovered that different people value him differently will discover it through this process.

Make it clear that the responsibility for development lies with the employee, not with you. If he wants to change himself, he takes the risks. A supervisor can predict only his own response to that change, not the response of others. If the employee decides to stay the same because everybody except you likes him that way, that is okay, too. Trying to dictate personality puts you on dangerous ground.

For this reason, avoid couching demands for personality changes in terms of management-by-objectives terminology. "I want you to set and achieve more difficult objectives" is the equivalent of saying "I want you to become a more striving and competitive person." Or, "I want you to do more marketing and make 50 percent more marketing trips next year" could be interpreted as "Become more comfortable with strangers, meet people easier, and be less tied to your home life."

A supervisor has the right to tell an employee what he wants, even to say that if he does not get what he wants, he will select another person for the job. But he has neither the right nor the power to insist—against the employee's will—that basic personality characteristics be changed.

A much better strategy is to try to help the person go in the direction he wants to go. Put it to the individual like this: "In this job, I need someone who enjoys meeting people more than you do presently. What would you like to do? We can get you training in interpersonal skills, or we can decide that you are going to have to travel and suffer until you get used to it. Or you and I can start to work out a different job for you."

Be specific when citing examples. A complaint that "you do not finish your work" should be accompanied by times and dates. Similarly, a compliment such as "customers really like you" should be amplified by stating who said what. Without supporting facts, how does the employee know that you are not just making things up as you go along? General statements do not sink in. To make your point, be specific.

Keep up to date. Appraisals should be made quarterly. People change fast, and appraisals are supposed to help them change, not be their final epitaph. Nor should feedback be delayed until the appraisal interview. Comment on the employee's performance at the time. Some supervisors give feedback as if they were computers without real-time capacity. They take their appraisal tape off the back shelf and supply the employee with a year's printout in one dose.

Trying to be nondirective is the human approach to appraisals gone overboard. The nondirective approach was designed for a particular style of therapy, not for appraisals. The best outcome of a nondirective appraisal is a clear picture of the employee's self-worth: People who like themselves tell you they are terrific; those who do not value themselves tell you they are awful.

It is useful to solicit the employee's opinion on his own performance and to request his reaction to the supervisor's appraisal. But it's the supervisor's job to give the appraisal. It's not fair to ask the employee to take the risk of revealing himself unnecessarily to the same person who is responsible for his future career. Nondirective therapists were never asked to recommend or deny pay increases for their clients. The two situations are immeasurably and obviously different.

The Personal Side of Management

Management has a personal aspect that can never be turned over to computers or robot-like human beings. This side of management is nowhere as apparent as in the appraisal process, which demands the utmost in human sensitivity and interpersonal skill. Advice to supervisors must be realistic and take into account both their human limitations and their organizational roles.

The supervisor cannot be bypassed. The organization must rely on his personal strengths as a human being to guarantee the development of its employees.

25

How Useful Are Exit Interviews?

WALTER A. JABLONSKI

The exit interview, usually held in the personnel department, is a good way to discover why an employee has decided to leave the company. It gives the employee an opportunity to speak his mind on problem areas, programs, procedures, and the supervisory technique of his superiors. At least, that's what the textbooks say. But in the real world, do exit interviews really provide such information? Does the employee have the opportunity to point out problems? Does the supervisor want a reflection of the impact he has had on the employee? Does management really want to hear what the employee has to say?

There are no all-purpose answers to these questions, because companies differ and managements differ—as do individual supervisors. The following discussion, however, can help you answer these questions for yourself and your company.

The exit interview can be considered from two angles. The first is the tone or emotional angle, which reflects the employee's feelings. This aspect is necessarily subjective, but it can be valuable. The second angle is the content, or what the person actually says. Although tone and content occur together, they vary independently. Almost any content can be expressed with any degree of feeling—even an apparently contradictory one.

Innocuous to Venomous

The tone of the departing employee can range from innocuous to sharply critical—even venomous. You may have heard innocuous statements like these: "I really hate to leave, but I have an opportunity that's too good to pass up." "I feel a need for a change to broaden my experience." "I want to go back to my home town." These statements convey mild feelings toward the company, and management has traditionally responded to them with little excitement.

At the other end of the spectrum, the most critical or venomous interviewees typically seethe with anger and spite. They are given to making such statements as, "The whole (adjective deleted) company doesn't care," or "Everyone is trying to (verb form deleted) everybody else," or "Mr. Brown is a real (noun deleted)." Such parting shots achieve at least one of their objectives: They attract attention.

However, although it is seldom stated or admitted, innocuous comments are usually considered to be more truthful and objective; venomous ones are most often viewed as the exaggerations or lies of an unreasonable and undesirable employee who, perhaps, should not have been hired in the first place. Why is this? Since innocuous statements are not a threat, they can be readily accepted—but venomous ones accuse or threaten time-honored practices or respected individuals and must be proved false.

Listen for the Tone

The tone of an interview is not always easy to categorize. Consider, for example, this statement made by a departing employee: "I'm just not totally happy, and I have an opportunity for a better position." Although this would sound innocuous to most interviewers, it was in fact an enormously hostile statement coming from the employee in question. It took him years of frustration and tolerating poor supervision to be able to admit that all was not well. But because his statement was seen as innocuous, it didn't receive much attention—and a very real problem went undiscovered.

Of course, the converse also occurs: Statements seen as extremely hostile to an interviewer may seem straightforward to the employee. In cases like this, investigation reveals that the employee has in some way exaggerated the situation even though he thinks he has spoken the gospel truth. Different viewpoints and biases account for such a wide disparity.

If a company seldom or never senses hostility in exit interviews, should it be considered an ideal place to work? Many managements like to think so. Even though employees are leaving, the conclusion is that they represent an irreducible minimum turnover and that otherwise, everything is just fine. This may be so where the majority of a company's exit interviews yield only innocuous comments—but not necessarily.

Fear of Retribution

The tone of the interview is controlled by the employee—specifically by the balance struck between his emotional and rational faculties. In an organizational atmosphere rife with fear and hostility, the employee may go in for sharp criticism to vent his pent-up frustrations. Or he may well be very cautious about what he says, since he knows that future positions may be affected by past references. If he fears that critical charges will trigger retribution or a desire to "get even," he may well choose to give a simple, innocuous interview. And why not? From his viewpoint, a hostile exit interview only gains him some minor self-satisfaction at the possible expense of a good job reference. Holding back during the exit interview is, unfortunately, a widespread practice.

Occasionally, interviewers and managements who recognize employees' reluctance to talk try to reassure them that there will be no retribution. But a person who is leaving because of some problem, and who feels that he has been let down by his boss or management, is not amenable to reassurance. It is naïve and insulting to tell an exiting employee that everything he says will be held in strictest confidence—that "nothing will go beyond these walls." Employees know that exit interviews lead to exit-interview reports, and that such reports are usually circulated to a number of people in the company.

The tone of the interview can be a key to recognizing and solving problems. But it is necessary to avoid either overreacting to venomous comments or minimizing seemingly innocuous ones.

Uncover the Criticisms

The content of the interview can also range from innocuous to sharply critical. As the content of the interview moves toward the critical end of the scale, employees typically have more to say. Thus, a good interviewer should guide the employee into as critical an interview as possible.

This does not mean that he or she has to accept the exiting employee's statements as the absolute truth. The employee's statements can be wrong, distorted, exaggerated, or inconsistent—but even so they may indicate hidden problem areas. The interviewer must take care to transmit the employee's feelings and complaints straightforwardly in preparing a follow-up report; he must never sugarcoat criticism or fictionalize the report to say what he thinks management wants to hear.

Employees don't leave without reason. A few leave for minor reasons, but most people do not take the drastic step of quitting a job unless there are more serious problems. If all jobs and working conditions were ideal, few employees would leave. Since jobs and working conditions are seldom perfect, there is always the possibility of improving them. The exiting employee knows the problems and procedures of his job in a way that no one else does, so the interviewer should try to get information from him that will lead to positive change.

The Real Motive

Let's look at a specific example. An employee resigns and tells the interviewer that he wants to return to his home town or state. The reason for leaving seems innocuous, to be sure, and the report will indicate that the employee resigned for personal reasons. This doesn't upset anyone—so no investigation is made, and no change takes place.

But the interview should not end there. The interviewer should seek underlying reasons as well as surface ones. Once, this employee was willing to leave his home state for the job—but now the reverse is true. Further questioning may prod him to say, "Well, when I came here I thought the job had more of a future."

In truth, the job may or may not have a future in terms of leading to higher level positions. If it is a dead-end job, and if the employee is resigning because of that, management may want to consider restructuring the position to be more satisfying for the next incumbent. On the other hand, there may be reasons that the position cannot be restructured. This is management's decision. In any event, the exit interview can encourage management to look at a potential problem—and when this happens, the exit interview becomes a valuable management tool.

Dig Deeper

The interviewer should never be satisfied with merely a statement or two, since further discussion may amplify a problem or suggest other problems. Suppose that the interviewer is able to determine through further questioning and his background knowledge that the position *has* a future, but that the exiting employee is unaware of it. What then? Perhaps the interviewer will discover that the employee was never sure about what was expected of him. If he had known, he might have qualified for a promotion or he might have been willing to stay on once he realized that future promotions were possible. This situation might indicate a serious lack of communication within the department—a possibility that should be checked out and corrected. Again, the exit interview is serving as a tool to point up weaknesses.

But the problem may not lie with the employee's superiors at all. A skilled interviewer may discover that the exiting employee does not really want to look at his future. The employee is doing the best he can in a job whose demands are just too much for him. He senses this, but to admit it even to himself is too painful. He knows he can never be promoted—but rather than seeing the cause as his own limitations, he takes the more comfortable approach of rationalizing that the position does not offer promotional opportunities.

In this case, the basic problem is that the employee is underqualified. The personnel department should take corrective action by re-evaluating hiring procedures. Personnel may also need to examine jobs more closely before recruiting and hiring for them.

Don't Overreact

The exit interview should not be viewed as a device for mounting an inquisition into the operation of a manager's department. Unfortunately, it is too often viewed negatively and is met with defensiveness and counterattack. If an exit interview indicates that a problem may exist, management should not overreact by trying to prove that the exiting employee is wrong—that a problem does not exist. Such defensiveness is not in the best interest of the organization.

Let's look at a case history. An employee resigned and presented himself willingly for the exit interview. His statements were critical, and top management viewed the tone as venomous and threatening. In a resultant investigation, a representative of the division vice-president interviewed the employee's supervisor and that supervisor's supervisor to get the truth.

The employee had joined the company a year before, primarily to be part of an inventory program that he thought would be an important and highly significant effort. But the program did not materialize, so he believed that his assignments were unimportant. He also felt that his supervisor's hands were tied—that even though he might speak to his supervisor, the superior would be unable to assign him valuable or interesting work to do.

A Go-Getter

Also, the employee felt that he did his work more rapidly and more efficiently than the other employees did theirs. He resented having to run the blueprint machine even though all the draftsmen of his rank shared the task. He worked hard and wanted to get ahead, but he had a misconception about the functions and level of his job. It was clear that he was expecting a more varied and challenging position than the one he held. Since the other men in the department were older, less aggressive, and content with the job the way it was, this employee stood out as unusual.

The employee's supervisor said that although they had talked frequently, the employee had never been content with the duties of the position and was always looking for something else to do. The investigator suggested that although the possibility of a communication problem remained, the actual problem appeared to be a placement error, since the man was too active, restless, and ambitious for the job.

Defensive Reaction

The operating supervisor and his boss didn't see it that way. They felt that the employee had attacked them by calling some of the duties "trash work." The exiting employee's statements were refuted completely; he was ultimately described as warped, and a request was made for the personnel department to develop a better procedure that would prevent future exit interviews of this kind. The head of personnel concurred (defensively), and the new procedure required future exit-interview reports to be cleared by the supervisors involved before they became final. The new procedure was heralded by just about everybody.

Let's consider some of the difficulties and results of this fairly typical procedure:

1. *Defensiveness.* Although the report of an exit interview is marked "personal" and "confidential," it is in reality a public document that many levels of management may see. This fact makes it awkward for a supervi-

sor to admit to any irregularity. In an ideal world, a supervisor could publicly admit a problem and find a solution without criticism or stigma. But this isn't an ideal world. Problem situations and mistakes are grounds for dismissal when they become too public. Successful managers have problems and mistakes, but they've learned to look critically at themselves and their operations to uncover and solve problems before they become public. Obviously, any exit interview procedure that forces public examination of a manager's operation is inviting defensiveness rather than critical evaluation.

2. *Distrust.* When a departing employee knows that his supervisor will comment on and possibly modify each statement he makes, the exit interview is not likely to be open and fruitful. This knowledge can only enhance the employee's belief that the interview is a sham and that management really does not want to hear what he has to say. The employee sees the situation as one in which management says one thing, but means another.

3. *Dysfunction.* If the feelings and statements of exiting employees are modified because of defensiveness, and if the employees are too distrustful to participate openly, how can the exit interview be used to determine when and where a problem exists? A management procedure that requires "clarification" of an employee's statements by his supervisor, or one that discourages him from talking, is self-defeating. Under such circumstances, the exit interview is useless and should not be conducted at all.

The Supervisor's Rights and Responsibilities

If all levels of management could accept the exit interview as a tool for possible improvement rather than a threat, attack, or source of embarrassment to be squelched, the report of an exit interview could contain only the unadulterated statements of the exiting employee. Under this procedure, the employee's immediate supervisor should be the first one to receive a copy of the interview. He could then ponder any criticisms and take any corrective action needed without being prodded by his superior. He should be able to appraise the exiting employee's statements to determine whether a problem exists. If it does, he should have the responsibility to change things; if a problem does not exist, he should be able to file the report with no action needed or taken.

Since a major objective of management is to develop subordinate supervisors, a procedure like this should be welcomed. It gives the subordinate supervisor an opportunity to solve problems on his own initiative and thus to grow. Too often, the first-line supervisor is the last person to see the report; that puts him in an awkward position, with little to do but resort to defensiveness.

Clearly, the exit interview becomes a useful tool only when those involved analyze and evaluate critically with an eye to improvement. If management is unwilling to admit and look at its own mistakes, the exit interview should be discontinued.

Part Nine

Alternative Forms of "Conferencing"

26

Assets and Liabilities in Group Problem Solving: The Need for an Integrative Function[1]

NORMAN R. F. MAIER

A number of investigations have raised the question of whether group problem solving is superior, inferior, or equal to individual problem solving. Evidence can be cited in support of each position so that the answer to this question remains ambiguous. Rather than pursue this generalized approach to the question, it seems more fruitful to explore the forces that influence problem solving under the two conditions (see reviews by Hoffman, 1965; Kelley & Thibaut, 1954). It is hoped that a better recognition of these forces will permit clarification of the varied dimensions of the problem-solving process, especially in groups.

The forces operating in such groups include some that are assets, some that are liabilities, and some that can be either assets or liabilities, depending upon the skills of the members, especially those of the discussion leader. Let us examine these three sets of forces.

Group Assets

Greater Sum Total of Knowledge and Information

There is more information in a group than in any of its members. Thus problems that require the utilization of knowledge should give groups an ad-

278

vantage over individuals. Even if one member of the group (e.g., the leader) knows much more than anyone else, the limited unique knowledge of lesser-informed individuals could serve to fill in some gaps in knowledge. For example, a skilled machinist might contribute to an engineer's problem solving and an ordinary workman might supply information on how a new machine might be received by workers.

Greater Number of Approaches to a Problem

It has been shown that individuals get into ruts in their thinking (Duncker, 1945; Maier, 1930; Wertheimer, 1959). Many obstacles stand in the way of achieving a goal, and a solution must circumvent these. The individual is handicapped in that he tends to persist in his approach and thus fails to find another approach that might solve the problem in a simpler manner. Individuals in a group have the same failing, but the approaches in which they are persisting may be different. For example, one researcher may try to prevent the spread of a disease by making man immune to the germ, another by finding and destroying the carrier of the germ, and still another by altering the environment so as to kill the germ before it reaches man. There is no way of determining which approach will best achieve the desired goal, but undue persistence in any one will stifle new discoveries. Since group members do not have identical approaches, each can contribute by knocking others out of ruts in thinking.

Participation in Problem Solving Increases Acceptance

Many problems require solutions that depend upon the support of others to be effective. Insofar as group problem solving permits participation and influence, it follows that more individuals accept solutions when a group solves the problem than when one person solves it. When one individual solves a problem he still has the task of persuading others. It follows, therefore, that when groups solve such problems, a greater number of persons accept and feel responsible for making the solution work. A low-quality solution that has good acceptance can be more effective than a higher-quality solution that lacks acceptance.

Better Comprehension of the Decision

Decisions made by an individual, which are to be carried out by others, must be communicated from the decision-maker to the decision-executors. Thus individual problem solving often requires an additional stage—that of relaying the decision reached. Failures in this communication process detract from the merits of the decision and can even cause its failure or create a problem of greater magnitude than the initial problem that was solved. Many organizational problems can be traced to inadequate communication of decisions made by superiors and transmitted to subordinates, who have the task of implementing the decision.

The chances for communication failures are greatly reduced when the individuals who must work together in executing the decision have participated in making it. They not only understand the solution because they saw it develop, but they are also aware of the several other alternatives that were considered and the reasons why they were discarded. The common assumption that decisions supplied by superiors are arbitrarily reached therefore disappears. A full knowledge of goals, obstacles, alternatives, and factual information is essential to communication, and this communication is maximized when the total problem-solving process is shared.

Group Liabilities

Social Pressure

Social pressure is a major force making for conformity. The desire to be a good group member and to be accepted tends to silence disagreement and favors consensus. Majority opinions tend to be accepted regardless of whether or not their objective quality is logically and scientifically sound. Problems requiring solutions based upon facts, regardless of feelings and wishes, can suffer in group problem-solving situations.

It has been shown (Maier & Solem, 1952) that minority opinions in leaderless groups have little influence on the solution reached, even when these opinions are the correct ones. Reaching agreement in a group often is confused with finding the right answer, and it is for this reason that the dimensions of a decision's acceptance and its objective quality must be distinguished (Maier, 1963).

Valence of Solutions

When leaderless groups (made up of three or four persons) engage in problem solving, they propose a variety of solutions. Each solution may receive both critical and supportive comments, as well as descriptive and explorative comments from other participants. If the number of negative and positive comments for each solution are algebraically summed, each may be given a *valence index* (Hoffman & Maier, 1964). The first solution that receives a positive valence value of 15 tends to be adopted to the satisfaction of all participants about 85% of the time, regardless of its quality. Higher quality solutions introduced after the critical value for one of the solutions has been reached have little chance of achieving real consideration. Once some degree of consensus is reached, the jelling process seems to proceed rather rapidly.

The critical valence value of 15 appears not to be greatly altered by the nature of the problem or the exact size of the group. Rather, it seems to designate a turning point between the idea-getting process and the decision-making process (idea evaluation). A solution's valence index is not a measure of the number of persons supporting the solution, since a vocal minority can build up a solution's valence by actively pushing it. In this sense, valence becomes an influence in addition to social pressure in determining an outcome.

Since a solution's valence is independent of its objective quality, this group factor becomes an important liability in group problem solving, even when the value of a decision depends upon objective criteria (facts and logic). It becomes a means whereby skilled manipulators can have more influence over the group process than their proportion of membership deserves.

Individual Domination

In most leaderless groups a dominant individual emerges and captures more than his share of influence on the outcome. He can achieve this end through a greater degree of participation (valence), persuasive ability, or stubborn persistence (fatiguing the opposition). None of these factors is related to problem-solving ability, so that the best problem solver in the group may not have the influence to upgrade the quality of the group's solution (which he would have had if left to solve the problem by himself).

Hoffman and Maier (1967) found that the mere fact of appointing a leader causes this person to dominate a discussion. Thus, regardless of his problem-solving ability a leader tends to exert a major influence on the outcome of a discussion.

Conflicting Secondary Goal: Winning the Argument

When groups are confronted with a problem, the initial goal is to obtain a solution. However, the appearance of several alternatives causes individuals to have preferences and once these emerge the desire to support a position is created. Converting those with neutral viewpoints and refuting those with opposed viewpoints now enters into the problem-solving process. More and more the goal becomes that of winning the decision rather than finding the best solution. This new goal is unrelated to the quality of the problem's solution and therefore can result in lowering the quality of the decision (Hoffman & Maier, 1966).

Factors That Serve As Assets or Liabilities

Disagreement

The fact that discussion may lead to disagreement can serve either to create hard feelings among members or lead to a resolution of conflict and hence to an innovative solution (Hoffman, 1961; Hoffman, Harburg, & Maier, 1962; Hoffman & Maier, 1961; Maier, 1958, 1963; Maier & Hoffman, 1965). The first of these outcomes of disagreement is a liability, especially with regard to the acceptance of solutions; while the second is an asset, particularly where innovation is desired. A leader can treat disagreement as undesirable and thereby reduce the probability of both hard feelings and innovation, or he can maximize disagreement and risk hard feelings in his attempts to achieve innovation. The skill of a leader requires his ability to create a climate for disagreement which will permit innovation without risking hard feelings. The leader's perception of disagreement is one of the critical factors in this skill area (Maier & Hoffman, 1965). Others involve permissiveness (Maier, 1953), delaying the reaching of a solution (Maier & Hoffman, 1960b; Maier & Solem, 1962), techniques for processing information and opinions (Maier, 1963; Maier & Hoffman, 1960a; Maier & Maier, 1957), and techniques for separating idea-getting from idea-evaluation (Maier, 1960, 1963; Osborn, 1953).

Conflicting Interests versus Mutual Interests

Disagreement in discussion may take many forms. Often participants disagree with one another with regard to solutions, but when issues are explored one finds that these conflicting solutions are designed to solve different problems. Before one can rightly expect agreement on a solution, there should be agreement on the nature of the problem. Even before this, there should be agreement on the goal, as well as on the various obstacles that prevent the goal from being reached. Once distinctions are made between goals, obstacles, and solutions (which represent ways of overcoming obstacles), one finds increased opportunities for cooperative problem solving and less conflict (Hoffman & Maier 1959; Maier, 1960, 1963; Maier & Solem, 1962; Solem, 1965).

Often there is also disagreement regarding whether the objective of a solution is to achieve quality or acceptance (Maier & Hoffman, 1964b), and frequently a stated problem reveals a complex of separate problems, each having separate solutions so that a search for a single solution is impossible (Maier, 1963). Communications often are inadequate because the discussion is not synchronized and each person is engaged in discussing a different aspect. Organizing discussion to synchronize the exploration of different aspects of the problem and to follow a systematic procedure increases solution quality (Maier & Hoffman, 1960a; Maier & Maier, 1957). The leadership function of influencing discussion procedure is quite distinct from the function of evaluating or contributing ideas (Maier, 1950, 1953).

When the discussion leader aids in the separation of the several aspects of the problem-solving process and delays the solution-mindedness of the group (Maier, 1958, 1963; Maier & Solem, 1962), both solution quality and acceptance improve; when he hinders or fails to facilitate the isolation of these varied processes, he risks a deterioration in the group process (Solem, 1965). His skill thus determines whether a discussion drifts toward conflicting interests or whether mutual interests are located. Cooperative problem solving can only occur after the mutual interests have been established and it is surprising how often they can be found when the discussion leader makes this his task (Maier, 1952, 1963; Maier & Hayes, 1962).

Risk Taking

Groups are more willing than individuals to reach decisions involving risks (Wallach & Kogan, 1965; Wallach, Kogan, & Bem, 1962). Taking risks is a factor in acceptance of change, but change may either represent a gain or a loss. The best guard against the latter outcome seems to be primarily a matter of a decision's quality. In a group situation this depends upon the leader's skill in utilizing the factors that represent group assets and avoiding those that make for liabilities.

Time Requirements

In general, more time is required for a group to reach a decision than for a single individual to reach one. Insofar as some problems require quick decisions, individual decisions are favored. In other situations acceptance and quality are requirements, but excessive time without sufficient returns also represents a loss. On the other hand, discussion can resolve conflicts, whereas reaching consensus has limited value (Wallach & Kogan, 1965). The practice of hastening a meeting can prevent full discussion, but failure to move a discussion forward can lead to boredom and fatigue-type solutions, in which members agree merely to get out of the meeting. The effective utilization of discussion time (a delicate balance between permissiveness and control on the part of the leader), therefore, is needed to make the time factor an asset rather than a liability. Unskilled leaders tend to be too concerned with reaching a solution and therefore terminate a discussion before the group potential is achieved (Maier & Hoffman, 1960b).

Who Changes

In reaching consensus or agreement, some members of a group must change. Persuasive forces do not operate in individual problem solving in the same way they operate in a group situation; hence, the changing of someone's mind is not an issue. In group situations, however, who changes can be an asset or a liability. If persons with the most constructive views are induced to change, the end-product suffers; whereas if persons with the least constructive points of view change, the end-product is upgraded. The leader can upgrade the quality of a decision because his position permits him to protect the person with a minority view and increase his opportunity to influence the majority position. This protection is a constructive factor because a minority viewpoint influences only when facts favor it (Maier, 1950, 1952; Maier & Solem, 1952).

The leader also plays a constructive role insofar as he can facilitate communications and thereby reduce misunderstandings (Maier, 1952; Solem, 1965). The leader has an adverse effect on the end-product when he suppresses minority views by holding a contrary position and when he uses his office to promote his own views (Maier & Hoffman, 1960b, 1962; Maier & Solem, 1952). In many problem-solving discussions the untrained leader plays a dominant role in influencing the outcome, and when he is more resistant to changing his views than are the other participants, the quality of the outcome tends to be lowered. This negative leader-influence was demonstrated by experiments in which untrained leaders were asked to obtain a second solution to a problem after they had obtained their first one (Maier & Hoffman, 1960a). It was found that the second solution tended to be superior to the first. Since the dominant individual had influenced the first solution, he had won his point and therefore ceased to dominate the subsequent discussion which led to the second solution. Acceptance of a solution also increases as the leader sees disagreement as idea-producing rather than as a source of difficulty or trouble (Maier & Hoffman, 1965). Leaders who see some of their participants as troublemakers obtain fewer innovative solutions and gain less acceptance of decisions made than leaders who see disagreeing members as persons with ideas.

The Leader's Role for Integrated Groups

Two Differing Types of Group Process

In observing group problem solving under various conditions it is rather easy to distinguish between cooperative problem-solving activity and persuasion or selling approaches. Problem-solving activity includes searching, trying out ideas on one another, listening to understand rather than to refute, making relatively short speeches, and reacting to differences in opinion as stimulating. The general pattern is one of rather complete participation, involvement, and interest. Persuasion activity includes the selling of opinions already formed, defending a position held, either not listening at all or listening in order to be able to refute, talking dominated by a few members, unfavorable reactions to disagreement, and a lack of involvement of some members. During problem solving the behavior observed seems to be that of members interacting as segments of a group. The interaction pattern is not between certain individual members, but with the group as a whole. Sometimes it is difficult to determine who should be credited with an idea. "It just developed," is a response often used to describe the solution reached. In contrast, discussions involving selling or persuasive behavior seem to consist of a series of interpersonal interactions with each individual retaining his identity. Such groups do not function as integrated units but as separate individuals, each with an agenda. In one situation the solution is unknown and is sought; in the other, several solutions exist and conflict occurs because commitments have been made.

The Starfish Analogy

The analysis of these two group processes suggests an analogy with the behavior of the rays of a starfish under two conditions; one with the nerve ring intact, the other with the nerve ring sectioned (Hamilton, 1922; Moore, 1924; Moore & Doudoroff, 1939; Schneirla & Maier, 1940). In the intact condition, locomotion and righting behavior reveal that the behavior of each ray is not merely a function of local stimulation. Locomotion and righting behavior reveal a degree of coordination and interdependence that is centrally controlled. However, when the nerve ring is sectioned, the behavior of one ray still can influence others, but internal coordination is lacking. For example, if one ray is stimulated, it may step forward, thereby exerting pressure on the sides of the other four rays. In response to these external pressures (tactile stimulation), these rays show stepping responses on the stimulated side so that locomotion successfully occurs without the aid of neural coordination. Thus integrated behavior can occur on the basis of external control. If, however, stimulation is applied to opposite rays, the specimen may be "locked" for a time, and in some species the conflicting locomotions may divide the animal, thus destroying it (Crozier, 1920; Moore & Doudoroff, 1939).

Each of the rays of the starfish can show stepping responses even when sectioned and removed from the animal. Thus each may be regarded as an individual. In a starfish with a sectioned nerve ring the five rays become members of a group. They can successfully work together for locomotion purposes by being controlled by the dominant ray. Thus if uniformity of action is desired, the group of five rays can sometimes be more effective than the individual ray in moving the group toward a source of stimulation. However, if "locking" or the division of the organism occurs, the group action becomes less effective than individual action. External control, through the influence of a dominant ray, therefore can lead to adaptive behavior for the starfish as a whole, but it can also result in a conflict that destroys the organism. Something more than external influence is needed.

In the animal with an intact nerve ring, the function of the rays is coordinated by the nerve ring. With this type of internal organization the group is always superior to that of the individual actions. When the rays function as a part of an organized unit, rather than as a group that is physically together, they become a higher type of organization—a single intact organism. This is accomplished by the nerve ring, which in itself does not do the behaving. Rather, it receives and processes the data which the rays relay to it. Through this central organization, the responses of the rays become part of a larger pattern so that together they constitute a single coordinated total response rather than a group of individual responses.

The Leader as the Group's Central Nervous System

If we now examine what goes on in a discussion group we find that members can problem-solve as individuals, they can influence others by external pushes and pulls, or they can function as a group with varying degrees of unity. In order for the latter function to be maximized, however, something must be introduced to serve the function of the nerve ring. In our conceptualization of group problem solving and group decision (Maier, 1963), we see this as the function of the leader. Thus the leader does not serve as a dominant ray and produce the solution. Rather, his function is to receive information, facilitate communications between the individuals, relay messages, and integrate the incoming responses so that a single unified response occurs.

Solutions that are the product of good group discussions often come as surprises to discussion leaders. One of these is unexpected generosity. If there is a weak member, this member is given less to do, in much the same way as an organism adapts to an injured limb and alters the function of other limbs to keep locomotion on course. Experimental evidence supports the point that group decisions award special consideration to needy members of groups (Hoffman & Maier, 1959). Group decisions in industrial groups often give smaller assignments to the less gifted (Maier, 1952). A leader could not effectually impose such differential treatment on group members without being charged with discriminatory practices.

Another unique aspect of group discussion is the way fairness is resolved. In a simulated problem situation involving the problem of how to introduce a new truck into a group of drivers, the typical group solution involves a trading of trucks so that several or all members stand to profit. If the leader makes the decision the number of persons who profit is often confined to one (Maier & Hoffman, 1962; Maier & Zerfoss, 1952). In industrial practice, supervisors assign a new truck to an individual member of a crew after careful evaluation of needs. This practice results in dissatisfaction, with the charge of *unfair* being leveled at him. Despite these repeated attempts to do justice, supervisors in the telephone industry never hit upon the notion of a general reallocation of trucks, a solution that crews invariably reach when the decision is theirs to make.

In experiments involving the introduction of change, the use of group discussion tends to lead to decisions that resolve differences (Maier, 1952, 1953; Maier & Hoffman, 1961, 1964a, 1964b). Such decisions tend to be different from decisions reached by individuals because of the very fact that disagreement is common in group problem solving and rare in individual problem solving. The process of resolving difference in a constructive setting causes the exploration of additional areas and leads to solutions that are integrative rather than compromises.

Finally, group solutions tend to be tailored to fit the interests and personalities of the participants; thus group solutions to problems involving fairness, fears, face-saving, etc., tend to vary from one group to another. An outsider cannot process these variables because they are not subject to logical treatment.

If we think of the leader as serving a function in the group different from that of its membership, we might be able to create a group that can function as an intact organism. For a leader, such functions as rejecting or promoting ideas according to his personal needs are out of bounds. He must be receptive to information contributed, accept contributions without evaluating them (posting contributions on a chalk board to keep them alive), summarize information to facilitate integration, stimulate exploratory behavior, create awareness of problems of one member by others, and detect when the group is ready to resolve differences and agree to a unified solution.

Since higher organisms have more than a nerve ring and can store information, a leader might appropriately supply information, but according to our model of a leader's role, he must clearly distinguish between supplying information and promoting a solution. If his knowledge indicates the desirability of a particular solution, sharing this knowledge might lead the group to find this solution, but the solution should be the group's discovery. A leader's contributions do not receive the same treatment as those of a member of the group. Whether he likes it or not, his position is different. According to our conception of the leader's contribution to discussion, his role not only differs in influence, but gives him an entirely different function. He is to serve much as the nerve ring in the starfish and to further refine this function so as to make it a higher type of nerve ring.

This model of a leader's role in group process has served as a guide for many of our studies in group problem solving. It is not our claim that this will lead to the best possible group function under all conditions. In sharing it we hope to indicate the nature of our guidelines in exploring group leadership as a function quite different and apart from group membership. Thus the model serves as a stimulant for research problems and as a guide for our analyses of leadership skills and principles.

Conclusions

On the basis of our analysis, it follows that the comparison of the merits of group versus individual problem solving depends on the nature of the problem, the goal to be achieved (high quality solution, highly accepted solution, effective communication and understanding of the solution, innovation, a quickly reached solution, or satisfaction), and the skill of the discussion leader. If liabilities inherent in groups are avoided, assets capitalized upon, and conditions that can serve either favorable or unfavorable outcomes are effectively used, it follows that groups have a potential which in many instances can exceed that of a superior individual functioning alone, even with respect to creativity.

This goal was nicely stated by Thibaut and Kelley (1961) when they

wonder whether it may not be possible for a rather small, intimate group to establish a problem solving process that capitalizes upon the total pool of information and provides for great interstimulation of ideas without any loss of innovative creativity due to social restraints [p. 268].

In order to accomplish this high level of achievement, however, a leader is needed who plays a role quite different from that of the members. His role is analogous to that of the nerve ring in the starfish which permits the rays to execute a unified response. If the leader can contribute the integrative requirement, group problem solving may emerge as a unique type of group function. This type of approach to group processes places the leader in a particular role in which he must cease to contribute, avoid evaluation, and refrain from thinking about solutions or group *products*. Instead he must concentrate on the group *process*, listen in order to understand rather than to appraise or refute, assume responsibility for accurate communication between members, be sensitive to unexpressed feelings, protect minority points of view, keep the discussion moving, and develop skills in summarizing.

Notes

[1] The research reported here was supported by Grant No. MH-02704 from the United States Public Health Service. Grateful acknowledgment is made for the constructive criticism of Melba Colgrove, Junie Janzen, Mara Julius, and James Thurber.

References

Crozier, W. J. "Notes on Some Problems of Adaptation." *Biological Bulletin* 39:116–129.

Duncker, K. "On Problem Solving." *Psychological Monographs* 58(5, Whole No. 270).

Hamilton, W. F. "Coordination in the Starfish. III. The Righting Reaction As a Phase of Locomotion (righting and locomotion)." *Journal of Comparative Psychology* 2:81–94.

Hoffman, L. R. "Conditions for Creative Problem Solving." *Journal of Psychology* 52:429–444.

Hoffman, L. R. "Group Problem Solving." In L. Berkowitz (Ed.), *Advances in Experimental Social Psychology*, Vol. 2. New York: Academic Press, 1965, pp. 99–132.

Hoffman, L. R.; Harburg, E.; & Maier, N. R. F. "Differences and Disagreement As Factors in Creative Group Problem Solving." *Journal of Abnormal and Social Psychology* 64:206–214.

Hoffman, L. R., & Maier, N. R. F. "The Use of Group Decision to Resolve a Problem of Fairness." *Personnel Psychology* 12:545–559.

Hoffman, L. R., & Maier, N. R. F. "Quality and Acceptance of Problem Solutions by Members of Homogeneous and Heterogeneous Groups." *Journal of Abnormal and Social Psychology* 62:401–407.

Hoffman, L. R., & Maier, N. R. F. "Valence in the Adoption of Solutions by Problem-Solving Groups: Concept, Method, and Results." *Journal of Abnormal and Social Psychology* 69:264–271.

Hoffman, L. R., & Maier, N. R. F. "Valence in the Adoption of Solutions by Problem-Solving Groups: II. Quality and Acceptance as Goals of Leaders and Members." Unpublished manuscript, 1967.

Kelley, H. H., & Thibaut, J. W. "Experimental Studies of Group Problem Solving and Process." In G. Lindzey (Ed.), *Handbook of Social Psychology*. Cambridge, Mass.: Addison Wesley, 1954, pp. 735–785.

Maier, N. R. F. "Reasoning in Humans. I. On Direction." *Journal of Comparative Psychology* 10:115–143.

Maier, N. R. F. "The Quality of Group Decisions as Influenced by the Discussion Leader." *Human Relations* 3:155–174.

Maier, N. R. F. *Principles of Human Relations.* New York: Wiley, 1952.

Maier, N. R. F. "An Experimental Test of the Effect of Training on Discussion Leadership." *Human Relations* 6:161–173.

Maier, N. R. F. *The Appraisal Interview.* New York: Wiley, 1958.

Maier, N. R. F. "Screening Solutions to Upgrade Quality: A New Approach to Problem Solving under Conditions of Uncertainty." *Journal of Psychology* 49:217–231.

Maier, N. R. F. *Problem Solving Discussions and Conferences: Leadership Methods and Skills.* New York: McGraw-Hill, 1963.

Maier, N. R. F., & Hayes, J. J. *Creative Management.* New York: Wiley, 1962.

Maier, N. R. F., & Hoffman, L. R. "Using Trained 'Developmental' Discussion Leaders to Improve Further the Quality of Group Decisions." *Journal of Applied Psychology* 44: 247–251.

Maier, N. R. F., & Hoffman, L. R. "Quality of First and Second Solutions in Group Problem Solving." *Journal of Applied Psychology* 44:278–283.

Maier, N. R. F., & Hoffman, L. R. "Organization and Creative Problem Solving." *Journal of Applied Psychology* 45:277–280.

Maier, N. R. F., & Hoffman, L. R. "Group Decision in England and the United States." *Personnel Psychology* 15:75–87.

Maier, N. R. F., & Hoffman, L. R. "Financial Incentives and Group Decision in Motivating Change." *Journal of Social Psychology* 64:369–378.

Maier, N. R. F., & Hoffman, L. R. "Types of Problems Confronting Managers." *Personnel Psychology* 17:261–269.

Maier, N. R. F., & Hoffman, L. R. "Acceptance and Quality of Solutions as Related to

Leaders' Attitudes toward Disagreement in Group Problem Solving." *Journal of Applied Behavioral Science* 1:373–386.

Maier, N. R. F., & Maier, R. A. "An Experimental Test of the Effects of 'Developmental' vs. 'Free' Discussions on the Quality of Group Decisions." *Journal of Applied Psychology* 41:320–323.

Maier, N. R. F., & Solem, A. R. "The Contribution of a Discussion Leader to the Quality of Group Thinking: The Effective Use of Minority Opinions." *Human Relations* 5:277–288.

Maier, N. R. F., & Solem, A. R. "Improving Solutions by Turning Choice Situations into Problems." *Personnel Psychology* 15:151–157.

Maier, N. R. F., & Zerfoss, L. F. "MRP: A Technique for Training Large Groups of Supervisors and Its Potential Use in Social Research." *Human Relations* 5:177–186.

Moore, A. R. "The Nervous Mechanism of Coordination in the Crinoid *Antedon rosaceus.*" *Journal of Genetic Psychology* 6:281–288.

Moore, A. R., & Doudoroff, M. "Injury, Recovery and Function in an Aganglionic Central Nervous System." *Journal of Comparative Psychology* 28:313–328.

Osborn, A. F. *Applied Imagination.* New York: Scribner's, 1953.

Schneirla, T. C., & Maier, N. R. F. "Concerning the Status of the Starfish." *Journal of Comparative Psychology* 30:103–110.

Solem, A. R. "1965: Almost Anything I Can Do, We Can Do Better." *Personnel Administration* 28:6–16.

Thibaut, J. W., & Kelley, H. H. *The Social Psychology of Groups.* New York: Wiley, 1961

Wallach, M. A., & Kogan, N. "The Roles of Information, Discussion and Consensus in Group Risk Taking." *Journal of Experimental and Social Psychology* 1:1–19.

Wallach, M. A.; Kogan, N.; & Bem, D. J. "Group Influence on Individual Risk Taking." *Journal of Abnormal and Social Psychology* 65:75–86.

Wertheimer, M. *Productive Thinking.* New York: Harper, 1959.

27

The Computer Conference: An Altered State of Communication?

JACQUES VALLEE, ROBERT JOHANSEN, *and*
KATHLEEN SPANGLER

Most of us communicate intuitively. We greet each other every morning without any thought of the contracting muscles of our vocal cords, the atmospheric support of sound vibrations, or the semantic intricacies of our language—all of which are necessary for our natural, face-to-face communication process. Suppose, however, that we had to explain face-to-face communication to someone who had never experienced it. How would we explain, for example, the necessity to be within vocal and visual range of other people? What about the possibilities for "body language," for interpreting all of the subtle visual cues, which accompany the vocal symbols of face-to-face communication? And how would you introduce vocal symbols to a person who has never depended on them to communicate? How do the social demand for immediate responses and our limited ability to remember words which vanish in the air define the nature of our communication?

Clearly, the task of explaining a communication process is staggering. Yet this is the task which we face in exploring the computer conference. Most of our intuitions about face-to-face interaction simply do not apply to this new and unusual form of communication. In computer conferencing, time and distance are dissolved. Visual cues no longer exist. Each person's "memory" of what has been said is accurate and complete. And everyone may speak at once or listen at leisure. With such features, it is not surprising that computer conferencing might actually establish an altered state of communication in which the realities of face-to-face communication are distorted and entirely new patterns of interaction emerge. Our research team at the Institute for the Future in Menlo Park, California, has often experienced this altered state of timeless, placeless, remote communication during the past two years, as we developed and experimented with a family of conferencing programs. Our computerized communication system, known as FORUM,[1] functions as an interpersonal medium for a variety of activities, including planning and forecasting, group conferencing, joint writing projects, electronic notepads (in which messages are stored in a computer instead of on paper), social simulations, and questionnaires. The system allows geographically separated people to communicate either simultaneously or on a delayed basis. We call these two basic usage modes "synchronous" and "asynchronous" conferencing. Participants do not need any technical expertise or even previous experience with computers, though they use a standard computer terminal. All of these characteristics combine to create social conditions that differ from face-to-face communication in at least three important ways: (1) the physical environment; (2) fewer time and space limits; and (3) the various communication structures which are allowed.

An Altered Physical Environment

Unlike face-to-face gatherings, FORUM gatherings are characterized by physical isolation of each participant. Alone with his terminal, each computer conferee depends on an unseen computer to communicate with his colleagues. All "conversation" must be typed on a computer terminal with a standard typewriter keyboard. As a result, accessibility and reliability of terminals, typing skills, and writing skills—factors which are not even considered in face-to-face meetings—all influence communication in a computer conference. For example, a slow or uncertain typist will probably become more selective in the questions he answers and in making his own contributions. On the other hand, many users have found that typing allows them to "give more consideration and focus" to their statements. Expressing ideas through a keyboard is not always a negative factor. Ernest Hemingway reportedly preferred a typewriter for developing dialogues even though he returned to longhand for narratives and descriptions.

The remote keyboard situation hints at some interesting changes in the ritual of "meeting" people. In a computer-based conference, there are no gestures, facial expressions, or vocal cues like pitch, intonation, pauses, or stress. In face-to-face communication, these cues often regulate the flow of a discussion; they also convey emotional feelings and attitudes toward other participants. FORUM greatly narrows this field of information, and many emotional messages simply seem to disappear.

When the sole context for "meeting" someone is through an impersonal keyboard and an equally impersonal printout, the person at the other end might seem inaccessible—a mere extension of the machine. Fortunately, this is not entirely true. Many of the messages ordinarily expressed in body movement or voice tones are translated into written form, either implicitly or explicitly. One conferee reported that "relationships were established easily, personalities came across, conversations could be established." In short, people can become recognizable personalities, even when their only means of expression is the printout of a computer terminal.

The computer itself is invisible in the communication process, but it may intrude upon the discussion in a couple of ways. First, a heavily loaded computer network may transmit messages irregularly. The resultant delay can be frustrating and confusing, since satisfactory communication usually depends on rapid feedback. This frustration is minimal, however, compared to the experience of a system "crash," when the computer stops and the terminal automatically prints out a message such as "DRUM FULL" or "HOST DEAD." (The "HOST DEAD" message created considerable shock among many of our users who attended computer conferences for the first time. A British researcher pointed out to us that a more gentle announcement, such as "HOST PASSED AWAY," might be less traumatic.) Unfortunately, we have had no control over network access or reliability.

Computer system failures are always annoying, but a failure in the middle of a conference dealing with intellectual and emotion-charged issues is devastating. Each person is suddenly and totally isolated in midstream; frustration is intense. A comparable situation in face-to-face communication might be the violent disruption of an assembly by armed bandits, or a sudden collapse of the building.

Alterations of Time and Space

When people in widely separated locations can interact at any time of day or night, their "real world" concepts of time and space are drastically altered. Most people have already had their sense of distance altered by the telephone, but FORUM further reduces the consciousness of distance since it typically costs no more to "talk" across thousands of miles than across ten feet.

Even more striking is the unique "suspended time" of a computerized conference. Participants may enter and leave the discussion at will, without risk of losing touch with the meeting. Time zones disappear since discussion can proceed without regard to the fact that one user is about to eat his supper in London, while a California user has just arrived at his office. If the London colleague unexpectedly joins the discussion while our Californian is busily entering his ideas, this "presence" suddenly adds a dimension of intimacy which restores the awareness of space and time.

Freedom from the constraints of time and distance can naturally reduce the obligation to communicate. No one is physically present, demanding a response. No ringing telephone demands an answer. There is only the knowledge that a conference is in progress and is available, at will, through the terminal. There are, of course, a number of motivations for joining: a need for information, the need to solve a problem, a professional sense of duty, or simply the desire to "be in touch."

Clearly, there are both advantages and disadvantages to such "self-activated" communication. A participant who is asked a question feels less pressure to respond immediately than he would in face-to-face discussion. He can take time to consult a library, review his own thinking, and present a well-prepared response. Still, this same lack of pressure may be an annoyance for someone who is eager to pursue a topic with an indifferent or preoccupied colleague; however, we have found that direct questions through FORUM have generally received prompt replies. And conference growth curves, which measure the number of entries, show that the majority of conferences have constantly or positively accelerated growth rates—an indication that the momentum of the conference can generate pressure to communicate. Nevertheless, the balance between motivation and lack of demand is strikingly different from face-to-face interaction. Thus, the communication might also evolve quite differently.

Altered Structures in Communication

Computer-based conferencing allows a great deal of control of communication structures. For example, users may send *public* messages, which are entered into the transcript and available to all, or *private* messages, which are sent to specific individuals and seen only by them. Functionally, the private message enables colleagues to "whisper" in the midst of a discussion without any breach of etiquette. In content, the public messages tend to be more formal than private messages, and more closely related to the discussion topic, while private messages include more personal interaction, sometimes quite unrelated to the main topic of group discussion.

Anonymous messages permit participants to state their views without divulging their identities—a possibility which does not exist in face-to-face meetings. Conferees have used this feature to express unpopular opinions, voice grievances, or make jokes in a way which is usually not possible.

A FORUM conference can vary from an open-ended discussion in which the topic is simply introduced and the discussion evolves without prescribed direction to a carefully preorganized discussion. In these more structured conferences, the FORUM program becomes a many-roomed meeting hall, dividing the conference into activities according to topic. For still more structured needs, FORUM will administer questionnaires or secret ballots and report the results.

In some ways, even the most unstructured computer-based conferences are more structured than face-to-face communication. FORUM discussions have been characterized by what appears to be a narrower range of topics, less diversion from the subject, and more explicit decision-making than in face-to-face conferencing. On the other hand, it is difficult to compel a FORUM user to direct his comments. It is impossible to shout down or interrupt any other person in the "meeting." All participants may "talk" at the same time; the computer simply records the entries according to the time at which the user began typing.

Mapping the Altered State

We have now begun to "map" the altered state of communications that arises from the special characteristics of a computer conference—physical isolation, dependence on the computer, suspension of time and space, reduced obligation to communicate, and a new set of communication structures. Each communication medium is a unique instrument with characteristics all its own. Because we are most familiar with face-to-face voice communication, we tend to make it a standard by which to measure other media. But we must be careful not to overlook the innovative patterns and opportunities of a new medium by clinging to our preconceptions of what communication really is. Just as it would be unfair to judge a piano by the narrow range of the human voice, it is misleading to evaluate computer conferencing as a simple substitute for face-to-face communication.

The social aspects of communications media have rarely been evaluated, and starting points are not easy to find. Perhaps as many as 50 researchers in the world are doing work on the social effects of different media in at least ten different locations. The theoretical basis for this work is rich, but scattered. The computer conferencing medium itself provides two powerful analytic tools for evaluating its social characteristics: (1) an up-to-date machine-readable transcript of every computer meeting is always available and (2) the computer can unobtrusively map interpersonal interactions to reveal patterns of communication among individuals, groups, and subgroups. Each of these points deserve elaboration.

1. A complete transcript of every computer conference is always available, current, and machine-readable. This transcript is automatically recorded exactly as it is typed, and members can review the record by subject, author, and date—during and after the conference. The possibilities for analyzing the content of the discussion are thus greatly improved over most other media. Using one analytic technique, we have classified entries by content, identifying them as regulatory comments dealing with the group process, comments on the substantive topics in the conference, humor, novel ideas, and similar classifications. In this way, we can evaluate a group's ability to focus on a particular task, and we can also determine where the time actually went (see Fig. 27-1).

The transcript also makes it possible to track specific discussion topics over time. We have thus identified a strong tendency for "threads" or "chains of thought" to occur in the conference transcript. These topic threads are frequently labeled ("re comment 13,"), but the tie is sometimes only implicit, requiring readers to review the earlier proceedings to find out what has been said on a particular topic. The review process is supported by the FORUM program: a participant can, for example, request the computer to search for any entries which mention a particular word, such as "energy." In general, our analysis of the topic threads shows that it is possible to discuss several topics at the same time, occasionally dropping one thread and then picking it up again later.

In addition to tracking the content of discussions, topic threads enable us to analyze the role that the different participants play. We find that some persons tend to introduce many new ideas, while others are best at developing them; still others function as synthesizers. The roles can vary greatly among persons and conferences, but we have noticed an apparent tendency for the "provocative" and "synthesizing" roles to be mutually exclusive. The provoker seems to push the discussion forward into new areas of thought, while the synthesizer ties the loose strands together. By examining the patterns of a FORUM conference, one can easily identify both the key persons and the key ideas.

2. The computer itself can unobtrusively map many dimensions of the interaction that may or may not be evident from the transcript. The ability to map these interaction patterns within a conference may be the most powerful analytic tool inherent in any communications medium. This capability of the FORUM program means that the detailed coding and painstaking observation of interpersonal communication that social psychologists must typically carry out in analyzing small groups can be done automatically here, without disturbing the normal communication process. Comparative participation rates, growth curves, daily activity, and other related indicators create new dimensions for assessing group interaction. Private message statistics, for example, may indicate the formation of subgroups, cliques, or coalitions. Such statistics even allow us to trace individual participation characteristics from one conference to another, perhaps as a function of topic and task.

In addition to individual characteristics of participation, we can also evaluate group characteristics with growth curves. When plotted for the content categories, for example, these curves can indicate if and when the conference has made a transition from the procedural questions inherent in any meeting to the solution of substantive issues.

It is difficult to think of another medium in which an analysis of group interaction can be automatically and unobtrusively generated with this level of detail. At the same time, the privacy of the conference is not violated. The statistics about interaction can be compiled independently of the content of the conference; conferees must grant their permission before we can make any comparison of personal interaction and content.

We have evaluated over 25 conferences using these and more traditional analytic techniques (including interviews and questionnaires). In general, our user groups have had the following characteristics: (1) little familiarity with computer systems; (2) a genuine need to communicate with each other; (3) group sizes ranging from 3–20, but averaging about 5; (4) tasks which were relatively unstructured; (5) time periods averaging several weeks; and (6) primarily asynchronous communication. After 5,000 conference hours with these groups, we are convinced that long-running field tests—as opposed to laboratory experiments—provide the most realistic environment for fully exploring conference styles and usage. FORUM was designed to be learned quickly, so that new users would be able to master its features after an introductory period of about 15 minutes. However, the styles of usage could vary greatly after persons and groups are more familiar with computer conferencing and with their own abilities to present themselves in the medium. In long-term tests, attitudes can be sampled over time, and evaluations become more credible as users integrate the medium with their everyday lives.

1. PROCEDURAL

2. SOCIAL

(195) Lipinski FRI 1 FEB 74 1:47PM
Good bye all, have a nice weekend. I am going to do some work in the garden.

(196) Johansen FRI 1 FEB 74 2:24PM
I hope that 195 does not mean that this will be taken as a 9-5, Monday-Friday conference. Actually, the machine is usually quite pleasant to use on weekends; and everyone is free to continue use in an asynchronous fashion as we have been doing.

(198) Kollen (Chairman) FRI 1 FEB 74 2:43PM
It would be appreciated if participants who are logging into the system would be so kind as to offer comments concerning the agenda of this conference (the five points set down for discussion) and remarks about the discussion of the present point 1. Thank you!

(199) Johansen FRI 1 FEB 74 2:57PM
I am not sure what was meant by 198, Jim. Does this mean you don't think we are sticking to the topic, or does it mean you wish more people would make comments?

(201) Johansen FRI 1 FEB 74 5:32PM
Several people have suggested that we develop an easy to use channel for collecting responses to FORUM conferencing as we go—something like a "gripe Mode." At present we need to set up a separate part of the conference to do this, and I would rather not do this for this conference. However, if you do have comments/criticisms of FORUM as we go, how about sending them to me in the form of private messages?

(202) Johansen FRI 1 FEB 74 5:38PM
As a reminder, the procedure for sending a private message is contained in entry 41, or you can just hit a ?.

(206) Johansen SAT 2 FEB 74 11:29AM
If I could make another procedural suggestion: since we are now working with a basic agenda, it might be helpful to review entries 93 and 62, which describe that agenda.

I am sure our chairman will keep reminding us when the discussion gets off the track. Please let me know if anyone is having any trouble with the review process in FORUM.

Fig. 27-1 Excerpts from the transcript of an actual computer conference. Participants discussed several topics simultaneously, occasionally

3. SUBSTANTIVE

(192) Lipinski FRI 1 FEB 74 1:20PM
There is a danger of confusing the richest with the ultimate (see 189). In fact, the end of the richness scale would probably be face to face with complete visual and aural record, a very uncomfortable situation in some circumstances. Thus, for different transactions, different degrees of richness may be appropriate, and too much may be as bad as too little. Unless one considers what kind of meeting one runs, there is a danger that data will be collected across the scale of "richness"

(194) Lipinski FRI 1 FEB 74 1:39PM
There must have been reasons surely, beyond inadequate publicity, why the TV conferencing was not a roaring success (in view of the savings).

(197) Kollen (Chairman) FRI 1 FEB 74 2:33PM
The answer to Mr. Lipinski's question in 192 is yes we have collected data on how business trips are distributed across corporate activities. We have 10,000 questionnaires which have data on the following: (etc.)

(203) Johansen FRI 1 FEB 74 5:50PM
To get back to the "spectrums of richness" question (I am afraid there are lots of different threads to this medium), wouldn't one end of the spectrum be telepathy, or complete "merging of the minds"? Though face to face certainly provides multiple inputs simultaneously, I see no reason to assume that this is the limit of communication richness.

(204) Lipinski FRI 1 FEB 74 6:00PM
I agree. In fact, science fiction has 3-d vision established firmly as their communications of the future. In one book of Asimov, the heroine and the detective eat dinner in 3-d, the barrier bisecting the table. However, there is still no common space, now that I think of it. Pity Gordon Thompson can't attend this conference! I would think that merging of the minds is beyond the present state of implementation; hence face to face remains, for all practical reasons, the richest form of communications we have.

(217) Kollen (Chairman) MON 4 FEB 7:09AM
Re 194. The Bell Canada Conference TV Trial was just that, a trial. It was not, and still is not, a market offering. It was conceived and conducted as an experiment; hence the comment about it not being a "roaring success" is not applicable as far as I can see.

(218) Lipinski MON 4 FEB 74 7:42AM
Re 194. I think you are too defensive. I hear (maybe Williams can comment) that the B.P.O. teleconference is not a great success either. Perhaps this is because we don't quite know why and how people communicate.

(219) Kollen (Chairman) MON 4 FEB 8:06AM
Re 218. Andy, I think that you may be right. Perhaps I overreacted to the words "roaring success" because I felt that there was no basis in E. Frohloff's remarks which warranted that particular criticism. Frohloff indicated that Conference TV was an experiment and not a service offering (as confravision in the U.K.)

dropping one topic "thread" and picking it up later. The communications shown here can be classified as procedural, social, or substantive.

Implications for the Future

A scant 100 or so persons throughout the world now use computerized conferencing on a regular basis. But the time may be fast approaching when far more people will be conferring through computers and we will begin to view computer conferencing as a "natural" way to interact.

In this new environment, "invisible colleges" may develop, since this medium can introduce and coordinate groups of people who may or may not have been in touch previously. Scholars, businessmen, and government officials would be able to interact outside the normal limits of time and space; they would no longer need to spend so much time exchanging journal articles, memos, and reports, arranging meetings, or traveling to conventions in distant places. (See Fig. 27-2.)

Perhaps we can enhance group creativity through a new communications style, forged in the computer conference. With everybody at a conference

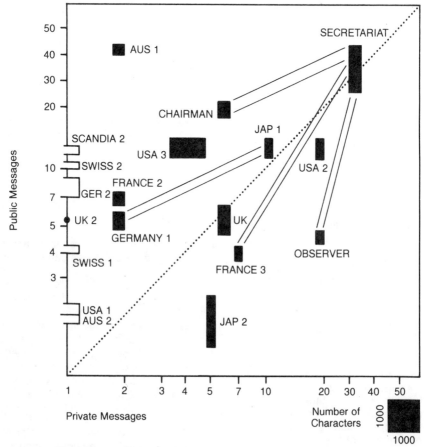

Fig. 27-2   Participation map for a simulated computer program[2]

thinking and expressing his thoughts in multiple streams, we might observe a process of "fast thinking" that would enhance our collective abilities to resolve conflicts, deal with crises, or improve decision-making capability. Or perhaps computer conferencing will spawn new types of poetry or literature.

From a practical viewpoint, a portable computer terminal may be hooked up to any standard telephone line, enabling persons immobilized with illness, or away from the office for any reason, to continue many of their regular duties. Computer conferencing also has great potential in providing handicapped persons with a channel to the outside world.

The "coolness" of the medium may also prove useful for such activities as encounter sessions, counseling, and discussions of personal values. Psychotherapy may also find uses for the medium: for instance, the altered environment for self-presentation may help in defining self-concepts (for example, in relating to persons of the opposite sex or of other races). Certainly a detailed analysis of self-presentation processes is possible in FORUM, and the FORUM communication environment may also be potentially less threatening than a face-to-face group. The major question is how such an environment could be used therapeutically to obtain results which could be transferred effectively to more "normal" communication situations.

On the other hand, we are not oblivious to the potential negative impacts of computer-based conferencing. Though costs are already encouraging (about $15 per terminal hour on a commercial computer network, with further cost reductions anticipated), computer conferencing is not yet a medium for the masses. And a type of electronic elitism is certainly a possibility as long as terminals and network access remain the privilege of a few.

Could computer communications replace much—or all—face-to-face contact? At present, "human contact" usually means being together "in person." For some people, the mere thought of a communication medium in which human bodies (or even voices) are irrelevant is frightening. Isaac Asimov, in his novel *The Naked Sun,* and E. M. Forster, in his 1929 story *The Machine Stops,* offer nightmarish projections of a future in which electronic communication replaces human contact as we now know it. Our research team has examined computer-based conferencing as a supplement to face-to-face communication, not as a replacement, but long-term negative possibilities deserve attention, if only so they can be avoided.

Our studies to date indicate that computer conferencing has unique potential for enhancing the exchange of ideas among people. In current field tests, we are exploring its usefulness in bargaining and negotiation, conflict resolution, crisis management, and some educational applications. However, as should be clear from this article, our work should only be viewed as a foot placed in an interesting door. We are convinced that this medium will change quickly and that it should not be evaluated by narrow criteria. We believe as well that the potential of computer-based communication remains largely unexplored.

Notes

[1] The FORUM system has been developed by a team composed of Roy Amara, Hubert Lipinski, Ann McCown, Richard Miller, Thad Wilson, and the authors of this article. This research is supported by the Department of Computer Research at the National Science Foundation (under Grant GJ-35 326X). The authors wish to thank Arthur Hastings for suggesting that computer conferencing might represent an "altered state." PLANET-1, a simpler version of FORUM, is now available on the TYMSHARE, Inc. computer network.

[2] Figure 27-2 was constructed with statistics *gathered directly* in a simulation of a computer-based international conference. In this test, the work of an International Telephone and Telegraph Consultative Committee Study Group was simulated by 18 graduate students at San Jose State University, assisted by several technical experts. The students played the roles of eight national delegations from which previous position papers were available. An analysis of user behavior with respect to negotiation and information exchange was then conducted. Rectangles represent each participant, indicating the number of private messages and public messages each has sent. The sides of the rectangles are proportional to the verbosity, defined here by the average length (in characters) of messages in private and public mode. This type of map can help define roles of participants; it also enables us to observe coalitions and subgroups and to track individual participation characteristics from one conference to another.

28

Telecommunications As a Travel Substitute: Some Psychological, Organizational, and Social Aspects

LESLEY A. ALBERTSON

Travel and telecommunications are better seen as interrelated elements in a social context which they help create.

Well before the year 2000 dawns the city office worker won't have to get up every morning to take the polluting commuter trail. He could be doing his job just as effectively from his living room at home. . . .

Break through the travel barrier with Confravision, the inter-city conference service at your door. . . .

In each of these statements, one taken from a discussion of the "home office"[1] in the popular press (5), the other from a British Post Office brochure advertising its teleconference[2] facility, it is assumed that video telecommunications are capable of replacing physical travel.

A number of writers in the fields of transportation and urban development, as well as telecommunications, make the same assumption. Dickson and Bowers (13) devote a chapter to the effects on transportation of substituting video telephony for business travel, but do not attempt to justify their assumption that such substitution is possible, other than by commenting that it has been "frequently suggested."

As one future urban form, the LUTSANC study (19) proposed a "cluster city," in which advanced telecommunications systems replace travel between nodes of population distributed over a wide area. Day (12) discusses travel-/telecommunications substitutability from several points of view, including the "behavioral reasons" for travel. In none of these cases, however, is it debated whether technologically-mediated interaction is a psychologically acceptable substitute for face-to-face communication, or whether using telecommunications devices over long periods of time might also have behavioral or social consequences.

In view of the importance to several areas of planning of the possibility that telecommunications could reduce the need for travel, it is surprising to find that such questions have been neglected, even by telecommunications specialists. This article therefore is concerned with developing a social psychological perspective on the use of telecommunications as a travel substitute, using the home office and video teleconferencing as focal points.

The absence, until recently, of any research into the question of whether video telecommunications allow business to be conducted as effectively as it is face-to-face is partly explained by the long-held belief of many telecommunications engineers that video telephony would provide "total communication." Those who accept this view argue that any differences observed between the two are a function of the limitations of present technology and, as this argument underlies the notion of substitution, it merits consideration in some detail.

Certainly some of the communication difficulties experienced using present video telecommunications are at least partly attributable to technological limitations. Surveys of teleconference users, for example, consistently report that "getting to know someone" is difficult over a video medium (2, 7, 27). Reid (23) has suggested that when only a voice channel is available, communicators create an image of the person speaking, which, while it may not accurately represent that person, is complete in itself. A low-definition video representation may be sufficient to interfere with the formation of such an image, while being too ambiguous to create a satisfactory image in its own right. "Maintaining friendly relations" is reported in these surveys as being less difficult, suggesting that the video image is sufficient to act as a reminder stimulus if the person is already known, although people using teleconference for regular meetings still experience the need to meet face-to-face about once in every three or four meetings (7). If Reid's explanation is correct, improving the quality of the video image could be expected to reduce this ratio.

But, if we imagine video technology as moving towards its ultimate state, with perhaps colored, life-sized holographs projected at the culturally appropriate communication distance, would there be a corresponding reduction in the perceived difference between the mediated exchange and an actual encounter? Although no empirical comparisons have been conducted, there are some *a priori* grounds for predicting that the relationship between technological improvement and the subjectively experienced quality of the communication medium is not so simple.

Conrath and Thompson (11) point out that when only a voice channel is used, the communicators share a common auditory space. With the introduction of a video channel, each communicator must present himself and part of his environment to the other. The inability of the communicators to share the visual environment or to move around in the other's environment could be partly overcome by designing a system which allowed camera control from the remote location. However, it seems likely that the feeling of discontinuity between the two environments would be increased as the visual image became increasingly lifelike.

Another problem which is often overlooked because of the strongly visual orientation of present Western culture is that telecommunications can only represent the auditory and visual dimensions, although our total sensory awareness also includes tactile, gustatory, and olfactory dimensions. Removing these dimensions obviously precludes some activities which are often associated with business meetings, such as shaking hands or sharing a meal; and although research in the area is limited, nonverbal communication theory (3) provides some basis for expecting that the absence of these dimensions may explain some of the difficulty experienced in getting to know someone over a video link. Although ingenious substitutes for some of these activities have been proposed, such as the hydraulically-controlled glove for remote hand-shaking, it seems unlikely that these dimensions can be telecommunicated in a psychologically meaningful way. Thus, improvement in the visual and auditory dimensions is likely to increase awareness of interdimensional perceptual discrepancies, the problem which Seyler (24) has termed "cross-modal mismatch." The other person may be observed drinking coffee or smoking a cigarette, but the accompanying stimuli in other modes (such as smell and tactile sensations) are absent.

Although the importance of these factors in communication effectiveness has not yet been empirically established, they are sufficient indication that even the ultimate in video communications cannot be assumed to be identical with face-to-face communication, and that there may be an optimum point beyond which technological improvement is self-defeating.

The First Systematic Attempt to Research the Question
of the Relative Effectiveness of Different
Telecommunications Media Was Made by the
Communications Studies Group at London University.

On one series of studies conducted by this group (10) persons were asked to use different media (usually telephone, closed-circuit television, or face-to-face) to perform a range of communication tasks. Such tasks included exchanging information, interviewing, problem-solving, persuasion, and negotiation. Perhaps the most important conclusion to emerge from these studies was that a communication medium as a whole cannot be located on a continuum of effectiveness in any simple manner. It was found that for less complex tasks, such as information exchange, the measured outcomes did not vary significantly with the medium of communication; a voice channel was found to be as effective as any other medium for this type of communication. In fact, one study (1) found that information recall was significantly better using the telephone than when the medium was either videophone or face-to-face communication, which leads to the conjecture that a visual image may act as a distractor under some circumstances.

However, for those tasks which involve interpersonal influence, such as persuasion or negotiation, outcomes were sensitive to the communication medium used. Morley and Stephenson (21) found that when simulated management-union negotiations were conducted over the telephone, the side with the case which had previously been rated as stronger was significantly more successful, a finding which was replicated by Short (see 10). The outcomes of studies of persuasion have been less consistent. The combination of four laboratory studies of persuasion (26) resulted in the finding that the greatest opinion change occurs in the audio-only condition. Video outcomes were intermediate between the audio-only and face-to-face conditions, but were more similar to the former than to the latter. Thus, although it seems that the physical presence of another person reduces the emphasis on communication content which occurs when only a voice channel is available, a video image (at least of the commercial quality used in these experiments) does not have the same effect.

These findings, however, do not provide any obvious basis for ranking media in terms of their effectiveness for interpersonal tasks, as this would involve a subjective judgment of which outcome was preferable. Evidence from teleconference users indicates that both audio and video telecommunications are perceived as less satisfactory for tasks such as negotiation than for simpler tasks such as information exchange (2, 25, 27). There is also evidence that attitudes towards communications media differ, independently of the purpose for which they are used. One study found that video systems are regarded as more "public" on a public-private dimension than either an audio system or face-to-face communication (8). This result is interpreted as indicating that the video medium creates a psychological sense of intrusion rather than a distrust of its actual security, as the only change between the video and audio condition in this experiment was that the video picture was turned off in the latter case.

The inherent problems of laboratory studies, such as the artificiality of subjects role-playing a situation in order to satisfy experimental demands and their short exposure to the medium, make it hazardous to generalize from these results to the real-life situation of remote working. But, even if it is accepted that it is possible to predict how effectively a series of tasks can be performed using a video medium, or how psychologically comfortable people are likely to be in doing so, the possibility of the home office also raises basic questions about the nature of work.

Professionals, managers, and office workers are the groups for whom the home office is usually seen as most appropriate. However, the work of many of these people is directly concerned with interpersonal communication. Managers in one large company were found to spend an average of 59 percent of their time in communicating with people, mainly face-to-face (18), a result which is within the range reported from similar analyses. As even the laboratory studies have shown that communication tasks involving interpersonal influence are sensitive to the communication medium, it is doubtful whether this part of a manager's work could be effectively conducted over a videophone. In addition, the extent to which this general category of "communication" can be adequately represented as a series of tasks is open to question. Mortenson (22) comments that to do so is to "reduce the complex and delicate process by which man somehow fashions a deluge of impressions into an orderly system . . . to the level of work habits required for laying bricks or digging foundations in a rainstorm."

It Is Perhaps an Indication of the Lingering Puritan Ethic Which Still Governs Many of Our Attitudes toward Work That the Social Context in Which Work Occurs Is Usually Regarded As Incidental to the Corporate Rationale.

However, some writers have recognized that this social context has a number of important functions which are relevant to both work performance and satisfaction. Carne (6) comments that "managers see their presence at the office as essential for direction, motivation and morale," and Harvey (16) that "the social organization of the workplace is the means by which people enhance their self-esteem as persons of competence, and satisfy their needs for companionship, affiliation and belongingness." Glover (15) interviewed a small group of people who had experienced working from home under present conditions and found that, in addition to the undoubted benefits, such as avoiding rush-hour travel and being able to complete projects without interruption, working in isolation from a social group also caused many of the drawbacks mentioned by interviewees. These included difficulties in making business contacts, the absence of fertilization of ideas or feedback, professional anonymity, and lack of social contacts.

Sophisticated telecommunications systems could be used to alleviate the difficulty of making social contacts, particularly if schemes such as a computerized method of meeting new people or video morning-coffee clubs were introduced. Nevertheless, the inherent limitations of the video medium, combined with the fact that telecommunications are primarily adapted to direct person-to-person communication, make it likely that under remote working conditions the other members of the organization would become less salient as a social group than is the case with face-to-face working.

This would have far-reaching effects on the nature of organizations. One consequence would be the erosion of corporate identity and the expectation that organizations have continuity over time. With employees' lessened affiliation with the work group and, as changing jobs would not involve a physical move, staff turnover could be expected to be much higher than at present. At the same time, organizations could be more flexible than at present; freed from the necessity to provide accommodation, organizations could tailor the number of people employed to meet changing needs, and conditions would be suitable for the formation of *ad hoc* organizations or task forces for carrying out particular projects. The removal of the social context would also mean that work would center around individual performance of tasks, which would present increased problems of coordination and control for the organization. Given the more fluid employment situation and the difficulties of using hours of work as a basis for payment, it seems likely that many people would work under relatively short-term contracts, with payment on the completion of specified projects.

> *To Counter the Obvious Possibility of the Individual*
> *Becoming More Open to Manipulative Control*
> *by Organizations, the Relevant Unions and Professional*
> *Associations Would Become More Active in Establishing*
> *Employment Conditions for Their Members.*

More attention would necessarily be devoted to work definition, measurement, and evaluation. It is also likely that such organizations would become a more important source of the person's sense of competence and professional identity. But, as it is doubtful whether an organization as large as a union would be able to fully satisfy the need for a meaningful social context, remote working would place sudden additional demands on both the family and the community.

Although working from a home office is, in one sense, a modern version of the situation which obtained before the industrial revolution, the social changes which accompanied industrialization preclude any simple "return" to the society of that time. Modern families are smaller, and an increasing proportion of people live alone. At the same time, partly as a result of material self-sufficiency, families have become more isolated from the community. For these reasons alone, the capacity of telecommunications to provide an adequate sense of interpersonal relating could become a crucial issue if remote working is not to result in psychological stress and a society in which people are increasingly alienated from each other.

Another important difference is that, in contrast to a lifestyle in which work and family were closely integrated, the two contexts are now not only physically separate, but give rise to distinctly different role behaviors which may have very little in common (4). The journey to work at present provides time in which the transition between roles can be accomplished smoothly, a transition which is assisted by appropriate changes in role symbols, such as dress. Performing both roles in the same context is likely to bring the two into sharp conflict, and much could depend on their successful integration. The possibility of the work role, with its requirement for "functional expertise and impersonal, detached attitudes" (28) invading the home role, in which the person's relationships are typically warmer and more relaxed (4), presents the danger of people losing touch with an important aspect of reality. However, the alternative possibility that working from home would result in a basic change in work role behavior is also likely to have enormous social consequences; even if Zijderveld's view that "modern bureaucracy is the general cohesive force in pluralistic society that keeps this society together as a functionally integrated whole" (28) is perhaps overstating the case, work roles are undeniably a major organizing principle in modern society.

Thus, although remote working holds out a promise for a new principle of social organization based on greater integration of work and home roles and a renewed sense of community based on contacts with other people, the inherent social dangers in making the transition from the present system are also great. In view of the magnitude of the changes which remote working would initiate, it is clear that decisions concerning the implementation of the home office cannot be made by considering only travel and telecommunicating. The changes in the nature of work and organizations, in individual lifestyles and in society and which would result from remote working, would also change communication needs and travel patterns to such an extent that to argue the substitution issue within an otherwise static social system is necessarily invalid.

In the Case of Teleconferencing, the Substitution Issue Takes a Somewhat Different Form, Being Centered on the Question of to What Extent Telecommunicating Is Likely to Replace Travel, Given That a Choice Between the Two Is Possible.

Teleconference systems are now operating in a number of countries, including Britain, Canada, the United States, Japan, and Australia. As all these systems are relatively new, the most effective ways to use and market them are still being explored. Substitution for travel to existing meetings is an obvious application, and this possibility has received renewed attention as a result of recent public concern with the issues of energy conservation and pollution. The existing links have been used mainly for real meetings since, unlike the desktop videophone, they have been made available as point-to-point facilities and hence do not involve the expense of installing a network. As a result, research has emphasized acceptability to the users, rather than experimental studies of their effectiveness.

Surveys have typically reported that more than 90 percent of users profess to be highly satisfied with such facilities (2, 14, 27). Nevertheless, relating satisfaction to subsequent use of the system, or to preferences for telecommunicating rather than traveling, has proved problematical. One reason is that the base for comparison is not necessarily an equivalent face-to-face meeting. Questionnaires completed by over 400 teleconference users (2) showed that although 92 percent of users "liked" the system, and 98 percent stated that they would like to use it again, 39 percent also considered that their teleconference was less effective than a face-to-face meeting would have been (although it should also be noted that 11 percent rated it as *more* effective). And, whereas some teleconference systems receive regular use, similar systems elsewhere are used seldom or not at all (10). Attempts to explain this finding include: attitudes towards travel, such as avoidance of long-distance travel to routine meetings (25) or a liking for travel and its associated "frills" (12); the perceived unsuitability of the system for particular types of meetings

(27); or the territorial implications of where the facility is located (7). In addition, the costs of video systems are generally high and are often greater than travel costs between the conference locations. But while these explanations may be correct in particular cases, a survey of more than 9000 businessmen traveling by air, road, and rail found that none of these or other explanations typically advanced in the research literature were significantly related to the respondent's reported decision to substitute telecommunications for the present trip (17). After finding no correlations large enough to usefully predict substitution, the researchers concluded that "either the decision to substitute may be an idiosyncratic one which the present study did not tap," or that "conceptualizing substitution of telecommunications as a *replacement process* rather than as a supplement to travel is ill-conceived."

Evidence from teleconference users concerning the relationship between their teleconference and travel lend partial support to this conclusion. In the survey previously quoted (2), although the majority of users (72 percent) considered that the option was "travel to a face-to-face meeting," not all the participants in the teleconference would have attended such a meeting. Twenty-two percent replied that they would not personally have been present, and a further 11 percent were uncertain. In 15 percent of cases, the exchange would not have occurred at all, and, with the exception of 5 percent who would have used a multi-party telephone call, the other alternatives involved a series of exchanges (for example, letters and telephone calls) rather than a meeting. Some of the face-to-face meetings would also have involved a multi-step process, such as a local meeting followed by sending a delegate to the remote location. These results suggest that, as well as replacing some existing travel, teleconferencing is also emerging as a communications medium in its own right; a greater number of simultaneous meetings occur than would otherwise have been the case, and many more people are directly involved in the communication than if traveling had been necessary.

However, these results represent only the initial phase of teleconference use. Other evidence suggests that if teleconferencing were used for a series of meetings between groups, the interrelationship between telecommunicating and travel would become more complex. One reason is that effective teleconferencing appears to require a proportion of face-to-face communication between the conferees; if they are not previously acquainted, teleconference users report that they need to speak more redundantly to ensure that the information is getting across (7), and even those who are acquainted feel the need for periodic face-to-face meetings (7, 25). In addition, teleconferencing is not perceived as suitable for more complex interpersonal tasks such as persuasion and negotiation (2, 27). A determined substitutionist who prohibited all travel would find that teleconferencing would become, if not less effective, certainly less satisfactory to the participants.

Thus, even if it is assumed that the total number of meetings remained constant, the involvement of more people in the meeting would also mean that whereas some people would travel less than at present, this would be to some extent counterbalanced by the fact that the additional conferees would need to travel occasionally if their participation were to be effective. However, there is little reason to assume that the total number of meetings will remain constant. Factors such as the multi-disciplinary approach to solving problems of various kinds, demands for union participation in management decision-making, and even the pressures for more open planning at all levels of government are likely to increase the need for meetings. But in addition to serving a proportion of the growing need for inter-group communication, the survey results quoted above suggest that the availability of teleconference facilities makes long-distance communication between groups more feasible, and hence is likely to result in more communication. And this, in turn, will generate a proportion of travel.

The Overall Impact of Teleconferencing on Travel
Is Therefore Difficult to Predict, but It Can Be Seen That
Even Extensive Use of Teleconferencing Would Be
Unlikely to Reduce the Present Overall Level of Travel,
and Indeed Seems More Likely to Increase It.

Although this conclusion may at first appear surprising, it is in fact consistent with the pattern of development of previous communication innovations. The opening of the transatlantic cable, for example, resulted in an enormous increase in both telecommunications traffic and travel across the Atlantic, partly because of the role of telecommunications in making transport systems safer and more efficient, and also because reliable communications made international operations a real possibility for the first time for many organizations. And, despite the conventional wisdom, television has not replaced other broadcast media in any simple sense, although overall use of the mass media has declined recently, at least in the United States (20).

But while substitution has not been the general rule, communications innovations have sometimes induced qualitative changes in the existing media, with the old and the new polarizing toward what each does best. Television, for example, has probably influenced program innovations in radio, such as audience "talkback," and cinema's increasing exploitation of its large screen size. By analogy, it would be expected that since transport cannot compete with teleconferencing as far as speed is concerned, travel advertising is likely to increasingly emphasize other advantages, such as the importance of "real" face-to-face communication, the possibility of useful encounters or the opportunity to relax away from the office.

Teleconferencing also provides new communication opportunities for organizations. However, the mere availability of teleconference facilities does not ensure that these will be taken up. In particular, teleconferencing is not likely to have a great impact on organizations if the facilities are provided mainly on a shared basis. Under these conditions their use is inhibited both by practical difficulties, such as the time required to travel to the studio and the need to make advance bookings, and by psychological factors, such as the territorial implications of where it is located (7) and forgetting about its existence (27). Even if it is assumed that organizations will gradually acquire their own facilities, introducing teleconferencing into organizations involves more than acquiring the technical apparatus or learning the most effective ways to conduct meetings over the system. If the new possibilities are to be exploited, teleconferencing needs to be integrated into the organization's functioning. This would require an analysis of the organization's patterns of communication, and how these relate to its aims, structure and functions. As a result of such an analysis, the constraints to the organization's aims which arise from existing communication patterns could be identified, and this would point to the specific ways in which teleconferencing would help these aims to be achieved more effectively.

Although the possibilities would vary with the particular organization, in general terms, teleconferencing could remove some of the gaps which result from the multi-step communication processes which are often necessary at present. And, by involving more people in direct communication, teleconferencing would increase dissemination of information throughout the organization, which would in turn improve job satisfaction and increase organizational cohesion and member identification with the organization's aims (16).

Thus, although teleconferencing would not have the major impact of the home office, it has the potential of subtly influencing the nature of organizations and the direction of their development.

In conclusion, while it is certainly true that video telecommunications can be used to replace travel in particular instances, there is no convincing evidence that such systems are likely to provide a departure from the positive relationship which has previously existed between telecommunications use and travel. Substitution provides an inadequate picture of the overall relationship between the two, partly because the medium itself is not subjectively experienced as the same as face-to-face contact, but, more importantly, because major communication innovations, particularly those of the order of the home office, would themselves initiate such vast organizational and social changes that it is inherently untenable to see communication needs as remaining static, with only the travel/telecommunications ratio changing. Travel and telecommunications are better seen as interrelated elements in a social context which they help create. In the case of teleconferencing, placing limitations on travel would not automatically increase telecommunications use by an equivalent amount; the more probable long-term effect would be that organizations would function in a more localized manner. Conversely, extensive teleconference use would not necessarily reduce the need for travel, although it would provide new opportunities for communication which could initiate changes in organizational functioning. And, while a decision to implement remote working could obviously reduce travel to a central business district, the need for an alternative social context to that presently provided by the workplace would generate travel which does not occur under present conditions.

Therefore, not only is consideration of the social implications of telecommunications innovation part of responsible planning, but the changes in communication patterns which result from such innovation are so intricately linked with the process of organizational and social change that it is virtually meaningless to debate the question for travel substitution independently of this context.

Notes

[1] Usually depicted as a complex of telecommunications systems based on the video telephone, and including such additional facilities as a keyboard, computer terminal, a unit for the visual display of information and a facsimile device for hardcopy printouts.

[2] "Teleconference" is used in this essay to include all telecommunications facilities which allow meetings between groups of people at two or more locations. These facilities may be audiovisual or audio-only.

References

1. Albertson, L. A. "A Comparative Study of Communication Effectiveness Across Media." Melbourne: Australian Post Office, 1973.

2. Albertson, L. A. "A Preliminary Report on the Teleconference User Opinion Questionnaire." Melbourne: Australian Post Office, 1974.

3. Argyle, M. *The Psychology of Interpersonal Behaviour.* Harmondsworth: Penguin, 1967.

4. Argyle, M., and Little, B. R. "Do Personality Traits Apply to Social Behaviour?" *Journal for the Theory of Social Behaviour* 2(1) (1972): 2–32.

5. Australian *National Times* (March 11–16, 1974).

6. Carne, E. B. "Telecommunications: Its Impact on Business." *Harvard Business Review* 50(4) (1972): 925–933.

7. Casey-Stahmer, A. E., and Havron, M. D. "Planning Research in Teleconference Systems." Report by Human Sciences Research, Inc., Virginia, for the Department of Communication, Ottawa, September 1973.

8. Champness, B. G. "Attitudes towards Person-Person Communications Media." *Human Factors* 15 (1973): 437–448.

9. Cherry, C. *World Communication: Threat or Promise?* London: Wiley-Interscience, 1971.

10. Communications Studies Group. "Interim Report, May 1972." Communications Studies Group, Joint Unit for Planning Research, University College, London, 1972.

11. Conrath, D. W., and Thompson, G. B. "Communications Technology: A Societal Perspective." *Journal of Communication* 23(3) (1973): 47–63.

12. Day, L. H. "An Assessment of Travel/Telecommunications Substitutability." *Futures* (December 1973).

13. Dickson, E. M., and Bowers, R. "The Video Telephone, A Preliminary Technology Assessment." Report prepared for National Science Foundation, Cornell University, June 1973.

14. Duncanson, J. P., and Williams, A. D. "Video Conferencing: Reactions of Users." *Human Factors* 15 (1973): 471–486.

15. Glover, J. "Long Range Social Forecasts: Working from Home." Long Range Intelligence Bulletin No. 2, Telecommunications System Strategy Department, British Post Office, 1974.

16. Harvey, L. V. "Interpersonal Communication." Paper presented at the annual conference of the Australian Psychological Society, 1971.

17. Kollen, J. H., and Garwood, J. "The Replacement of Travel by Telecommunications." Paper presented at the Psychology and Telecommunications Symposium, 18th International Congress of Applied Psychology, 1974.

18. Link, P. L. "Future Communications Systems in Australian Business Organizations." Unpublished master's thesis, Department of Economics, Monash University, Melbourne, 1973.

19. Land Use/Transportation Structure Alternatives for New Cities (LUT-

SANC). "New Structures for Australian Cities." Report prepared for the Cities Commission under the direction of Maunsell and Partners Pty., Ltd., Canberra, February 1975.

20. Maisel, R. "The Decline of Mass Media." *Public Opinion Quarterly* (Summer 1973).

21. Morley, I. E., and Stephenson, G. M. "Interpersonal and Inter-party Exchange: A Laboratory Simulation of an Industrial Negotiation at the Plant Level." *British Journal of Psychology* 60(4) (1969): 543–545.

22. Mortenson, C. D. *Communication: The Study of Human Interaction.* New York: McGraw Hill, 1972.

23. Reid, A. A. L. "Comparison between Telephone and Face-to-Face Conversation." Paper presented at the 5th International Symposium on Human Factors in Telecommunication, London, 1970.

24. Seyler, A. J. "On Some Fundamental Aspects of Teleconferencing." Unpublished report, Australian Post Office, Melbourne, 1974.

25. Short, J. "A Report on the Use of Audio Conferencing Facility at the University of Quebec." Communications Studies Group, Joint Unit for Planning Research, University College, London, 1973.

26. Short, J. "The Effects of Medium of Communication on Persuasion, Bargaining and Perception of the Other." Communications Studies Group, Joint Unit for Planning Research, University College, London, 1973.

27. Williams, E. "The Bell Canada Conference Television System: A Case Study." Communications Studies Group, Joint Unit for Planning Research, University College, London, 1973.

28. Zijderveld, A. C. *The Abstract Society.* Harmondsworth: Penguin, 1973.

Part Ten

Dynamics of Small Group Decision Making

29

Communication in Micro-Networks

RICHARD V. FARACE, PETER MONGE, *and* HAMISH M. RUSSELL

When people in social systems talk with one another on a regular basis, the patterns created by the messages they exchange are called communication networks. If the communication occurs in small groups the resultant patterns are called "micro-networks." If the communication patterns occur in large organizations they are called "macro-networks." This distinction is important because books on communication frequently discuss communication networks, but almost exclusively in terms of micro-networks. Large organizational macro-networks receive scant attention.

Knowledge about micro-networks developed out of research on whether different kinds of communication networks affected group performance. The question makes sense from an organizational viewpoint because organizations can exercise some degree of control over how members are organized and who may talk to whom.

The initial work that described micro-networks was published by Bavelas (1948, 1950) and Leavitt (1951), who developed procedures for studying communication networks in the small-group laboratory. Using a laboratory setting the researchers positioned people (initially five) around a table that was partitioned off so that each person was physically isolated. The only way group members could communicate was by sending messages through slots in the partition walls. The group was then assigned a task which required the participation of all group members. The specific network was imposed upon the group by controlling the slots each member could use to transmit messages. Some slots were open and some were closed, depending upon the network pattern.

Several types of networks were studied, utilizing both symmetrical (two-way) and asymmetrical (one-way) channels. Leavitt employed the circle, chain, Y, and wheel patterns. These four, as well as other networks that have been studied, are presented in Fig. 29-1.

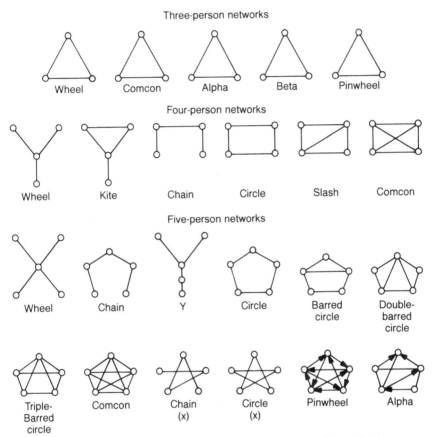

Three-person networks

Wheel   Comcon   Alpha   Beta   Pinwheel

Four-person networks

Wheel   Kite   Chain   Circle   Slash   Comcon

Five-person networks

Wheel   Chain   Y   Circle   Barred circle   Double-barred circle

Triple-Barred circle   Comcon   Chain (x)   Circle (x)   Pinwheel   Alpha

Fig. 29-1 Communication networks used in experimental investigation. Dots represent positions, lines represent communication channels, and arrows indicate one-way channels.[1]

The theoretical position articulated by Bavelas suggested that two kinds of descriptors should be developed for networks: (1) those for individual positions within a network, and (2) those for the network as a whole. In general, indices for the network as a whole are simple sums of the individual measures. Leavitt (1951) argued that two concepts, centrality and peripherality, were of prime interest in the study of networks; he presented metrics for each.

Subsequent investigation has examined the influence of several other variables. Shaw (1964) organizes these under three categories:

1. *Network-related variables:* group size, changes in network, opportunity to organize;
2. *Information-input variables:* noise, information distribution, reinforcement; and
3. *Group-composition variables:* ascendance, authoritarianism, leadership style, and popularity.

These variables have been studied in relation to their effects on problem-solving efficiency, communication activity, organizational activity, and member satisfaction. They are typically measured by observational or questionnaire techniques.

Of the several dozen studies that have been conducted over the past two decades, only one consistent finding has emerged; it pertains to the concept of centrality. Centralized nets (e.g., wheel, Y) are more efficient—they permit faster problem solution with fewer errors—when dealing with simple tasks. Decentralized nets (e.g., circle, comcon) are more efficient when the task is complex. Decentralized nets, however, are more satisfying to group members, regardless of whether the task is simple or complex. The effects of other variables listed above have been reviewed, summarized, and tabled by Glanzer and Glaser (1961), Shaw (1964), and Collins and Raven (1969).

Unfortunately, there are several problems in attempting to apply the findings from small-group studies to larger organizations. First, the findings of the various studies are inconsistent and often contradictory. Nearly a quarter of a century of research has produced surprisingly little agreement among scientists as to the role that networks play in group processes.

Second, it is difficult to generalize the findings to small groups actually existing in large organizations, because the behavior of groups in the laboratory differs considerably from groups *embedded* in an organizational setting (e.g., Cohen, Robinson, and Edwards, 1969). The point that Cohen and his associates make is that groups in an organization usually have a history, are clearly aware of power and status relations, and operate within the norms of the organizational context. Most small-group laboratory research, on the other hand, has used ad hoc, randomly formed groups without histories or a normative operating context.

Third, it is difficult to generalize the findings to groups larger in size than that used in the experimental design, since the findings seem to change as group size changes. Differences occur in the performance of three-, four-, and five-person groups, a fact which makes it unsafe to extend the findings to larger groups. This problem is all the more important if one considers that many if not most of the groups which operate within large organizations are larger than, say, the typical laboratory small group.

A fourth problem stems from the fact that virtually all studies have been designed to examine networks as a causal variable; i.e. they examine the effects that networks have on some aspect of group performance. Because virtually no research has been conducted to determine those factors which produce alternative network formations, little is known about the conditions which lead to the development of a circle or chain or Y or wheel network, or even to a more centralized (versus decentralized) network.

This problem of the evolution, or emergence, of group networks focuses not on the end-state of network formation, but on the process itself. The issue is change in communication patterns—how fast, through what intermediate states, and to what stabilization points? This point is well illustrated in a chapter on group structure and performance by Davis (1969). He says:

> One strategy for the study of group structure under controlled conditions is to *impose* a structure upon a small group. Structure is thus treated as an independent variable, and the consequences of a particular structure may be observed with regard to group performance, interpersonal responses, and the personal reactions of members. A second strategy is to regard group structure as an *emergent* phenomenon—the interpersonal consequence of a set of persons' interaction over a period of time. Group structure is thus regarded as a dependent variable.[2]

While Davis's chapter, like the other available literature, does treat imposed structures, it does *not* deal with emergent structure.

Fifth, it is apparent that the micro-networks (such as the circle, chain, wheel, and Y) are highly atypical networks for real groups. Granted that an organization could arrange its work groups in one or more of these particular configurations, the fact remains that they are not "typical" organizational networks. Other arrangements are possible, occur more frequently, and are perhaps even more desirable.

Finally, previous micro-network research differentiates networks by creating discrete, private links between people. But differentiated patterns of interaction also exist in small groups where everyone talks *openly* in front of everyone else (called the *com*pletely *con*nected micro-network, or comcon). Even though everyone could talk to everyone else, not everyone does. Discussion typically centers around one or two persons; several may say almost nothing at all; others may maintain their own private dialogue (perhaps under their breath) throughout the entire discussion. Thus, people are not equally connected and a more highly differentiated structure would appear to exist.

Recognition of these problems forces us to raise serious questions regarding the usefulness of the entire network concept, at least as studied in the laboratory, for organizational analysis. Were our knowledge of networks limited to what has been provided by the micro-network research, the conclusion would most likely be that little is known and even less is useful. Here is where the distinction between micro- and macro-network becomes helpful, however, for macro-network analysis can and has been a highly useful tool for organizational analysis even though micro-network research has not.

Notes

[1] M. E. Shaw, "Communication Networks," in L. Berkowitz (ed.), *Advances in Experimental Social Psychology.* Vol. I (New York: Academic, 1964), p. 113. Reprinted with permission.

[2] From J. H. Davis, *Group Performance,* 1969, p. 88, Addison-Wesley, Reading, Mass.

References

Bavelas, A. "A Mathematical Model for Group Structures." *Applied Anthropology* 7 (1948): 16–30.

Bavelas, A. "Communication Patterns in Task-Oriented Groups." *Acoustical Society of America Journal* 22 (1950): 725–730.

Cohen, A. M; Robinson, E. L.; and Edwards, J. L. "Experiments in Organizational Embeddedness." *Administrative Science Quarterly* 14 (1969): 208–221.

Collins, B. E., and Raven, B. H. "Group Structure: Attraction, Coalitions, Communication, and Power." In G. Lindzey and E. Aronson (eds.). *The Handbook of Social Psychology,* Vol. IV, 2nd ed. Reading, Mass.: Addison-Wesley, pp. 102–214.

Davis, J. H. *Group Performance.* Reading, Mass.: Addison-Wesley, 1969.

Glanzer, M., and Glaser, R. "Techniques for the Study of Group Structure and Behavior: II. Empirical Studies of the Effects of Structure in Small Groups." *Psychological Bulletin* 58 (1961): 1–27.

Leavitt, H. J. "Some Effects of Certain Communication Patterns on Group Performance." *Journal of Abnormal and Social Psychology* 46 (1951): 38–50.

Shaw, M. E. (1964). "Communication Networks." In L. Berkowitz (ed.), *Advances in Experimental Social Psychology,* Vol. I. New York: Academic, pp. 111–147.

30

Phases of Decision Building

BONNIE McDANIEL JOHNSON

When Robert Bales wrote *Interaction Process Analysis* in 1951, he observed that the process of human interaction in groups had largely been ignored. Instead of looking at what people say to one another, researchers had been content to relate personality traits of individual members to outcomes of the group process such as the quality of decisions. His research was among the first to investigate how people actually communicate in the process of deciding. This section presents four descriptions of the phases which groups go through in building decisions. Unlike the normative theories developed for this process, these theories of decision building are empirical. They are theories of how groups have been observed to decide; they do not prescribe how groups should decide.

Bales's Three-Phase Process

Bales and Strodbeck[1] have observed several hundred groups. They found that the category of talk varied by time. Early in the discussion people tend to give and ask for orientation. They called this first phase the "orientation phase." Then the conversation shifts and most of the talk involves the giving and asking of opinions. This constitutes the "evaluation phase." Finally, people begin to give and receive suggestions. They called this the "control phase." They also found patterns of positive and negative reactions. In the control phase, for example, negative reactions characterize the beginning; positive reactions characterize the end. This analysis of three phases of group development was one of the first descriptions of how people actually do solve problems.

Janis's Cumulative Process

Irving Janis, in his study *Victims of Groupthink,* approached the task of describing group decision making in a different way. His intent was not simply to describe how groups decide. Rather, he sought to describe how integrative processes—especially pressures to conform—can affect decision making. His claim is that "The more amiability and esprit de corps among the members of a policy-making in-group, the greater danger that independent critical thinking will be replaced by groupthink."[2] Groupthink refers to a mode of thinking in which members' strivings for unanimity override their motivation to realistically appraise alternative courses of action.

In the process of describing the manifestations of groupthink, Janis indirectly presents a description of how any group builds decisions. Although his concern is not with "phases," he is concerned with the chronological development of ideas or "themes" in a discussion. The description following is largely my abstraction and extrapolation of ideas about group decision building from Janis's description of groupthink.

The process of reaching a final decision involves many subdecisions. Group members explicitly or implicitly decide upon what kinds of information are relevant and valid. Group members decide which "experts" are credible and relevant to the problem at hand. They arrive at some kind of consensus to be used to evaluate proposed decisions. Any group member who criticizes the group's assumptions about information, criteria, or possible proposals risks censure and exclusion. The process of excluding a person may happen so subtly that group members do not realize what they are doing. When members of a group fall into the groupthink syndrome, they simply censure their own comments to avoid the risk of group censure. They refrain from making remarks contrary to commonly held assumptions of the members. Janis describes the kind of group process which results from groupthink:

1. The group's discussions are limited to a few alternative courses of action (often only two) without a survey of a full range of alternatives.
2. The group fails to reexamine the course of action initially preferred by the majority of members from the standpoint of non-obvious risks and drawbacks that had not been considered when it was originally evaluated.
3. The members neglect courses of action initially evaluated as unsatisfactory by the majority of the group. They spend little or no time discussing whether they have overlooked non-obvious gains or whether there are ways of reducing the seemingly prohibitive costs that had made the alternatives seem undesirable.
4. Members make little or no attempt to obtain information from experts who can supply sound estimates of losses and gains to be expected from alternative courses of action.
5. Selective bias is shown in the way the group reacts to factual information ... Members show interest in facts and opinions that support their initially preferred policy and take up time in meetings to discuss them, but they tend to ignore facts and opinions that do not support their initially preferred policy.
6. Members spend little time deliberating about how their chosen policy might be hindered by bureaucratic inertia, sabotaged by political opponents or temporarily derailed by common accidents that happen to the

best of well-laid plans. Consequently, they fail to work out contingency plans.[3]

Implicit in this description of the groupthink syndrome are four behavioral tendencies of people engaged in decision building. Janis was concerned with "faulty" decision methods. The principles discussed below must be inferred from what he says. I have labeled the four principles:

The Rabbit in the Hat Principle: Version 1
The Rabbit in the Hat Principle: Version 2
The Rich Get Richer Principle
The Ala Kazam! Principle

The *Rabbit in the Hat Principle* reminds us that problem solvers are not magicians. Unlike magicians, the only rabbits which problem solvers can pull out of a hat are those which they put into the hat. Version 1 states that a group chooses its solution to a problem from among those alternatives it discusses. This means that people in the group must communicate the ideas they have to others. Groups do not choose from among all possible alternatives. Before a possible alternative becomes an actual possibility in a discussion, it must first occur to a member of the group. Furthermore, the person to whom it occurs must risk describing the proposal to others. Any number of interpersonal factors such as "groupthink" may cause an individual to be unwilling to risk offering a particular proposal for consideration. Limitation of group discussion to only a few alternatives results from such individual members censuring their own ideas.

Version 2 of the Rabbit in the Hat reminds us that problem solvers do not use all relevant information to solve a problem. The only information they use is what they obtain and perceive to be important. Thus, the quality of group solutions depends on the aggressiveness of members in searching for information. (Again, information is not a rabbit which appears by magic. Rather, it must be searched out and then shared.)

The *Rich Get Richer Principle* states that ideas are not "born equal" or given equal consideration. Ideas initially preferred by the majority, as Janis observes, are given preferential treatment throughout the discussion process. Information which confirms the majority's original position is more likely to be considered by the group than information which reflects badly on the majority's position. Likewise, ideas originally frowned upon by the majority are disadvantaged. When a group member offers a proposal, the initial reactions (though often unreflective) result in a biased treatment of the proposal. Group members selectively interpret information in favor of proposals which they initially found attractive. The "rich get richer."

The final principle is concerned with the nature of the group "product." An important characteristic of a collective decision is that it is "announced," either formally or informally. Distinction should be made between the announcement of a decision (which is a set of symbolic displays and/or documents) and the actions which people take in interpreting the announcement.

Implementation of a decision is part of the decision itself because it is the interpretation of the announcement in the form of actions. When group members think of desirable "products" of their deciding process, therefore, they must think of implementation as well as announcement.

The *Ala Kazam! Principle* is concerned with the confusion of implementation and announcement which characterizes much decision building. In Janis's words, "group members spend little time deliberating about how the chosen policy might be hindered by bureaucratic inertia, sabotaged by political opponents, or temporarily derailed by common accidents." The process of deciding is inevitably directed toward producing some kind of message (announcement) as the solution. Decision building is symbolic activity (talk). The only direct output of symbolic activity is symbols. Decision-building groups therefore can directly produce only symbols. But the goal of such groups is seldom to produce only symbols. They want to have an impact on the problems they discuss.

The Ala Kazam! Principle states that a group in producing a symbolic message (statement of a solution) does not ipso facto solve the problem. The solution can result only from actions taken in interpreting the message. This principle obviously has implications for how groups should go about building decisions.

Underlying Janis's conceptions of how people decide collectively, there is the notion of decision building as a cumulative process. Decisions are built as ideas occur to people, as they share ideas, evaluate ideas, announce decisions, and implement decisions in action. The talk which occurs at each phase influences what happens in the next. The expectations of a group—the roles, norms, agenda, and intention—can either encourage or discourage unusual ideas and frank evaluation of ideas in a group.

Scheidel and Crowell's Spiral Model

Thomas Scheidel and Laura Crowell have developed a "spiral model" to describe the process of decision building.[4] They criticize classical models such as reflective thinking as grossly "inaccurate in portraying the reasoning process in small groups." The reflective thinking model insists that for rational thinking to take place group members must proceed in a linear fashion. Members "complete" one step and then proceed to the next. In the reflective decision-making model, the topic is introduced; the problem is defined, possible solutions are offered, the best solution is selected, and finally the action is determined.

Scheidel and Crowell support their argument that ideas are not developed in a linear fashion with analysis of talk from several small groups. Their data indicated that only 22 percent of all talk in sample groups was devoted to the initiation, extension, modification, and synthesis of an idea. By contrast, 33 percent of the talk was spent substantiating and accepting an idea already under discussion. They interpret this to mean that:

> Group-thought seems to move forward with a "reach-test" type of motion, that is, one participant reaches forth with an inference which seems

to be elaborated at length with movements of clarification, substantiation, and verbalized acceptance. Little wonder that group thinking often proceeds slowly when the anchoring of thought takes up practically half of the time.[5]

The spiral model of idea development suggests that when people collaborate to build decisions, one person "moves" the discussion to a "higher" level and then the talk of several people solidifies group consensus about that idea. The "movement" comments are those which initiate, modify, and synthesize ideas. The solidifying comments accept and substantiate. A spiral is a good metaphor for the "building" of decisions. It emphasizes the cumulation of group consensus through a process of "anchoring" thought. The announced decision results from a group's resolving its position on many lesser ideas.

Fisher's Four Phases of Decision Emergence

Aubrey Fisher, in his theory of "decision emergence," combined features of the spiral model and models of "phases" of decision making into a more sophisticated conception of decision building. According to Fisher, there are four phases in "decision emergence." These phases can be identified by the kinds of talk which people engage in. The first phase is orientation. Much of the talk in this phase is "clarifying" and "agreement." People are trying to understand what the others are saying. The talk is generally "first encounter style"; people stick to safe topics, so there is little disagreement.

The second phase is conflict. After members of a group have talked enough to get to know one another, there are attempts to confront their differences. When this happens, conflicting opinions are voiced. People feel freer to respond unfavorably to ideas they do not like. Also there are more comments which are intended to substantiate an idea being debated. In groups such as those described by Janis, the conflict phase is brief. Groupthink suppresses conflict. In other groups, the conflict may be so bitter that the group dissolves before any decision emerges. According to Fisher, however, most groups move from conflict to a phase which he calls emergence.

The emergence phase is characterized by: (1) a decline in the proportion of unfavorable comments, (2) an increase in comments which modify the speaker's previously dissenting opinion, and (3) an increase in the proportion of comments indicating some change in stance toward what proposals should be accepted. Fisher says that during this phase people emphasize differences of opinion. They use their talk to make clear their individual points of view. In order for a group of people to agree to a common set of symbols as their "decision," they typically begin to describe their position in more general terms.

For example, two people may be in conflict because a particular proposal would cause immediate benefit to one and immediate harm to the other. During the conflict phase they argue strongly the pro and con of the proposal. As they realize that they must come to an agreement, they search for alternative ways to define the problem as well as for alternative proposals. They find that if the proposal is modified slightly, it will serve the long-run interests of both.

Thus, they redefine the nature of the problem in light of a desirable solution. (Note that this is in contrast to the linear description of problem solving, in which the problem is defined only at the very beginning.) They say that "after all" the immediate costs will not be so great. By concentrating on the ambiguous "long-run" and by talking about mutual benefits, each is able to get out of being locked into his or her conflicting positions. Each saves face. A collective decision is possible. In the emergence phase, talk becomes more ambiguous, proposals get modified, and people modify their objections.

The final phase is reinforcement. The comments of group members are more favorable; typically there is little or no dissent. People talk about their unity and how "really good" their decision is. In the emergence phase, people modify proposals being considered. In the reinforcement phase, people recognize that they have reached agreement on how to solve the problem being discussed. Fisher describes the building of decisions like this:

> A specific point in time at which decisions are made is not apt to be found. In fact, the emergence process presupposes that groups achieve consensus on their decisions *after* those decisions appear to have been made. The very final stage of interaction then fulfills the purpose of procuring members' public commitment, the essence of consensus, to decisions already reached.[6]

Goals may be described as "retrospective." This means that while we have some idea about what we want, we do not have a very clear idea until after we get it. This same idea applies to Fisher's description of how groups solve problems. Members of a group have some general ideas about what they want to accomplish. They can set down in the beginning of a discussion some general criteria which any solution to a problem must meet, but specific criteria become evident and agreed upon during the discussion. Only during the final, or reinforcement phase, can the goals be made explicit. In the process of telling one another what is "good" about the decision, group members are practicing how to sell the idea to others, and they are convincing themselves that it is a good idea. They are "announcing" the decision to themselves.

Notes

[1] Robert F. Bales and F. L. Strodbeck, "Phases of Group Problem-Solving," *Journal of Abnormal and Social Psychology* 46 (1951): 485–495.

[2] Irving Janis, *Victims of Groupthink* (Boston: Houghton Mifflin, 1972), p. 13.

[3] Ibid.

[4] Thomas Scheidel and Laura Crowell, "Idea Development in Small Discussion Groups," *Quarterly Journal of Speech* 50 (1964): 140–145.

[5] Ibid.

[6] Aubrey B. Fisher, *Small Group Decision Making: Communication and the Group Process* (New York: McGraw-Hill, 1974), p. 140.

31

Characteristics of Effective Decision Building

BONNIE McDANIEL JOHNSON

Empirical theories of how groups solve problems are helpful in understanding the general process of decision building. They suggest the cumulative nature of the decision-building process. They point to the role of talk in constructing the set of symbols which is the "collective decision," but for those of us who have sat through hours of unproductive conferences, empirical theories do not seem to be of much immediate benefit. What we want to know is how can we improve our meetings, not simply what is likely to happen in these meetings.

Empirical theories are not directly informative about what people should do. For example, if an investigator finds that in most groups there is a concentration of disagreement in the middle of a discussion, what are the pragmatic implications? We cannot conclude that talk should be concentrated in the middle. We would hardly want to train people not to make any statements of disagreement until one third of the discussion is completed.

Some researchers have investigated factors in group discussions which seem to be related to more effective decision building. Jay Hall suggests that group effectiveness results from four factors: commitment, conflict, creativity, and consensus.[1] Note that the first three refer to feeling states or climates. I describe each factor and its relationship to decision construction in informal groups below.

Commitment

Commitment, according to Hall, is a feeling of "attraction, belonging, and ownership of the group ethos"; it is the "unifying force which holds the group together."[2] Commitment is what some people call motivation because it is a personal feeling which leads people to take actions because they want to do so. People who are committed to a group are actively involved in the talk which goes into the announced decision and then actively attempt to translate the words into actions.

In the group decision phase which Bales and Fisher have called "orientation" members attempt to secure commitment of people to one another and to the common task. Fisher says that there is a high proportion of talk classified as "clarifying" and "agreeing." Clarifying talk enables people to understand what is happening. When people state their agreements with one another, they build some foundation for commitment to one another.

The need for commitment is not concentrated in the opening of a discussion, though it is necessary throughout the decision-building process. We have all been in groups in which people seemed highly committed at first. All the members were actively participating; all were looking at one another; no one was doodling or engaging in other activities "on the side." Then as the discussion progressed, one by one people "dropped out." Most of them stayed in their seats, but only two or three people did the talking. Some of the non-talkers still watched. Occasionally, one would attempt unsuccessfully to break into the conversation. Some others seemed not to listen to what was being said. Members of such a group have lost their commitment. They display their lack of commitment by their failure to participate actively in what is happening.

Hall investigated the relationship of acts of verbal participation and feelings of involvement. His study involved approximately four hundred people participating in small group discussions. About two-thirds of the people reported they were "active participators" in the discussion. Hall instructed one hundred people (one or two in each group) to remain silent throughout the discussion unless someone extended to them a direct invitation to participate. About forty people who had not been so instructed reported that they were largely silent during the discussion. After the discussion, the people completed questionnaires which asked them to describe their feelings about the group and its decisions.

Two of the questions are of particular importance here. Item three asked, "How much responsibility for making the decision work would you feel?" Those who perceived themselves as active participators felt much more responsible for the decision they helped to construct than those who felt they did not participate. The relationship of commitment to participation is also evident in answers to question four: "How committed do you feel to the decision your group made?" Those who reported high participation also reported feeling committed to the decision. It should be noted, however, that members who did not participate rated the *quality* of the decision about as high as those who did participate.

According to Hall, this rating indicates that nonparticipators may be silently saying to the others: "We have heard your arguments, and they are sound. On the basis of facts—which we all heard and assessed—the decision you reached is a good one. But don't expect me to be satisfied with it, feel responsible for its success, or be committed to it." Hall continues: "The feeling tones associated with noninvolvement would seem to overshadow the logical appeal of decision content. The data from this exercise clearly reveals a paradox of human systems. What may be logically acceptable is not necessarily psychologically acceptable."[3]

In other words, decisions we "accept" in the sense that we are willing to take action are those decisions we feel we have helped to create. The most logical decision created by other people is their decision. Let them do what is necessary to make it work! Securing commitment, then, is a continuing problem of all decision-building groups. Special attempts are made during the first few minutes of a discussion to secure initial commitment, but initial commitment does not insure its continuation. People must be motivated to participate throughout the discussion. In this sense, the task of group members is analogous to that of interviewers or public speakers. All must secure initial commitment and then continuously motivate integration of all members of the group.

Conflict

Conflict is Fisher's term for the second phase of decision emergence.[4] After an initial period in which group members stick to safe topics about which they can agree, they begin to offer proposals for solving the problem. Because these proposals are usually controversial, conflict ensues. Janis stresses that conflict is essential to the effective functioning of a decision-making group.[5] According to Janis, those groups who develop norms which suppress conflict are not capable of critically evaluating ideas presented to the group. As the result, they are led toward poorer decisions.

It is not simply the presence or absence of conflict, but the meaning of a conflict situation which distinguishes ineffective from effective groups. According to Hall, members of ineffective groups tend to believe that conflict is necessarily unhealthy. He states: "The earmark of the ineffective group is often the unarticulated feeling that speedy resolution of task demands is the sine qua non of effective functioning, and that anything, particularly dissenting points of view, which frustrates closure is seen as detrimental to the group."

Conflicts are seen as impeding the "efficiency" of a group. When people voice disagreeing opinions it means that others must take time to answer the objections. It is easier to agree on a solution if people do not voice their objections. When people define their job as getting to a group decision as quickly as possible, anything which slows them down must be seen as bad. Conflict, then, is necessarily defined as a bothersome disturbance. Conflict can also cause hard feelings among group members. Members of ineffective groups tend to view interpersonal relationships as fragile. People must like one another if the group is to do its job. Therefore, they tend to define conflict as bad because it may damage the good interpersonal relations among group members.

Maier and Hoffman investigated the relationship of a discussion leader's attitude toward a dissenting member and the quality of the decision constructed by the group.[6] Some leaders reported that they appreciated the contributions of the dissenter. The dissenter reminded the group of risks they had overlooked. He or she made members explain the logic of their position. In short, for some leaders, the dissenter was a positive force helping the group construct a better decision. For other leaders, dissenters were "troublemakers" who did not really care about the group. Dissenters kept the group from being more effective.

Maier and Hoffman found that those groups led by people who saw dissenters as positive contributors were much more effective than the other groups. Their decisions were better than the other groups. The researchers conclude that the leader's perceptions have a powerful influence on how group members define their situation. Leaders who see dissenters as troublemakers create (with others' help) a set of expectations in which people are reluctant to disagree. Leaders who see the value of conflict subtly reward people for disagreeing and thus contribute to a norm which encourages open expression of doubts and disagreements. Thus, the meaning which the leader has is related to the meaning the group adopts to define conflict.

In effective groups, according to Hall, conflict means that

there is less than optimal sharing of the group frame of reference; conflict is treated as a symptom of unarticulated rationales or latent feelings from which, once they are verbalized, the group may be able to profit. Getting to the bottom of conflicts, drawing out deviant opinions so that they may be tested for feasibility, and seriously attending to far-out member insights have more often than not sparked a reappraisal of group thinking to such an extent that group positions are revised and performance enhanced. . . . Differences are encouraged and handled by the effective group in a "clearing the air" working-through manner which increases the likelihood that end products will reflect the contributions of all.[7]

People act in a situation according to how they define it. Groups who establish a collective definition of conflict as detrimental not only develop expectations which discourage conflict, they also develop methods for suppressing and circumventing those conflicts which do arise. In some groups, one or more people develop the role of "peace maker." People learn to acquiesce to the compromises suggested by this person. Other groups use majority rule to prevent open conflict. Whenever a conflict arises, the matter is immediately put to a vote. Those in the minority are expected to remain silent.

Another method might be called "reciprocal payoffs." It is the expectation that if a person "gives in" on one issue, he should be allowed to win on a later issue regardless of how unreasonable an argument he presents. Conflict is avoided because people simply take turns in influencing what the collective decision will be. It is like two people deciding about a vacation. One wants to go a thousand miles away and fly. The other wants to go two hundred miles and drive. They compromise. They go a thousand miles and drive!

A final method groups use to avoid controversy is changing the subject. When debate over an issue gets under way, one person brings up an issue which may be largely unrelated to the debate. Group members drop the controversial topic; everyone then speaks in favor of (or opposed to) the new idea and the appearance of agreement is maintained.

Successful handling of group conflict is not easily achieved. People must express their doubts and disagreements. In order for this to happen, they must expect that others will try to understand their position. The expectation that others will try to understand does not mean that others will agree. Successful handling of conflicts results in people developing equivalent meanings for common symbols (and symbolic actions). It is a process of coorientation.

Creativity

According to Hall, creativity is dependent upon conflict. Groups without conflict over ideas are not as likely to produce "creative" ideas as those who must talk out differing opinions in order to reach a collective decision. In order to measure the creativity of discussion groups, Hall had research subjects list possible solutions to a problem before engaging in a discussion. These prediscussion judgments were rated for quality. The higher their quality, the higher the group's "average resources" for problem solving. After the group discussion, the collective decision was rated for quality and also to determine whether one or more group members had listed it as a suggested answer prior to discussion. Decisions which had not been suggested by anyone were termed "emergent."

Hall found that those groups in which the prediscussion suggestions were diverse more often produced emergent decisions. He calls this the "high conflict condition"; there is little initial agreement on what must be done, and therefore, people must present and discuss differing ideas. These groups were more creative because they had to do more than merely accept a decision which several people felt to be best before the discussion began.

All emergent decisions are not equally "creative." Hall found a difference in quality between groups of strangers meeting for a brief period only (ad hoc groups) and established groups.[8] The collective decisions of *ad hoc* groups were consistently inferior to the members' average predecision judgment under conflict conditions. However, the emergent decision of established groups were vastly superior to their prediscussion judgments. One inference from these findings is that the established groups had more stable procedures for handling conflicts when they arose. Groups of strangers are unlikely to have worked out consensual expectations for managing conflict. Their relationship is more fragile than relationships in established groups. They are more uncertain about how to talk to one another when there is conflict.

Hall states two ways in which conflict, if adequately managed through supporting group norms, can facilitate creativity. First, "one effect of conflict in groups may be to achieve a more tentative opinion stating among members which, in turn, facilitates decision flexibility of the type needed for creativity."[9] This reason is similar to Fisher's description of what happens in the "conflict" and "emergent" phases of discussion. Group members state opinions and disagreement ensues. This disagreement is followed by more ambiguous, or in Hall's words, "tentative" statements of opinions. Group members become more flexible. It is this flexibility or ambiguity which allows group members to find creative decisions. A second way in which conflict facilitates creativity is through subjecting ideas to examination and modification. Hall states:

> Effective groups seem to recognize intuitively that where there is a conflict there is a need for both more data and a closer examination of existing inputs. Out of such additions and re-examinations frequently come those "aha" kind of insights which not only have a compelling quality of logic once articulated, but which underlie and lead to creativity as well.[10]

Creativity, then, is a third factor in group effectiveness. Creativity results when group members question one anothers' assumptions (often their unrealized assumptions). When disagreements force people to justify their ideas to one another, when people thus force one another out of comfortable paths of thought, they may hit upon less obvious but better solutions to problems. They may construct decisions more acceptable to everyone. If the norms and roles of a group allow the expression of conflict without personal defensiveness, the result can be collective decisions which are better than the best individual judgments.

Consensus

According to G. M. Phillips consensus is the distinguishing characteristic of small groups.[11] Consensus is often thought of as perfect agreement, but consensus does not mean that everyone in a group holds the same values or sees the world the same way. When a small group reaches a "consensus," it means that every person in the group accepts the collective decision as his or her own with understanding of what the decision means to others. Any person might have really preferred another decision, but all people feel committed to the group decision.

Hall explains consensus as both a set of expectations which constitutes a "decision rule" and a performance goal for which members strive. As a performance goal, consensus is the idea shared by group members that their final collective position or decision will reflect (at least) the tacit approval of every member. "Tacit approval" is not disgruntled silence. All members must "say"—in words or silent symbolic displays—"Yes, I can live with that decision."

Consensus as a decision rule means that all members actively seek out the opinions of other members. The job of constructing a collective decision is one of putting together many smaller decisions. At each decision point members of a group operating under a decision rule of consensus ask one another to express opinions.

I saw consensus work best as a decision rule with a group of "Outreach Workers" employed by metropolitan New York City Y.M.C.A. The group's task was to suggest some organizational goals. The discussion lasted several hours before they produced a set of goals on which they could all agree. In the process, however, they scrupulously attended to each others' attitudes and feelings. The most common comments I heard them use were questions to one another such as, "What do you think about that idea?" "Are we all agreed?" "How would that go in your district?" "You're not saying anything, what's the matter?" Thus, they not only reached consensus on their announced decision in the end, they secured consensus on the validity of each idea they discussed. They would not proceed until everyone agreed he understood what was being said at that time and until they all had an equivalent sense of how relevant the issue was to the decision they were constructing.

Consensus as a decision rule is a means for accomplishing group effectiveness through commitment, conflict, and creativity. When group members' opinions are actively sought, they are more likely to participate, and therefore to feel commitment. By insisting on consensus, those who disagree are invited to express their opinions and feelings.

Consider the expectations of people who have learned that consensus is a decision rule in their group. First, they expect to be supported when they raise objections. Being "supported" does not mean others will necessarily agree with their ideas. Rather, it means that they will not be personally censured as a troublemaker for having said them. Everyone's opinions will be seen as contributing to a better decision in the end. Also, group members can expect that regardless of how much conflict there is over ideas, they will resolve the conflict. A person does not have to worry that in introducing conflict he may be destroying the group because the expectation is that people will talk about their disagreements until a consensus is reached. Such expectations are sure to lead to people being more willing to disagree and more able to sustain conversation until a creative solution is found.

Notes

[1] Jay Hall, *Toward Group Effectiveness* (Conroe, Texas: Teleometrics International, 1971).

[2] Ibid., p. 2.

[3] Ibid.

[4] Aubrey B. Fisher, *Small Group Decision Making: Communication and the Group Process* (New York: McGraw-Hill, 1974).

[5] Irving Janis, *Victims of Groupthink* (Boston: Houghton Mifflin, 1972).

[6] Norman R. Maier and L. R. Hoffman, "Acceptance and Quality of Solutions as Related to Leaders' Attitudes Toward Disagreement in Group Problem Solving," *Journal of Applied Behavioral Science* 1 (1965): 373–386.

[7] Hall, *Toward Group Effectiveness,* p. 4.

[8] Jay Hall and M. Williams, "A Comparison of Decision-Making Performances in Established and Ad Hoc Groups," *Journal of Personality and Social Psychology* 3 (1966): 214–222.

[9] Hall, *Toward Group Effectiveness,* p. 6.

[10] Ibid.

[11] Gerald M. Phillips, *Communication in the Small Group* (Indianapolis: Bobbs Merrill, 1973), p. 15.

32

Communication Roles in Small Group Interaction

MICHAEL BURGOON, JUDEE K. HESTON, *and* JAMES
McCROSKEY

Within a group, there are several roles or functions that need to be fulfilled if the group is to complete its task and maintain its cohesiveness. These
are classified as task and maintenance roles. A third category are dysfunctional, self-centered roles that need to be avoided. These three categories include the range of constructive and destructive functions that group members
may perform (Benne and Sheats, 1948). We will discuss each of these individually.

Group Task Roles

These roles involve the communication functions necessary for a group to
accomplish its task, whether it is decision making, problem solving, education
and information exchange, or conflict resolution. Not all, but most, roles are
required in each situation. No roles should be played by a single individual;
each person should perform multiple functions. The good participant will fulfill most, if not all, of these roles.

1. *Initiator*—proposes new ideas, procedures, goals, and solutions. He gets
   the group started. Since getting started on any task is usually difficult, his
   is an important role. New ideas and perspectives are also essential to the
   continued life of a group.
2. *Information giver*—supplies evidence, opinions and relates personal experiences relevant to the task. We have discussed earlier the necessity of an
   abundance of information. In addition to quantity, quality information is
   needed. The quality of a decision or solution can be no better than the in-

formation that produced it. No information may be better than erroneous or biased information.

3. *Information seeker*—asks for information from other members and seeks clarification when necessary. This role is equally as important as giving information; if we fail to ask others for their information, relevant evidence may be overlooked.

4. *Opinion giver*—states his own beliefs, attitudes and judgments. Usually, there are a few people in a group who are more than willing to present their opinions. The concern is that everyone, including the introverts and communication apprehensives, give their views. Group effort has an advantage over individual efforts; it produces both a wider range of ideas and more creative contributions. This principle presupposes that all members participate. The ineffective participant withholds his opinions out of fear of criticism; the effective member expresses them.

5. *Opinion seeker*—solicits the opinions and feelings of others and asks for clarification of positions. Too often, we are so concerned with presenting our own views that we neglect to ask the opinions of others. The effective participant actively seeks others' attitudes and convictions, especially those of members who are hesitant to speak. Questioning for both opinions and information can play a vital role in group communication. It should not be overlooked as an effective discussion technique.

6. *Elaborator*—clarifies and expands the ideas of others through examples, illustrations and explanations. As long as his elaborations are relevant to the task, this role is valuable. It is especially useful with others who are unable to express their own ideas adequately.

7. *Integrator*—clarifies the relationship between various facts, opinions, and suggestions and integrates the ideas or activities of other members. The integrator ties together elements that might otherwise seem unrelated and disjointed. This linking function makes contributions as useful as possible by incorporating ideas that might otherwise be disregarded.

8. *Orienter*—keeps the group directed toward its goal, summarizes what has taken place and clarifies the purposes or positions of the group. Essentially, he insures that the group has a direction and that it heads in the "right" direction. Without orientation, a group may easily "get off the track" onto trivial or irrelevant issues. This role is necessary to define or clarify continually the group's intermediate and ultimate goals so that the group's activities can be checked, at any given time, for consistency with the desired outcomes.

9. *Energizer*—stimulates the group to be energetic and active. By this person's communication and example, he motivates the group to reach a decision or to be more involved. The energizer's drive contributes to greater group efficiency and productivity.

Group Maintenance Roles

These roles build and maintain the group's interpersonal relationships. They determine the socioemotional atmosphere of the group. If these roles are not performed, conflict may arise and group cohesiveness is reduced; if they are performed, the group interacts more smoothly, with greater satisfaction as an outcome.

1. *Encourager*—praises and agrees with others, providing a warm, supportive interpersonal climate. The accepting orientation, discussed as an input, is evidenced by how well a person shows encouragement and support for others. This function is valuable in producing solidarity in the face of conflict.

2. *Harmonizer*—attempts to mediate differences, introduce compromises, and reconcile differences. The harmonizer's conciliatory communication is directed toward reducing conflict and encouraging a pleasant socioemotional atmosphere.

3. *Tension reliever*—introduces a relaxed atmosphere by reducing formality and interjecting humor. This role, like the harmonizer, must be filled when conflict arises. This is not an easy assignment; when tension increases, people become less flexible and more emotionally involved. The effective participant attempts to suppress his own emotional reactions while trying to deemphasize the conflict for others. If he is good at telling jokes or making others see the humor of a situation, his intercession may go a long way in relieving tension.

4. *Gatekeeper*—controls the channels of communication, providing proper balance in the amount of participation of each member. The gatekeeper encourages those to talk who might otherwise not speak, while cutting off those who tend to monopolize the discussion. In conflict situations, he attempts to reduce the amount of communication by highly dissident or argumentative members, while increasing participation by more moderate, conciliatory members. However, if the situation warrants a confrontation, the gatekeeper opens up channels to the opponents so that the catharsis can take place. His overall purpose is the satisfactory continuation of the group. By his attention (or lack of it), by his body orientation and eye contact, and by the members he addresses, he can control the flow of communication.

5. *Follower*—acquiesces to the wishes of others. Although we do not generally recommend the follower role, in circumstances where the group's cohesion is disintegrating, this role is constructive in furthering maintenance of the group, because it does not contribute to conflict. It serves, rather, as a neutralizing element. The good participant may be advised, therefore, to adopt this role under stress situations, as long as he is following a leader who is trying to resolve conflict. If he is following one of the disruptive members, this role becomes a destructive one.

Dysfunctional Roles

We have recommended that the effective participant function in as many of the task and maintenance roles as possible. The roles that are about to be discussed are ones that the good participant should avoid. They are self-centered roles played by a person who is more concerned about personal needs than the group's interest. These roles reduce group productivity, cohesion, and satisfaction.

1. *Blocker*—constantly objects to others' ideas and suggestions and insists that nothing will work. He is totally negative. As the name implies, the blocker prevents progress. He may belabor points that the group has finished discussing or repeatedly oppose recommendations. The blocker is always complaining, always dissatisfied. He is the type you forget to inform about meetings or plan them during times when he is busy.
2. *Aggressor*—insults and criticizes others, shows jealousy and ill will. Like the blocker, the aggressor is discontented and disapproving. His malevolence is evidenced by jokes at others' expense and efforts to deflate others, whom he distrusts and dislikes. He may have alienated or anxious personality traits.
3. *Anecdoter*—tells irrelevant stories and personal experiences. He is a little like the elaborator, only he gets carried away with irrelevant anecdotes. He is motivated by a need for attention (as are the others who take disruptive roles). While the stories and jokes may be entertaining, they retard group progress.
4. *Recognition seeker*—interjects comments that call attention to his achievements and successes. He boasts while trying to appear not to do so. For example, the recognition seeker might say, "When I won the state swimming meet, I noticed that that problem was occurring . . ." He needs the sympathy and recognition of others.
5. *Dominator*—tries to monopolize group interaction. He wants to lead the group and will use whatever tactics he feels necessary, such as flattering, interrupting, and demanding to get his own way. He has the "spoiled brat" syndrome: he is not happy until he is running things his way.
6. *Confessor*—uses the group to listen to his personal problems. The confessor seems compelled to reveal his shortcomings, fears, and needs to the group. He involves the group in his problems, using it for catharsis. Unless the group is intended to be therapeutic, this role is disruptive, sidetracking the group from its goals.
7. *Special-interest pleader*—represents the interests of a different group. He pleads for favors or attention for the group whose interest he represents. The special-interest pleader's loyalties lie outside the group.
8. *Playboy*—distracts the group with antics, jokes, and comments. He is uninvolved with the group's purpose, preferring to entertain himself and the other members through his horseplay or sarcasm. The label "playboy" does not derive from his flirtatious behavior, although this may be part of it, but for his affinity for "play" rather than "work." Nor should the label imply that only males are guilty of this behavior; females can be playboys just as easily.

Each of us may recognize within ourselves some tendencies toward these dysfunctional behaviors. If we are to be effective participants, we must consciously control these inclinations, while striving to perform the more constructive task and maintenance roles.

References

Benne, K., and Sheats, P. "Functional Roles of Group Members." *Journal of Social Issues* 4 (1948): 41–49.

Part Eleven

Creative Problem Solving

33

Creativity Techniques: Toward Improvement of the Decision Process

IRVIN SUMMERS *and* MAJOR DAVID E. WHITE

Individual managers and members of management teams are engaged in an almost continuous process of decision making and problem solving; any technique that can improve the decision process and improve the performance of the organization is important to the function of management.

Although creative activity may be present in most decision making situations, the potential contribution of explicit creativity techniques has not been fully exploited. Existing organization constraints encourage solutions that are safe and fail to challenge existing assumptions. Creativity techniques have the potential to provide the elegant and unusual solution that is required by complex organizations and complex technology.

The purpose of this paper is to develop interest in, and stimulate the use of, creativity techniques as tools for improving the decision process in organizations. The creativity techniques discussed and sources cited are not exhaustive; they are intended to provide only initial direction for those interested in implementing creativity techniques in the decision process.

Whiting defines the creative process as:

> that mental process in which past experience is combined and recombined, frequently with some distortion, in such a fashion that one comes up with patterns, new configurations, new arrangements, that better solve some need of mankind (25, p. 2).

Whiting also distinguishes between original thinking and creative thinking: original ideas may not necessarily be useful, but a creative idea must be useful and satisfy some need. For the purpose of this paper the term *creativity techniques* will be used to label explicit techniques that are deliberately used to facilitate the decision process by utilizing the creative ability of individuals within the organization.

Illustrative Creativity Techniques

We know much and at the same time little about creativity; that is, there are many descriptions but no accepted theory. The problem is that the creative process is obscure, unknown, unperceived, and unverbalized even by the creator, and therefore it is uncommunicated to others (24, p. 655).

Numerous techniques for exploiting human creativity have been developed and many of those techniques seem to be similar. Fulmer (8) places the various implementing techniques into four categories.

Free-Association
    Brainstorming
    Synectics
    Gordon or Little technique
    Phillips 66 buzz-session
    Organized random search
    Black box technique

Forced-Relationship
    Catalogue technique
    Listing technique
    Focused-object technique

Analytical
    Attribute listing
    Input-output
    Grid analysis, matrix analysis

Eclectic Approaches
    Combinations or extensions of the other techniques

A detailed description of the several creativity techniques is beyond the scope of this paper; a brief description would add little to the descriptions that have been provided by Fulmer (8), Webber (24), and Graham (11). For illustrative purposes four techniques are described briefly: the comparatively unstructured technique of *brainstorming,* the comparatively structured technique of *synectics,* an eclectic technique developed by deBono, and the non-interacting technique of *nominal group process.*

Brainstorming

Brainstorming is probably the best known creativity technique. It was developed by Osborn (20) to help solve advertising problems and is used to improve problem analysis by providing more possible solutions and unusual approaches to the problem.

A typical brainstorming group consists of six to twelve individuals who get together to search for solutions to a problem. Most brainstorming experts recommend that the group members have a variety of backgrounds in order to facilitate the analysis of the problem from different points of view (25).

Osborn (20) suggests four rules necessary for the utilization of brainstorming. Judgment is withheld; ideas may be criticized and evaluated later. Wild ideas are encouraged; ideas are easier to modify than to originate. Numerous ideas are desired; more ideas increase the possibility of obtaining an excellent idea. The participants are encouraged to utilize the ideas of others to develop additional ideas. Other recommended procedures include: the sessions should be recorded because some ideas may be missed during a meeting; sessions lasting from forty minutes to one hour are most effective; the problem must be manageable, even if it requires breaking large problems into smaller parts; samples should be available if products are being discussed (25).

Brainstorming reached its height of popularity in the 1950's (3). Enthusiasm for brainstorming declined after a study conducted at Yale University in 1958 concluded that individuals working alone could produce more unique ideas than could a group. Further research by others supported this finding (2). While individuals may perform better than groups in certain situations, there are situations in which groups are best. Groups are usually better if the information is scattered among different people. A high quality individual decision may not be as acceptable to others as a lower quality group decision; and acceptance of new ideas and decisions is generally greater if they originate from the group that must implement the decision (2).

For additional information pertaining to the implementation and the limitations of brainstorming as a creativity technique the reader is referred to the work of Bennett, Bouchard, Crosby, Luthans, Oates, and Whiting (1, 2, 3, 16, 19, 25).

Synectics

Synectics, developed by Gordon (10) in 1944, is not as well known or widely used as brainstorming. The purpose of synectics, based on the assumption that creativity can be described and taught, is to improve the quality of creative output from those assigned to a synectics team (3).

The people selected to participate in a synectics group determine the group's success. For this reason team members are chosen only after very thorough testing and screening in order to insure selection of the best combination needed to solve the problems of a specific organization. The selection process results in a tailor-made synectics team composed of individuals best equipped, intellectually and psychologically, to deal with problems unique to their organization. After selection members are assigned to the synectics team on a full time basis and begin studying the creative process and learning the use of synectics. A synectics team solves problems for the entire organization, similar to operation research or system analyst groups, and must be fully integrated into the organization (3).

The synectic process involves: (a) making the strange familiar, and (b) making the familiar strange.

The first step, making the strange familiar, requires that the problem be understood and that the ramifications be considered. Assuming that the mind tends to emphasize one's own experiences and forces strange ideas into an acceptable pattern, it is easy to become buried in detail and those details become ends in themselves.

The second step, making the familiar strange, involves distorting, inverting and transposing the problem in an attempt to view the problem from an unfamiliar perspective. To assist in viewing the problem from different angles (making the familiar strange) synectics uses four mechanisms:

1. *Personal analogy.* Members of the group try to identify, metaphorically, with elements of the problem. For example, when a synectics group attempted to develop a new constant-speed mechanism, each member of the group metaphorically entered the box and, using his or her body, tried to effect the speed consistency required. This eventually resulted in an efficient and economical model.

2. *Direct analogy.* Parallel facts are compared. Bell used direct analogy by studying the human ear when he invented the telephone. Biology is an excellent source for direct analogies.

3. *Symbolic analogy.* Objective and impersonal images are used to describe the problem. In one case symbolic analogy was used in developing a jack to move large heavy objects such as houses or freight. The synectics group was making little progress until a member made a symbolic analogy with the Indian rope trick. This analogy proved to be the key and resulted in an innovative jacking mechanism.

4. *Fantasy analogy.* Fantasies are used to solve the problem. For example, a vapor-proof closure for a space suit was developed using a fantasy analogy of little insects closing the opening. This analogy lead to the development of a complex spring mechanism for closure.

The familiar has been made strange when an appropriate analogy has been found (10).

Eclectic Technique

As the name denotes, an eclectic technique is a combination of other techniques. The best elements of other techniques are adapted and combined to form techniques that are satisfactory to the user or developer. An organization does not necessarily totally adopt an existing creativity technique; it may modify, adapt, and combine techniques to its own needs. Undoubtedly many comparatively unknown eclectic techniques exist.

Edward deBono (4, 5) has developed an eclectic creativity technique. The technique has elements similar to elements of other creativity techniques categorized above under Free-Association and Forced-Relationship. The deBono work does not appear to be widely known and is seldom referenced in publications directed toward management or business in the United States. His techniques are primarily directed toward learning to use one's ability to think creatively. Basic to deBono's technique is the utilization of the signal or word *Po* to indicate that customary communication and thinking constraints and patterns do not apply. When the signal or word *Po* is inserted into the communication the participants are to understand that the usual communication restrictions are not applicable.

The *Intermediate Impossible* (Po-1) technique is similar to brainstorming. The habit or thinking pattern of immediately evaluating or applying value judgments to ideas or statements is to be broken. Ideas occur because the situation is free of evaluation and value judgments and the situation is viewed in a new way. The situation is to be considered in the most unlikely and outrageous way possible to see where it leads.

The *Random-Juxtaposition* (Po-2) technique is of the Forced-Relationship category and is similar to the synectic process of making the familiar strange. The random juxtaposition provides a starting point that is different from the usual or established pathways. The assumption is that the brain stores such a vast amount of information that one does not know when and what type of link-up is apt to occur; the random juxtaposition provides a new entry point with the hope for new link-ups. The correct utilization of this technique requires that no juxtaposition that pops into one's mind be rejected; if selection is occurring the juxtaposition is no longer random.

The Po-3 technique, *Challenge for Change* is a way to produce alternate ideas or alternate ways of viewing a situation. Perhaps the most important elements of this technique are the direct attack on dogmatic and arrogant inputs, and the examination of existing assumptions. The objective of the technique is to challenge an idea without rejecting it—to bypass the usual yes/no judgment and ask for a change. When an individual has given an answer it may be necessary to challenge the answer—but not by rejecting it—to get additional answers or input. The challenge implies that the original input is fine, but there may be other answers and other viewpoints, i.e., the input is not judged right or wrong—only the uniqueness of the input is challenged.

Nominal Group Process

The nominal group process technique utilizes a component not contained in any of the techniques previously mentioned; the group does not vocally interact, so the group is labeled *nominal*—group in name only.

The nominal group process is implemented as follows:

1. Without discussion, group members write their ideas pertaining to the problem.
2. Individuals' written lists may be divided into lists centering around feelings (fear, anxiety, etc.) and lists centering around organization dimensions (structure, costs, resources, etc.).
3. Lists are read round-robin fashion. Each person reads his or her first item, each person reads his or her second item, etc., until all lists are ex-

hausted. The items from each individual's list are recorded in clear view of all, as they are read.

4. The highest priority items may be identified by a voting system.

The relatively simple and easily understood procedure is a distinct advantage of the nominal group process technique.

Delbecq and Van deVen (6) list advantages of the nominal group process:

1. Non-interacting groups do not inhibit the performance of members, as may interacting (e.g., brainstorming) groups.
2. Non-interacting groups do not tend to focus on a single train of thought, as may interacting groups.
3. Tension created because others in the group are industriously writing causes one to become fully involved in the task.
4. The process avoids early evaluation and the distraction of elaborate comments.
5. Round-robin procedure allows risk-takers to state risky problems and self-disclosure dimensions early, thus making it easier for the less secure to engage in similar disclosure.
6. Use of personal and organizational categories encourages the stating of social-emotional dimensions.

Interacting groups have one potential to stimulate thinking that is absent from the first step of the non-interacting nominal group process. The desirable delay of evaluation is obtained by restricting vocal input within the nominal group process; however, also delayed is the stimulus to thinking that may occur when hearing others' ideas.

Several references provide additional information and sources pertaining to the nominal group process (6, 7, 12, 13, 14, 23).

The above techniques illustrate the wide choice of creativity techniques available to organizations. Numerous other techniques exist and more can be created by combinations and adaptations. The technique selected or developed for a specific decision is contingent on the decision situation and the requirements of the organization.

The Utilization of Creativity Techniques

Industry Week (2) reports a study conducted at the University of California indicating that the thirteen fastest growing companies in the United States have programs to encourage employee innovation and creativity. Whiting (25) discusses creativity programs in General Electric, General Motors-A.C. Division, and United States Steel. The purpose of the General Electric program was to develop creative product designers; graduates of the eighteen month course are reported to have averaged three times as many patents as General Electric engineers who had not completed the creative course. The A.C. Division of General Motors initiated a program of creativity training in 1953; a 400 percent increase in the number of suggestions and a 600 percent increase in the number of suggestions accepted is reported. The Gary, Indiana, facility of United States Steel started a creativity program for supervisors in 1956; through 1958 more than one thousand supervisors had completed the program and sixty task forces worked on company problems using brainstorming and similar creativity techniques.

The above experiences with implementation of creativity programs are from 1958 and 1971 references. The writer interviewed personnel, public relations, and training staff members at General Motors, 3M, General Electric, and United States Steel and failed to identify any explicit use of creativity techniques in those corporations as of December 1974. It seems reasonable to conclude that creativity techniques are not an explicit part of their corporate decision making process.

The under utilization of creativity techniques probably results from their contribution not being fully identified and their failure to meet the user's expectations. The precise contribution of creativity techniques to the decision process is difficult to identify and measure because the contribution may be ambiguous (3). The acceptance of creativity techniques is detrimentally affected when organizations attempt to use them as miracle-workers or perceive them as the solution for all decision making quandaries (21).

Considerations Fundamental to the Decision Process

Prior to selecting a specific creativity technique to be used in the decision process it is important to examine the conditions under which decisions are made and the steps applicable to that process.

The complexity of any two specific decisions may vary from the very complex to the very simple. McFarland (17) has classified decisions into the categories of *basic* and *routine;* the distinction is a matter of relative impact on the organization. *Basic* and *routine* identify the extremes of a continuum, with the location of a particular decision being determined by judging the degree of complexity and importance of that specific decision. *Basic* decisions are complex and long-range decisions involving large amounts of the organization's resources. A basic decision is critical to the organization's existence. *Routine* decisions are the commonplace, relatively simple, and repetitive decisions that, when totaled, account for most of the decisions made within the organization. Routine decisions, in their total effect, may be important to the success of an organization, but individually they have little impact on the organization. Creativity techniques are applicable to either basic or routine decisions. However, when the decision is basic the commitment of resources necessary to implement creativity techniques is justified, while utilizing creativity techniques for routine decisions may require more time and other organization resources than is practical.

Decision making is hazardous because the outcome cannot be precisely known in advance. Categories frequently used to define conditions under which decisions are made are *certainty, risk,* and *uncertainty. Certainty* and *uncertainty* may be viewed as conditions at the extremes of a continuum; *risk* is the condition at all points between (16). Under a condition of *uncertainty,* one has no experience or knowledge about the problem or the outcome—it is not reasonable to attempt decisions when there is absolutely no knowledge about the decision situation. Under a condition of *certainty,* perfect knowledge of the problem and the outcome is required—a most infrequent condition. Therefore, most decisions occur within the area of *risk*—and the amount of risk is determined by the quantity and quality of the information about the outcomes of various alternatives. The use of creativity techniques may reduce the uncertainty of any specific decision by providing additional information or unique solutions.

Regardless of the conditions under which the decision is made the decision process can be subdivided. Newman, Summer and Warren (18) divide the process into four parts: (a) making a diagnosis and defining the problem, (b) arriving at alternative solutions, (c) analyzing and comparing alternative courses of action, and (d) selection of a solution. Creativity techniques can be utilized during the decision process to increase the number and quality of alternative solutions and to provide assistance in analyzing and comparing alternatives.

To summarize, the use of creativity techniques can contribute to the decision process in several important ways. Creativity techniques have the potential to increase the quantity and the quality of decision information during steps (b) and (c) of the decision process—seeking alternative solutions and analyzing alternatives—and as a result improve the quality of the decision. Committing the resources necessary to utilize creativity techniques is justified when the decision is *basic* and is a *risk* decision tending toward the *uncertainty* side of the continuum. The explicit use of creative techniques is probably too expensive for routine decisions and may not be necessary for decisions that tend toward certainty.

Expected Improvements in Organization Performance

When resources are expended, improvement in organization performance is desired. If the organization is profit-seeking an increase in profit is sought; if not-for-profit, increased efficiency and quality of service are sought. The following hypotheses link the expected results from creativity techniques to improvements in organization performance.

1. When the amount of applicable information is increased the amount of uncertainty is reduced.
2. An increase of feasible alternatives increases the likelihood that the best alternative is known.
3. When unusual or unique solutions are known, the solution may exceed the requirement of satisfying and tend toward maximizing.
4. The commonplace solution is readily available to all; the unusual solution provides competitive advantage.
5. Improvement in decision quality reduces the number of decisions that must be revised after implementation; reduction of changes in implemented programs improves organization efficiency.
6. The scalar bureaucratic structure does not facilitate the development of

unusual and extraordinary solutions; implementation of explicit creativity techniques encourages the unusual and extraordinary.
7. Specific job assignments and role definitions may utilize a small part of an individual's total ability; the organization's resources are used more efficiently when more of an employee's total ability is utilized.
8. In most organizations, the challenging of existing assumptions is difficult and risky for the individual; creativity techniques provide an acceptable and safe method for an individual to challenge existing assumptions.

Limits and Impediments to Implementation

Organizational constraints may limit and impede the implementation of creativity techniques. Not all organizations and individuals are equally receptive to the change and openness required for implementation of creativity techniques. Considerable management discretion is necessary when selecting the situation and individuals where techniques are applicable.

The individual most gifted in contributing to the organization's use of creativity techniques may not be well perceived in the organization's usual employee evaluation process. Indeed, the individual may be perceived as a bit of a trouble maker (8, 15). Further, the socialization process of the organization does not encourage the maintenance of an individual's creativity.

Schein suggests three responses that are available to the individual when faced with organizational socialization (22).

Type I   Rebellion: Rejection of all norms and values.
Type II   Creative Individualism: Acceptance of only pivotal values and norms; rejection of all others.
Type III   Conformity: Acceptance of all values and norms.

The Type I response will be tolerated by few organizations and the individual will be separated from the organization. The Type II response will be very difficult for the individual to maintain because of the constant pressure, from those evidencing a Type III response, to accept all of the values and norms of the organization. Also, "to remain creatively individualistic in an organization is particularly difficult because of the constant resocialization pressures which come with promotion or lateral transfer" (22, p. 9). To obtain the full potential from creativity techniques, the Type II response must be encouraged and maintained. The encouragement and maintenance of the Type II response is contained within creativity techniques that legitimize the unusual idea and the challenging of existing organization assumptions.

Some would argue that the utilization of the creativity techniques does not fit into traditional organization patterns, may provide a unique status to a few individuals, and is a duplication of the activity that management groups in the organization are already supposed to be doing. These objections are realistic. Creativity techniques do have the potential to disrupt existing organizational relationships. However, all change in an organization is potentially disrupting. A creative reaction might be to utilize the *Challenge for Change* technique by asking: do some of the existing relationships require examination from a new point of view?

Creativity techniques do not replace the judgment of experienced managers and others who must determine what risk is acceptable. Creativity techniques can be used to improve the search for solutions and to choose the alternative or select the course of action. However, the final selection of the appropriate alternative and the determination of acceptable risk remains the domain of discriminating management judgment.

Summary

Creativity is probably present in all human decision and problem solving processes. However, the use of explicit creativity techniques has the potential to improve those processes by more fully utilizing the ability present in the organization. Commitment of resources necessary to implement explicit creativity techniques is justified when the decision is crucial to the organization.

The usual and expected is encouraged by the socializing process within organizations. Improvement in organization performance, especially to cope with rapid change and complex technology, requires the unusual, the elegant, and the challenging of existing assumptions. Creativity techniques have the potential to modify the socializing process toward acceptance of challenges to the *status quo.*

Existing organization assumptions and decision making procedures inhibit organizations from attracting individuals with the most ability to provide unusual solutions. Implementation of explicit creativity techniques can attract these individuals to organizations and provide legitimacy and psychological safety for them.

Creativity techniques do not replace management judgment in the risky process of decision making. These techniques do have the potential to improve the process by improving the quality and quantity of inputs to those that must make the final decision.

References

[1] Bennett, Keith W. "Tomorrow's New Products, Today, by the Hunch Bunch." *Iron Age* (May 18, 1972): 49.

[2] Bouchard, Thomas J. "Whatever Happened to Brainstorming." *Industry Week* (Aug. 2, 1971): 26–27.

[3] Crosby, Andrew. *Creativity and Performance in Industrial Organization.* London: Tavistock Publication, 1968.

[4] deBono, Edward. *Lateral Thinking: Creativity Step by Step.* New York: Harper and Row, 1970.

[5] deBono, Edward. *Po: A Device for Successful Thinking.* New York: Simon and Schuster, 1972.

[6] Delbecq, André L., and Van de Ven, Andrew H. "A Group Process Model for Problem Identification and Program Planning." *The Journal of Applied Behavioral Science* 7 (1971).

[7] Delbecq, André L., Van de Ven, Andrew H., and Gustafson, David. *Group Techniques for Program Planning: A Guide to Nominal and Delphi Processes.* Glenview, Illinois: Scott, Foresman and Company, 1975.

[8] Fulmer, Robert M. *The New Management.* New York: Macmillan, 1974.

[9] Gordon, William J. J. "Operational Approach to Creativity." *Harvard Business Review* 34 (1956): 41–51.

[10] Gordon, William J. J. *Synectics.* New York:

Harper and Row, 1961; paperback, Toronto: Collier-Macmillan, 1968.

[11] Graham, Gerald H. *Management: The Individual, The Organization, The Process.* Belmont, Calif: Wadsworth, 1975.

[12] Green, Thad B. "An Empirical Analysis of Nominal and Interacting Groups." *Academy of Management Journal* 18.

[13] Green, Thad B., and Pietri, Paul H. "Using Nominal Grouping to Improve Upward Communication." *MSU Business Topics* 22, (1974).

[14] Green, Thad B., and Vroman, H. William. "The Nominal Group: A Model to Facilitate Change Through Quantitative Analysis." In Ted F. Anthony and Archie B. Carroll, eds. *Contemporary Perspectives in the Decision Sciences. Proceedings of Southeastern AIDS,* 1975.

[15] Hicks, Herbert G. *The Management of Organizations.* New York: McGraw-Hill, 1967.

[16] Luthans, Fred. *Organizational Behavior: A Modern Behavioral Approach to Management.* New York: McGraw-Hill, 1973.

[17] McFarland, Dalton E. *Management,* 3rd ed. New York: Macmillan, 1970.

[18] Newman, W. H., Summer, Charles E., and Warren, E. Kirby. *The Process of Management.* Englewood Cliffs, New Jersey: Prentice-Hall, 1967.

[19] Oates, David. "The Boom in Creative Thinking." *International Management* (December 1972): 18.

[20] Osborn, Alex F. *Applied Imagination.* New York: Charles Scribner's Sons, 1963.

[21] Porter, Donald E., and Applewhite, Philip B. *Studies in Organizational Behavior and Management.* Scranton: International Textbook, 1964.

[22] Schein, Edgar H. "Organizational Socialization and the Profession of Management." In D. A. Kolb, I. M. Rubin, and J. M. McIntyre. *Organizational Psychology, A Book of Readings,* 2nd ed. Englewood Cliffs, New Jersey: Prentice-Hall, 1974.

[23] Van de Ven, Andrew H., and Delbecq, André L. "The Effectiveness of Nominal, Delphi, and Interacting Group Decision Making Processes." *Academy of Management Journal* 17 (1974).

[24] Webber, Ross A. *Management.* Homewood, Ill.: Irwin, 1975.

[25] Whiting, Charles S. *Creative Thinking.* New York: Reinhold, 1958.

34

The Boom in Creative Thinking

DAVID OATES

Recently the Swedish firm, Perstorp AB, wanted to take a fresh look at some of its problems. So the chemical and plastics group decided on a novel approach; it asked a group of two dozen school children, aged 15 and 16, to come up with suggestions.

Under the guidance of British creative thinking expert Edward de Bono, the teen-agers generated a number of ideas for making three-shift work more attractive, creating a receptive attitude to change within the workforce and finding new uses for existing techniques. The company terms the suggestions "realistic" and "very mature."

Perstorp is only one of many companies which are turning to creative groups to solve knotty corporate problems. Brain-storming sessions, which originated some 40 years ago in the U.S., have recently come into vogue in management circles. Using brain-storming techniques, groups of employees can generate large numbers of ideas in a short time. Many specialist consultants have developed variations on brain-storming, such as synectics, and the use of artificial stimuli to force participants away from normal thought patterns.

The common thread for all the techniques is creativity, which Sidney Parnes, professor of creative studies at the Buffalo State University College in the U.S., describes as "finding a fresh and valuable new association, making the irrelevant relevant." Parnes is the *protégé* of the late Alex Osborn who is credited with having invented brain-storming. He is president of the Creative Education Foundation, which Osborn founded.

Experts attribute the awakened interest in creative thinking techniques to the need for firms to keep pace with the rapid changes in technology and in consumer tastes.

Increasingly, companies are seeing creative techniques as a quick and efficient way of reaching solutions that would take a great deal of time to arrive at by conventional analytical procedures. Creative thinking is being used for such diverse purposes as generating new product ideas, creating new approaches to marketing, finding new ways to cut costs and developing new banking methods.

But even the most ardent supporters of group creativity sessions are unable to think of anything akin to the law of gravity, the invention of the steam engine or the theory of relativity ever emerging from a brain-storming session.

"I don't believe a group will ever produce anything on the level of Einstein or Pasteur," concedes George Prince, president of Synectics Inc. of the U.S., as he leans back in one of the folding canvas chairs dotted around his Cambridge office. "But a group can be very close to the genius level if it is operating really well."

To get groups operating well, consultants first attempt to free them from deep-seated thought patterns, inhibitions and defense mechanisms that they have developed over the years. "The child is inherently imaginative," notes Parnes. "Not creative: imaginative. By the time he gets to be an adult all that imagination has been squelched. Everybody has told him to be serious, be sensible."

Perstorp has traded heavily on this idea in actually using school children in problem-solving sessions. But most consultants simply attempt to unchain the child's imagination in mature corporate employees.

Such was the case at a recent course in which the UK-based PA Management Consultants Ltd. exposed a group of newly recruited consultants from France and Germany to brain-storming techniques. The tutor, senior consultant Geoffrey Rawlinson, devotes a third of his course to making them aware of the barriers which normally prevent them from giving free rein to their creative faculties.

He starts by giving his class some mathematical problems to which there are precise answers. He then goes on to point out that there are many problems to which there are no single solutions.

Rawlinson then asks the class members to list all the possible uses they can think of for a paper clip. Most of the participants can think of only three or four uses, and most of them involve fastening things together. Then Rawlinson unwinds the clip into a straight piece of wire and goes on to illustrate a vast variety of uses ranging from a coat hook to a back scratcher. Later he poses the same problem with a belt, and this time the students are using their imaginations more freely, suggesting it can be used for such things as a noose or a whip.

This prepares the class to accept more readily the four major rules under which brain-storming is conducted. These are: suspend judgment; generate ideas in quantity rather than quality; allow the mind to "free-wheel;" cross-fertilize ideas.

Suspending judgment prevents the participants from criticizing each other's suggestions and thus killing many promising ideas before they are given the chance to lead to something worthwhile.

Brain-storming is intended to generate vast quantities of ideas. Quality is not important until a later evaluation stage. During a normal brain-storming session it is quite common to generate 200 ideas in the space of 20 minutes. The leader of the session, or a specially appointed scribe, writes them down as fast as they are suggested. Rawlinson notes the ideas from his sessions on large sheets of paper which he attaches to the walls of the room. At the end of a good session the walls are plastered with dozens of such sheets.

Free-wheeling means the participants should let their imaginations run freely and not refrain from mentioning an unlikely idea for fear of appearing foolish in front of the others.

The cross-fertilization rule lies at the heart of all creative thinking approaches. It underlies the need to bring together unlikely combinations—the juxtaposition of elements which are not normally associated with each other.

"Every PA consultant is made aware of the value of brain-storming," says Rawlinson, "and many of them use it to help find solutions to clients' problems."

It is the unexpected, and often initially ludicrous, sequence of ideas which invariably sparks off the most innovative breakthroughs in real brain-storming sessions. This was the case earlier this year when Minnesota Mining & Manufacturing Co. (3M) in the UK ran a brain-storming session to find ways to counteract falling business in its office equipment sector. Nine of the firm's leading managers concerned with dealer relations took part in the session. A humorist among them suggested that an improvement in relations with the firm's 1,350 dealers might be achieved if women managers were employed. This led to the facetious suggestion that girls should be given as prizes in a dealer sales contest. This initially unproductive train of ideas eventually led to the more sensible suggestion that women should be employed in the sales department. Finally they suggested that women telephonists should be used to contact dealers for orders. The firm has already put this final concept into operation by employing an outside agency which supplies women telephonists for such purposes.

An equally controversial suggestion at the 3M session was that the manager in charge of dealer relations should be fired. This led to the suggestion that all the firm's dealers should be replaced, and then to the idea that at any rate the least successful of them should be dispensed with. This was finally turned into a positive idea that has since been implemented: the firm should identify its top 25% of dealers and concentrate its energies on creating better business with them. This suggestion was based on the theory that, broadly speaking, the top 20% of salesmen in any organization generate 80% of the business.

"The reason we called our managers together for this session," explains Guy Talbot, a 3M divisional marketing manager, "was because our business had been falling and we felt the reason was lethargy on the part of our dealers. The session generated about 350 ideas, of which about 150 were finally acted upon."

The result was that three months later the firm's trading in office equipment had more than doubled and this rate of new business was still being maintained five months later.

Top management at 3M was so impressed with the turnaround in business in the office equipment sector that it is introducing brain-storming as a problem-solving technique to other divisions. The technique is also being used at several of the firm's UK manufacturing plants to find ways to cut back overhead costs as part of a corporate campaign.

Not all firms use brain-storming primarily as a means to generate new ideas and approaches, however. Barclays Bank International Ltd. in the UK uses the technique because it feels it helps its executives to participate more in the running of banking affairs.

"The trouble with bankers," says Bernard Cowley, head of Barclays International's management development programme, "is that they tend to think that, if at the end of the day all the figures balance, there are no other problems they need concern themselves with. Brain-storming opens their minds and makes them think. It gives them the feeling they are contributing, and as a pure by-product you probably get some good ideas."

Barclays International recently began including brain-storming as part of its senior management training course. Cowley has also introduced brain-storming among his own training staff, because he felt they needed motivating. He wanted them to become more involved in running the training operation from their own initiative. The first session produced about 90 ideas for improving training methods.

Shortly afterwards some members of the training department came to Cowley and suggested that a brain-storming session should be run to devise uses for the video-recorder the department had recently acquired. One of the unusual ideas to come out of this session was that the video-recorder should be used to record customer movements at the bank. The bank needs to keep track of customer movements to help it plan the layout of future branches. Previously this was done laboriously with a tally man standing at the door timing customers in and out of the bank. The video-recorder dispenses with this task.

Cowley stresses that brain-storming "demonstrates that people in banks, whether clerks or super-clerks, have minds and can think clearly. After 20 years of subjugation in a bank it can come as a complete surprise to many of them to realize they have a brain. They go away from the brain-storming sessions in a state bordering on euphoria."

Despite many examples of the successful application of ideas generated from brain-storming, attempts are being made to develop the basic concept into more sophisticated approaches. For example, synectics is a creative technique that puts greater stress on developing and evaluating ideas as they are suggested, rather than simply generating a vast number of ideas.

Prince and a colleague, William Gordon, are credited with developing synectics. They began experimenting with creative thought processes while working at Arthur D. Little Inc., another U.S. consultancy. Prince, attired in sporty bermuda shorts, gives his former employer credit for being a "wonderfully tolerant kind of place. Like if we had a problem we would all get drunk and see if that helped solve the problem, and they would turn a blind eye to that kind of thing." After several entreaties to "settle down," Prince and Gordon left to found a company which they named after their new technique.

Synectics is similar to brain-storming in that it brings together groups of people to solve problems imaginatively. But whereas in brain-storming a basic rule is to suspend judgment on every idea thrown up, synectics tries to judge each suggestion in a positive way. Explains Vincent Nolan, of Abraxas, a UK management research organization: "Synectics employs a basic behavioural rule called 'itemized response'. It means that if you comment on anybody else's idea, you must first say what is good about it and then go on to express any reservations or concerns you have."

For example, Nolan recently ran a synectics session at a car manufacturing firm which was looking for ways to sell its vehicles by emphasizing their road safety qualities. One of the issues was: what can be built into the car to make people more aware of road safety? Somebody facetiously suggested that a spike attached to the windscreen and pointing at the driver's head would be a good and constant reminder to the motorist of the dangers of driving. Normally, such an outrageous suggestion would have been dismissed without further discussion. But under the rules of synectics a member of the group came back with the positive response: "Yes, this would certainly be a constant reminder to the driver of the need to drive cautiously, it would be simple and cheap to put it on the market. But how could we achieve this result without killing off a high proportion of drivers?"

The spike suggestion, because it was not killed stone dead at the outset, eventually led to a tangible idea. From the spike, the idea progressed to the suggestion that there should be a radar display panel on the windshield, similar to those in aircraft, to keep drivers posted of traffic conditions. This was eventually dismissed because of cost factors. Then the idea was proffered that a "black box" device similar to the flight recorders fitted to aircraft should be installed in the cars to record the circumstances leading up to an accident. The firm concerned is now exploring this possibility.

Comments Nolan: "The effects of this 'itemized response' rule can be very far-reaching. Criticizing other people's ideas is built into our culture and educational system."

"We've been astonished at the destructiveness that goes on during meetings, the way people are put in a position that makes them feel they are losing," says Prince. "They will get back at people even though they are both dependent on the outcome of what they are doing."

Créargie, a Paris-based consultancy which specializes in advising firms on how to manage innovation, has also found brain-storming inadequate in the raw form. It reinforces the basic concepts of brain-storming with different kinds of stimuli. For example, it sometimes uses check lists of words which can put a new light on an idea when injected into a creative session. It can be based on a series of verbs, such as "add," "subtract" and "multiply." The members of the creative group ask themselves: "What can we add to this idea to make it more feasible?" Or: "What can we subtract from it?" Or: "How would it be if we multiplied it by a certain factor?"

A similar system employs "flash words." Such words as "slow," "fast," "hard" and "soft" are injected into the brain-storming session at given intervals. This stimulates the participants to look at ideas from a different perspective. These words can be pre-recorded on tape and timed for transmission at given intervals. Pre-recorded music can similarly be injected into a brain-storming session as an added stimuli. Also, thought-provoking slides can be projected.

Abraxas even urges creative groups to day-dream. The technique recently proved successful in helping an international football star to start a new career, after he had to give up football because of injury. An informal group of friends and consultants was given two key words: "famous" and "archeology."

The group was then invited to let their imaginations meander freely. After a time one of the creative group was asked to describe what was in his mind at that particular moment. He said that he saw a tourist coach in front of the Colosseum in Rome. The footballer was the tourist guide and was passing on information to the people in the coach. The rest of the group developed this scene further. And out of their discussions came the suggestion that the footballer should become an estate agent dealing in property. The suggestion appealed to him and that is what he became.

Another technique which is gaining favour as an enhancement to brain-storming is the method of using an analogy or metaphor for the problem under discussion. The idea is to side-track the creative group, to get them away from their conventional problem-solving methods. Their development of the analogy is later translated back to the specific problem, often sparking new concepts.

Jean-Claude Willig, a Créargie consultant, recently used this technique to help a creative group at a client firm design a system for automatically washing windows. Willig and members of the firm spent days trying to solve the problem working from a basis of logical analysis, but they failed to invent anything innovative. Using the analogy technique, they began to examine the components of the human eye and how they operate. They investigated the eye's system of cleansing itself with the use of its lachrymal glands. They also looked closely at the function of eyelashes. Although they were unable to imitate nature directly, their research on the eye gave them a vital clue in their search for an automatic window-washing system, which is still a closely guarded secret.

Creative consultants say all these techniques can be learned and practiced by all grades of executives. They get away from the old-fashioned notion that, to develop creative ideas, firms need an elite group of highly imaginative people who meet periodically as a think tank.

Gilbert Rapaille, joint managing director of Créargie, discovered the elitist approach mistake some years ago when he was asked to form a creative group inside the marketing department of a French firm. Rapaille formed a marketing think tank, but despite sophisticated efforts to spark creativity its efforts were unsuccessful. The reason, according to Rapaille, was that "we put creative thinking into the hands of a small group. We made a little tribe inside a big tribe. It was the best way to enhance resistance to change. Other people asked, 'Why can't I have ideas? Why can't I work in this group too? If they are supposed to have all the ideas, I'm not going to make suggestions any more.' "

It became clear to Rapaille that isolated pockets of creativity in a firm did more harm than good. What he had to do was deal with the innovation process as it applied to an entire company.

"What we are introducing into firms," he says, "is a kind of therapy for sane people—to recover the creative faculties they have lost maybe because of our education system or because of their traditional working patterns."

35

Using Nominal Grouping to Improve Upward Communication

THAD B. GREEN *and* PAUL H. PIETRI

Communicating with subordinates is one of the most crucial activities of a manager. Its importance is rivaled only by its difficulty. Particularly troublesome is the manager's need to feel the pulse of that part of the organization which functions under his leadership.

In examining the internal communication system of an organization, one generally finds greater managerial dedication to downward, rather than upward, communication. Much of this undoubtedly stems from the obvious importance of downward communication. No organization could function efficiently without the downward flow of objectives, policies, rules, and work assignments. Unfortunately, however, many managers visualize the upward communication function narrowly. They view it in terms of how well their downward communications have been followed. Are objectives being met? Are policies and rules being adhered to? Are assignments being carried out? Although it is frequently overlooked, there should be an upward flow of additional information. Upward communication may include information about such things as subordinates' feelings and attitudes toward their jobs, special problems encountered in performing work activities, and ideas for alleviating these problems. Normally, communicating downward is facilitated by a number of formal media. Subordinates are bombarded from above by devices such as bulletin boards, policy statements, conferences, company newspapers, pay inserts, and formal addresses. Yet, the only formal upward communication mechanisms that frequently exist are the ancient suggestion system and a so-called open door policy.

This article investigates the widespread potential of the relatively new nominal grouping technique or process as a communication tool. The idea of using nominal grouping as a communication technique is new, but it is rapidly gaining acceptance. It is one of those rare approaches that does not have to be sold. It is eagerly being bought on its own merits—simplicity and intuitive soundness. Management practitioners generally are not familiar with nominal grouping, but once aware of it, they become successful users. Among communication experts there is not a widespread awareness of nominal grouping either. In fact, an extensive survey of the literature reveals only a single source suggesting the use of nominal grouping in a communication context.[1] But the technique is being advertised and publicized—by word of mouth among satisfied customers.

The authors are aware of the use of nominal grouping as a communication tool in a wide variety of organizations including General Motors, the U.S. Department of Agriculture, Wachovia Bank, Mississippi Medical Center, CECO Corporation, a number of state employment agencies, and in colleges and administrative offices of several major universities.

What Is Nominal Grouping?

Nominal grouping is a technique formulated through the collection of diverse, proven features embodied in a variety of research on small group dynamics, including brainstorming and "pooled individual effort." The nominal grouping procedure described here is a modification of a model first identified in 1970 as a technique for program planning.[2]

Nominal grouping is a method in which several assembled individuals (usually five to ten) follow a highly structured, noninteracting format to achieve an assigned goal. It is this noninteracting characteristic from which nominal grouping derives its name; *nominal* means "in name only." Relative to the operating mode of a typical group, a nominal group is indeed a group in name only. The process begins with the grouper[3] asking each person to respond, in writing, to a specific question designed to generate the desired information, such as any of the following hypothetical queries:

- What changes do you feel should be made to improve your working environment?
- What solution approaches do you see for the departmental morale problem?
- What problems exist in the organization that deserve special attention?
- What is the general employee attitude regarding unionization?

Regardless of the nature of the question and the extent of controversy it may provoke, discussion is not permitted during the listing phase in which each person generates a personal list of items in response to the question presented.

A recording phase follows after a specified time limit (usually twenty minutes is adequate). The grouper calls on someone to read the first idea from his written list. The grouper records this verbatim on a large sheet of paper in full reading view of all group members (taped to the wall, for example). Each successive person is called upon to read an item for recording, with this process continuing in round-robin fashion until all items from each group member's list have been read and recorded.

A voting phase follows to obtain a consensus regarding items of greatest importance. Having the group collectively identify the five most important items, for example, enhances the utility of the total information set.

A set of instructions for the grouper describing the nominal grouping process in greater detail is shown in Exhibit 1. The highly structured yet simple format facilitates the ease with which it is employed. This structural feature coupled with the absence of discussion enables the grouper to perform effectively in the absence of the special, but seldom present, leadership skills so essential in typical discussion groups.

The quotes which follow are typical of those that might originate in almost any organization. They contain a common thread: upward communication is being suppressed for one reason or another. Properly used, nominal grouping offers a valuable opportunity to help alleviate these and other upward communication problems that are difficult to solve. Nominal grouping lubricates the machinery of upward communication by providing subordinates with a vehicle for expression that cuts across the maze of red tape and standard operating procedures, and even closed doors. The extent and value of information received from subordinates is limited only by management's lack of ingenuity in developing topics to be handled in a nominal grouping session. These quotes are typical:

> Boy, does the old man have a temper! He asks for an honest opinion on the new sales control reports which my salesmen have to fill out each day, so I tell him what I think. Boy, did he ever hit the ceiling! Accused me of undermining top management. You can believe me that I'll never make the mistake of telling him something that he doesn't want to hear. It's not worth it!

> My boss is an o.k. guy, if you know what I mean. He gives you a job to do and you do it well and you get treated fairly. He's always asking my feelings about things in the plant and my ideas about how the company could be doing better, but to tell you the truth, I always agree with him. Oh, I've got some pretty good ideas, but I just don't think it's my place to tell him how to run things. He gets paid for that. I don't think my people should be having to give me ideas that I'm paid to come up with either. The whole nature of a manager's job is to make decisions for other people, otherwise you have no business being in a manager's position. That's what you're paid to do.

Exhibit I
Instructions for Nominal Groupers

Listing Phase
1. Arrange subjects, including yourself, to sit in a circle.
2. Discuss the purpose of the meeting, emphasizing that the organization is genuinely interested in getting ideas from individuals.

3. Indicate to the group that they will be working with a technique called *nominal grouping*. Briefly describe nominal grouping by outlining how the group will operate in each of the three phases (listing, recording, voting).
4. Request that everyone be concise in his or her written responses during the listing phase, using short phrases or key words rather than complete sentences. For example, in a group that was identifying management problems, two persons identified the same problem. One stated it as "The company does not do an adequate job of training employees." The other simply stated "inadequate training." The meaning of the short statement is as clear as the longer statement, but is much easier and faster to record.
5. Point out to the group that there is to be no discussion during the listing phase.
6. Indicate the time period to be allowed for the listing phase. (Usually fifteen to twenty minutes is sufficient.)
7. Hand out to each person a sheet of paper which specifically states the task he is to address. (This should be a concise statement of the "purpose of the meeting" which was generally described in step two above.) Read the statement aloud, then allow time for those who may have questions.
8. Request group members to write their responses on the sheet distributed to them, and encourage each person to generate a list as long as possible—"the more items the better."
9. Ask if there are any final questions, then begin the recording phase.

Recording Phase

1. Have the group stop writing, and prepare to record the items by writing them on a chalkboard or large sheets of paper taped to the wall in full view of all group members. (Recording on paper usually is preferred since it provides a permanent record of all that is recorded.)
2. Indicate that no discussion is allowed during this phase.
3. Impress upon the group the need to record all items listed, regardless of how trivial they may seem.
4. Have an individual read aloud the first item he has listed so it may be recorded. Write it verbatim unless the item is too long. If necessary, ask the reader to condense it; don't help condense and don't allow anyone else to help. Place a check mark by the item for each member who has essentially the same item listed on his sheet. (Simply ask for raised hands to determine this.) If some member of the group does not understand the item and needs clarification, the reader of the item should offer clarification. But there is to be no discussion of the item.
5. Have the next individual read aloud his first item for recording, following the same procedure as in step four above.
6. Proceed in this round-robin fashion until all items are recorded.

Voting Phase

1. Distribute voting ballots to the members, asking them to assign priorities (the top five, the top ten, or whatever is deemed appropriate) to the items

that have been recorded. They should ask themselves "What is the most important item on the list? The next most important?" and so forth.
2. Remind the group that no discussion is allowed.
3. Collect the ballots and terminate the session.
4. Any number of methods can be used to tabulate the votes, a simple one being to give five points for a first place vote, four points for a second place vote, and so forth, to the "top five" items.

Keep the Boss Out

One way nominal grouping facilitates upward communication is related to the homogeneous composition of the group. The groups should be composed of individuals of equal rank and authority. This homogeneity neutralizes the role of formal authority and status, two factors which research has shown will strongly mitigate against free, honest, and upward communication in organizations.[4] Face-to-face communication with the boss may be perceived as risky by the subordinates; anonymous conveyance of information is far more acceptable.

Communicating in a noninteracting way and in the absence of superiors depersonalizes individual inputs and reduces the fear of reprisal by one's superior. Not only does a homogeneous group mitigate against the need to withhold distasteful information, but the absence of superiors reduces the need to communicate what the boss "expects" to hear. One member stated after his initial nominal grouping session:

> You know, we came in here with definite reservations about this. We were probably each wondering about how honest other members sitting in our group would be about listing their real feelings on the subject. But man, we came out with things that we never would have told the boss to his face. Face to face you have a tendency to tell him about how well things are going along down here. But there are a heckuva lot of problems that he ought to know about, but doesn't. Our group really told it like it was, and it's a good feeling to know you've gotten some of these things out in the air. I only hope the boss takes these things in the right manner and not personally. But I guess that he wouldn't have done this unless he wanted to hear it like it really was.

Group Meeting with No Discussion

At first glance, the fact that nominal grouping does not allow a discussion of individual inputs appears to be inconsistent with *good* communication practice. However, this is not the case. It has been long recognized that "two heads are better than one," yet research indicates interaction among group participants often has a damaging effect on both creativity and productivity.[5] Nominal grouping is structured to bring a group of individuals together, but discussion is not permitted. This is a way of eliminating factors which otherwise inhibit group performance. A variety of inhibiting forces are overcome with the "no discussion" feature of nominal grouping. Richard C. Huseman suggests three sources which are subdued: (1) with no criticism allowed, participants are more willing to share ideas that are not yet well developed; (2) since there is no discussion, the nominal groups do not fall in a rut by focusing on one particular train of thought; and (3) because contributions are not evaluated, the nominal group can concentrate all of its time and energy on the specifically assigned task.[6] Beyond this, (4) nominal grouping prevents dominance of strong personalities (formal or informal group leaders) since they have no persuasion opportunity.[7] Also, (5) the expression of minority opinions and ideas is encouraged since criticism is not allowed.[8] Finally, (6) incompatible, conflicting ideas are more likely to be expressed because feelings of inferiority or defensiveness among group members are minimized.

The Ultimate Goal Is Information

Another characteristic of nominal grouping which contributes to effective communication is the ultimate goal of the group. The expected group output is information. Such an objective has a forcing effect upon group members to communicate feelings and ideas that might ordinarily have little opportunity or probability of being communicated through normal organizational channels. When management brings a nominal group together, it is essentially saying to the group: "You have some valuable inputs which we'd like to have. Will you please give them to us?"

Some typical upward communication barriers which retard normal upward communication flow and which the "forcing" effect of nominal grouping helps overcome are:

- tendency of managerial authority to suppress accurate upward communication;
- lack of availability for interpersonal communication. Many managers simply do not make themselves available for interpersonal contacts by their subordinates;
- the fact that many subordinates don't ordinarily view upward communication as part of their normal work role;
- poor listening habits by managers. Because of listening ineptness, managers discourage subordinates from communicating upward. Poor listening habits might include lack of concentration or attention; extreme ego protection or defensiveness; and the tendency to become overly emotional when receiving unpleasant information.

If a manager can recognize his own limitations as well as those of his subordinates, the nominal grouping approach can provide a valuable source for information which might have little chance to pass through normal communication channels.

Who Can Use It?

Nominal grouping can be an important tool for improving communication at all levels in an organization. The attractiveness of the process is reflected by its potential use by any individual manager. As shown in Fig. 35-1, manager A can use the technique to receive valuable information from his immediate subordinates, B_1, B_2 and B_3. Moreover, B_1 can use the technique with his own subordinates, C_1, C_2 and C_3. Managers B_2 and B_3 can also employ the process with their own subordinates.

In addition to two-level usage, nominal grouping can be utilized more comprehensively to include any number of lower level inputs. For example, a higher level manager (manager A in Fig. 35-1), may employ the process on a multi-level basis (see dashed line in Fig. 35-1) when:

1. He strongly suspects that important information from lower levels (Level C in Fig. 35-1, for example) is being "filtered" by intervening managerial levels (such as Level B in Fig. 35-1).
2. He feels that a number of managers within his jurisdiction (B_1, B_2 and B_3, for example) have negative attitudes toward upward communication which discourage lower levels (such as Level C) from communicating relevant information.
3. He suspects that adverse conditions exist between various levels (between Levels B and C, for example) or within subunits that fall under his jurisdiction (such as within units C_1, C_2 and C_3).
4. He feels that an occasional "purging" is necessary to allow short circuiting of formal organizational channels so that information can be received directly from lower levels (C).

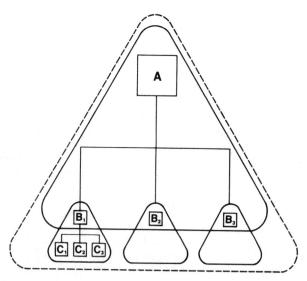

Fig. 35-1 Nominal grouping as a tool for individual managers

When a manager decides to employ nominal grouping on a multiple level basis, several important factors must first be considered. Among them is determining which organizational subunits will be included in the sessions. How many levels of the organization should be involved? Which particular subunits should be included? Who will be charged with conducting the sessions? Will the nominal groups be conducted by the manager who makes the decision to utilize the process, by an appointee or staff assistant, or even by an outside consultant?

Another important decision to be made concerns the disposition of the data generated. Will they be made available to all levels of management (including the by-passed levels) or shared only among a few managers? Answers to this question undoubtedly depend upon the given purpose of the sessions, and the nature of the data received.

A Technique for Multi-Directional Communication

Nominal grouping is a technique for multi-directional communication. When subordinates meet together for the purpose of communicating upward, lateral communication unavoidably takes place. The information items which participants generate and read aloud in the recording phase are a reflection of their interests, attitudes, and concerns; also, perhaps, an indication of their perceptiveness and intelligence. This kind of idea sharing among peers often goes beyond the typical degree of lateral communication. Nominal grouping also allows for downward communication if the total information sets generated by superiors are made available to subordinates. In the same way, diagonal communication, whether downward or upward, can also be a planned by-product advantage. Deliberate, overt action is necessary to achieve the downward and diagonal communication, and circumstances dictate the procedure of doing so. However, lateral communication is a natural, unavoidable by-product of the technique.

Information Is Generated

Nominal grouping can do more than simply facilitate the communication of existing knowledge. One principal advantage emanates from its utilization for the purpose of "idea generation." For example, the process may be used in this way to identify various solution approaches for a specific problem. The purpose here goes far beyond the simple role of communication. It embraces the creativity/information-generation function. Evidence indicates that the nominal grouping environment is highly conducive to the intense, searching pattern necessary for "idea generation."[9]

Participation Par Excellence

Nominal grouping is a vehicle for participative management. Conducting the sessions per se is a form of participation, but the way and extent to which the process is employed dictates the degree to which participative management is operationalized. Asking several groups of five to ten employees to communicate with management by means of the nominal group setting is a minimal form of participation. Participation can be maximized, however, by using the same people to identify problem areas and to decide (by voting) which ones are to receive attention first, and further allowing them to identify problem solutions and to decide which are to be implemented.

With either approach, however, employees are participating, and the simple act of using the technique is a demonstration of management's interest and confidence in its subordinates (a form of downward communication). For many individuals, this results in an increased feeling of importance, an enhanced self-image and a greater level of self-confidence. For some peer groups, the effect may be stronger group identification and cohesion, and an eager, excited, productive attitude. A general feeling of "at last, respect from our superiors and the opportunity to really be involved and to contribute" may well be generated. This is summarized by Huseman who notes that the use of nominal grouping "creates a type of 'Hawthorne Effect' with the employees involved." The authors have experienced this same display of enthusiasm by participants in a wide variety of nominal grouping situations.

Nominal grouping can be used to provide the necessary impetus to overcome the status quo. For example, if employees are asked to identify problem areas in their work environment, the inference is that management intends to resolve them. This creates an "expectation for change" on the part of employees (that is, an environment conducive to change), and serves as a productive stimulus for management actions.

Another by-product advantage which almost invariably results from the use of nominal grouping is the identification of training needs. Almost any nominal grouping session in which problems are identified (communication inadequacies, managerial problems, and so forth) provides indications of training needs.[10]

Although many of the problems are best solved through managerial decisions and action, others often can be resolved only by providing the employees with appropriate kinds of training. Designing training programs from this informational base results in a program more nearly tailored to specific individual needs.

It Is Not "Something for Nothing"

For the potential user of the technique, several caveats are in order. Utilization of nominal grouping gives birth to the expectation for action, and the process should not be used if positive change is not desired. Nominal grouping is a commitment to action and the information communicated in the sessions may open a "can of worms." The process has no place where management is not interested in identifying and solving problems. Nominal grouping is perceived as a threat to some employees, and should not be used if identifying and strengthening weaknesses is not considered beneficial. Using the process for multi-level purposes may mean re-channeling communication and by-passing superiors. If the value of this improved communication does not exceed the detriment of a by-passed link in the chain of command, then the process should not be used in a by-passing way. Finally, nominal grouping does require time—about one and one-half hours per session. But this is a nominal cost in absolute terms and especially relative to other techniques (such as discussion groups) and to the value of the information generally communicated.[11]

Notes

This article is based on a paper originally presented at the annual meeting of the Southern Management Association, 9 November 1973, in Houston, Texas.

[1] Richard C. Huseman, "Defining Communication Problems within the Organizational Setting," *Journal of Organizational Communications* (Summer 1972): 19–20.

[2] Andre L. Delbecq and Andrew Van de Ven, "Nominal Group Techniques for Involving Clients and Resource Experts in Program Planning," in T. J. Atchison and J. V. Ghorpade eds., *Academy of Management Proceedings* (San Diego, California: Academy of Management, 1970), pp. 208–27.

[3] The leader of a nominal group is called a *grouper,* rather than leader, since he does not assume a typical leadership role.

[4] Chris Argyris, *Personality and Organization* (New York: Harper and Row, 1957), pp. 159–60.

[5] Donald W. Taylor, Paul C. Berry, and Clifford H. Block, "Does Group Participation When Using Brainstorming Facilitate or Inhibit Creative Thinking?" *Administrative Science Quarterly* 3 (1958): 23–47; and Marvin D. Dunnette, John Campbell, and Kay Jaastad, "The Effect of Group Participation on Brainstorming Effectiveness for Two Industrial Samples," *Journal of Applied Psychology* 47 (1963): 30–37.

[6] Huseman, "Defining Communication Problems," p. 20.

[7] Andrew Van de Ven and Andre L. Delbecq, "Nominal versus Interacting Group Process for Committee Decision-Making Effectiveness," *Academy of Management Journal* (June 1971): p. 207.

[8] Ibid.

[9] Ibid.

[10] Thad B. Green, "The Utilization of Nominal Grouping To Determine Needs" (Paper presented at the thirty-fourth annual meeting of the *Academy of Management,* August 1974, Seattle, Washington).

[11] For additional references on research and applications of nominal grouping see Thad B. Green, "An Empirical Analysis of Nominal and Interacting Groups," *Academy of Management Journal* (forthcoming); Donald C. Mosley and Thad B. Green, "Nominal Grouping As An Organization Development Intervention Technique," *Training and Development Journal* (March 1974): pp. 30–37; and H. William Vroman and Thad B. Green, "The Application of Nominal Grouping to Health Care Distribution Systems" (Paper presented at the first annual Miami Conference on Progress and Prospects in Health Care Distribution Systems, Miami, Florida, November 1974).

36

The Delphi Technique:
A Long-Range Planning Tool

RICHARD J. TERSINE *and* WALTER E. RIGGS

Group decisions are necessary when the scope of a problem is such that no individual has sufficient expertise and knowledge to effect a solution. Group processes are also functional in disseminating information and providing instruction. However, grouping "experts" together causes a number of hindering side effects. Emergent leaders (high status, expressive or strong individuals) tend to dominate activities either because of their knowledge or informal influence. Personalities and organizational status affect decisions because credibility is influenced by perceptions of the person offering an idea, or his position. Generally, *compromise* decisions are obtained as opposed to *consensus* decisions.[1] Group processes often leave participants exhausted, discouraged and frustrated because of endless meanderings and a lack of resolution.

Advantages of Delphi

In an effort to eliminate these negative side effects, the RAND Corporation developed a technique called *Delphi,* to be used in long-range technical forecasting where a group of experts from diverse backgrounds are called upon to make decisions. Delphi is a method to systematically solicit, collect, evaluate and tabulate independent opinion without group discussion. This quasi-objective, or subjective, technique replaces direct debate with a carefully designed program of individual interrogations, usually conducted by a series of questionnaires. The control of interaction among respondents is a deliberate attempt to avoid the disadvantages of the more conventional use of

366

experts via round table discussions, committees and conferences. The experts are not identified to each other in any way, and there is usually a greater flow of ideas, fuller participation and increased evidence of problem closure.

Delphi has many advantages over more conventional means of gathering opinions on matters not subject to precise quantification. Most of these advantages are the result of keeping the identities of the participants unknown, to eliminate bias. A participant finds it much easier to change his mind if he has no ego involvement in defending an original estimate (only he knows if he changes his mind). He is less subject to the *halo effect,* where the opinions of one highly respected man influence the opinions of others. Also reduced is the *bandwagon effect* which encourages agreement with the majority. A significant advantage of Delphi is that it forms a consensus of opinion by requiring justification for any significant deviation from the group average.

Since Delphi does not require the participants to meet at a common time in a common location, geographical dispersion presents very little difficulty and fewer demands are put on panel members. In face-to-face groups, full participation by individuals is restrained as the size of the group increases. Delphi imposes no such limitations and there is no restriction on the number of participants. Delphi encourages individual thinking, forces a panel to get on with the business at hand, and forces respondents to move towards a consensus, unless strong convictions to the contrary are held.

Eliminates Confrontations

The central idea is to eliminate any direct confrontation of the experts and to allow their projections to reach a consensus based upon increasingly relevant information. A series of questionnaires are distributed or interviews are conducted with each participant. After the initial response, individuals are asked to request any information they need or specify what information they have which can aid others in the decision process. Opinions are left out and only facts are considered relevant to the entire group. Following tabulation of each questionnaire, the participants are given the information that other participants contributed. The process is continued through an iterative number of rounds until there seems to be sufficient convergence of opinion.

The last step is to apply a correction process to the results to bring into line those responses that may be the result of inappropriate assumptions or misinterpretations of data. Therefore, the results are based upon not only a consensus of end product, but a consensus of assumptions and uniform interpretations of the importance and effect of the data.[2]

Although in actual application the specific procedures of Delphi vary, the following example is typical: A forecast is initiated by a questionnaire which requests estimates of a set of numerical quantities (dates by which specific technological events will occur, probabilities of occurrence by given dates, event desirability and feasibility, and the like). The results of the first round are summarized, and the median and interquartile range of the responses is computed and fed back to the respondents with a request to revise their first estimates where appropriate. On succeeding rounds, those individ-

368 INTERCOM: READINGS IN ORGANIZATIONAL COMMUNICATION

uals whose opinions deviate greatly from the majority (outside the interquartile range) are requested to give the reasons for their extreme opinions. A collection of these reasons is presented to each participant, along with a new median and interquartile range, and participants are given another opportunity to reconsider and revise earlier opinions or estimates. The process is continued until a consensus is reached. Instead of starting with a preconceived list of questions, sometimes preliminary questionnaires are used to select and develop questions for which estimates can be obtained.

Wide-Ranging Uses

The Delphi technique has been applied to a variety of problems. The most predominate use has been for long-range technological forecasting. It was originally developed in the early 1950s and applied to problems of a military nature, but nonmilitary applications were developed in the 1960s.

One of the first reported corporate applications was to explore a firm's future external environment and to analyze evolutionary product lines. Delphi has been used to predict likely inventions, new technologies and product applications. In education, it has been used to design a new curriculum and to predict the impact of socioeconomic developments on future school systems. In retailing, Delphi was used to indicate future changes in department stores. Other applications of the method have been to predict the impact of a new land use policy; information systems relative to development planning; and to identify problems, set goals, establish priorities and obtain solutions in health care programs. Delphi has become a multiple-use tool, and has proved to be an effective method of forecasting future events in both business and government. Cities and municipalities are just beginning to adopt the technique and it is likely they could become its largest user.

The Procedure

The steps of the Delphi technique can vary somewhat based on the intended application, but a basic diagram of the process is shown in Fig. 36-1.

Forming a Work Group

Before the questionnaire process begins some initial steps must be completed. A work group consisting of decision makers and staff members must be selected. The decision makers are individuals who must act on the conclusions of the study; they should play an active role in the process to insure their complete understanding of the events leading to the consensus. The staff members are the professionals who conduct the Delphi process; they do the typing, sending and receiving of the questionnaires and make a preliminary analysis of the results. The decision makers and staff members must work in conjunction to analyze, appraise and revise the questionnaires in succeeding rounds.

The staff members must interview each of the decision makers to determine what information should be obtained from the experts and how that information will be utilized. Then the design and structure of the questionnaires can be developed. This step is very important to the success of the undertaking, and plenty of time should be allowed for this process.

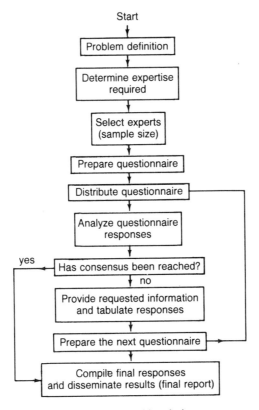

Fig. 36-1 Delphi technique

Selecting Experts

A second group which must be selected is the panel of experts, or respondents. These are the people whose judgments are being sought and who agree to answer the questionnaires. The composition of this group is critical in determining the effectiveness of the Delphi technique. Respondent selection is very important to the value of the process, and five basic criteria should be considered in choosing participants:

They must have a basic knowledge of the problem area and be able to apply that knowledge.

They must have a good performance record in their particular areas.

They must possess a high degree of objectivity and rationality.

They must have the time available to participate to the conclusion of the program.

They must be willing to give the amount of time and effort to do a thorough job of participation.[3]

The composition of the respondent group must also be considered, and will vary with the nature of the problem. If the problem is highly specific and technical, all of the respondents should have technical expertise. If the problem is general and abstract, a team of interdisciplinarians might be more effective.[4] Many problems fall between these extremes, so a balance of specialists and generalists may be desirable. Also, a proper balance of theoreticians and pragmatists should be sought. The knowledge and composition of the panel will depend on the nature of the forecasting problem.

The sample size is the next major item for consideration, and will vary with the homogeneity of the respondent group and the amount of work the staff can adequately handle. If the group is homogeneous, between ten and fifteen respondents should be sufficient to generate effective results. However, as the degree of homogeneity declines, a larger number is necessary to achieve reasonable quality. The University of Virginia used 421 respondents in one study, and achieved workable results.[5] The general feeling is that the sample size should be the minimum necessary, thereby avoiding much administrative staff work, but there are no specific guidelines for determining the optimum number of panel members to use.

Contacting the respondents is the next step in the process. The nominator or panel of nominators who initially chose the respondents should convey to them the following points: the purpose of the study, the primary question/problem to be analyzed, the part they will play in reaching a solution, the importance of a concerted effort on their part to successful results and the uniqueness of their abilities in the total effort. As is usually the case in such processes, some will decline to participate and additional new respondents will have to be chosen.

The First Questionnaire

There are two conceptual approaches to the development of the first questionnaire. First, if the primary question or problem is of such a nature that it can be stated in specific terms, it should be set forth in the greatest detail possible. In this case, each response will contain one opinion about the primary question, the respondent's reasoning, the facts which he considered important and his requests for additional information needed to make future responses.

The second approach is used when the primary question or problem is stated in general terms, thus requiring further specification. The questionnaire will then contain one or more open ended questions that will attempt to better define the problem. Also included will be questions regarding reasoning, facts and additional information requests.

Regardless of which approach is followed, a short cover letter should accompany the questionnaire, explaining the instructions and thanking the respondents for their participation. Include a self-addressed stamped envelope for returning the response, and set a specific completion date deadline.

Upon receipt of the completed questionnaires, the tabulation process will begin. The staff will examine each questionnaire to determine the areas of agreement and disagreement. The items requiring clarification and additional information will be identified and summarized, creating the material for the next questionnaire.

Subsequent Questionnaires

A composite of responses to the first questionnaire, along with an explanation of any misconceptions on the part of any respondents, will form the base of the second questionnaire. Usually some measure of central tendency, such as the mean or median response, and some measure of dispersion, such as the interquartile range, are provided to the respondents. Each participant will be asked to revise his opinion based upon the new data and responses of his peers. If an expert's response falls outside the interquartile range, it is customary to have him give the reasons for his extreme position. These justifications are summarized and distributed in succeeding rounds so that other group members can take exception to a stated position. The purpose of information feedback is to produce more precise predictions and to encourage opinion convergence. The tabulation procedure is repeated in a similar manner for subsequent questionnaires until convergence is obtained. The number of questionnaires varies, but generally a minimum of three is necessary to achieve a reasonable consensus of opinion.

The Correction Process

The final step in the Delphi process is the correction phase, which takes many different approaches. The RAND Corporation took the median of the responses as the consensus and then gave some consideration to the trend of responses.[6] A weighted average of the component estimates has also been used with the weighting factor being the relative expertise of the individual participant.[7] A final report should summarize the goals, processes and final results of the study.

Extensions of the Technique

There are several extensions and modifications of the Delphi technique. One modification is known as cross-impact analysis. This process takes into consideration the impact of the occurrence of one event on a subsequent event when several events are interrelated. Usually the analysis will develop a series of conditional probabilities for events. An iterative process helps to insure the elimination of contradicting predictions.

Another modification is called System for Event Evaluation and Review (SEER). SEER modifies the process by establishing an initial list of forecasts that have been constructed through a series of interviews prior to the beginning of the Delphi process. It can reduce the number of questionnaire rounds, thus saving time. Also, participants can be asked to answer questions in only their area of expertise. This aids in eliminating possible distorted responses caused by lack of knowledge in a particular area.[8]

Although Delphi tends to be futuristic, it can also be used to investigate opinions about the past. As a form of cybernetic arbitration, experts could be placed at terminals on-line to a computer so that the time of the Delphi process could be reduced considerably.

Limitations

Several limitations to Delphi deserve discussion. First, the crucial step in the entire process involves the selection of the participants. The mechanics of the Delphi can be completely negated by poor panel selection and poor motivation. The length of time required for the analysis also presents a problem— it can take several weeks for a three round Delphi. If the results do not come quickly, participant motivation can wane. Adequate time must be available to use the technique.

Delphi should not be considered for routine decision making. Its use is for issues requiring wide and representative input. When aggregate, individual judgments are desirable, it can be most helpful, but the following issues must be resolved during the process: whether to use open-ended or structural questions; how many questionnaires are required; the number and design of feedback reports needed; guidelines for aggregation of panel judgments.

Delphi compares favorably to other group processes on such items as number of working hours required, cost of utilizing committees and the proximity of group participants. It usually requires the least amount of time for participants. However, the calendar time required to obtain judgments from respondents can be a disadvantage. (On long range considerations, calendar time to decision is not usually that relevant.)

The final problem lies in the action that is taken as a result of the forecast. Executives will generally assign a rather low priority to events likely to occur far in the future due to their concern for more immediate problems. Implementation of results can be a problem, but it is not exclusive to Delphi.

Validation

The validation or testing of the accuracy of Delphi predictions is difficult particularly when the events will not take place for many years. There are two approaches to Delphi validation. The first compares Delphi predictions with actual occurrences. A study of eight groups of 20 people satisfactorily predicted 32 out of 40 short-range questions in a two round Delphi.[9] Experimental results indicate that Delphi is at least a "good" predictor with predictions relatively close to actuality.[10]

The second approach compares Delphi predictions with those of conventional confrontation methods. One study that compared Delphi and direct confrontation groups found Delphi more accurate in thirteen of sixteen cases, less accurate in two cases, and in one case the two methods were equal, indicating that Delphi was more accurate than direct confrontation.[11] Unfortunately, comparison studies are practically nonexistent at this time, but it appears that Delphi is at least as good as, if not superior to, other long-range forecasting techniques.

Long-range planning has been a constant source of difficulty for many organizations. Because of the interrelated factors which must be considered in decisions of major magnitude, it becomes necessary to rely on group decision making. The problems associated with traditional methods are well known. Delphi eliminates some of the more glaring difficulties, particularly those associated with personality domination and status of the contributors.

The Delphi technique is a general methodology for achieving a reliable consensus of opinion from a group of experts concerning the impact or implications of some unknown or uncertain future event. It is accomplished through the use of a series of intensive questionnaires interspersed with controlled opinion feedback. The process is based on the notion that single experts may hold incorrect opinions regarding future occurrences, but increased accuracy is achieved by collecting the opinions of a number of experts. That is, the collective opinion corrected for individual biases and misinformation will result in a more reliable forecast or estimate.

Long-range forecasting has increased substantially in organizational importance. Realizing that survival in the future depends on effective planning, organizations are adopting more elaborate and sophisticated forecasting approaches and it is timely and appropriate that the Delphi technique be considered an effective approach to such long-range predictions since judgmental decisions are best facilitated by judgmental techniques.

Notes

1 Andre F. Delbecq and Andrew H. Van, *Techniques for Program Planning* (Glenview, Ill.: Scott, Foresman, and Co., 1975), pp. 83–107.

2 Norman Dalkey and Olaf Helmer, "An Experimental Application of the Delphi Method to the Use of Experts," *Management Science* (April 1963), pp. 458–467.

3 Richard N. Farmer and Barry M. Richman, *Corporate Management and Economic Progress* (Homewood, Ill.: Irwin, 1965), pp. 328–359.

4 Ibid.

5 Frederick R. Cypert and Walter L. Gant, "The Delphi Technique: A Case Study," *Phi Delta Kappan* (January 1971), pp. 272–273.

6 Dalkey and Helmer, pp. 458–467.

7 Farmer and Richman, pp. 328–359.

8 Alan R. Fusfeld and Richard N. Foster, "The Delphi Technique: Survey and Comment," *Business Horizons* (June 1971), pp. 63–74.

9 N. C. Dalkey, "Comparison of Group Judgment Techniques with Short-Range Predictions and Almanac Questions," (New York: RAND Corporation, R-678, May 1971).

10 Robert C. Judd, "Delphi Method: Computerized 'Oracle' Accelerates Consensus Formation," *College and University Business* (September 1970), pp. 30–34.

11 John Pfeiffer, *New Look at Education* (New York: Odyssey Press, 1968), pp. 154–155.

Part Twelve

Conflict and Socialization Processes

37

Conflict: An Overview

OLGA L. CROCKER

Conflict—the word conjures visions of disagreement, strikes, picket lines, fighting, and a host of other negative images. It results when two or more incompatible forces meet. Each party, through its behavior and actions, attempts to win, to defeat or suppress an opponent and to create an imbalance in power in favor of itself.

Although each of us has experienced conflict, we have great difficulty in understanding it, managing it, and resolving it. Behavioral scientists provide limited help. The study of conflict involves problems of timing. The observer must be in the midst of the action, privileged to the inside story and the thoughts and feelings of the parties. He or she must not become involved; involvement provides vision through biased spectacles. Unfortunately, from an observer's point of view, an audience changes the actions of the participants. They become intimidated; they grandstand; they become more reasonable or exhibit other behaviors atypical of the unobserved situation.

Nonetheless, we do know a few things about conflict. We know, for example, the parties to a conflict and the sources of the problem. We can analyze whether conflict is functional or dysfunctional for each of the parties. We are beginning to know something about those factors that increase and decrease conflict. This article will discuss each of these points in turn.

Parties to Conflict

Conflict may be classified according to the individuals who are involved: (a) the individual personally (intrapersonal or internal), (b) two individuals (interpersonal), (c) the individual within the group, or (d) two or more groups.

Internal Conflict

The inner struggle an individual experiences is attributable to role conflict and role ambiguity.

Role ambiguity results when the individual is uncertain what actions and behaviors are expected. This uncertainty results from a lack of clarity about responsibility, a lack of knowledge about how a task is to be performed, and a lack of knowledge regarding the standards and expectations that will be applied in deciding whether satisfactory performance has occurred.

Role conflict, on the other hand, is generally categorized into four types: inter-role, intra-role, person-role, and role overload. *Intersender* or inter-role conflict results when pressure is exerted by different senders who perceive the individual's role from different viewpoints. A professional woman, for example, must not only be a leader, but she must often be a wife, a mother, and a housekeeper. Satisfactory performance of one role makes the other one difficult or impossible to perform. *Intra-role* conflict is the product of conflicting or contradictory demands made by one person or a given situation. Who has not experienced the three-day task and the words of the boss who wants no efforts spared in performing an exceptionally good job—by tomorrow morning! *Person-role* conflict results when action is required that violates the codes and standards by which the person prefers to live. At times, a clash occurs between a desire for personal independence and the authoritarian demands of the organization or group to which we belong. There may also be a clash between obligations incurred because of friendship or kinship and obligations to society at large. The last type of role conflict, *role overload,* is the consequence of too many expectations. Each expectation may be legitimate and compatible; together, they are impossible to complete within the given time restrictions.

A certain amount of inner conflict that results from role ambiguity and role conflict tends to increase an individual's effectiveness. If these levels become too high, however, productivity and physical and emotional health may be affected.

Interpersonal Conflict

Conflicts between individuals are what movies are made of. Two heroes fight over the same heroine. Two girls argue about the rules of a game. An editor and a reporter argue the merits of a story. Four men vie for the presidency of an organization. Two executives disagree on where a new computer installation should be located, each desiring it for his own department. Spiderman fights for his life against one of his innumerable foes. Conflicts between individuals are familiar and legendary.

Individual Within a Group

When an individual first joins a group or an organization, many negative aspects appear to dominate. He or she is not accepted and does not fit within the group. After some time, the individual learns the argot of the group, the tricks of the trade, and the social skills required to be part of the group. Conflict has subsided and socialization has occurred. The group has influenced the individual to accept its goals and values.

The individual may also be in conflict with the group when an attempt is made to gain influence, leadership, or power over the group. In that case, the individual is resisting the socialization process that the group is attempting to impose.

Group Conflict

Within groups and organizations a law of interorganizational conflict appears to exist—i.e., every group is in partial conflict with every other group. Israel and Egypt, line and staff people, vice-presidents of different departments, the hard sciences and the social sciences at the university, labor and management; all these groups are in conflict with each other. Conflicts occur because different groups have different goals and values, because they share resources, and because they must depend upon each other to accomplish their own goals.

Sources of Conflict

Basic to any conflict episode are at least one of three causes: (a) the desire for power, (b) communication, and (c) unresolved prior issues. Power or the desire to change the power structure includes differences attributable to values and ideologies, goals and methods, and interdependencies. Communication can cause problems because the receiver and the sender do not perceive information in the same way, because words do not have the same meaning, and because different importance is attached to the same facts. Unresolved prior issues are the unsolved problems and residual of feelings each party brings to the present relationship. They result from previous interfaces between the two parties.

Power as a Source of Conflict

The control of people and the ability to direct money and other resources to desired ends or goals is the essence of power. It is for this reason that there is conflict over the setting of goals and over the means to achieve these goals. Power conflicts arise in the value differences of people and because they are dependent on others to achieve their goals.

Ideologies and Values

The desire for power begins in the ideological or value base of individuals. Some people have a strong need to be liked and accepted and would avoid conflict if possible. Others have a strong need to excel and achieve and, therefore, might ignore conflict. For a third group of individuals, the strongest need involves a desire to control the environment and others within that environment; in other words, a need for power.

A factor in power conflict is attributable to racial differences, especially if one group feels that there is a superiority of particular genes. During World War II, the Nazis in Germany perceived themselves as the superior people of the world. In the southern States, South Africa and Rhodesia, the superiority of whites was an unquestioned ideology for many decades.

Conflicts over power are the result of differences in value orientations. Each person perceives the world in terms of personal experience, training, and background. This uniqueness means that different aspirations and different types of tangible and intangible goods are valued by different people. Within organizations these values translate to different expectations of the same leader, to differences in time perspectives, and a desire for the same organization to assume different forms of structure.

In other words, some people within the organization prefer tall hierarchies and autocratic leaders who lay down the law and expect to be followed. Others value the lower, flatter organization with its greater participation and the opportunity to be consulted and to share in the decision processes.

University students are at least somewhat future-oriented; they look for situations in which they will reap generous rewards in the not-too-distant future. Young people born and living in a ghetto want their rewards here and now; they have little faith and trust in an uncertain future.

Conflicts result when the organization cannot satisfy, to an equal degree, the values and expectations of all these different kinds of people because of their differences in attitudes, tolerances, and ideas of justice.

Interdependencies

Interdependencies exist not only within the organization, but also in interpersonal relationships. Others have power to the extent that there is a dependency on them to fulfill needs or to the extent that common resources are shared. Power is the right to give commands and expect obedience, to reward, and to punish. Power is the extent to which an individual has knowledge that is needed and the extent to which the individual is admired. The need exists for this admiration to be reciprocated.

Where no dependencies exist, there is no power and no potential for conflict. The president of a university has considerable power, but his power over students in a particular class is much less than that of the professor who teaches them. The professor, on the other hand, treads lightly in the presence of the departmental secretary. When a dependency exists, when individuals have to share resources or wait for the outcome that another can provide, the power exerted and the potential for conflict is considerably increased.

Goals

Goals are the expression of intentions. They serve as targets of behavior; they provide motivation; they determine the direction of expenditures and efforts; and they decide how resources will be utilized.

One might think that the goals of a group or an organization are very simple to identify—to make money, to heal people, to provide welfare. A look at the concept of profit shows the difficulty in determining goals. What is profit? Is it cash in the bank? Is it the money value of the items sold? Is it the margin on each item? What if it costs more in overhead to sell one item than it does another? What about turnover of goods? Is profit dependent on the number and kinds of units produced or on the number and kind of units sold? Would the production department, the sales department, and the credit department agree on one definition? The production department wants to minimize costs. This is accomplished by minimum shut-downs and minimum retooling and by producing large quantities of a few products. Salesmen require a great variety of products, some of which are loss leaders (the company loses money on these but produces them to retain customers), and very liberal credit terms. The credit department must collect accounts; they want minimal credit and then only to A-1 customers.

Surely the goal of healing people in a mental hospital is more easily defined! Are drugs and shock to be used in healing? Is it to be therapy? Both? In what quantity? Would the psychosomaticist and the psychotherapist perceive the solution in the same way? If therapy requires that the patient spend a portion of time working with normal people outside the walls of the institution, would everyone agree? Is the goal of the mental institution to protect society by confining these people? What about the ward aide? How does he or she translate patient progress and healing? By the patient's display of individualism? By his or her challenge to authority? Or is the ward aide's life easier if the patient is subdued and submissive?

And so it goes. The perception of organizational or group goal differs, depending on the role one has in attaining that goal.

Goals also depend on the vantage point of the individual. A senior leader might look outward—to profits, public acclaim, re-election, or growth. At the operational levels, the important goals are units per hour or survival in a hostile world. These two types of goals are not generally compatible. That individual who is close to the power source, who controls the goals or objectives of the organization and the methods by which these will be achieved, controls the people and resources of the organization. This situation invites conflict.

Communication as a Source of Conflict

Conflict results because the communication transmitted is misunderstood or does not reach the individual who could best influence the conflict situation. This occurs because the message is (a) distorted by the sender; (b) distorted, suppressed, or unintentionally dropped while it is being transmitted; or (c) distorted or misunderstood by the receiver.

The communication process has at least four elements: the sender, the message, the channel, and the receiver. The sender brings to the situation certain values, experiences, training, background, and an emotional and cognitive state. The message is translated into physical, semantic, and symbolic forms—i.e., into some type of vocabulary, body language, gestures, and facial expressions. It travels through a channel as verbal, written, and/or visual symbols. These forms are retranslated and interpreted by a receiver who has his or her own values, experience, training, background, and cognitive and emotional states of mind. This individual transmits a reaction to the interpretation of the message by other symbolic or physical forms (by ignoring it, by smiling, by frowning, by a rigid posture, etc.). With each element of the communication process, the potential exists for increasing or decreasing the degree of conflict.

The clarity of the message depends on the motivation and communication skills of the sender. The sender may condense the message (because of a desire for brevity) or distort it to retain power. (The possession of required information gives the holder expert power over others.) In transmitting the message, the sender may state a personal view as if it were a certainty—i.e., he or she may attempt to obtain closure by making the information appear to be more precise and definite than it is. Of course, some individuals are more competent at communicating; others are less so. Conflict may be increased because the sender cannot or does not adequately convey the intended message, and the intent of the communication is misunderstood by the receiver.

Situations may exist where a message is lost in transmittal. This can occur intentionally or unintentionally. Within groups and organizations, gatekeepers exist who assume the responsibility of filtering and interpreting information. At other times, the loss may be unintentional—the message was not read, was not salient and thereby ignored, or was only partially heard or understood. Some unintentional filtering occurs as a result of specialization. Specialists interpret the message in terms of their area of expertise, omitting or not understanding the significance of those elements that appear inconsistent with their experience and knowledge.

The receiver is also important in the communication process. He or she filters the message because of differences attributable to perceptions and the interpretation of words used. A denial or selectivity process may be used so that mental choices established earlier and personal cognitive consistency are maintained.

There is, however, an additional problem. Although the correct message may reach the receiver and all aspects may be correctly understood, it may come so rapidly or in such quantity that information overload occurs. When overload results, conflict may be prolonged or aggravated because the receiver (a) is unable to process the information and omits all or a portion of it; (b) processes it incorrectly; (c) mentally files the received information, hoping to use it later; and (d) stereotypes or is influenced by a dominant characteristic of the opponent. This overload leads to a distortion, not only of information but also of the motives and the attributes of the opponent.

An example from a labor-management negotiation situation, which the author had the opportunity to witness, may help indicate the importance of communication in the abatement or exacerbation of conflict. In this instance, the labor negotiator prided himself on being tough and hard. Frequently he mentioned that "schoolin" was unnecessary, that he had become a leader in spite of his minimal educational level. The management negotiator who sat across from him had never worked on the shop floor. This man was equally proud—that he had been university educated, that he had received a law degree.

The labor negotiator spoke of factory problems in the vernacular of the plant. The lawyer did not share this vocabulary. Other factors also may have influenced this man's perceptions. He may have been listening selectively, hearing and seeing only that which he understood or wanted to hear. He may have been evaluating the message in terms of his opponent and basing this opinion not on the leadership and negotiating qualities displayed, but on the lack of education and the coarseness of behavior exhibited. Certainly the lawyer might have had personal problems; perhaps he was thinking that he himself would not have a job if he did not drive a sufficiently hard bargain.

Time after time, the management negotiator misunderstood and misinterpreted what was being said. Each time he would reiterate the company position. And each time, the labor negotiator would explain the problems and the solution. Ironically, both men were saying the same thing: the company was in financial difficulty; it was mandatory that it remain in business; some improvement in wages and conditions would be necessary so that the employees would not leave the company.

A number of factors contributed to the conflict. There was a lack of common background, an inability or unwillingness to recognize this lack of commonality, a reluctance to express feelings and bring them into the open, and an introduction of many smoke screen issues. The tendency to speak in shop floor vernacular, in generalities, or in legalese presented a barrier to meaningful communication and heightened conflict to almost nonreconcilable levels. Both parties recognized the same goals, were satisfied with the prevailing power balance, and were willing to compromise on the same settlement. In spite of the fact that there was no basis for conflict, conflict did exist; neither man could understand what the other was saying!

Residual Issues as a Source of Conflict

The third source of conflict is residual issues. The relationship that existed between the parties in the past affects the present relationship. To understand this concept, it is necessary to understand the process of conflict and its seven elements—i.e., latent conditions, perceptions of these conditions, a felt injustice, action, retaliation, resolution, and residual or aftermath.

Before conflict can occur, undesirable conditions must exist (latent conditions) within the environment or in the relationship between two individuals or groups. At least one party must perceive that this injustice exists and experience some emotional discomfort regarding the situation. Conflict begins when action is taken to right the injustice and a retaliation results.

Resolution of the conflict leads to an "aftermath." At the time of resolution, some issues are solved, others are not. Feelings and emotions that were developed in the course of the conflict are retained by both parties. These three outcomes are the "aftermath" or residual issues that are carried over into the future relationship between the two parties.

The potential that this carry-over has for future conflict depends on the type of solution reached. In a problem-solving situation, both parties may attempt to resolve future mutual problems jointly. In a domination or annihilation, one party will be supreme; the other will either not dare to challenge or will be unable to challenge. If a temporary truce is reached, one or both of the parties will likely retrench to gather forces and attack again. The potential for future conflict is heightened if the struggle was bitter, if the solution for at least one party was unsatisfactory, and if an opportunity for retaliation exists. The perceptions and feelings aroused in the prior conflict and the outcomes in terms of resolved and unresolved issues are carried over and affect the parties in future relationships.

Functional or Dysfunctional

Contrary to popular belief and the impression that may have been given in this article, conflict is neither good nor bad. It merely leads to functional or dysfunctional results.

Conflict is functional to the extent that it increases effectiveness. This can occur in a number of ways. Conflict can prompt a search for new facts and solutions. It can act as a safety valve. If small problems can surface and be resolved satisfactorily, a major blow-up may be prevented. Conflict can increase the motivation and energy that is available. It can increase group cohesiveness and performance. During conflict, members tend to close ranks to achieve a superordinate goal or to defeat the superordinate enemy. Conflict can also decrease group cohesiveness. It can promote a circulation in leadership and a reevaluation of goals. Last, but not least, conflict provides an easy measure of an individual's or group's own power relative to the opponent.

Whether conflict is dysfunctional depends on the viewpoint of the participants. Within the group or organization, it is dysfunctional if it decreases effectiveness. It is dysfunctional to the organization, for example, when superiors deliberately create dissension so they can gain stature in the eyes of constituents when they solve the problem. The individuals concerned, however, would view this dissension as functional; it achieved the purposes desired. Conflict used as a cover for empire building can be viewed in the same way. Conflict is dysfunctional to all parties involved, however, if it becomes personalized. When this occurs, individuals direct more energies to self-defensiveness than they do to solving the real problems and issues. Conflict is dysfunctional also to the extent that it rigidifies the group and to the extent that it leads to gross distortions of reality.

Whether the results are favorable or unfavorable depends upon the measures and actions used in resolving the conflict, on the attitudes of the opponents toward each other, and the values and orientations of the party making the judgment. It is not unusual for conflict and the outcomes of conflict to be viewed favorably by one party and unfavorably by another party.

Factors Affecting the Resolution of Conflict

Whether conflict can be resolved and the quality of that solution depend upon (a) the attitude of the parties towards conflict itself, (b) the environmental component, and (c) the personalities of the parties involved.

Attitude of the Parties toward Conflict

Three attitudes toward conflict exist: avoidance, management, and inter-actionist.

Avoidance

The earlier scientific management view (which is still used in many organizations) stated that conflict must be avoided at all costs. It is dysfunctional for the organization. It is used as a cover for empire building; it becomes personalized and results in bitterness; it rigidifies the groups; it leads to distortions of reality; it undermines the control management has on employees. In short, it threatens the existing situation and power structure.

Managers who believe that conflict must be avoided take precautions to ensure that it does not exist or is not acknowledged. These leaders are of two types—those who rule with an iron hand (dispensing justice at the slightest deviation) and those who "bury their head in the sand." No matter what occurs in the organization, they do not wish to know about it. When this is the dominant view of conflict, it is the responsibility of subordinates to resolve the problem by whatever method they can and to keep it from surfacing.

Management

The management view of conflict is at the same time a complement and a contradiction to the human relations point of view, which recognized that conflict was inevitable within the organization. Minor dissensions would always surface, and they should be controlled. The role of the manager under this system is to manage conflict and control people. Performance is judged by how well participants are manipulated and by the minimal disruptions that occur to the organization as a result of these minor scrimmages.

Under this view, managers learn not only human relations skills—how to be leaders, how to motivate workers, and how to use communication channels—but a multitude of survival tactics best described a number of centuries ago in Machiavelli's *The Prince.*

Interactionist

Higher levels of education and an introduction of employees to differing philosophies and methods of supervision have made functioning difficult for those who would control and channel conflict. These two aspects have led to the interactionist approach, which states that conflict should be brought into the open.

This approach sees conflict as good for the organization. Conflict acts as a pop-off valve, prompts a search for new solutions, increases group cohesiveness, provides a measure of power, provides a means for settling a participant's own internal conflict, and promotes a reevaluation of goals and a circulation of leadership. Conflict can provide entertainment and a release from tension as well. There are those who enjoy the challenge of battle and those who enjoy watching the sweetness of success and the bitterness of defeat. In short, conflict keeps the organization viable and striving.

For interactionists, conflict is an organizational process. They utilize it in brainstorming, in Delphi techniques, in conferences, and at every opportunity within the organization.

To effectively use the interactionist approach, organizations must be ready to effect change. When the black rights movement began, for example, the blacks wanted change—a change in leadership and a change in goals and values. The institutions they sought to influence wanted to maintain the status quo; conflict would not serve that purpose. For the interactionist approach to be used effectively, a change in mental attitudes on the part of all participants is necessary.

The Environmental Components

The surroundings and the physical and social structure often work to determine if and to whose advantage a conflict situation will be resolved. Basically, home territory, room and seating arrangements, and the presence of time limits act as moderators. The presence of an audience also influences the conflict relationship.

The Physical Environment

Home territory generally provides the host with an advantage. Control can be exerted over the physical arrangements in such a manner as to offset any advantage the opponent may have, or as a compensator for lack of status, ability, or personal power. Home territory also gives the host a psychological advantage. It is not known why, but at least three reasons have been suggested. Since the host knows the home territory, it is expected that he or she will look after details and the guest will accept these arrangements graciously—whether he or she likes them or not! The guest may retain a fear and distrust that the host will use the knowledge of home territory to personal advantage. This puts the guest on the defensive; energies are channeled, not toward the conflict, but toward being alert to the possibility of fouls or of displaying this defensiveness in an overt manner. In familiar situations, there is a tendency for the individual to become more assertive and to win more frequently.

Seating arrangements can influence the relationship between the parties. Close arrangements (right angles, side by side) force opponents to look at each other and to interact. This makes it more difficult to tell a lie or to bluff, and it makes conflict resolution easier. Distant seating arrangements (across the ends of a long table, for example) make it more difficult for the opponents to see and hear each other. Under these circumstances, it is easier to avoid direct visual contact and intimate interaction. For the same reasons, round tables tend to increase the informality and the closeness; long oblong tables tend to decrease the opportunity for communication and thus increase the coldness and the formal nature of the conflict resolution process.

The use of artistic objects, such as flower vases and abstract sculptures, tends to facilitate informality and affiliation; the use of books and magazines tends to inhibit these processes.

The presence of time limits can often affect the resolution of conflict because it places pressure on the participants to settle their differences or accept the consequences. If the consequences are sufficiently severe, each party will lower the least favorable terms under which it is willing to settle and lower its expectations of what it can obtain as a result of the conflict.

Social Environment

Research in social psychology indicates that the individual's judgments, perceptions, attention, and motivation become different when he or she is watched or is a member of a group. Groups make riskier decisions and are more willing to take riskier action. At the same time, there is greater peer pressure to conform to the norms and expectations of the group, and the individual directs more effort toward pleasing others and being positively evaluated by the group and by onlookers. This issue becomes particularly crucial in situations when an individual involved in a conflict represents or is accountable to constituents. Energies become directed, not toward solving the problem, but toward gaining or retaining the approval of constituents.

The Role of Personality in Conflict

Personality is an illusive variable. Some people are pleasant; some are aggressive; some are introverts; some are neurotics; and some provoke conflict everywhere they go. When it comes to specifying the characteristics of these individuals, however, the task is more difficult. It appears that there are four types of individuals who are generally the focal point of conflict.

The first type is the group of people who are very sensitive to threatening clues within their environment and reveal this sensitivity in a negative manner. This tends to invite hostility and aggression from others. These individuals may lack self-esteem, may be insecure, or may be personally aggressive.

A second group of individuals who invite conflict are those who are dogmatic and authoritarian. Because of their rigidity and inflexibility, they do not listen and cannot hear arguments that differ from their own point of view. It is not unusual for these people to continue to argue at length and often belligerently after a point has been conceded by their opponent.

A third group of individuals who are generally in the midst of conflict are those who perceive the world and the behavior of others with distrust and suspicion. This attitude has, of course, its own self-fulfilling opportunity. If we expect people to act suspiciously, we will look and find indications of this behavior. Having found these indications, we confirm our original suspicions, and the cycle continues to escalate. When these feelings and perceptions are telegraphed to others, they respond with hostility and self-defensiveness, thus confirming the original suspicions.

The last group of individuals who provoke conflict exhibit none of the characteristics named above. Indeed, these people may be exactly the opposite. The energy, the creativity, the assertiveness, the nonconformity, and the independence of these individuals may trigger resentment and aggression in others. Too frequently these people elicit a feeling of guilt in others and are perceived as a threat, either from a materialistic or a self-image point of view.

A great many studies of other personality traits and how they affect conflict have been carried out. Unfortunately, these studies are often contradictory in their findings. It appears that personality is not a variable that can be studied separate from the environmental world in which it exists. There appears to be an interaction between personality and the physical and social aspects within which an individual functions.

Concluding Remarks

This overview of conflict has examined the parties to the conflict; three sources of conflict (power, communication, and residual issues); how differences in ideologies and values, interdependencies, and goals act to increase conflict; whether conflict is functional or dysfunctional; and some of the factors that determine how readily a conflict might be resolved or escalate.

Much of what has been stated is based on laboratory experiments, on observations, and on conjecture. Conflict is difficult to observe and more difficult to analyze. Perhaps the time will come when behavioral scientists have the ability to examine inner thought processes; we then may find a more precise method of learning about conflict, its true causes, and all of its outcomes.

References

Crocker, Olga L. "Precipitators of Job-Related Stress," M.B.A. thesis, Edmonton, Alberta, University of Alberta, 1974.

Filley, Alan C. *Interpersonal Conflict Resolution.* Glenview, Illinois: Scott, Foresman and Company, 1975.

French, J. R. P., and Raven, B. H. "The Bases of Social Power." In Dorwin Cartwright, ed. *Studies in Social Power.* Ann Arbor: University of Michigan Press, 1959.

Hall, Richard H. *Organizations. Structure and Process.* Englewood Cliffs, N.J.: Prentice-Hall, Inc., 1972.

Pondy, Louis R. "Organizational Conflict: Concepts and Models." *Administrative Science Quarterly* (September 1967): 296–320.

Robbins, Stephen P. *Managing Organizational Conflict. A Nontraditional Approach.* Englewood Cliffs, N.J.: Prentice-Hall, Inc., 1974.

Rubin, Jeffrey Z., and Brown, Bert R. *The Social Psychology of Bargaining and Negotiation.* New York: Academic Press, 1975.

Webber, Ross A. *Management. Basic Elements of Managing Organizations.* Homewood, Illinois: Richard D. Irwin, 1975.

Wieland, George F., and Ullrich, Robert A. *Organizations: Behavior, Design and Change.* Homewood, Illinois: Richard D. Irwin, 1976.

Winter, D. G. *The Power Motive.* New York: Free Press, 1973.

38

Socialization in Groups and Organizations: Toward a Concept of Creative Conformity

PATRICIA HAYES BRADLEY

The reasons individuals become members of groups and formal organizations are divergent and often multi-dimensional. For one person, group membership represents security and belonging; for another, it connotes prestige and power; and for still others, organizational affiliation offers the opportunity to exert concerted effort toward the common goal of creating a qualitatively better, safer society. However selfish or altruistic an individual's motives might be, whether they are riveted on private financial gain, oriented toward public service, or perhaps more commonly, projected toward a combination of these two goals (and many, many more), William Whyte's notion that we are all "organization men"[1] and women is a commonplace observation of American life during the last decades of the twentieth century. Yet, many have decried the homogenizing effects of organizational membership.[2] In fact, attacks levied against bureaucracy, the most prominent organization form, often center on the tendency of bureaucratic structures not only to dehumanize and alienate but also to give birth to dull, gray organization beings, persons stripped of their individuality and creativity, nonthinkers, conformers.

Yet, it is almost a paradox that the society that bewails bureaucracy for its alleged robbery of personal assertiveness and independence, at the same time anguishes over those who perch on the opposite end of the conformity-anticonformity continuum—the deviates, persons who seem always to be offering contrary views, those who jumble the apples with unceasing predictability, the hapless souls who seem never to fit into the role models and opinion molds fashioned for them. This paper considers the social influence phenomenon as it operates within groups and organizations by (1) *exploring some of the theories that seek to explain why groups exert pressure for uniformity and why individuals comply;* (2) *examining some of the major research findings relating to conformity, deviation, and social influence;* (3) *considering the consequences of and reactions to opinion deviation;* and (4) *developing a concept of creative conformity as an appropriate approach to human and organizational behavior.* First, however, it is important to define some of the terms central to a thoughtful consideration of social influence, particularly *organizations, norms, conformity, anticonformity,* and *independence.*

Basic Definitions

Basic to the concept of organization is the notion that individuals alone are often unable to fulfill all of their needs and wishes. Moreover, as several people coordinate their efforts toward common goals, they usually find that they can do more with relative effectiveness than any one of them could have done alone. To achieve efficiency within organizations, most are structured to divide labor and to differentiate responsibility. Thus, an organization is, as Schein has noted, "the rational coordination of the activities of a number of people for the achievement of some common explicit purpose or goal, through division of labor and function, and through a hierarchy of authority and responsibility."[3] As organizations go about the task of coordinating the efforts of individual members, norms develop. Typically, the term "norm" refers to a set of expectations held by group members concerning how one ought to behave. As such, norms usually exist on such evaluative scales as appropriate-inappropriate, good-bad, just-unjust, and moral-immoral. An individual's compliance with a norm is most readily measured by public behavior; but implicit in a broader understanding of norms is the notion that they are often *assumed* to extend to private feelings and attitudes.

While some norms apply to all persons at all levels of a given organization, others differ according to the position or role of a particular person. Thus, all employees of an industrial organization might be expected to show up for work regularly, but assembly-line workers would normally wear work clothes and managers might typically wear more formal ("white collar") attire. In every organization some norms are *explicit,* that is, formally stated. *Implicit* norms, on the other hand, are generally unstated, but among enduring members of groups and organizations, they are known and understood. Together, implicit and explicit norms constitute a potentially powerful regulatory mechanism for achieving uniformity of opinion and behavior among those who aspire to maintain or perhaps even enhance their group membership.

If norms refer to expectations regarding behavior, then clearly the conforming individual is one who fulfills these expectations. Even so, several distinctions must be made. First, there are those who conform because they desire reward from others, primarily their approval. Deutsch and Gerard refer to this type of behavior as *normative social influence,* that is, conformity to the "positive expectations of another"; and they distinguish it from *informational social influence* where the conforming person simply accepts information obtained from others as being correct, that is, as supportive "evidence about reality."[4] In the latter case, the person conforms because, having considered alternative views, s/he is actually convinced that the majority is correct. Pleasing the group is not the point; supporting a correct decision is. We often find, not surprisingly, that normative social influence is associated with public compliance, and informational influence, with private acceptance. Nevertheless, the two often work together, and there is some evidence to demonstrate that public compliance may eventually lead to private acceptance. Festinger and his colleagues have found that whenever a person's attitude is discrepant with his/her overt behavior, there is a tendency for the attitude to change toward closer agreement with the behavior.[5] Thus, while we normally assume that behavior is a reflection of a felt belief, it is also possible for an action to alter an attitude.

A final conceptual issue worth exploring is the distinction between *independence* and *anticonformity*. Hollander and Willis have pointed out that *pure conformity* exists when there is a great deal of movement toward greater agreement with the majority view.[6] There is no *one* opposite to pure conformity, for the nonconformist may be demonstrating either independence or anticonformity. According to Hollander and Willis, the truly independent person is well aware of what is expected of him or her. These expectations, however, do *not* function as guidelines for the individual's behavior; in fact, often the independent person is completely indifferent to them. The anticonformist, on the other hand, is quite another matter. This person is also cognizant of the group's norms and consistently reacts by moving away from these social expectations. In a very real sense, then, the group does guide the anticonformist's behavior, for anyone who knows the norm can predict the person's behavior with precision. While independents give no weight to the norm in making a judgment, both pure conformists and anticonformists notice the group's norm to an unusual degree: the conformist, in order to accept the norm and the anticonformist, to disagree with it.[7]

Theories of Social Influence and Conformity

Before considering the individual and situational factors most likely to encourage or inhibit conformity behavior, two important theoretical issues should be addressed: (1) *why do groups exert pressure for uniformity?* and (2) *why do many individuals conform to existing norms?* One approach to providing an answer to the first question can be found in Festinger's *group locomotion hypothesis.*[8] Organizations (and certainly small groups within them) have any number of goals to which they are committed. If these groups are unable to achieve their goals, they are likely to have difficulty maintaining themselves as a unit. Festinger points out that groups typically try to function so as to facilitate goal achievement. If it is assumed that this can best be accomplished when members conform to certain norms, and such is often the belief, then majority members become motivated to pressure deviates into conforming. In some situations, continued deviance may be only irritating, but on other occasions, it may become totally disruptive of the group's completion of its task. If, for example, a religious organization has a minister who decides to grow long hair and a beard, this behavior could cause a variety of reactions ranging from wild enthusiasm on the part of the youth to mild disapproval among the general congregation to actual withdrawals of church membership and financial support. In the latter instance, where goal achievement is clearly hindered, the deviating minister will undoubtedly experience pressure for uniformity toward what is probably an implicit church norm: only conservative hair styles are appropriate for preachers!

Another interesting approach to understanding group pressure may be drawn from Festinger's *social comparison theory.*[9] Most individuals do not need to consult the views of others to validate their perceptions of physical reality. A stove is hot; an elephant is big; a car is red. With matters of opinion and belief, however, the individual often finds comfort and reassurance in knowing that other persons share his/her views. Whenever members of a group or organization share common beliefs, values, or opinions, they create a kind of social reality for the validation of those views. This social validation process works best when group members are uniform in their beliefs; that is, according to social comparison theory, deviance destroys or seriously weakens the social reality that allows for opinion validation.

Finally, a number of theorists have advanced *balance theories,* parts of which may be relevant in explaining the group pressure phenomenon.[10] According to this perspective, groups prefer to exist as balanced systems. Consider the following example where imbalance or inconsistency has become a problem. A small group of executives meets regularly to make policy decisions. The group is close-knit, and there is a feeling of shared liking. Suppose further that member A strongly opposes the other four members on an important policy decision. Among the several options available to the majority members are (1) avoiding discussion of the issue, (2) deciding that the issue is not as important as they had first believed, (3) deciding that member A must not really understand the policy or has been misinformed, or (4) deciding that member A is not as likable as they had once believed. Either of the last two approaches are particularly relevant to social pressure, for if the third interpretation is made, the result would be a number of attempts to inform, elaborate, and persuade the deviate. If this strategy fails, then another way to create balance is to choose alternative four and direct negative sentiments toward the deviate while reinforcing all conforming others. Research has shown that both of these approaches are common occurrences, particularly among highly cohesive groups who are making important decisions.

In addressing the second major question concerning why individuals often conform, two of the theoretical perspectives already discussed are of relevance. First, the *group locomotion hypothesis* is important in that if the individual group member is committed to helping the group attain its goals, and if the person further believes that his/her conformity will facilitate goal achievement, then s/he should be internally motivated to conform. Organizations that demand unanimous votes for major policy decisions often inspire individuals to feel that a dissenting vote would not simply indicate symbolic protest, but would prevent the organization (here represented by the group's majority) from moving forward toward a generally desired goal. Also potentially useful in understanding motivations toward conformity behavior is *balance theory*. Like the group, the individual strives for consistency throughout his/her life. If group or organizational membership is valued, then the knowledge that one does not agree, fit in, or meet the expectations of others is potentially dissonance producing. Thus the individual is often motivated to agree, to conform, and to become more similar to other group members in order to achieve a personal sense of balance or consistency.

Not unlike social comparison theory, Campbell's *epistemological weighting hypothesis* focuses on the extent to which individuals rely on others for validating their perceptions.[11] Campbell believes that knowledge may be acquired through either personal modes (such as trial and error or the observation of inanimate objects) or social modes (for example, observation of others or receiving instructions regarding appropriate and inappropriate behavior). From this perspective, what determines an individual's conformity is the relative weight given to the personal and social modes of knowledge acquisition. It should be noted, however, that Campbell's theory only works with informational social influence. Moreover, Campbell himself is quick to point out that on some occasions the individual conforms because of desired rewards or in an attempt to escape the costs of nonconformity. As a result, knowledge acquisition may not be terribly relevant.

A final approach to explaining conformity behavior is the *social-exchange view,* which construes conformity as a social process in which positive effects are brought about in interactions with others by manifestations of expected behavior.[12] Thus conformity becomes either a deserved reward to others that smooths the path of interaction and provides for further prospects of rewarding exchange or as a payment in advance for anticipated rewards. Conformity then might be thought of as a technique of ingratiation[13] or perhaps as a way to amass credits in one's status "bank."[14]

Research Findings: Personal and Situational Variables

The area of social influence has suffered from no paucity of empirical investigations. Taylor was one of the earliest organizational researchers to be concerned with norms and their effects on industrial productivity.[15] Studies contributing to the human relations movement later pointed to the salience of informal work groups in establishing norms, sometimes at variance with the organization's notion of acceptable quantities of output.[16] Within the laboratories of social psychologists, the earliest experiment on social influence was conducted in the 1930's by Muzafer Sherif whose research with the autokinetic effect demonstrated that in a *group* situation, individual judgments soon converged over a number of trials.[17] One of the most extensive investigations of social influence was conducted by Solomon Asch.[18] He confronted naive subjects with the unanimous and erroneous opinions of several confederates on tasks involving simple perceptual judgments and discovered marked movement in the direction of the majority. In fact, only one fourth of Asch's naive subjects remained *completely* independent, but one third of the subjects displaced their estimates toward the majority judgment in half or more of the trials. It is important to note, too, that these line discrimination tasks were of no intrinsic importance to the subjects, the naive subject was unacquainted with the other group members, and they, in turn, made *no overt* attempts to influence his views.[19]

One of the implications of Asch's research is the seeming dichotomy between the independent subjects and the conformists. In an attempt to differentiate these two basic "types" of individuals, a number of investigators have sought to discover personality characteristics that might be associated with yielding behavior. Crutchfield's research was one of the earliest to unearth a kind of differential character profile.[20] He found that the independent person demonstrated great intellectual effectiveness, ego strength, leadership ability, and maturity of social relations. At the same time, s/he seemed to lack inferiority feelings, rigid and excessive self-control, and authoritarian attitudes. Finally, the independent was free from a compulsion to follow rules and was adventurous, self-assertive, and high in self-esteem. In contrast, Crutchfield reported that "the overconformist had less ego strength, less ability to tolerate ambiguity, less ability to accept responsibility, less self-insight, . . . less productive originality, more prejudiced and authoritarian attitudes, . . . and greater emphasis on external and socially approved values."[21]

The quest for personality characteristics that might be predictive of yielding behavior has received less attention in recent years. Although individuals do possess more or less enduring attributes, research has demonstrated that these attributes are modifiable by situational or contextual factors. It is not uncommon to find that the same individual is confident and self-assertive in one situation and reticent and uncertain in another. Thus so-called "universal traits" are extended or extinguished, depending upon the nature of the task being performed, the kind of people who surround the person, the nature of their interpersonal relations, and even other factors totally external to the group itself (such as the existence of an emergency or a particular political climate).[22] The point is that situational factors can prove so powerful that they break through the habitual response patterns and intensify or weaken the enduring attributes of personal character.

What are the situational variables that seem salient in affecting social influence processes? What, for example, are the contextual factors that seem most likely to produce conformity? Previous research points to the importance of a *unanimous majority.* Asch found that the inclusion of a single person who disagreed with the naive subject reduced the conformity rate by thirty percent.[23] In explaining this finding, Asch hypothesized that a fellow dissident both lowered the group consensus and provided the deviant member with social support for his/her private views. Follow-up research by Allen and Levine found, however, that unanimity was not necessary with subjective judgmental tasks where complete consensus was not anticipated or needed for significant social influence to occur.[24]

The *size of the majority* needed to achieve optimum pressure has also received a good deal of attention. Varying the size of the incorrect majority from one to fifteen, Asch found the effects of group pressure more pronounced when the unanimous opposition consisted of either three or four persons.[25] Other researchers, however, have failed to find a significant relationship between group size and conformity. Goldberg reported no significant difference between majorities of one, two, and three.[26] At the other extreme, Gerard and others found the most group-influenced judgments in a group of eight.[27] It is highly probable that group size is not nearly so important as the role relations among the members of the group. *One* powerful organizational executive exerting pressure for uniformity may be more influential than several lower-level employees in changing the publicly stated views of a would-be deviate.

Yet another important variable is *situational* or *stimulus ambiguity.* If an individual initially disagrees with a group's judgment on an issue that is unclear, uncertain, ambiguous, or difficult to understand, s/he is more likely to accept the group's position than if s/he perceives the issue to be more clearcut and certain. After all, ambiguous matters are always open to interpretation; that is, they inherently involve degrees of correctness and incorrectness rather than absolutes of right or wrong. Thus especially on matters of opinion, belief, and attitude, the group's interpretation could easily be correct— or, at least, no more incorrect than the individual's.[28]

One final situational variable focuses on the nature of the interacting group and has to do with its degree of *cohesiveness.* Shepherd defines cohesiveness as "the quality of a group which includes individual pride, commitment, and meaning, as well as the group's stick-togetherness, ability to weather crises, and ability to maintain itself over time."[29] Highly cohesive groups demand, and usually get, great loyalty and conformity from their members. As a social-emotional quality of small groups, cohesiveness has been both lamented and applauded. People who belong to highly cohesive groups are usually there for positive reasons, often associated with their genuine liking for other group members, their feeling that the group's task is important, or perhaps their sense of pride in being affiliated with the group. If the highly cohesive group demands positive behaviors, attitudes, or outcomes, its chances of getting them are better than are those of a group lower in cohesiveness. On the other hand, the highly cohesive group that establishes less positive standards or attitudes (such as low productivity, racial prejudice, or intolerance of divergent views) is also more likely to maintain its norms and achieve its goals. Thus cohesiveness is neither good nor bad per se. Rather, it is a quality that enhances the potency of the group's norms and goal achievement potential, whatever they happen to be.[30]

The personality and situational variables discussed in this section are not exhaustive but only suggestive of some of the significant personal and contextual factors associated with social influence and conformity behavior. But what of the deviate? How specifically do groups exert pressure for uniformity? How does the deviant member respond? Finally, what happens to the person who ultimately fails to conform?

The Deviate: Treatment and Impact

One interesting observation noted by the human relations researchers was the tendency of small informal work groups to develop verbal and non-verbal methods of getting deviating members "back in line." Tactics such as teasing, ridiculing, or punching and shoving the deviate were not uncommon.[31] Perhaps the first systematic investigation of the characteristics of pressure for uniformity was conducted by Schachter who found that groups may exert forces for uniformity through increases in the *quantity* of communication.[32] He noted that communication quantity interacted with task relevance and group cohesiveness such that communication attempts increased throughout the discussions in all groups *except* for the highly cohesive groups dealing with important tasks. In those latter groups, communication to the deviate reached a peak midway through the session and then proceeded to decline steadily, leading ultimately to rejection. Subsequent research by Taylor focused on the verbal behavior of majority members facing an opinion deviate.[33] He found their communication was characterized by dominance, reasonableness, and hostility.

Of all the variables that might affect a deviate's treatment, none is more important than his/her position within the group. An individual's group position is often measured on a scale reflecting status, usually thought of as the significance, value, or prestige associated with a given role. In most instances, we know that high status persons can "get away with" more in terms of deviant behavior; that is, given the performance of identical deviant acts (ranging from opinion deviation to illegal behavior), the low status deviate is usually more severely sanctioned than his/her high status counterpart.[34] An intriguing explanation for these findings has been advanced by Hollander whose "idiosyncrasy credit" model looks upon conformity as one input to the accumulation of status in the form of positive impressions or "credit" awarded by others.[35] This credit then permits greater latitude for nonconformity under certain conditions. A basic feature of this model is that there is *not* a fixed norm or set of norms to which all must comply equally. Rather, nonconformity behavior is defined differently by the group *depending upon how the individual group member is perceived.* Thus the same behavior is seen as deviant (in the negative sense) when performed by member A and as creative innovation when performed by member B. In this sense, conformity becomes person-specific and functionally related to status. Of course, this model is of great relevance to leadership. Leaders are usually great conformers to group norms,[36] but, at the same time, they are often initiators of change (reflected in seemingly nonconforming behavior). What often happens is that early conformity to group norms combined with such attributes as perceived competence may serve to enhance the acceptance of a leader's later nonconformity.

Yet, high status roles do carry with them high expectations. While there are wider latitudes of deviation for the high status person in some areas, there are greater restrictions in others. Extremely serious deviation, for example, may be more severely sanctioned when attributed to a high status actor than to a low status person.[37] There are, according to Hollander, at least two reasons why the role obligations of high status persons are so severely delimited.[38] First, high status is believed to hold greater self-determination; therefore, those in high status positions are assumed to be more responsible for their actions. Second, and perhaps just as important, high status carries with it role demands that are more likely to affect important outcomes for the members of the group. So long as norm violations can be construed as instances of "productive nonconformity,"[39] then the high status deviate's behavior will be accepted and perhaps even welcomed. If, however, his/her actions are seen to hurt the group or organization, the high status person will be held *more* responsible than would a low status member. As Hollander puts it, "It is true that the acts of the high status person are less likely to be perceived negatively than those of a low status person, but given that the evaluation of acts is equally unfavorable, the high status person will pay the higher social price."[40]

Responses of the deviate to group pressure vary. But for most, being in a position of opposition to other group members is accompanied by uneasiness. As early as 1936, Smith demonstrated that college students become emotionally aroused when they learn that their peers disagree with them.[41] This arousal is greatest when the disagreeing peers challenge opinions that are strongly believed. Assuming the arousal is unpleasant, it should motivate attempts to lessen the disagreement; and one way to do this is to accept the majority position. Asch, too, was interested in discerning why yielding behavior occurred. Through post experimental interviews, he discovered that the frequent yielders reported three types of reactions: (1) they actually "saw" the majority estimates as correct (perceptual distortion); (2) they believed, contrary to what they saw, that their perceptions were probably incorrect and that the majority was probably right (distortion of judgment); and (3) they yielded because of a desire not to seem different from the other group members (distortion of action). Among those who remained totally independent, there were also several reactions: (1) complete, vigorous confidence; (2) withdrawn, introverted independence, and (3) doubtful, tension-ridden nonconformity. It should be noted, however, that no one of these groups (including the so-called "completely confident" category) was immune from some tension and experience of conflict. Finally, Bradley's study of the verbal behavior of deviates undergoing pressure for uniformity revealed some interesting patterns.[42] She found, for example, that opinion deviates made few early attempts at influence or leadership. As the discussions progressed, however, they expressed their ideas in a more assertive, influential manner. When this strategy proved futile, dominance tendencies regressed rapidly. In addition, deviate emotionality increased from the beginning to the end of the discussion sessions while reasonableness declined. Bradley speculated that when the discussion has progressed to the stage where the deviate sees that the exhibition of sound judgment and well-balanced thought is proving futile, s/he abandons them as useful persuasive tools. Even so, emotional involvement continues to rise.

There are situations, of course, in which the expression of deviant views may influence the ideas of the rest of the group. Grove found that the attitudes of both deviates *and* majority members are affected by the presentation of opposing views during group discussions. Moreover, while both majority group members and deviant group members appreciably changed their positions as a result of mutual interaction, majority convergence was greater than deviate convergence.[43] A recent study by Bradley, Hamon, and Harris further revealed that an articulate, intelligent deviate is capable of influencing the publicly expressed views of majority group members; that is, in group discussion settings, majority group members will use a significant number of the deviate's arguments, actually reciting them as their own.[44]

Group members who are valued by the group and/or are in positions of leadership may find it possible to engage in constructive deviation without sanctioning. Dittes and Kelley found, for example, that subjects believing they had high acceptance in their groups felt great freedom to express deviant views.[45] Certainly there is something to be said for the democratic assertion that all opinions, however deviant, should be aired. The old notion of playing the "devil's advocate" clearly implies that ideas will be better for having stood the test of argument. Many approaches to group problem-solving recognize the importance of gathering a divergent sampling of views *prior* to interpretation or evaluation; thus, they variously employ brain-storming, nominal grouping, and other techniques to encourage the expression of unstifled thought. One of Irving Janis' advocated solutions to *groupthink* was to bring in different points of view (often from outside the group), to expect *each* group member to play the role of critical evaluator, and to avoid overly directive leadership, particularly the statement of personal preferences. Thus in overcoming the natural "ingroup" tendency to agree, it is important to welcome and respect the freedom to disagree.

So far, we have looked at theories and research of the past in an attempt to assess the nature, kinds, strategies, processes, and outcomes associated with the social influence phenomenon. The last section of this work will focus on an approach to using this knowledge for the effective functioning of organizations and the fulfillment of individuals within them.

Creative Conformity

All organizations engage in socialization. They have goals, values, norms, and preferred ways of doing things that are taught rather systematically, both overtly and covertly, to all new members. Schein differentiates *pivotal norms* (required for organizational membership, such as belief in the free enterprise system) from *peripheral norms* (desirable but not essential, such as holding conservative political views). He believes that organizations should seek creative individualists, persons who accept all pivotal norms while rejecting all others.[46] Schein's view is close to the one espoused in this work, but it differs in some important respects.

First, it is not possible to delineate a model organization person. There are simply too many kinds of skills involved, jobs to be performed, individual personalities to consider, and so forth. The kind of creativity needed among top level executives is clearly not the same as that desired among factory workers or even among leaders in different executive divisions (for example, the vice president for finance as opposed to the vice president for research and development). Even so, we can *begin* to discern an effective approach for organizations to pursue with many of their employees. And the approach originates with an assessment of the organization's norms and expectations. What are the values to which the organization is committed at a *behavioral level?* How are these made manifest? What are the implications for workers who spend their lives trying to be fruitful and fulfilled within this formal structure? Is the organization honest with itself about its values, and does it attempt to honestly communicate those values to employees at a time when such knowledge could make a difference, such as during the selection interview? The interviewing department chairman who tells a would-be assistant professor that "teaching and research are equally valued at this university" should probably ask him/herself, "*if* they are equally valued, why are they not equally rewarded?" In short, the organization must recognize the nature of its goals, expectations, and values before it can critically assess them and communicate them to employees.

Likewise, workers need to undergo a specific process of self-assessment prior to entering the organization and continuously throughout their productive lives. This assessment should focus on education, work experience, and developed skills as well as goals, expectations, and values. Only when both parties have evaluated themselves with directness and candor can a good "fit" between organization and individual occur. It is my view that the creative conformity suggested in the title of this work can only occur when there exists just such a "fit."

Consider the notion of the psychological contract. It implies that individual and organization have a variety of mutual expectations. These expectations not only cover the amount of work to be performed for a certain amount of money, but also the whole pattern of rights, privileges, and obligations between workers and organization. Many of these expectations are never written into formal agreements between employee and organization, but they continue to operate as powerful determinants of behavior.[47] From the organization's point of view, the psychological contract is implemented through the concept of *authority.* A decision to join the organization implies a commitment to accept its authority system.[48] Authority in this sense is *not* the same as pure power, for the former implies the willingness on the part of subordinates to obey *because* they *consent;* that is, because the employees understand the organization's expectations, they *agree* to accept certain roles or positions within the organization. It is crucial to note, however, that from employees' points of view, the psychological contract is implemented through their perception that they *can* influence the organization of their own immediate situations sufficiently to insure that they will not be taken advantage of. The mode of influence is not so important as the fundamental belief that the power to influence exists. The psychological contract, then, is based on acceptance of mutual influence, an understanding of mutual expectations, and a willingness to behave reasonably and fairly within the confines of the agreement.

If this contract is to be mutually satisfying, extensive agreement must exist between the standards of the individual and the expectations of the organization. This is to say that individual creativity can most meaningfully occur within an organizational context where individual needs and values and organizational goals are congruent. Thus for the most part, the individual does conform and quite probably in more than the pivotal areas—but s/he does so because it is natural. The person behaves as s/he normally would behave, and that behavior *is* in keeping with organizational expectations simply because employee and employer are well matched. Etzioni writes of three types of involvement that individuals may have as they approach their organizational responsibilities: (1) *alienative* (where the person is coerced into belonging); (2) *calculative* (where the person works to achieve a valued personal end—usually money, security, or prestige); and (3) *moral.*[49] This latter involvement concept is central to the discussion of creative conformity, for it means that the person intrinsically values the mission of the organization and his/her job within it and performs the job, not for reward, but because s/he values it!

Early in the history of our nation, one of the most valued of personal characteristics was "rugged individualism." While independence is clearly important in many contexts, in recent years the American value trend has moved in the direction of *interdependence.*[50] Thus the emphasis is upon cooperatively striving for common goals with a respect for the person's individuality and a simultaneous recognition of the strength of concerted effort.

But there is still another implication to the notion of interdependence that takes us beyond the organization's boundaries. For most organizations, the ability to grow is commensurate with adaptability to and management of change.[51] Every organization exists in a dynamic environment. As technological change proceeds at an incredible rate, organizations face constant problems of obsolescence. Moreover, social-political changes throughout the world are creating an undiminished demand for new services as well as the expansion of existing products. Organizations have changed further with the advent of computers and automation—needing highly educated managers, far exceeding the present supply.

The relationship between every organization and its environment is one of interdependence. Without reciprocal exchanges, adjustments, and mutually influencing interactions, neither can benefit the other. Given the dynamic state of the organization's surroundings, then, perhaps the most critical capacity to be developed by organizational members is the ability to meet a variety of new problems with creativity and flexibility. More important, this quality is not merely an attribute to be possessed by management, but by all of the organization's human resources. Flexible managers may alter the structure, policy, or even the goals of the organization in order to adjust to environmental changes. But if the employees themselves are inflexible, then altering the company's blueprint will have but minimal impact on the actual operation of the organization.

When organizations become committed to such "norms" as creativity, innovation, and flexibility, it is not only possible, but more highly *probable,* that organizational members can practice creative conformity in a personally fulfilling and professionally productive way. Given the presence of normative social influences, a virtual fact of group and organizational life, there is every reason to attempt to use these powerful social stimuli for the encouragement of positive group and individual goals. Deutsch and Gerard were among the first to recognize that social influence might be used to buttress, as well as undermine, individual integrity! They stated: "Groups can demand of their members that they have self-respect, that they value their own experience, that they be capable of acting without slavish regard for popularity. Unless groups encourage their members to express their own, independent judgments, group consensus is likely to be an empty achievement."[52]

In some senses, the creative conformity perspective represents an ideal. To apply it at all levels of all organizations would be an impossibility. But movement in the direction of the approach seems warranted in view of (1) the survival demands placed on the organization for adaptation and innovation and (2) the internal needs of the individual for self-actualization through organizational affiliation. Creative conformity, not unlike Schein's concept of creative individualism, stresses the acceptance of major organizational policies, goals, and values. But creative conformists are also free to accept most of the organization's relevant peripheral norms since their commitment to the organization is rooted in *value congruence*. They know what the organization stands for, accept it, and are committed to it at a personal level. Their relationship to this particular organization is simply one major manifestation of their over-all value orientation. And it is a mutual commitment, for the organization pledges to encourage innovation, to reward creativity, to applaud adaptability, and to nurture human growth in a context of organizational development.

Notes

[1] William Whyte, *The Organization Man* (New York: Doubleday and Company, Inc., 1956).
[2] See, for example, J. Bensman and B. Rosenberg, "The Meaning of Work in Bureaucratic Society," in A. Etzioni ed., *Readings on Modern Organizations* (Englewood Cliffs, N.J.: Prentice-Hall, 1969).
[3] Edgar H. Schein, *Organizational Psychology*, second edition (Englewood Cliffs, N.J.: Prentice-Hall, Inc., 1970), p. 9.
[4] Morton Deutsch and Harold B. Gerard, "A Study of Normati ⸱ and Informational Social Influences upon Individual Judgment," *Journal of Abnormal and Social Psychology* 51 (1955): 629.
[5] Leon Festinger, *A Theory of Cognitive Dissonance* (Stanford, California: Stanford University Press, 1957).
[6] Edwin P. Hollander and Richard H. Willis, "Some Current Issues in the Psychology of Conformity and Nonconformity," *Psychological Bulletin* 68 (1967): 62–76.

[7] *Ibid.* It is important to note here that these distinctions do not connote a typology of persons, but rather a differentiation of responses.
[8] Leon Festinger, "Informal Social Communication," *Psychological Review* 57 (1950): 271–282.
[9] Leon Festinger, "A Theory of Social Comparison Processes," *Human Relations* 7 (1954): 117–140.
[10] See, for example, Fritz Heider, "Attitudes and Cognitive Organization," *Journal of Psychology* 21 (1946): 107–112; Festinger, *A Theory of Cognitive Dissonance;* and Charles E. Osgood and Percy H. Tannenbaum, "The Principle of Congruity in the Prediction of Attitude Change," *Psychological Review* 62 (1955): 42–55.
[11] Donald T. Campbell, "Conformity in Psychology's Theories of Acquired Behavioral Dispositions," in Irwin A. Berg and Bernard M. Bass eds., *Conformity and Deviation* (New York: Harper and Row, 1961), pp. 101–142.

[12] For example, see J. Stacy Adams, "Inequity in Social Exchange," in Leonard Berkowitz ed., *Advances in Experimental Social Psychology* Vol. 2, (New York: Academic Press, 1965), pp. 267–299; Peter M. Blau, *Exchange and Power in Social Life* (New York: Wiley, 1964); George C. Homans, "Social Behavior as Exchange," *American Journal of Sociology* 63 (1958): 597–606; and John W. Thibaut and Harold H. Kelley, *The Social Psychology of Groups* (New York: Wiley, 1959).

[13] Edward E. Jones, "Conformity as a Tactic of Ingratiation," *Science* 149 (1965): 144–150.

[14] Edwin P. Hollander, "Competence and Conformity in the Acceptance of Influence," *Journal of Abnormal and Social Psychology* 61 (1960): 361–365.

[15] Frederick W. Taylor, *The Principles of Scientific Management* (New York: Harper and Row, 1911).

[16] F. Roethlisberger and W. Dickson, *Management and the Worker* (Cambridge, Mass.: Harvard University Press, 1939).

[17] Muzafer Sherif, "A Study of Some Social Factors in Perception," *Archives of Psychology* 27, No. 187 (1935).

[18] Solomon E. Asch, "Studies of Independence and Conformity: A Minority of One Against a Unanimous Majority," *Psychological Monographs* 70, No. 416 (1956).

[19] See Dorwin Cartwright and Alvin Zander, "Pressures to Uniformity in Groups: Introduction," *Group Dynamics*, third edition (New York: Harper and Row, 1968), pp. 139–160.

[20] Richard S. Crutchfield, "Conformity and Character," *The American Psychologist* 10 (1955): 191–198.

[21] *Ibid.*, 196.

[22] L. B. Rosenfeld, *Human Interaction in the Small Group Setting* (Columbus, Ohio: Charles Merrill, 1973).

[23] Asch, No. 416.

[24] See, for example, Vernon L. Allen and J. M. Levine, "Social Support, Dissent, and Conformity," *Sociometry* 31 (1968): 138–149 and V. L. Allen and J. M. Levine, "Social Support and Conformity: The Role of Independent Assessment of Reality," *Journal of Experimental Social Psychology* 7 (1971): 48–58.

[25] Solomon E. Asch, "Opinions and Social Pressure," *Scientific American* 193 (1955): 31–35.

[26] Samuel C. Goldberg, "Three Situational Determinants of Conformity to Social Norms," *Journal of Abnormal and Social Psychology* 49 (1954): 325–329.

[27] Harold B. Gerard, R. A. Wilhelmy, and E. S. Conolly, "Conformity and Group Size," *Journal of Personality and Social Psychology* 8 (1968): 79–82.

[28] Stimulus ambiguity is clearly not reserved to matters of attitude and opinion. Sherif's autokinetic situation, for example, is extremely ambiguous, and as Sherif has demonstrated in subsequent research, the group's judgment may be accepted for as long as a year.

[29] C. Shepherd, *Small Groups* (Scranton, Pa: Chandler Co., 1964).

[30] Irving Janis' work on "groupthink" is one of the best contemporary examples of the negative outcomes historically associated with highly cohesive groups, such as the development of an illusion of invulnerability, excessive rationalization, shared stereotypes, and a tendency toward self-censorship.

[31] F. Roethlisberger and W. Dickson.

[32] Stanley Schachter, "Deviation, Rejection, and Communication," *Journal of Abnormal and Social Psychology* 46 (1951): 190–207.

[33] K. Phillip Taylor, "An Investigation of Majority Verbal Behavior toward Opinions of Deviant Members in Group Discussions of Policy," (Unpublished Ph.D. dissertation, Indiana University, 1969).

[34] See, for example, Leonard Berkowitz and J. R. Macaulay, "Some Effects of Differences in Status Level and Status Stability," *Human Relations* 14 (1961): 135–148; Edwin P. Hollander, "Some Effects of Perceived Status on Responses to Innovative Behavior," *Journal of Abnormal and Social Psychology* 63 (1961): 247–250; and J. A. Wiggins, F. Dill and R. D. Schwartz, "On 'Status-Liability,'" *Sociometry* 28 (1965): 197–209.

[35] Edwin P. Hollander, "Conformity, Status, and Idiosyncrasy Credit," *Psychological Review* 65 (1958): 117–127; and E. P. Hollander, *Leaders, Groups, and Influence* (New York: Oxford University Press, 1964).

[36] George C. Homans, *The Human Group* (New York: Harcourt-Brace, 1950).

[37] Ralph Wahrman, "Status, Deviance, and Sanctions: A Critical Review," *Comparative Group Studies* 3 (1972): 203–224.

[38] Hollander, *Leaders, Groups, and Influence*, 277.

[39] Pauline Pepinsky, "Social Exceptions That Prove the Rule," in Irwin A. Berg and Bernard M. Bass eds., *Conformity and Deviation* (New York: Harper and Row, 1961), pp. 424–434.

[40] Hollander and Willis, 243.

[41] C. E. Smith, "A Study of the Autonomic Excitation Resulting from the Interaction of Individual Opinions and Group Opinion," *Journal*

of Abnormal and Social Psychology 30 (1936): 138–164.

⁴²Patricia Hayes Bradley, "Pressure for Uniformity: An Experimental Study of Deviate Responses in Group Discussions of Policy," *Small Group Behavior* 9 (1978): 149–160.

⁴³Theodore G. Grove, "Attitude Convergence in Small Groups," *Journal of Communication* 15 (1965): 226–238.

⁴⁴Patricia Hayes Bradley, C. Mac Hamon, and Alan M. Harris, "Dissent in Small Groups," *Journal of Communication* 26 (1976): 155–159.

⁴⁵J. E. Dittes and Harold H. Kelley, "Effects of Different Conditions of Acceptance upon Conformity to Group Norms," *Journal of Abnormal and Social Psychology* 52 (1956): 100–107.

⁴⁶Edgar H. Schein, "Organizational Socialization and the Profession of Management," *Industrial Management Review* 9 (1968): 1–6.

⁴⁷Chris Argyris, *Understanding Organizational Behavior* (Homewood, Ill.: The Dorsey Press, 1960).

⁴⁸Schein, *Organizational Psychology*, pp. 12–13.

⁴⁹Amitai Etzioni, *A Comparative Analysis of Complex Organizations* (Glencoe, Ill.: Free Press, 1961).

⁵⁰E. L. Trist, "Urban North America: The Challenge of the Next Thirty Years," in W. H. Schmidt ed., *Organizational Frontiers and Human Values* (Belmont, California: Wadsworth, 1970).

⁵¹Schein, *Organizational Psychology*, p. 19.

⁵²Deutsch and Gerard, p. 635.

Part Thirteen

Seeking Affiliation with the Company

39

Job-Hunting As an Information Search

RICHARD NELSON BOLLES*

At its heart, job-hunting is basically a search for information. It is not—as some alleged experts claim—*basically* a "marketing problem," although the abundance of workshops and seminars on such subjects as "How to Market Yourself to an Employer" might lead us to think so. Such seminars are frequently run by management people who have learned all about marketing and sales from the business world. When they turn to look at job-hunting, they say to themselves, "Why, this is just another marketing problem. All the know-how that I picked up in the business world ought to qualify me for teaching job-hunting and interviewing techniques." Voila. Another seminar is born.

To be sure, "selling yourself" to an employer, once you've found him or her, can be very difficult. This sort of expertise is needed, at the end. But it is that finding of an employer which is basic to job-hunting, and this is an information search of the first order. Here we need the help not so much of "management people" but of "research experts."

In his excellent book, *Finding Facts Fast,* Alden Todd points out that there are four groups of people in this country who are especially expert at information searches. These are (1) reference librarians, (2) university scholars, (3) investigative reporters, and (4) detectives.[1] We might also add (5) spies, or intelligence officers. We would expect these people to be able to shed much light upon the topic "Job-Hunting As an Information Search." It is a subject that is "right up their alley." Therefore, it is hardly surprising that a leading expert today in creative methods of job-hunting, John Crystal, was formerly (a) a university scholar and (b) an intelligence officer. This training is thoroughly evidenced in a major work *Where Do I Go from Here with My Life?*"[2]

* For further help with the job hunt, see Richard N. Bolles, *What Color IS Your PARACHUTE?* (1979 edition), from which this chapter is excerpted. Published by Ten Speed Press, Box 7123, Berkeley, CA, 94707.

How to conduct job-hunting in the light of what we have learned from such information search specialists as Crystal is perhaps best illustrated when the job-hunt has to be conducted from long distance. In such a hunt, the principles which should guide *all* job-hunting stand out especially clearly. To illustrate the point, we can use two recent inquiries which came across my desk. A communication from a soldier in Germany read:

> I am presently assigned in Germany and am getting out of the Army October '77. Area of interest: Corporations—Department of Mental Hygiene. I am having trouble getting information on the field since it is a relatively new field. Any help on resources? Trying to make contacts over 500 miles of water is tough!

From a woman in New York State came a similar inquiry:

> I am having trouble finding organizations I qualify for in far-away places. Non-profit organizations. I am also having trouble finding out what their problems are from long distances. I am interested in locating in Kentucky, western North Carolina, or upper Tennessee.

In seeing how we might counsel these individuals to deal with their problems, we can see the principles that underlie the job-hunt as information search.

The Principles of Information-Searching at a Distance (Or up Close)

1. Be clear about the different kinds of information you will need for your job-hunt.
   You will need information about the following (use this as a check list):
   a. What Your Skills Are
      (1) That you have already demonstrated
      (2) That you enjoy
      This list must be in detail, clustered into families, and ordered in terms of priorities, ranking your six or so favorites. If you fail to do any of these three steps (in detail, clustered, and ordered in priorities), you will seriously hamper your subsequent information search.
   b. Where You Want to Use These Skills
      Someone who has the skill of welding can use that skill to weld the casing for a nuclear bomb or to make a wheel for a cart. In what way do you want to use your skills? In the service of what? To accomplish what? Simply to say you want to do welding is not sufficient and will seriously hamper your subsequent information search.
   c. What Kinds of Organizations
      (1) You like
      (2) Either already use people with your skills in the service of your goals, or
      (3) Ought to and perhaps could be persuaded to do so

(4) In the geographical area (or areas) on which you have focused
The last step above is the precondition for answering the other three.
Our soldier, for example, cannot really do his information search
about corporations' departments of mental hygiene until he has *first*
selected at least an area of the country, and preferably two or three
cities in that area, by name.

d. What Are the Names of Such Organizations in the Cities upon
Which You Have Focused
The more specific and detailed you have been in step "c" above, the
easier this step "d" will be. The more general you have been, the
harder this step will be. For example, "corporations" is too general.
In a particular city, that will turn out to be a very long list. "Corporations with not more than 200 employees, which produce some
product" would result in a much shorter list, in any particular city or
a country area. Likewise, the phrase "non-profit organizations" is
too general. That again will produce a long list.

e. Who in the Organization Has the Power to Hire You
Identifying this individual is critical in the creative job hunt. For the
level of job at which you are likely to be aiming, it will not be the
Personnel Department which will do the hiring.

f. What Are the Problems of the Man or Woman Who Has the Power
to Hire You?
After locating places that look interesting to you, your task is to uncover the problems of that organization so that you may, in the interviews you later secure, interpret your skills in terms of their
problems. This is the aspect of creative job-hunting which baffles so
many people. There are several guidelines which may be helpful to
you in your information search:

(1) You don't need to discover the problems of the whole organization (unless it's very small); you only need to discover what
problems are bothering, concerning, perplexing the man or
woman who has the power to hire you. If you did a thorough
information search, you may already have met that individual
in the course of gathering your information. So he or she is
more to you than just a name. If it's a committee that has the
power to hire you, you must decide who is the one individual
(or two) who *sway* the others, the one whose judgment the others respect. How do you obtain this information? Using contacts is one way. Someone will know someone who knows the
whole committee and can pinpoint the *real* leader. It's not necessarily the one acting as chairperson.

(2) You shouldn't assume the problems are huge, complex, and
hidden. The complexity of the problems will frequently be correlated with the level at which you want to work. For example,
if your application is at the clerk or secretary level, the problems are fairly predictable: absenteeism, too long coffee or
lunch breaks, not caring about the subject matter, not accepting

the supervisor's priorities about what work needs to be done first. If you wish to work at a higher level, the problems are likely to be more complex.

(3) Don't assume that what *ought* to be bothering the employer will be his major concern. In your research you may be thinking to yourself, "This firm has a huge public relations problem; I'll have to show them that I could put together a whole crash P.R. program." That's the large complex problem that you think *ought* to be concerning the man or woman who has the power to hire you. In actual fact, what may be of primary importance to this person is whether you're going to get to work on time, not be out sick too often, and take assigned coffee breaks. Don't overlook the small, simple, and obvious problems that bother almost every employer.[3]

(4) In most cases, your task is not that of educating your prospective employer, but of trying to read his/her mind. To be sure, you may have uncovered, during your information search, some problems that the employer himself may not recognize. You may be convinced that for you even to mention these issues may win you his undying gratitude. Perhaps. But don't bet on it. Our files at the National Career Development Project are filled with testimonials like the following: "I met with the V-P, Marketing in a major local bank on the recommendation of an officer, and discussed with him a program I devised to reach the female segment of his market, which would not require any new services, except education, enlightenment, and encouragement. His comment at the end of the discussion was that the bank president had been after him for three years to develop a program for women, and he wasn't about to do it because the only reason, in his mind, for the president's request was reputation enhancement on the president's part."

Inter-office politics or other considerations may prevent your prospective employer from being receptive to your idea.[4] Your research must be devoted to finding out what already *does* motivate him/her to hire someone for the position in which you're interested, not what *might* motivate. In other words, you're trying to find out what is already going on in his/her mind. In this sense, your task is more akin to mind-reading than to education.

(5) There are various ways of finding out what's going on in his/her mind; don't limit yourself to just one way. You may analyze the organization at a distance and make some educated guesses. If the organization is expanding, they may well need more of what they already have; what they already have, with different style and/or added skills; or something that they don't presently have, a new kind of person with new skills doing a new function or service. If the organization is continuing as is,

they may need to replace people who were fired (find out why, what was lacking), to replace people who quit (find out what was valued about these individuals),[5] or to create a new position because of existing assignments being reallocated or because of newly perceived needs. If the person in charge of hiring is available, talk directly to him/her in the early stages of your information search.[6] Talk to his/her "opposite number" in another organization similar to the one that interests you and find out what kinds of problems perplex this individual. For example, if you are interested in working for a Senator out West, you can talk to a Senator's staff where you presently live first. The problems will probably be similar. Talk to the person who held the job before you or to the person in a similar organization who holds that position. No one will know the problems of a superior so well as someone who works, or used to work, for him. While the person still on the job will have a huge investment in being discreet, the ex-employee rarely has such needs or values.

(6)   Beware of the language that you use to express yourself. Most of the people who have the power to hire you for the position that you want do not like the word "problems." It reminds them that they are mortal, have hangups, haven't solved something yet, or have overlooked some area of concern. Express your ideas in terms of the employer's priorities, values, concerns. For example, speak of "an area that you probably are planning to move into" or a "concern of yours" or *anything* except "By the way, I've uncovered a problem you have." Use the word "problems" in your own head, but don't blurt it out with your prospective employer, unless reference has already been made in those terms.

An example of approaches to use in presenting your skills in terms of the organization's problems is as follows:

Employer Was Concerned About:	*You Emphasize That:*
Your predecessor had all the skills but was too serious.	You have all the skills (name them), *and* you have a sense of humor.
The organization is expanding and needs a training program for its employees.	You have all the skills to do the training, especially in the specific areas of major concern to the employer.
The manager wishes that he had someone to attend to details which he presently is having to handle himself.	You are very good with details and follow up.
This magazine probably isn't covering all the subjects it should, but	You have done a complete survey of the magazine's tables of contents

there's been no time to confirm it or to decide what areas could best be added.

for the last 10 years, can show what has been missed, and have outlined sample articles in those missing areas.

2. In review, these are all the areas about which you will need information: your skills; where you want to use these skills; what kinds of organizations most interest you; names of specific organizations in cities or locations in which you have decided to focus your search; who in these organizations has the power to hire you; and what are the problems of the organizations, especially in the areas in which you will be applying. The next step in the creative job hunt is to set down on paper which of the above information searches you can do where you are and which require the help of others in the cities of your choice. Normally, you can determine your skills and where you want to use these skills where you are, since this is potentially a self-directed information search. To aid the job hunter in doing that part of the information search, I have devised a "Quick Job-Hunting Map," a beginning version for high school students and others who are entering the world of work for the first time and an advanced version for those who have had considerable experience or who wish to change careers. If, even with the map, you have difficulty identifying your skills and locating where you want to use them, you should solicit the aid of mate, a friend, or business acquaintance to help you work through the map; or you should seek help from professional career experts such as your university career-planning or placement office or from professionals trained in workshops such as the National Career Development Project.[7]

Once these steps have been accomplished, you are ready to go on to the other information searches previously listed. If there is a good library where you are, or if that library (however small and limited) is on an inter-library loan system, you can do some research on the kinds of organizations that most interest you, names of specific organizations in cities of particular interest to you, and the potential problems that the organizations may be experiencing.

3. Determine how much time you have before you *absolutely have to find* a job.

It would be encouraging to think that you could conclude your information search—successfully—within the month. However, it is not at all unusual for a job hunt to take nine months, or longer. Decide how much time you have, at the outside limit. The earlier you can get started, the more lead-time you can give yourself, the better.

4. Figure out if there isn't some way during that time that you could go visiting the city or cities of your choice.

Does a vacation fall within the time period between now and the date you must finalize your plans? Could you visit the city on vacation? Take a summer position there? Go there on leave? Attend a convention in that city or get appointed to a group or association that meets there? Think it through. You will *have* to go there, finally (in almost all cases) for the actual job interview. If no other way seems possible, arrive a week or so ahead of that interview, but in time to look over the scene in person.[8]

5. Until you can go there, use every resource and contact you have in order to explore the answers to questions raised in the preceding discussion.

It will be doubly apparent by now how crucial it is for you to choose *by name* two or three cities or towns where you wish to locate and to concentrate your efforts, at least initially. If it's a country area that interests you, identify the general area and then the name of the nearest city or town(s). Starting with the city or town that's on the top of your list, use the following resources in your information search:

a. The Local Daily or Weekly Newspaper

Almost all papers will mail to subscribers anywhere in the world. Subscribe for a six month period or for a year. Many of the answers to your questions will appear in the daily newspaper. Additionally, you will note businesses that are growing and expanding in the city you are researching.

b. The Chamber of Commerce and City or Town Hall

These are the places whose interest it is to attract newcomers and to dispense information on the city's businesses. Write and ask them, in the beginning, what they have about the city or town in general. Then later, don't hesitate to write back to them with more specific questions.

c. Your Contacts

Most of you will know people in whatever city or town you're researching during your job-hunt-as-information-search. Write to your old high school and get the alumni list for your graduating class. Do the same with your college or university. Subscribe to your alumni bulletin for further news, addresses, and hints. If you belong to a church or synagogue, write to the church or synagogue in your target city and request help in your information search. ("I need to know who can tell me what non-profit organizations in your city deal with X.") ("I need to know how I can find out what corporations in your town have departments of mental hygiene.") For further contacts, ask your family, relatives, and friends whom they know in the target city or town of your choice. You know more people in the city who could help you than you think.

d. The Appropriate State, County, and Local Government Agencies and Associations

Ask your contacts to tell you what those appropriate agencies might be.

6. Regard the city or town where you presently reside as a replica of the city or town in which you are interested, so that some of the information search can be done where you are, and then its learnings can be transferred.

Suppose, for example, you know that you are skilled in counselling people, particularly in one to one situations, that you are knowledgeable about and well-versed in psychiatry, and that you love carpentry and plants. You are trying to answer the question "What kinds of organizations would most interest me?" You must first translate all of the above identifications into people (counselling-counsellor), (psychiatry-psychiatrist), (carpentry-carpenter), (plants-gardener). Next ask yourself: "Which of these persons is likely to have the largest overview?" This is often (though not always) the same as asking: "Who took the longest to get his training?" The answer here is psychiatrist. In the place where you presently live, go to see a psychiatrist. If there is no other way, pay him or her for fifteen minutes of his/her time; or go to see the head of the psychiatry department at the nearest university or college. Ask the person whom you consult: "Do you have any idea how to put all the above together in a job? If you don't, who might?" Eventually you will be told: "Yes, there is a branch of psychiatry that uses plants to help heal people." Having acquired this information, you can then write to your target city or town to ask, "What psychiatric facilities are there, and which ones, if any, use plants in their healing program. Thus can you conduct your research wherever you are and apply to the place you want to go.[9]

One of the best ways of describing the present job-hunting system in this country is Neanderthal. Despite the fact that the majority of American men and women will be involved in the job-hunt at some point in their lives, the average individual is condemned to go about the job-hunt as though he were the first person in the country to have to do it. The average individual will face the same problems, make the same mistakes, and endure the same frustrations as have countless thousands before him. In the end, he may still end up either unemployed or *under*employed, working at the wrong job in the wrong field, far below the peak of his abilities. He may discover that the "experts" know little more than he does and that the best plan they can suggest to him is the "numbers game." By "numbers game," I mean the following: In order for a job-hunter to get a job he/she really desires, he/she should have a choice of two or three offers. Securing these offers entails first getting *at least* six interviews at different companies. In order to get six interviews, the applicant must mount a direct mail campaign, sending out X resumes to prospective employers, usually with covering letters. Surveys indicate that the job-hunter having six interviews as his target must send out at least 500 resumes, with some experts saying 1000, 2000, or more. The applicant keeps a card file and records the outcome. That is the "numbers game," sold by U.S. personnel services, many job counsellors, and most of the books in the local bookstore. For many people, the "numbers game" is a demoralizing and unrewarding pursuit, just as are the processes of contacting executive search firms, answering and placing newspaper ads, going to employment agencies and college placement firms, and using executive registers or other forms of clearinghouses.[10]

When you consider the amount of money that is involved in the career you have decided to pursue and when you consider the time that you must spend in the position, investing all that you can give to a creative job hunt should seem to be a worthwhile endeavor. No one knows your abilities, desires, and ambitions better than you yourself. As such, you are your own best counsellor. Every organization needs the creative job hunter, for he/she is a man or woman who has already demonstrated initiative, a sense of purpose, and a knowledge of and interest in the organization he has chosen. He/she has not made the most fatal assumptions that the average job hunter makes: (1) That being vague about what he/she wants to do, he/she is then free to take advantage of whatever vacancies may be available. (2) That he/she should spend a great deal of time identifying whatever organizations might be interested in him/her, regardless of where they are located and how attractive or unattractive they appear.[11]

Finding the right job is not easy. It involves time, energy, and commitment. Some people say that job-hunting is the hardest work you will ever have to do. After all, it necessitates defining yourself, your abilities, what you want, and where you are going with your life. John Crystal notes that the absolute first lesson that must be learned in job-hunting is that there *are* no shortcuts, and hurrying through the process can be devastating.[12]

Notes

[1] Alden Todd, *Finding Facts Fast* (New York: Morrow Paperbacks, 1972).

[2] John C. Crystal and Richard N. Bolles, *Where Do I Go from Here With My Life?* (New York: Seabury Press, 1974).

[3] Peter F. Drucker, *Management: Tasks, Responsibilities, Practices* (New York: Harper & Row, 1973). Also see *Work in America*, Report of a Special Task Force to the Secretary of Health, Education, and Welfare, M.I.T. Press, 1973; and David Noer, *Jobkeeping: A Hireling's Survival Manual* (Chilton Book Company, 1976).

[4] Remember, however, in this whole process that you are the screener, and it may well be that when you find out that person is not open to your idea, *that* factor alone will lead you to cross that organization off your list of possibles. Don't give up your values just in order to get a job.

[5] Beware of assuming that the new person (hopefully you) should have the same skills as the previous employee. Maybe he/she helped start things, but different skills are needed to keep things going.

[6] Phase II, page 22, "The Quick Job-Hunting Map," Ten Speed Press, Box 7123, Berkeley, California 94707.

[7] Referrals may be obtained from NCDP, P.O. Box 379, Walnut Creek, California 94596. Enclose stamped self-addressed envelope.

[8] How to research a city or town in person is thoroughly described in John Crystal, *Where Do I Go from Here with My Life?* pp. 187–196.

[9] For further information on how to conduct the job-hunt, see John C. Crystal and Richard N. Bolles, *Where Do I Go from Here with My Life?* pp. 102–112, also pp. 120–148. Also see Richard N. Bolles, *What Color Is Your Parachute?* (Berkeley, California: Ten Speed Press, 1977).

[10] Richard N. Bolles, *What Color Is Your Parachute?* pp. 9–33.

[11] Ibid., pp. 39–40.

[12] Cited in Richard N. Bolles, *What Color Is Your Parachute?* p. 43.